WORKING
IN THE 21ST CENTURY

WORKING

IN THE 21ST CENTURY

AN ORAL HISTORY OF AMERICAN WORK IN A TIME OF SOCIAL AND ECONOMIC TRANSFORMATION

MARK LARSON

A MIDWAY BOOK

AGATE

CHICAGO

Grateful acknowledgment is made to A.D. Carson for permission to reprint a portion of the lyrics from "Do Nothing."

First printed in February 2024

Printed in the United States of America

Library of Congress Cataloging-in-Publication Data

Names: Larson, Mark, author.
Title: Working in the 21st century : an oral history of American work in a
   time of social and economic transformation / Mark Larson.
Description: Chicago : Agate, [2024] |
Identifiers: LCCN 2023032451 (print) | LCCN 2023032452 (ebook) | ISBN
   9781572843332 (hardcover) | ISBN 9781572848825 (epub)
Subjects: LCSH: Working class--United States--Interviews. | Working
   class--United States--Attitudes. | Labor--United States--History--21st
   century. | United States--Economic conditions--21st century.
Classification: LCC HD8072.5 .L367 2024 (print) | LCC HD8072.5 (ebook) |
   DDC 331.0973--dc23/eng/20230712
LC record available at https://lccn.loc.gov/2023032451
LC ebook record available at https://lccn.loc.gov/2023032452

10 9 8 7 6 5 4 3 2 1   24 25 26 27 28

Author photo: Sarah Elizabeth Larson

Midway is an imprint of Agate Publishing. Agate books are available in bulk at discount prices. For more information, visit agatepublishing.com.

Again, for Mary, Sarah, and Emily.

And in memory of my parents, Dorothy and Roy.

"[That] interesting phrase 'making a living' [. . .] intrigues me so much. We make a living doing what the institution or the organization does, but we're also making a living, a life, with the people we're making that living with."
—Marilyn Halperin, *director of education at a theater*

"I've worked with people who like to say, 'I like being able to shape the skyline, to say, I was part of that.'"
—Shahara Byford, *a president and founder of a construction company*

"What I worked for was having a job without having to compromise my values."
—Nick Madden, *a former coal miner*

"I *have* a job, right? It's called raising my kids. *That's* my job. *That's* what I do."
—Justin Rosario, *a stay-at-home parent*

A job ain't nothing but work,
and I don't wanna put on no pants or shirt,
so I'm a do nothing today.
You should probably do the same.
—from "Do Nothing" by Dr. A. D. Carson, *a hip-hop professor and performance artist*

CONTENTS

INTRODUCTION

Why I Showed Up Again

My work day, as it has for decades, invariably begins before dawn, including weekends and holidays, in sickness and in health. I watch the sun rise from my desk, a fresh start implied. I began this practice when I was working as the director of education at Chicago's Lincoln Park Zoo, scrounging for scraps of time for a writing project. I'd wake early, drive to a coffee shop near the zoo, and get as much done as I could before my paid job began. Now, in what passes for retirement, it is a habit I can't break.

From the start, my work history has been eclectic. I began as a paperboy, aiming newspapers at front doors before school. I swept floors at a local five-and-dime, cleaned houses, washed dishes at a restaurant, worked the nightshift at a video arcade, cleaned a Burger King from midnight till 7 in the morning, and tried selling *Time* magazine subscriptions over the phone, where I was instructed not to relent until I got a sale. I quit after a kind elderly woman whom I was trying to cajole into saying yes finally said, "My dear, I cannot talk to you any longer. I lost my husband this morning." I briefly sold vacuum cleaners door-to-door and tended to begin my pitch with "Please don't feel like you have to buy this. . . ." I later sold tap shoes, equally effectively. I was a puppeteer for a large production of *The Hobbit* that traveled to universities across the country in a mobile home. I worked as "special assistant" to Burr Tillstrom, who created *Kukla, Fran and Ollie*, and I drove Carol Channing to and from her Chicago performances of *Hello, Dolly!* I enjoyed 14 years as a high school English teacher, a profession I still hold in high regard but left when I was offered a position in educational leadership at the Field Museum, then Lincoln Park Zoo, and finally National Louis University. Now retired, I devote my time to works like the one you are reading.

This morning, before I opened my work on this introduction, I opened Facebook (an appalling habit), and I found, gazing back at me, the face of Broderick Love, an Amazon warehouse worker who appears in these pages.

He, too, was at work. His look was weary. "Currently trying to make sense of why I showed up, again," he posted. Though our work and our circumstances are quite different, I found myself wondering the same as I sat at the desk I've returned to pre-dawn after pre-dawn without questioning whether or why. That's the thing about habits, appalling and otherwise: thought is replaced by triggered reflex—it's almost dawn; ergo, begin again.

In 1974, half a century ago, I read Studs Terkel's just-published oral history, *Working*, for which 133 disparate American workers talked with him, as his subtitle clarifies, about what they "do all day and how they feel about what they do." I was 22 then, and deeply moved and fascinated by both the minutiae of the speakers' work and the candor of their voices, all of them searching in their own ways for meaning in what they do. The "why" they showed up, again. Here were the voices of the people who parked your car, poured your water at the diner, sold you shoes, built your cars, told you to put your seatback in the upright position.

I was struck by Studs's curiosity about the people who are not often handed a microphone nor called into the spotlight. He wanted to know what brought them to this work, what were their joys, fears, pet peeves, longings, dreams, dashed hopes, sources of pride? He and his readers came to know each of them as multifaceted human beings rather than nameless functionaries.

Sydney Lewis, who would become Studs's transcriptionist for several books and assisted him with his memoirs, for example, says in the prologue to my book that she met Studs when she was a "waitress," as they were known then, and served Studs and his party. He peppered her with questions of genuine interest until she said, "You know, Mr. Terkel, I've read *Working*, but right now I *am* working." I can imagine his delighted cackle. He favored authenticity. That brief encounter was the beginning of a decades-long professional association and friendship.

Working and Studs's own sensibility have had an indelible and traceable impact on my own worldview about the significance of individuals like his server that night, regardless of shallow societal markers of status like the size of their income, their fame or anonymity, the power they hold or lack, or the company they keep. Studs's guiding inquiry for *Working* and throughout his oeuvre seemed to be, as he sometimes put it, "to know what it's like to be you, whoever you happen to be." It was as simple and as complex as that.

Twenty years after reading *Working*, I twice had the honor of sitting on Studs's couch at his home on Castlewood Terrace in Chicago and speaking into his cassette recorder. He wanted to know what it was like to be me, then a high school English teacher. His opening question was "Who are you?" So simple; so complex. I also sat with him in the WFMT radio studio as he conducted a live interview for his daily radio broadcast, *The Studs Terkel Program.* Through these encounters, I experienced firsthand the power of his uncommon attentiveness, empathy, and curiosity. His questions were sometimes alarmingly astute, always probing. They were also often ordinary, but it was his way of listening, I found, that had summoned a candor I don't normally share. When I'd see him in social situations, he could be a chatterbox, albeit a fascinating one, but when we sat on the couch, he handed the mic to me and mostly listened, pressing his shoulder firmly against mine to compensate for his hearing loss.

Studs writes in his introduction to *Working* that while working on the book, he found himself "possessed by the mystique of work," a feeling I now share thanks to the intuitive suggestion of my publisher, Doug Seibold. Early in 2020, as the COVID-19 death toll was beginning to climb steeply and much of the world locked down, he asked me what I thought of my doing a book inspired by *Working* but for the 21st century. I immediately reread (and relived) *Working* and began conducting interviews of my own. The more people I talked to, the more keenly I recognized the fact that both Studs's interviews and mine, though separated by half a century, were conducted in times of radical social upheaval and rapid, sometimes wholly unexpected change.

As Studs peered at the work world through his speakers' eyes in the early '70s, America was emerging from the tumultuous '60s, a time rocked by a seemingly endless war, devastating assassinations, the Watergate scandal, and determined movements that demanded equal rights for all. At the same time, the incipient feminist movement was just beginning to significantly alter the face of the American workplace, and personal computers were on the verge of colossally and irrevocably changing (and challenging) our lives and work in ways few could have envisioned at the time.

Today, we read Studs's workers' stories through the lens of our own times and experiences and in so doing we reflect on how much the world and our own work have changed since then. And how much they have not.

Our nation now faces multiple unprecedented challenges and threats. We are again in the throes of rapid, radical, and increasingly violent social change fueled

---

* The one-hour program was broadcast each weekday between 1952 and 1997 on WFMT radio in Chicago.

by widely disseminated hate talk and misinformation, thanks in part to the computer and the internet and worsened by the proliferation of firearms unfettered by meaningful regulation. The seemingly relentless succession of killings of unarmed Black citizens at the hands of police officers has brought to the fore a long-overdue racial reckoning, compelling many professions, some willingly, some not, to rethink their practices and the long-unquestioned lack of equitable representation and opportunity.

Dr. Lawrence Taylor, a Black podiatrist from the Midwest, recounts facing blatant racism and questionable, but expensive, legal obstacles when he relocated his practice to Mississippi. Due to unrelenting intimidation, he ultimately moved back north to Minneapolis. There, he would bear witness to the death of George Floyd, a 46-year-old Black Minneapolis resident accused of using a counterfeit $20 bill. Floyd died of cardiopulmonary failure under the knee of a hometown police officer. Dr. Taylor recalls the optimism of his youth in the '60s and '70s. "Hope springs eternal when you're young," he says. "But now, to see all that come crashing down—I cry too easily these days."

Perhaps most unexpectedly, a global pandemic brought a protracted standstill to countless businesses and professions, some of which may never return, while others are reopening in an attenuated form. Still others have thrived because what they had to offer matched the current conditions, like delivery and streaming services, video conferencing programs, and the gaming industry.

Many workers discovered during the shutdown that they can do their work just as, if not more, efficiently from home. Drew McManus, a small business owner, laughs, "I still can't wrap my head around how people spend time commuting every single day. That's time that you could either sleep in and be better rested or have more work time [. . .] instead of getting from point A to point B, especially if you don't *really* need to be at point B to begin with." Others, though, don't have that privilege. Labelled "essential workers," they have little choice. If they want to keep their jobs, they *have* to show up. Sayda Ragheb, an assisted living nurse, talks about the toll of her workplace being short-staffed due to the pandemic. "COVID, when that hit," she says, "was our biggest test. We lost quite a few nurses and CNAs because of medical conditions they had, or because they had other jobs and they kind of worked both jobs, or, honestly, just from the fear of getting COVID."

Irrevocable and increasingly devastating environmental change also has led to accelerated changes in many professions. Jack Victor, a federal wildland firefighter, speaks of the vastness and intensity of the blazes he faces today, and how much more difficult his work is from what soon-to-retire colleagues faced for most of their careers. I ask if this is the "new normal." "I hate that," he replies. "I wouldn't want to ever use that language because we shouldn't accept it as the new normal, but it *is* what's happening. And the problem has grown, but the work-force hasn't, so there is the same workforce for quite a bit more work, and more dangerous and risky work."

Bigotry, racism, and political vitriol and their all-too-common deadly mani-festations in spaces we once assumed were havens, like schools, places of worship, shopping malls, and nightclubs, frequently target vulnerable communities and indi-viduals. The quite real and quite present danger to American democracy from some of our own fellow citizens and leaders is making the future ever more uncertain and perilous. "Teachers are leaving in droves," says two-time Georgia State Teacher of the Year, Tracey Lynn Nance, commenting on increasing governmental restrictions on what can be taught. "It used to break my heart when I saw teachers sharing online about leaving [the profession]. I'm like, 'No, don't promote that idea. We don't want educators to leave.' And now, after everything that's happened, I have to say I understand. I get it."

And as I write this, teachers, artists, journalists, and countless other profession-als are just beginning to fathom the impact and transformative potential that the emerging field of artificial intelligence holds for the future of work and our world. Andrew Goldstein, a lawyer who specializes in intellectual property and informa-tion technology, for example, mentions in passing that he had just read that a judge had ruled that "an AI program cannot be listed as an inventor of a patent." After a pause, he adds, "This is wild stuff."

Against the backdrop of this turbulent moment in our history, my own version of Studs's guiding inquiry is accented on what it is like to be you doing this work in *these* times. We begin with a doula and conclude with a funeral director. In between is a sampling of what 102 disparate American workers do and how they feel about their work at this moment, while a handful look back on their now-concluded careers and wonder what they still have to contribute. Several of them yearn to be able to show up again, to feel they still matter. Linda MacLennan, a now-retired news anchor, speaks of the pleasures of retirement, then adds, "But at a certain point, you go, 'I need a purpose.' I need to be feeling valuable, I guess. I still feel like I have a contribution to make somewhere."

When I contact Broderick Love to ask about this morning's post about showing up again, he tells me he wrote it in reference to "my mood during the shift. My words," he adds, "come from an honest place." I believe the words of all the speakers in this book come from an honest place. Each person seemed to enter the conversation with a willingness to explore and question, to make sense of rather than explain, justify, or argue. None of these speakers is meant to represent their profession. They represent only themselves, offering a glimpse of the world as they see it. They do so candidly and with neither performative humility nor grandiosity. Though they sometimes share their political views, absent is the vitriol that fills our airwaves. What is evident, however, is the impact of these rancorous and unsteady times on their lives and work. I owe them a huge debt of gratitude. I, too, prize authenticity.

◣ ◤

A few notes on process: An inevitable question in an endeavor like this is, who is included and why? An asset as well as a burden of this work is that quite literally anyone who is breathing and working or *has* worked is eligible for inclusion because each is part of the fabric of the American workplace. So, where to begin? I began by chasing my own interests, allowing serendipity to do its indispensable work, and then the search branched and branched again from there. A carpenter might lead me to a firefighter who leads me to a nurse who leads me to a welder, and on it goes. Social media, for all its foolishness, was a helpful tool for casting the net wider. Several people who heard that I was working on this book even volunteered themselves.

Once I had a critical mass, motifs emerged on their own. Some remain from Studs's time: the search for personal meaning in our work, the desire to matter and to have something to point to and say, "I did that." Present-day themes include the impact of the pandemic, the effects of constantly being connected via the internet, rising sociopolitical tensions, our collective uncertainty about the future, and, through it all, the centrality of children in our lives. Once I'd identified these, I began to select voices that explored one or more of them.

I took a cue from Studs, who chose to not include persons with access to significant forums for expressing their views—politicians, corporate heads, and pundits, for example. "I was interested," he wrote in the introduction to *Working*, "in other counties not often heard from." There are a few exceptions in this book—an author, an actor, a political satirist—as there are in *Working*, which I include because the speakers' reflections on the challenges of their work set against the background of these times explore one or more of my themes from their uncommon perspective.

I include my own questions and comments only occasionally to facilitate a transition or offer clarification, or because the exchange between the speaker and myself revealed something about what Studs liked to refer to as the "feeling tone" of the time we spent together. I do this because it is from that tone that all the rest emerges.

As I have noted elsewhere, the ear is more forgiving of speech than the eye is of the written word. I therefore have reshaped some sentences so the meaning that my ear caught by inference, but which did not translate clearly to the page, would not be confusing or misleading to the reader. I also rearranged the order of some passages for the sake of a cohesive narrative. This will sound counterintuitive, but all changes were made solely with the aim of remaining faithful to the speaker's intention and tone as I moved from spoken to printed word. I gave each speaker an opportunity to see and comment on such changes. I saw this work as a collaboration.

I hope you'll discover echoes of your own work life, whether past or present, in the narratives they share, irrespective of profession or social status. With this aspiration in mind, I organized the book by theme—for example, "voice," "community," and "a better world for our children"—rather than by type of work so you can explore these themes through the lenses of various professions.

As you engage with the stories within these pages, join Broderick Love and the other speakers here in contemplating why *you* chose to show up again today—or why you did not.

PROLOGUE

AT THE SCHOOL OF STUDS
SYDNEY LEWIS

She is currently senior editor of transom.org, finance director of Atlantic Public Media, Inc., and the author of three oral history books. For almost 30 years, she was Studs Terkel's associate, close friend, "amanuensis" (his word), and "nanny" (her word) "because," she says, laughing, "he's like a hyperactive 3-year-old." She was also his transcriptionist for "five or six" of his books. In the final two years of his life, she assisted him with his second memoir, Touch and Go, *published in 2007, and his final book,* PS: Further Thoughts on a Lifetime of Listening, *published posthumously in 2009. It is dedicated to Sydney.*

We talk on Zoom. She sits on her back deck on a scorching hot day in Massachusetts under a bright orange umbrella. She has just been swimming. "I don't have AC, but just down the lane is a pond. That's my air conditioning."

I met Studs when I was waiting tables at the Quiet Knight, the legendary nightclub. There was a fundraiser for the Wobblies, and I had the center section with a big round table where he was sitting with [his wife] Ida and some other people. I don't remember who they were. It was very crowded, loud. I knew who he was because I had read *Working,* and it had left a huge impression on me.

I was trying to get the drink order, and he started interviewing me. I hadn't lived in Chicago very long, so I still had a sort of a vague New York accent. He asked me where I was from and how long I had been there and how did I like Chicago? "Hey, kid, you know who the Wobblies are?" I said yes, and he was impressed with that. Finally, I said, "You know, Mr. Terkel, I've read *Working,* but right now I *am* working."

Later I was looking for work, and there was an opening at WFMT[*] [in the mid-'80s]. I was hired to be [a] secretary. I ended up doing a lot of temp work near Studs's office. And he would walk by, and we would chat. Cathy Zmuda, who was his first transcriptionist—I call her the real transcriptionist, got cancer and was suffering, so I started filling in a little bit because she just wasn't able to keep up with all the work. When she passed, I inherited the job. After I left 'FMT, I just kept working with him in whatever way he needed help.

A piece guiding my path in life was something my father said: "Don't ever do work just for money; do what you like." And that book [*Working*] reinforced that feeling immensely. I just always followed whatever showed up in my path. And Studs showed up in my path.

I got a transcriptionist machine from WFMT, one of those with a little foot pedal, which I confess I stole when I was fired. Was that right? Well, Lois Baum[†] actually "stole" it for me. She said, "It's just gonna get dusty." I would get cassettes from him, and I'd put on the headphones, and [type what his interviewees said]. He always wanted nonverbal sounds noted as well, from a laugh, to a sigh, to the creak of a chair, to an emotional tone, to tears, to a pause. He wanted the nuance, if possible. Was it a harsh laugh or a belly laugh? A very long pause or just a pause? Sometimes I would comment in the margin, say something was funny, or that I really liked something or teased him about something. Then I would hand him the transcript, and he would edit it, and later he would hand it back to me and I would decipher his hieroglyphics and make a new version.

You know what a Luddite he was. After computers, the first time I was going to send a manuscript in on a floppy disk, I brought it over to his house and said, "Okay, it's all done. It's going to The New Press today." And he said, "Where is it?" "It's *here*, Studs." He just could *not* get it. That visual aid was not sufficient.

Did you ever think about the fact that you were literally the first person to hear what would later become part of our cultural history?

I wasn't thinking of it in the context of cultural history. Nah, I wasn't thinking of that. I'm thinking of this person's voice in my headset, and I want to get it as accurate as I can. I actually liked transcribing. I liked it because I love radio. I

---

[*] A fine arts and classical music radio station in Chicago where Terkel hosted a live one-hour interview show for 45 years (1942–1997).

[†] Associate program director at WFMT (1964–2000).

loved having the voice right in my ear. I concentrated on trying to capture with commas and all those other marks the feeling of what was happening in the room and getting the flow of the speech right. It's a little thing, deciding where the commas and periods go, but it makes a difference.

Studs would often talk about the editing process as "panning for gold." André Schiffrin* talked about how, in *Working* [Studs's third oral history], a lot was cut, but Studs became more aggressive in cutting as time went on to make the work stronger. He would really find and distill the essence of what they were sharing, saying, thinking, feeling, whatever it was, and he would help you, the reader, get the strongest version of that.

He dove into everything, you know? A meal, a conversation, music; he just was all in. I think that all that complete openness to experience translated into an openness to you—*you* were the experience he was having. What he did with people was get them to reveal to themselves what they felt or thought and then he would further burnish that so that the reader got the cleanest, most powerful version of it without the other distractions you find in conversation. He lived in the words. He went through them and through them and through them and through them and would feel his way to put the best *you* into the story that he was going to give [the reader]. His editing was soulful as opposed to technical. He was like a fine musician finding the music.

One of the things that always amazed me about him was his eyes. His eyes were so intense. I just remember feeling like this is what it would be like to talk to a . . . whale. (Laughs.) He had that level of ancient *something* in his eyes. Ancient what? Something like ancient wisdom, ancient perception. Well, I believe in reincarnation. So I always felt like he had been here a lot of times.

His eyes were not like, emotional, they were just so deep. It's hard for me to put it into words, but I always felt like part of how he connected with people was the gaze. The gaze that he gave you allowed you to reveal yourself because you weren't being judged. He had the capacity to be accepting of the frailties that he so often referred to. He was so sensitized to people who had been humiliated or felt lesser than or been made to feel small or worthless.

But it wasn't a sentimental gaze. I think there was a detachment. He would be totally present for your story, but he wouldn't get *enmeshed* in your story. He would be supportive of your feelings, but he wouldn't feel it *with* you. I think it's

* Studs's longtime editor, first at Pantheon and then at The New Press.

a really amazing kind of detachment, and probably why he could talk to anybody. It was seeing, acknowledging, accepting, and treasuring, celebrating the fullness of human experience in its highest and lowest forms.

Studs always had to have something to be working on. André, whenever they were well into whatever book they were working on, would start thinking about what would be next because Studs needed something to throw himself right into. [In 2005] Studs had been in the hospital for quite a while, a couple of months. He had pneumonia and a heart attack and one thing after another. It was a very long, slow process of getting out of the hospital and getting home, and his spirits were down.

I was going to Chicago to visit him in the hospital just for moral support, and I would spend about a week a month, just hanging out. André knew Studs and I enjoyed each other and how I would cheer him up, so he said, "Well, how about we make a contract where you can go and record Studs? I will give you an advance to help fund your travel and time. If a book comes out of it, fantastic. But if a book doesn't come out of it, it will have given him something to be excited about and energized by." Who does that kind of thing? The publisher of the only nonprofit publishing house in America, that's who. It was because André loved him and wanted to do whatever he could to help him. And this was something he could do to help him.

Also, when André left Pantheon˙ [in 1990] and set out on this venture to try to start a nonprofit publishing house [which became The New Press], Pantheon offered Studs all kinds of things to stay, and there was a big uproar about [his book] *Race*, which was just about done. Studs held the book [for him] and said, "André gave me my publishing career. I wouldn't have had any of that without him, so of course I'm going to wait and see if he can start this new publishing house." My favorite part of that story is that he was mystified by why people would think he'd do anything else.

So, I came [to Chicago] for a week at a time and taped Studs. I remember one day—and he was still in serious recuperative shape—he spoke for eight hours. We took breaks, but the total time was eight hours! I was exhausted. Him, not so much.

I don't think we had a huge plan. I just had to ask him a question. That's really all you had to do. You could pretend that you were going to direct an

---

˙ Pantheon had published Studs's oral histories in the beginning.

PART ONE:

FUNDAMENTALS

CHILDREN

"I'm having to put myself back in the forefront again."
IDA MUSONI

She is a doula and founder of Mother's Milk Doula Services. "I had been in advertising and marketing. I worked at HARPO [Studios] for like a hot second, and then went to another ad agency. "I was laid off from that agency, and I had to figure out how to be a doula full time."

I started this because when [my son] Victor was 6, I was cleaning the house on a Sunday, just vacuuming or whatever, and Mr. Profound Child that he was, he's like, "So, Mom, who's Ida?" And I was like, "I'm your mom." He's like, "Yeah, but who else are you?" I'm like, "Oh. I don't know. Why are you asking me this ridiculous question? I'm vacuuming." I was struggling so hard with an answer, but I couldn't answer it. Who else am I outside of being a mom?

I've been Victor's mom for 21 years, now. And when he was 6 years of age, I had started losing sight of Ida in a big way. Now I always tell my clients that your children chose you to come through, and they chose you because you're a good mom for the direction that they need to go in. So you have to really be careful not to lose sight of who *you* are. You have to be their guide in that.

My service's mission statement is "Empowering mothers around the world to achieve their full potential in motherhood and in life." So how do we show up in the world to support—not just the baby, because we always focus on the baby, of course—but how do we show up to support the mother because postpartum is forever. I will never be able to go back to the time before I had a baby. Your body goes through such a surreal transition and metamorphosis, so every layer of your being is affected.

[So being a doula] is also for the mother and making sure she gets to use her voice, and not just use her voice before she's giving birth, not just to use her voice during labor, but to use her voice postpartum as well. Because it's amazing to see how fast you're silenced. People always have their opinions about your pregnancy, how you're going to give birth, *when* you're going to give birth, how you take care of your kid, where to go to school. So you start to question your own self, and you start to question your choices, and some people feel like, "Well, my focus should just be my kid because if I focus on myself, then that's wrong." That's a huge problem.

In your experience, is being a doula looked upon by the medical profession as legitimate?

I think in the beginning not every doctor was excited about having a doula in the room. They're like, "Oh, god, another tree hugger, another whatever," you know? I think it's become more legitimized over the years. In the very beginning, I had some doctors glare at me when I walked in the room. They're like, "Oh, god, here's this," you know. And so I had to really navigate these kind of hard spaces. I think also, being a person of color in these spaces, I had to separate like, are you not trusting me because I'm a doula or is it because I'm a person of color? So it's having to break down these walls.

But I've been told by the nurses and some medical staff like doctors and of course my lovely midwives that I work with how invaluable we are. I'm the consistent in the room. Nurses come in every 30 minutes to do vitals; doctors or your midwife come in sometimes every four or six hours, sometimes less, to check in. I, as the doula, I'm there the whole time until baby shows up and maybe two hours after that baby comes. That's what our role is. It's consistent care.

A lot of the midwives that I've been working with, I've had long enough relationships with them that they've come to me and said, "How do we [better help] our clients?" I've had some of their Black clients hire me specifically because, of course, I'm a woman of color. And so, I can see them, and I see the traumas. I can go to midwives and say, "Hey, your client has felt this way. I'm just letting you know that this is what they're feeling in your practice." It's my goal to make them aware. I can't always do it in the moment, you know, because the focus, again, is on the mother and she might not see something wrong. Or she might, and she doesn't even realize that she's living deep in the biases that always put people of color in that space, so she's not speaking up because she's afraid.

I think of one mom that I had who was white, and another mom who was Black, and they both had the same questions and challenges. My one mom was like, "I don't want to get any needles. I don't want to have the Hep-Lock." It's a port that is put in your wrist usually to make sure that if there's an emergency, they have access to a vein. They don't *have* to do that. The white mom was like a hardcore "*No!* Absolutely not. No, no, no, no, no." Like, yelled *No-o-o-o!* Whereas my Black mom? Right? There were no [medical] issues with her either, so there was no real reason that she would need it. She's like, "I really don't want this." And the responses to both of them were so different. White mom had a midwife from the hospital come in to calm her. They were like, "Alright, if this is not what you want to do, this is what we're going to do, instead."

With the Black mom, they're like, "Absolutely not. These are rules, and you just have to follow them." I said, "Can we speak to her doctor? Could we speak to somebody else about this?" Like, "Nope, these are the rules, and we have to abide by them. There is no need to question this. You don't know what you're talking about. Get over it." And so that mom was just like, "It's okay. It's fine. It's okay."

Now, *I'm* pissed, and I want to fight. It was not about her anymore, so I have to pull back again, because she's resigned herself to it. I have to reset the room to make it feel good for her again, in a different way, and give her control over something else to make sure she still feels like she has autonomy. I just wanted to give her back some power again and remind her that she had that. Being in those rooms, it's so frustrating at times, I just want to scream.

I've worked with multimillionaire mamas and families, and young women who are homeless. And guess what? Sometimes [the latter] have more resilience than these women that have everything because her whole being has been about the fight and showing up and just doing what you got to do. You're not thinking about it, you just do it. You don't have all of the tools, you don't have all of the information at your fingertips, you just know that you got to show up and you got to do what you got to do. And so, birth just feels and looks different for you, but I just want you to remember that your birth is not less important because you don't have the same bank account as some of these other folks that I've worked with.

What are you still finding that you need to get better at?

I think balance. It takes a lot to do this work, and I give a lot. But I have to remember the power of my *own* "No." I've struggled with that word for years and being able to say no to folks is really challenging. So it's just being able to balance that and show up for my clients because I've refueled. Thank God for therapy.

Now I'm empty nesting since August for the first time. So, yeah, it's recent. It's been so much harder than I thought . . . and my kid lives in this state! (Laughs.) You know? In the same city as me! But for the last 21 years my life has been led by me being this person's mother, and now I'm having to put myself back in the forefront again. That's been a whole new world and a whole new challenge. I think I'm just coming out of the sadness. And I'm super proud. But

I think it's so important to hold on to yourself through it. So I've been going through a whole self-discovery of like, who I am at *this* stage of my life outside of being my son's mother, because that's not my leading charge anymore.

So, you return to a question once asked by a 6-year-old.

Yes. My son likes to take credit for my journey.

"The most good I can do."
DR. HILLARY MCLAREN

She is 33 years old and has been an obstetrician gynecologist for six years. She works for a large university hospital and is also contracted out to work with a free-standing abortion clinic. She recently completed a two-year fellowship, which is additional training after OB-GYN focusing on abortion and complex contraceptive care.

"That was really an effort to focus my clinical practice on abortion care. I always knew I wanted to do the full spectrum of OB-GYN. Philosophically, I do not think that abortion care should be any different from other health [care] that we provide. I think it is part and parcel of being a reproductive health care provider. Fifty percent of what I do is abortions."

She is about to complete a summer sabbatical. "I'm looking forward to returning to work. I think physicians are, generally speaking, people who like to be busy. I like my respite, but I think I do better when I'm working."

We talk on Zoom two months after the Supreme Court overturned Roe v. Wade in the Dobbs v. Jackson Women's Health Organization case.

I didn't become a doctor because I wanted to be *any* sort of doctor; I became a doctor because I wanted to provide reproductive health care. And yes, abortion was something that was tied into [my decision] because I saw it as providing health care to help women take charge of the course of their lives. I think, historically, there has been a lot of agency that's been taken away from people, and I thought this work was a really empowering way to help individuals and change the course of our society in general. You pick this job because you think it's the most valuable thing you can be doing in the world.

I'm a born and raised midwesterner, if you can't tell by my accent, and I always knew I wanted to be providing abortion care in the Midwest. It became abundantly clear that there were fewer and fewer places [in the country] where I was actually going to be able to do abortions. So sticking around Illinois was a big deal for me because I recognized that that is where people from Wisconsin and Michigan and Indiana and Iowa are going to come [for care]. That was a huge thing for me.

This is not a job that you choose because it pays well or is easy. You choose it because it's a calling, and it's a passion, and you believe that people have this bodily autonomy, right? This really *isn't* an easy job to do. There's safety issues, the difficult logistical issues, and a lot of administrative barriers. The amount of controversy that comes with providing abortions means that there are lots of hospital systems that don't want to provide it at their hospitals or have their doctors providing that care, even if it's not at their hospital. You'll find a lot of private hospitals or private practices actually have clauses that say you cannot provide abortion care, especially in hostile states that aren't supportive of abortion access. You'll find that a lot.

"Hostile states." Is that a term used in your profession?

It's part of the lexicon, yes.

Those of us who work in abortion care knew this was coming and have been preparing for this to happen for a long time. All bordering states of Illinois have severely restricted abortion care, and there has been a huge uptick [of women coming to us]. Folks much smarter than myself have been preparing and working towards expanding services to accommodate this. I mean, Mississippi, Tennessee, Texas, Kentucky—not just Wisconsin and Iowa and Ohio. People are coming from everywhere.

This is the unfortunate reality presently, and I think this is not going to change in the short term. I think there are going to be states where people can get abortion and there are going to be states where people cannot get an abortion. I think people who have the capacity to travel, will, and people who don't have the capacity will be forced to carry pregnancies they don't want to carry. I think we might have to see some really sad and terrible things happen to those people who are forced to carry their pregnancies before we flip the coin and make abortion care more accessible again. But if we think about how long it took to get here—50 years of *Roe* being in place before it was overturned—I think we've got decades of our current situation before we're going to see any real change.

Do you or have you ever had an ethical debate in your own mind about whether abortion might be wrong?

It was never an ethical question for me. It has never been difficult for me to reconcile the value of a person having control over their own body. I can certainly understand how that might be an ethically challenging question for other people. But bringing my own belief system to the table, I think bodily autonomy is central to my personal belief system. And so that was never anything I really struggled with, quite frankly.

Abortion is a personal decision. I think if you believe that abortion is wrong, that is your personal belief, and I would *never* ask you to have an abortion. You get these scenarios where a woman is pregnant and her life is at risk. There's that question of, what would I do? And I know with 100 percent certainty that I would end the pregnancy, but I know there are people for whom dying themselves is preferable to having an abortion. I would never ask anyone to do anything that was against their belief system. But it's a *personal* belief system. When we extend those beliefs to other people, that's what I think is wrong. We can't legislate belief.

There is talk among policymakers, as we speak, about federalizing a ban on abortion. Do you ever ask yourself, "Would I perform an abortion unlawfully if somebody really needed it?"

Yes, I do. It could happen. It could. And I think that's just scary. It's really scary. And I am a risk-averse person. I don't think I would be the first one to break the law, I'll tell you that. Abortion care is part, *part* of what I do. I would certainly be a resource and a support system. And I would want to be part of a network of folks helping patients get care, but "know thyself," right? I think I know that I don't want to be the one to break the law.

Does religion play any role in how you perform and think about your work?

This is something I do offer a lot of thought to. I am not a religious person, but I was raised on church and Sunday school. I have no religious affiliation presently, but I am a spiritual person. And I do believe in God, and I do believe in a higher power that kind of connects us all. I do think the work that I do is good work. And I do think that God, how I understand them, wants me to do the most good I can do on this earth. I do think I'm doing that in being an abortion provider.

I think we offer a lot of space for people to weaponize their religion to not have an abortion or to vilify abortion or vilify people who get abortions or provide abortions. I don't think we provide a lot of space for those of us who feel like being an abortion provider really is part of our conscience. I think it's a disservice to all the people who have trusted me for me to not practice to the fullest of my capacity. I do think abortion care is an enormous part of my practicing to the fullest of my capacity.

In addition to providing abortion care, you are also present when people are experiencing one of the greatest highlights in their life: the birth of their child. Do you internalize their emotion, whether high or low?

I have attended hundreds and hundreds of births in various shapes and forms, and it never gets old. As much as it is routine and it's doing the same thing over and over again, it is special every single time because it's just really rewarding to be with someone in one of the most memorable days of their lives, and to see someone see their baby for the first time. It is just a wealth of emotion that cannot be recreated. It's just really a beautiful thing. Birth, when it goes really well, is the highest of highs, and for the vast majority of the time, it goes that way.

But there are some really terrible things that can happen to people, and I'm speaking specifically of a fetal demise or what we might call a stillbirth. I think those are the absolute saddest things to be a part of.

I spoke to an ER nurse[*] who told me that after a death on her unit, there is a kind of reverent moment among the team who worked on the patient. She said "You go, Wow, that was . . . sad. It sounds plain to just say it was sad, but it's so . . . sad." And then they move on to the next thing.

The energy in that room is a really different vibe. That moment you just described of like, "Wow, that was sad," I know that moment. I think we have our professional barriers that we put up, that armor that we have to put on because I can't sit around and be sad all day, and I can't sit around and be elated all day long about every baby I deliver. But I certainly carry that with me. I wouldn't do the job if it didn't bring me some sort of joy and gratification. But it's also a job that requires you to, like you said, keep marching forward.

You said earlier that you want to play a role in changing the course of society. What is the change you want to see?

[*] Meghan Hilliard, p. 105.

Not to wax too philosophical, but this notion of a person's control over their reproductive freedom really does determine the course of their life. I think as we allow individuals to have more control over their reproductive lives, we are going to see a better, more equitable society with more diverse voices sitting at tables where big decisions are being made and are really going to serve us as a society much more. I mean, I didn't invent that thought; I think Ruth Bader Ginsburg probably said that first part much more eloquently than I did, but I really do believe that one of the driving tenets of my life is that we can make the world a better place by helping people control their own lives more thoroughly.

"There's no break."
MIKE GUISTOLISE

He is a stay-at-home parent and has two preschool-age children. His wife is a clinical psychologist. We talk via Zoom the morning after the January 6 assault on the capital.

"I was driving around listening to the beginning of the proceedings, and then I heard the first objection. I'm like, 'Okay, well, here we go. We knew this was going to happen.' And then I got home and had to take care of the boys and this and that. [I saw it on TV] and then I'm just like, 'What in the world is going on?'

"I had my Bluetooth earpiece on, listening to the news while keeping an eye on the boys. I'm just glad that they're too young to know what's going on, because how do you explain that to kids? How do you explain that?"

I don't really have a professional identification; I have my real estate license. I don't want to use the words "part-time real estate agent" because that gives the notion that you're not committed, in a sense. But I don't have the time, now, to be a real estate agent because I'm taking care of an almost-3-year-old—he'll be 3 next week—and a 1-and-a-half-year-old. I'm a stay-at-home dad, but I'm also a real estate agent. I just don't have the time to commit to it. Kids are more important. I love it. It's exhausting. It's hard. But you know, that's what my family needs at this time.

We had a full-time nanny, and half of my money was going to that. Well, what's the point? You might as well just have one of us stay at home. And since my wife has a nice-paying job with good benefits, it's like, well, let's just have me be the stay-at-home. It's like this: why have somebody else raise our kids?

I guess every day is the same, but yet different. It's always Groundhog Day. I've got to. . . . Wait, all of a sudden my son wants an apple, so now I've got to go peel an apple. This is why it probably would have been better to do this interview on the phone. You'll just have audio, now. (He leaves the room.) It's interesting, though. . . . Can you hear me?

Yes.

It's interesting, though, I was just telling my dad that you'll go through, at the same moment, multiple emotions, like, the extreme love you have for your kid, but also extreme frustration, wanting to pull your hair out. You have all those emotions at the same time.

I think maybe it's intense because, in a sense, there's no break. It's not like going into an office where you can go to the "watercooler," so to speak, and talk about "Hey, did you see this?" There's no interaction with adults on a regular basis. So you're dealing with kids who are very emotional and needy. I find myself talking more and rambling more when I'm finally talking to an adult again. It's hard to explain, but day-to-day interaction with adults is a skill and the less you do it, the harder it is to do it well. It's hard not having regular contact with adults outside of my family.

[Since the pandemic and the lockdown], my wife is working from home every day by Zoom upstairs. She meets with people from 7:30 to 5:30. Sometimes my oldest, he'll have a meltdown, and he'll go to the bottom of the stairs and scream, thinking that my wife is going to come down, but she can't. Sometimes she'll get a cancellation or there's a no-show. But in general, she goes 7:30 to 12:30, has lunch 12:30 to 1:30, and then goes back with patients from 1:30 till 5:30.

So there's really no chance for her to relieve you for a few minutes?

No. Sometimes, if she has a cancellation, she'll come down. But if she comes down and starts interacting with the boys, well, they struggle with her having to go back to work. So we try to schedule it so she comes down for lunch, and when they finish their lunch, we put them to bed for their nap, and then she goes back to work. But it doesn't always work out that way. But we're working at getting it to that. It's gotta be hard on her because she's talking to people, and they can hear [in the background] somebody's screaming for their mom.

What are you learning about yourself from this?

One thing I'm sensing now is I'm becoming more impatient. I don't know if that's because you have two toddlers whining. I don't know if that's the catalyst for me becoming less patient. But it's the whining. I don't know, I'm becoming less tolerant towards whining. But that's because I'm probably around it alone for a good portion of the day.

But you try to stay calm because, obviously, they need something, and they don't have a way to express what they need. They're not rational. They're just emotion. I don't mean that in a negative way. But you know what I mean? I'm learning, I guess, that I need to be more patient, which maybe that's going to help me down the line. Because if you can get through a day with two kids screaming, then you can probably get through anything.

Do you ever wish you could just go run an errand on your own?

Every. Day. Because it's like they're whining, and I just need to get out of the house. Even if it's just to go to Walgreens to get a pack of gum. I mean, if I can just get out for 15 minutes, just to go outside and not be in the house. . . . Our backyard goes right up to a park, but now it's winter, so you're stuck inside and you just—oh my gosh, you want to get out.

I talked to another stay-at-home dad who's been doing it for 13 years.*

That's how long he's been doing it? Oh, geez.

He said that as he anticipates starting to do job interviews again, he's not sure how to account for those years and how much he learned and the valuable skills he's acquired as a stay-at-home parent. Does that make sense to you?

It absolutely does. I still—maybe this is naive, but I don't see why there should be anything negative about being a stay-at-home dad. I think the negative thing is the fact that our country has made it financially, in some cases, so that both parents have to work.

I completely understand why both parents would need to work. You have a mortgage and now the increased expenses of a child and that second income may be necessary. Further, you have invested so much to get where you are in

---

* Justin Rosario, p. 240.

your industry, and if you are absent for an extended period of time, it's possible that you will be passed over for promotions you have definitely earned. And it's unfortunate that that is the case.

People always say to me, "You're doing a great job." And I think, I'm just doing what I'm supposed to do. I think deep down, though, I could be doing more. I get worried, like, am I doing enough? Does [my son] know enough? Should I spend more time trying to teach our youngest letters or shapes? Or, maybe I shouldn't have done this or that. Or, maybe I should focus more on them; you can always do laundry later. And there's the guilt of, okay, now I have to put on the TV because I have to make them lunch and then clean up the dishes after the lunch. So, it's like, well, *should* I do that? Or should I just let dishes pile up all day and then do it at night? This sense of guilt that maybe I could be doing more for them.

Eventually, I will rejoin the workforce, and wherever I end up, I plan on using my time as a stay-at-home as a strength and not something that is negative.

"A sacred work."
ANA CAROLINA (NINA) SANJUAN

She and her husband, Anthony, live six months in Colombia, where she was born and raised, and six months in Minneapolis, where they share a home with Anthony's parents. She is a stay-at-home parent. He is a cook at a café and a musician. Our Zoom conversation is delayed 90 minutes. Their 20-month-old daughter, Anna, did not want to go to sleep. "I guess she is having a lot of discoveries in her life, right now. She doesn't want to sleep because life is too fun."

Staying home with Anna for her early years was a decision Anthony and I made. I do see it as a job because I am helping another person to be alive, to be warm, to be fed. My mom and Anthony's mom are really supportive of my decision. They are like, in my team. They really understand that this is very important. And they support us. Allowing us to live here with them, for example, is a really big support. Because if not, we will have to pay for rent. How things are in America, right now, I would have to work for sure.

Before Anna was born, I was working in a community of farmers markets and organic producers in Colombia. I was part of a network in Colombia where we basically, with other people, would grow food. And then Anthony and me would . . . *transform?* this food. How do you say this in English? We . . . *cooked* it, right? And sell it in farmers markets. And also, we would cook for events that were part of this community.

For a while in my life, I lived in a community of six families in a farm where they were all raising the children together. All their children were like brothers and sisters, even if they were made by different couples that were living in the same space. So, for example, one mom or two moms will take care of all of [the kids] while the other moms were doing projects for the farm, creating medicine, creating the food, working with the ground to grow food, and building the houses and other projects in the community. But in the setup here [in America], people work—grandma work, grandpa work. I feel like it will be very exhausting because in these first two years [of Anna's life] she wakes up at night, so nap-time for me is so sacred and so important for me to rest, too. But if I had a job, I wouldn't be able to rest. Right?

I feel like, in the capitalistic world, to feel being independent and being autonomous is so important. But I feel like it has been so, so, *so* valued. We are humans, and we are born from a mom and a dad. I feel like the importance of mothers that take care of their kids is that we are remembering the importance of nurturing others, of offering others our life. It's like you would call it a sac-rifice, but not in a suffering way. But more in a way where it is a sacred office, a sacred work. The word *sacrifice* comes from the sacred word of being in service to another human being.

The way I do it, like for example, is Anthony and I play a lot of music together. So I feel like [Anna's] a person that is receiving from her early child-hood, the vibe, the medicinal vibration of music. Music can help you in moments where you feel stuck in your life, and you just like, allow yourself to move your body to dance with your emotions, to dance with your thoughts. So I feel like I'm passing that to her. I'm trying to create freedom for her, you know, trying to nurture her in the way that I feel it's healthy. But if I bring her to a daycare, I have to accept the way they treat her—for example, have her use screens, which I don't do that.

So it's a lot of work because of the way that I'm doing it. I literally spend all my day with her. So, for me, it's very important to value, again, the work of women and the feminine energy that lives in women—and men, but *we* embrace it more—the energy of caring for others, nurturing others, rocking others to soothe them, all of those qualities. I feel like there is a big need to balance that out, here in America. Because the capitalism and patriarchy has only valued a lot the work that has an economic result, like a product, but not the other work of raising and loving and caring for others in a way, in a place that is not paid.

I work a lot, because raising a kid is a lot of work. But the rhythm of the day is very slow and smooth and flowy. I can just play with her and walk and enjoy nature and breathe. I lay down the yoga mats when we stretch together. I'm very grateful because I have been able to do this. I know that is a possibility that not everybody has.

Do you ever feel like people misunderstand your choice?

A lot of people does. Yeah, a lot of people does. There is two types of people. When I go to the park or to the library there is people that really embraces [my choice] and really wants to take care of their kids in the first years of their life, so they do a lot of changes to do this. They create like a network of help to be able to raise these kids and not have to work so many hours and are able to be with the kids. But there is other people that are like, "I just [got my diploma]!" and right away they go to work, like super fast. And then their kids are all day with people in daycare.

But even in my own mind, sometimes I'm like, "What am I doing?" Sometimes I ask myself this because of this importance of work and building a career and being successful, economically. Being able to buy a house, buy a car, have like, commodities to live your life. And baby care and spiritual care and all of those things are put in a second place.

I would describe myself as a—how do you say that in English? Auto—?

An autodidact?

Exactly. But it's like this thing with time, this rush, this cultural rush, that sometimes I feel like I'm behind. Even in Colombia, even in Colombia, where people has a more slow rhythm, there is a lot of pressure like, "What is your career?" And "What have you done?" And "Why don't you work in a company where you get paid way better?" I have never applied for a job. I have always created my work, my offerings, my workshops, my food that I sell in farmers markets. And, of course, I'm not economically wealthy, let's say, but I feel like I have had the time to create so many other things.

Do you remember, when you were growing up, what you thought that you wanted to do with your life?

When was I growing up? That's a hard question. I think I'm still figuring that out, and *remembering* what I wanted to do is a big part of it.

POSTSCRIPT: *A year after this conversation, she tells me, "My life has changed. Now I'm a teacher at a Waldorf school. My daughter comes with me! It's the perfect transition for her. They focus on offering a home-like, loving environment and lots of free outdoor play!"*

"Kids are my North Star."
ABBEY ROMANEK

She is a domestic relations judge. "Everybody starts in Traffic, everybody. And actually, I loved Traffic, but it's a funny place to start because most of the public who, in their lifetime, if they will meet a judge, it will be in traffic court. It's kind of funny because those are really the newest judges; it's a training ground. But I loved it because it was fun. You did quick little trials. But it came time to move on. I went from there to Evictions, which was a step up, believe it or not. I ended up there for about a year. And that was awesome. Sometimes I had to evict people, though, which I didn't love."

She is now a judge in the Domestic Relations Division, a merging of divorce court and parentage, which includes "child support, visitation, deadbeat dads, and things of that nature." She is 61 years old.

I see a lot of heartbreak, but the reason I like this better [than what I was doing previously], is that now I have a wider range of economic demographics. I've got the ultra-, ultra-, ultra-wealthy, as well as the poorest of the poor, people who don't work, haven't worked, can't work, whatever it is. The heartbreaking part for me is always the children. They are what I focus on at all times. Money and property, while really important, don't hold a candle to the life of and the well-being of a child. That is where I can make a real difference.

I find that people try to use their children as weapons, and that's something I will not abide at all. What I hear about the law and litigants in criminal court versus family court is that criminal court are the worst people behaving their best. And family court is all people, and often the best people, at their worst, which is really true. People come in and they're mad, they want to hurt the other person, they want to take everything they can get. I have cases with multi-multimillion-aires and all they want to do is make sure their soon-to-be ex-wife gets nothing. They want them living in the gutter . . . and it's the mother of their children!

That sounds like revenge.

Oh, there's a lot of that. Yeah, there's plenty of revenge, unfortunately. And again, when it hurts the children, it's not something I have any patience for.

It sounds like kids are your North Star.

They're absolutely my North Star. Yeah. I mean, I also hear orders of protection where people come in for domestic violence cases, whether [the violence] is against the spouse or the child. And, of course, when it's against the child, those are the hardest ones. I mean, they're not hard decisions, but they're really hard to hear.

When I decided to become a judge, it was because I wanted to serve the public in the best way possible. And I think the best way to do that is to give people closure. And that requires me to make a decision. I don't have to be right. I mean, that's the other thing that I think about. I *want* to be right; I *hope* I'm right, but I'm not always. But that's what the appellate courts are for. But nevertheless, at least they move from point A to point B. At least now you have a decision. You may not like the decision I make, but even if you don't like it, you're still moving forward. It's not just stagnant. And I think that's my job: to move these cases forward, get these people moving on.

A big issue that's interesting to me is you've got women who are staying home. Obviously, I've never been a stay-at-home mom. Under the law now, you really *can't* be one once you're divorced because you have to be imputed a wage when it comes to any kind of child support. It's called the income shares. Everybody has an income, even though you may not actually have it. So the child support gets to be less. There might still be maintenance issues, but that's a separate calculation. Moms who stay home could do that if their husbands were out working—or vice versa, because that happens a lot, too—but now that you're divorced, your life's different. You *have* to go to work now. And you know, it is the best way to move on with your life anyway. You have to make a change in your life.

You make decisions that can dramatically change a person's and a family's life. Knowing that, how do you make your decisions?

Like you said, I have a North Star. I love that term. It is all about the best interest of the child. I end up having to figure out, is Dad or Mom going to see the child Tuesdays and Thursdays or Mondays and Wednesdays? Twice a week or three times a week? I have trials, I mean, *long* trials fighting over one extra day a month. I think, "Why don't you save that money for your child's college education?"

Do you ever find yourself second-guessing a decision later?

You know what, I don't because of my—I love that "North Star"—because of my own North Star. I mean, I believe I have made the best decision with the information I have *for that child.* Maybe sometimes, on some money issue here and there, I've second-guessed, and when they come back, maybe I'll change it, or they'll do a motion to reconsider. Maybe I'll change my mind on some of the small things, but when it comes to the kids, no, because their best interest is what I'm looking for and what I'm listening to. I have to say that these decisions don't tend to be that difficult.

SCHOOL

"We're living in history right this second."
BRADLEY TARRANCE

He is 39 years old and has been a middle school principal for three years, though he has been an educator for 20 years.

"Our school is about 54 percent Latinx. We have a small population of refugees from Africa, usually from central Africa, the Congo, and some from Western Africa. That's about 10 percent. We're about 22 percent African American, and then probably about 16 percent white. We're sitting on the outskirts of Grand Rapids; we bump up against it, and a lot of our kids come from there. Our graduation rates are extremely high, so there's been a tradition of students coming to us."

We talk on Zoom, 10 months into the pandemic. He sits in an empty classroom.

I think we first got a sense in February 2020 that everything was going to change. Our superintendent would come back from superintendent meetings and say, "Hey guys, we're maybe looking at teaching school very differently." And then it started picking up a lot, and it was all hands on deck. It was a lot of hours to adjust and to figure out what our community, which was dependent upon our school, needs.

We're a "school of choice,"* so kids can opt into our school. Because of this, the student population does not mirror the specific neighborhood where we are. The demographics have changed exponentially over the last 20 years. There used to be a factory around the corner and that shut down, so a lot of the folks that live here in our community are older white people that worked on the factory lines and now have retired, and they just stayed in the neighborhood.

We're beginning to see younger families buying homes, now. But when I say "younger," I mean, younger working class and people living in poverty in Section 8 housing that's popping up in our area. So we're really transitioning. Knowing that [because of the pandemic] we're experiencing things nobody's ever experienced and that we're going to be making decisions that historically we've never made and that we'll be making mistakes, we said, "Let's ground ourselves wholly in our core beliefs and mission and values. And then we can base all decision-making on those values." I would meet with my community coordinator probably two, three times a week. We started getting a list together of the families that we had been dropping food off for and that we were giving counseling services to. And then we started with a design-thinking model around, what does that mean and look like *now*? And what do we have to do to be able to still do those things in these circumstances? So "nothing is impossible" is really the framework that we thought about.

There are days when I'm dropping off weekend meals to six different families in the community to make sure they have food because they lost their jobs or whatever it is. And it's not just me going to my own bank account, getting out a hundred dollars and giving it to a family to keep their lights on or to feed their family. It was a matter of looking at where the community needs are and being responsive to those needs and making sure we're meeting those needs. I think that's going to help build relational trust and help people see us modeling the behaviors that we want to see in society.

I think as the leader of the school, my role is to be calm and say, "Hey, we're okay. Here's our core. This is who we are." And then, because we do not have a lot of folks that voted for the current president [Trump], when they would hear him speak and would get perturbed or irritated or nervous with his nonsense [regard-

---

* In Michigan, "school of choice" provisions allow local school districts to enroll nonresident students and count them in membership without having to obtain approval from the district of residence.

ing the pandemic], they turned to the school for information. It was difficult. It absolutely came to the absence of strong political federal leadership.

We tried, instead of making the [conversations] about the absence of political leadership and letting it become a complaining session with parents, we tried framing it as, "This is the information that our president currently has, and he's trying to calm everybody." But when the media took this and said, "This is what our president is saying, but here's the reality," it perpetuated the community's nervousness. So we held parent meetings, both virtual and in person, and said, "It's going to be okay. Here's what we know so far." And we were transparent in everything that we were sharing, saying, "Please bear with us while we adjust."

And this was while I was simultaneously dealing at home with my own kids [ages 4 and 7], wondering, are they going to be going remote with *their* school district or not? And as a parent saying, "Okay, what do I have to do to get my kid to do the work?" All those things everybody is going through, now. So it was a balancing act between my two major roles: father and principal.

What was your own emotional experience while this was all unfolding?

I think, while trying to be the calming factor, inside I was nervous, terrified, all these feelings. In front of my families and in front of my parents, I knew I needed to be transparent and let them know that, yes, I have anxiety because of this, but we're all in this situation together, and that we are built to be able to thrive in uncertain times. That was a huge mindset piece that I looked at. I thought, "Okay, I have been *built to thrive in uncertain times*, and staying grounded in our core beliefs and values, now is my time to ensure that my community and my own family are able to thrive in these times, too. But it really weighed heavy on me and my physical health during that time.

In addition to the pandemic and economic downturn, this is a time of much social unrest. How has that impacted your school and community?

Huge. Huge. There were demonstrations that became riots in Grand Rapids this year, sparked by the murders of George Floyd and Breonna Taylor. She was born in Grand Rapids and some of her family still lives here in our school district. So that hit really close to home with all of us. When we were down protesting, there were a lot of folks there, but it was peaceful.

And then, toward evening, when people started to leave, a different crowd started coming in. You could just feel a different energy. I saw pallets of bricks that just showed up. I don't know how, but they showed up in the corners of downtown. As I was walking away, I could see the difference in the folks coming in. They were not wearing protest shirts and carrying signs. They had baseball bats and other things. That night, windows downtown were busted out. There were choppers all night and things going on.

I walked back down the next day with my family. We saw National Guard trucks arriving in the city and buses, just regular school buses, with military people in them. And we saw a community coming together and cleaning up, painting and leveraging the strengths of our community. Artists were painting these beautiful murals on the boards where windows used to be.

I got with my community coordinator at the school, and we said, "We're living in history right this second. We have to allow our children to see that and embrace it." So we got a photographer to take some photos, and then we framed them and put them around the school with descriptions and quotes.

I identify as an actively anti-racist educator. When I was hired here three years ago, I brought that to the table, and they knew that about me coming in. So we talk about both COVID-19 and "COVID 1619" with students. And when we did parent meetings, too. We brought up both of those pandemics. "Let's first talk about COVID-19. What do you need in order to feel safe to send your children back to our school?" And then we said, "We cannot deny that there are other things happening in our society right now, too." And we talk about COVID 1619. I think owning the fact that that is going on and not denying that it is impacting our community greatly, greatly, greatly, is important. We have allowed staff to include that in our curriculum. We have to *say* these things, we have to bring these things up.

We had two board members that were actively against us using the phrase "Black Lives Matter." One man said, "All lives matter." And he claimed that we didn't know the community. We said, "Hold on, you're talking about the community that lives right here geographically, not the community of our school that you're serving. So let's look at those percentages and break those down and then talk about what *that* community wants."

We took it as an opportunity to educate our board. And so, we did a full session in a board meeting on the Black Lives Matter movement and what it means. We had parents and students speak and showed a video to help explain.

It opened him up and pushed him further, and opened up another person, too, that had voted against saying, "Black Lives Matter" in the district, to saying, "We absolutely need to be saying it."

I hope our students are actually realizing that wow, *this* is history. It will be written about, the way that we transitioned away from education [as we knew it]. I think it would have a larger impact if we don't go back to—quote, unquote— normal, if we *don't* come back to schooling the way it was and this *really* changes our trajectory as a nation and as a world. I think that if we're able to leverage this to *change* that trajectory, I'm hoping for a *huge* change in that trajectory. But I'm also thinking and being open to saying, "Okay, it may just be a small change in the trajectory for now, but how can we get people to realize, 'Oh, wait, there's an opportunity here for me never to come back to school again in a building and sit in chairs and desks'?" Really rethinking education, rethinking what it means to be a school, rethinking what it means to be in a society.

I anticipate a strong push to try to get back to normal. I anticipate also us having to do the hard work as leaders to push against it going back to normal, to push it forward. I think that that for me is one of the biggest things. I don't want to go back to the way it was. I want to go forward. I want this movement to keep going.

"How are we going to be better for this?"
SUZANNA GORDON & HAROLD AVILA

They teach at the same public magnet high school in the San Fernando Valley where they had met as students. "I'm the English department chair," Suzanna says, "and I teach AP English Literature, Honors Freshmen English, English Language Development, and I coordinate a program called AVID [Advancement Via Individual Determination]. I also coach our school's academic decathlon team."

Harold teaches culinary arts. "I am also co-chair for the union at our school, and I'm the CTE [Career Technical Education] chair as well." His students call him Chef.

"We're what's called a span school," she says. "We span the fourth through 12th grades. This is an integration magnet school that was created as part of California's integration initiative, and 60 percent of the student body is minority students. We're also socioeconomically diverse. We're 57 percent Title I, which means 57 percent of our students are on free or reduced lunch. And that was before the pandemic hit. That number will probably only go up."

They have two children, ages 7 and 11. We talk on Zoom 10 months into the pandemic, during their winter holiday.

SUZANNA: As department chair, I got a text message from our principal in March: "I need you to get a substitute teacher for the day. I'm having all of the department chairs come in to meet and figure out how we're going to handle a shutdown if we have to go out." We could kind of see the writing on the wall, but it was a mad scramble to figure it all out.

HAROLD: I remember our last normal day. We were working on proteins—how to properly cook it, the proper temperatures, how to cut it so it's more tender. I had bought all these tri-tips that we were going to grill. But then we shut down. Three months later, I ended up coming home with like 30 pounds of beef because I got a call from our campus saying the electricity was going to be shut off. So, "if you have anything in the freezers or the fridge, you better get rid of it." I distributed them to different teachers.

SUZANNA: Initially, the kids were kind of relishing having an elongated break. That was exciting to a lot of them, and to a lot of teachers, too. But it was interesting because shortly thereafter, the students very much missed coming to school. I think they were very surprised by the realization of how much they actually *missed* going to school. There's been a very real loss, the lack of togetherness, of community, of unity.

But our school is a really wonderful place. I think we did a really good job of getting computers to kids who needed them and getting them what else they needed to be able to do this remotely. But I think students were very surprised by their own reaction.

HAROLD: As a teenager, you want nothing to do with your family. All you want to do is hang out with your friends. And that's a huge thing. But when you've grown up with these same friends from fourth to 12th grade, being away from them for this long. . . . Well, you can tell that it's a strain on them, for sure.

How has remote teaching worked out for you, Suzanna?

SUZANNA: A lot of people are surprised to find out teachers have been instructed by the district—and I think this is across the board in every state—that we cannot require students to turn their cameras on. So it's really, really tough. You just see a box with their name or photo. You'll ask them a question to see if they're even there. It's a very big deal. As a teacher, I look for facial clues to see if they're understanding what I'm talking about or not. It's so important to me to be able to see them, even aside from the kind of communal aspect of it, which is important, too. A lot of parents are surprised to find out that teachers are not allowed to require that.

HAROLD: At first, I had, on a daily basis, 10 kids show up, total, the whole day. I had a hard, hard time with that. Part of the problem was that the district had made it so that we couldn't give kids D's or fails or take attendance or give them a lower grade than they had earned up to that point.

And then I started to think about what I was going to do if this continues. I thought, "Okay, I have to promote my class in a way that the kids are going to enjoy it and want to be here." So I started researching technical equipment that I could use. The district gave us $5,000 to use how we wanted. I got cameras and the whole setup. I built a little display in my garage with webcams. I started to get really tech savvy and was able to do really good demos and give kids a close up, personal view of things. I've definitely found a little niche out of this. Now it's giving me more opportunities and advantages.

SUZANNA: Your attendance is now, what, 85 percent?

HAROLD: 95 percent. It was interesting for me to go from that first semester where I felt so hopeless to this new semester where I feel more empowered.

SUZANNA: My concern was, how am I going to create a classroom culture without a physical classroom? I decided my buzzword this year is going to be *community*. What am I doing that's going to make my kids *want* to tune in? What am I going to do differently that's going to make them *want* to turn on their camera and *want* to be a part of it and *want* to be seen? So you end up having to be a lot more intentional and spend a lot of time doing that.

HAROLD: For me, my "dad jokes" just don't hit the marks as well as they normally do in person. (Laughs.)

SUZANNA: I just want to state the obvious, which is that there is no replacement for in-person teaching, not even close. To be honest, if this was what teaching was 19 years ago, I don't think I would've gone into it. This has been really, really tough.

How do you balance being a teacher and being a parent when you're all at home together?

HAROLD: When we first started, Suzanna was very panicked about the whole situation.

SUZANNA: We were going to have four Zooms happening at the same time. And where was that, logistically, physically going to be? And did we have the Wi-Fi that would support it? We don't have a home office, so what do we do? Yeah, I had this moment of like, "Oh my god, we've got to make sure we have the best upgraded Wi-Fi." For my desk, I'm using the dresser in my bedroom. He's using the kitchen, and each of our kids are in their bedrooms. Luckily, we happened to get them desks at the start of the school year.

And then on top of that, there was the issue of, aside from the logistics, our little guy was just starting second grade. What if he needs help with any of this and what's going to happen, and it's not fair to ask our sixth grader to be the one to help him, that's *our* job. Harold was much calmer and reassuring.

HAROLD: I looked at it like, we're going to make it work. What was going on in my mind at the time was that it's a pandemic, and—excuse my language— shit's going to happen. It's about how we deal with it. If I lose Zoom during class—and I've seen my son's and my daughter's teachers freak out—I'm just like, "It's okay. We'll get back on in time."

SUZANNA: As a parent, it was important to me to say, "Okay, so I'm going to be teaching at home while my children are going to school in their rooms, and I need to say, no matter what, *their* needs come first. Their physical and emotional needs, whatever they are, I have to be a parent before I'm a teacher." And that's interesting because even though that is normally always in the back of your head when you're at your school and they're at their school, it didn't really take on the same kind of gravity that it does now. I was glad that I had made that promise to myself and to them, because there have been times where you're kind of pulled in multiple directions, and that's when I would go back to, "Nope, they come first." I don't ever want my own biological children to think that I love my students more than them.

But I'm lucky. I am *able* to say that my kids come first. I have a lot of students whose parents don't have that luxury. Some are essential workers and have to go to work and leave their child alone at home to "go to" school or not, or to watch younger siblings. And especially for my ESL students whose parents are immigrants or recent immigrants, it's really difficult for them to use the tech. A lot of them have had trouble logging onto Zoom, or their Wi-Fi was so spotty, they would lose connection, or it was super glitchy. So trying to make sure to advocate for those kids and to help them and talk to parents to see what can be done has been a huge, huge struggle.

The pandemic has really highlighted social inequities. What I think most needs to be highlighted and addressed is that there are opportunity gaps in lots of places. I keep thinking about, how are we going to be better for this? I hope seeing these inequities means that we will all work to address those. My worry is that we will go back to normal, and we won't have learned to do things differently. I really hope that all this can matter. I hope we'll be able to say, "Yeah, it was terrible, but we came out of it better than we went into it," and not that it was just a complete loss. I don't know.

One thing I've learned, though, from teaching as long as I have, is that kids are incredibly resilient, much more so than adults. And they will, for the most part, bounce back from things that would put an adult flat on their backs. So I keep reminding myself of that.

Teachers are gonna make it work no matter what. And we are finding ways. I keep saying to my colleagues, "Guys, eventually we're going to get really good at this! And hopefully we never have to do it again." God willing, we'll never, ever have to be here again.

"This is the wheelchair and me. We're buddies; we come together."
GABRIELA SALGADO

She is 27 years old and lives in a western suburb of Chicago. She volunteers at an elementary school and is seeking a position as a school counselor. She has cerebral palsy and uses an electric wheelchair.

Not many people know this story, because I don't like to share it. I hold it very close. It was during my student teaching. That's where the trouble started, and if it's okay with you, I'd rather not use the school's name, because I've left that behind, in a way. But that's where the problem started, because to me it seemed like my abilities or capabilities were coming into question simply because I use a wheelchair. But I would have an assistant with me— not so much in the classroom, but to help me take care of my personal needs throughout the day. So, the school also wanted to know what my assistant's role would be in the process.

Early on, the school wanted to have a meeting with me. It was myself, members of the university community from the school of education, and the assistant superintendent and assistant principal of the school where I'd be student teaching at. I had an idea going in that they had some concerns, and I basically had to put them at ease and let them know that everything was going to be okay. Telling myself, "Don't get defensive; don't let them think that they got you, because they don't."

I was basically being asked how I would handle certain situations if they were to arise given my physical situation or my "circumstances"—to use their word—because I was in a chair. For example, "How would you deal with a child that ran out of the room? How would you handle a situation of a fire alarm? What would you do?" I sat there, and I answered them all. I said, "Well, if a child ran out of the room, I certainly wouldn't be running after him, because I would have 20 to 18 other students to look over, so I would have to reach for the phone, call the office, and tell them."

I basically had to sit there and "defend" myself, for lack of a better word, and kind of prove that I could do this and that I *did* belong here. But when I was first told that they wanted to have this meeting, it kind of felt like, you're basically telling me that you don't think I can do it. After that, I felt like I had a target on my back. I felt like people would be watching me a little bit more because I was in the situation, I was in the circumstances that I had.

It was after I taught my first lesson that I noticed I was having issues writing on the board because of the angle and everything. I asked the teacher for some feedback afterwards. "How do you think I did?" And she said, "Let's talk about that later." I was like, oh boy. I knew, in the pit of my stomach I knew that something was wrong. I just didn't know what. Toward the end of the day, she pulled me aside, and she said, "I don't know how to put this. I'm sure you're intelligent, you're smart, the kids love you, but I don't think you can do this. I was watching you during the lesson; it didn't seem like you were able to maintain control of the class and answer their questions while they were asking them. And I wouldn't feel comfortable leaving you in my class alone or having you take complete control of my class."

When she said that, oh wow! It was like I had just been punched in the gut. The wind had been literally knocked out of me, and I kind of zoned her out after that. I was there physically with her, but I wasn't there. She continued on to say, "If you want, we can have another meeting with school administrators and people from the university and try to figure out what we can do to fix this."

I said, "Well, what difference would it make? I'm giving it all I have. What if I had my assistant write on the board for me? I would dictate to her what needed to be written on the board, and she would write it for me." She said to me, "Then who would be teaching?" I said, "It would be me, but I would just be doing it in a different way, you know?"

But it was after that that she's like, "Let's just have another meeting to see what we can do. Go home tonight, think it over." Then she's like, "If you want to, you don't have to even go back in the room today." She went back in the room for me and got all my stuff, and I just left because I had a class that night.

What not a lot of people know is that my assistant was actually my mother. She's my primary caregiver at home. She wanted to do this for me, too. I left the school, and she saw the look on my face. (Pauses.) It's so hard to talk about. She saw the look on my face, and I just burst into tears, and she said, "What happened?" I said, "She doesn't think I can do it." She's like, "What are you talking about?" And then I tried to explain it to her in the midst of my bawling my eyes out. But after I'd calmed down, I told her what happened, and she's like, "Well, go see the people from the college of education. Talk to them about it. See what they say, what we can do, what are your options?"

That's exactly what I did. I went to see the person in charge of student teachers, and she called the certification officer, and I explained the situation. And they're like, "Well, do you want to have another meeting?" I said to them at that point that I was done. I was done because I had given everything that I could possibly give, and for me to sit through another meeting and have everyone talk about me or talk at me while I'm sitting there watching them, I was like, "You know what? No." It was a difficult decision to make, but I was like, "No. You know what? I'm done." But I wanted to say goodbye to the children. She said, "That's fine."

And that was the hardest part. That was the hardest thing I've ever had to do, aside from making the decision that I did earlier. I basically told them that I had been assigned to another school. I was very surprised at the attachment that they had formed so quickly to me. I handed out pencils as a gift, and there was one student who didn't want to use her pencil. I asked her why. She's like, "I want to use it to remember you. If I use it, I won't have it anymore." So that was really hard, that was extremely difficult.

I finished with a master's of education in school counseling. I went into an interview for an internship, and I was nervous. I went in there scared, thinking that it was going to be a repeat of what had happened to me three years earlier. I was sweating because I thought the first thing that was going to arise is something related to my wheelchair and how would I do whatever I had to do with the wheelchair. But no. My advisor was very aware of the situation that had happened to me in the past. She assured me. She said, "I'm not going to let that happen." I was nervous and I was stuttering and I was completely freaking out. But I had decided beforehand that I was going to be completely honest. That I was going to be completely upfront. I was going to say, "Look. This is it. This is the wheelchair and me. We're buddies; we come together."

And I got the position.

What would you want people to know and understand about the fact that you're in a chair?

To not look at the chair, but to look at the person that's in the chair. Believe it or not, we have so much more to offer than you think that we do. I think people, when they see the chair, it startles them. It intimidates them, and they're afraid to ask questions because they don't know how people would react to them, to the questions that they're being asked because people might think they're being nosy or being rude, so they think they're just better off not asking any questions, but I don't mind people asking questions. I wish they would.

POSTSCRIPT: She later earned a counseling certificate, but in an email, she shared with me that her certificate expired, due to her inability to obtain a full-time position. She now devotes her time to volunteering for a nonprofit organization that strives to empower adults with physical disabilities. In addition, she is a vocal advocate about societal issues that impact individuals with disabilities. Most recently, she was a collaborating author on a book that shared the stories of individuals living with cerebral palsy.

"I'm a question-asker."

ELEANOR HAMM

She teaches middle school science and life science in the same southwestern Virginia community where she grew up and raised her four children. She is one of two Black teachers in a school where the student body of 300 is mostly white.

She is 61 years old and has four adult children. She sits in her classroom. We talk on Zoom at the end of the third full day of classes at the start of her 22nd year as a teacher.

I was in business management for 15 years, and then went to teaching. I think I was always supposed to be a teacher. I had managed an apartment complex for a while that was low-income housing, and there were a lot of kids there that needed extra help, so we did some after-school programs. I kind of helped with the kids in the property. And when I left there and started managing an outlet retail store, I hired local high school students to come work for me, and they lacked a lot of social skills. They lacked basic skills of communication, working together, just doing stuff. And I'm like, "Something's wrong with these kids." When I started teaching, my oldest son was in the seventh grade, so they were getting ready to enter the system. I thought, I need to make a change. I need to have an influence on this. And I'm not going to be able to help these kids unless I get in there right where they are, in the school.

This is an agricultural area. A lot of families aren't employed, but if they are, they are working at a major truck plant that is close by; a lot of our parents work there. My husband actually works there. We have a Gatorade plant that is in our county, too. A lot of parents work there and in a couple of other industries. But manufacturing plants is where most of our parents work. And if not there, they're doing fast food.

We have a high percentage of our students here who live with grandparents or they live in foster care. A lot of what we have is very low income. We have a high percentage of students that are free and reduced lunch. I don't know exactly what the percentage is, but right now we're under a grant where all of our students get free lunch and free breakfast.

I try to instill in these kids that I teach now that one important thing that they have is a future, and it can be anything they want it to be. They do not have to stay where they're at. They can dream big and go big and leave this area and be anything they want to be. But my son did some research when he was at UVA, and he said only 10 percent of the students in our county even take the SATs. So it's not a high percentage of students who go on to a four-year college. Now we offer a free six-semester program at our local community college. Some of them do participate in that.

I think some of our families feel like, if you go away, you're going to get lost because you're not ready. We've had a lot of our students leave and go to college and then come home because they just couldn't get adjusted to it. One thing we experience and battle the most is lack of motivation. There's not much motivation in the homes. Part of that is the community has a high opioid addiction problem. And so, we do deal with a lot of parents that are incarcerated due to drug abuse or for other reasons. And we have children that are removed from homes because they're being neglected. So there's not a lot of motivation encouraging students to go. Hopefully, it's trending away from that. But I have experienced that a lot myself that there's not an expectation to go to college. There were eight kids in my family. Two of us have four-year college degrees.

You tell your students they can be anything they want to be. Do you get frustrated by the lack of motivation?

I try not to. Because I understand where some of them are and where they're coming from. And I just encourage the ones that I can. I guess—(she looks over her shoulder toward her open classroom door)—I get frustrated with the adults. It's really tough to have all this stuff that you want to do and everybody's not as into it as you are. And it gets pushed to the side. I'm like, "It's for the *students*!" But it's not seen that way, to my frustration.

I do have to deal with adults. I do have to deal with discipline. I do have to deal with the paperwork and things that I don't always want to deal with. But I do love working with children that want to learn. But I don't really love dealing with kids that don't want to be here and don't want to learn, and who don't respect me because I'm a woman. And the color of my skin.

We live in a culture here where some male students are not brought up at home to, first, respect a woman; second, respect minorities. I recognize that most of them do keep it under control, but I can tell by the way they interact with me whether they're going to be respectful to me.

What about the adults?

My first two years teaching, I was observed twice by a school board member, a white gentleman. I realized that it wasn't just a classroom observation. It was more like a literacy test that voters used to have to do to be allowed to [vote]. But I didn't even think about it until I transferred schools. And then the principal that was there, he was looking at my file, and he said, "I've *never* seen an observation from a school board member. And you've had it twice." I said, "Maybe it's because I was a career switcher, and I was a little older when I started to teach."

But after doing this workshop,* I found out a lot of stuff about myself, and that the things that I thought were running smoothly, really weren't. I am still being looked at and tracked as a minority, even though I felt like I wasn't. I thought that they weren't seeing me as a Black, that they were seeing me as a teacher. I don't care if you see me as being Black; I'm fine with that because I *am* Black, but see me for what I am, not the color I am. I really thought that things were going well, but then after I had to look at some things a little closer [at the workshop] and talked to my children, I realized.

I mean, I went to school in the '60s and '70s. I know what it was like then; I know what I dealt with. And then I found out that my own children went through some of the same things I had gone through in the same school system. I told them that when I was in fourth grade, I had asked to read a passage. And the teacher stopped me and said, "Oh, no, no, no. I want you to read something else." She wanted me to read Booker T. Washington.

My daughter said that the same thing happened to her when she was in elementary school, and she had never told me that. I realized I had thought things, in all these years, had changed and that my kids were living a better life. They really weren't. They were still under a microscope because of the color of their skin.

As a country, we're going through a harshly political and fraught time. How does it impact your work there in Virginia?

Most of these kids here are Trump supporters. We now have a policy in our school that you cannot have a confederate flag on anything that you wear to the school. It was last year around November that it actually got put into the policies for the county. So we were going through the new dress code and talking about offensive things on your clothing and that you cannot have anything that's offensive, or hurtful, or all these different things, nothing tobacco related, and all this. My students said, "Well, can we wear a Trump shirt if somebody's offended by it?" I said, "This is the deal. If you wear something to school, you're taking responsibility for what you've put on to wear. If it creates a disturbance or disruption in my classroom, and I have to stop teaching to calm you down or to address

---

* She had attended a workshop over the previous summer that focused on ways teachers could address the killing of George Floyd when the new school year began.

this situation, I will ask you not to wear it again." We do have some very strong political voices on both sides.

I don't agree with parents having some say in what's being taught in the classroom. I think some of these things that they're bringing up to be taught are a bit much. Like when the whole critical race theory thing came out, and it got really blown out of proportion really quickly. We're in a Bible Belt. I don't think people understood what it was all about. I still don't know what they were expecting us to teach. I said, "If you're going to allow a particular person to say someone's been oppressed in some way, there's a possibility for that to happen in any race or any ethnic origin or any culture if, for some reason, they could feel that they've been oppressed by something." We have a lot of our Caucasian or white population that say affirmative action oppressed them. So we had those debates going on, and I did hear some of those debates. And now we have the proper pronouns to use in the classroom. People feel very strongly about that, too.

Also, I have to teach evolution. When I say the word evolution, people get their back straight and they want to see what's coming next. I have been advised by administration that I need to send a notice home before I start teaching evolution. I don't do that. I don't think there's any reason for me to alert a parent of something that they could misunderstand. I just teach it properly in the way it was supposed to be taught and move on. I don't have to dwell on it.

But I'm just going to be honest with you. I don't spend a lot of time watching and keeping up with a lot of these things because it kind of hurts my soul to watch the news. I'm a very faithful Christian woman, and I am devoted to serving the Lord the best that I can. And one of the things that has been in me and works in me is that I may not care for this or that person, but Jesus cared enough to die for them. So I need to at least care about a certain person because He cared about them. If I'm going to be a Christ follower, they need to be important to me. So that's kind of how I've tried to live my life now. But I have my moments. I've had my moments, so . . . We'll just, you know, leave it at this: I'm not going to be anybody's doormat. Leave it at that. But I do try to be fair to everyone.

Twenty-two years after you started, do you still love this work?

Yeah. I don't say that very often. But yeah.

"How do we live in this brave new world?"
KATHRYN HARMON

She is 40 years old and a library media specialist living and working in a small, rural coastal town in Oregon. "Where I live and work, it's a long strip of the coast. There are some farms and homesteads that are just out in the middle of nowhere. We have kids on the [school] bus for upwards of an hour each way. We're predominantly white, but I feel like that is shifting a little bit. We're getting some more families of color on the coast, and I am thrilled to have a little more diversity in my classes instead of it just all looking the same."

I have a 10-mile commute to school, and I do not have one stop sign, stoplight, or stop anything between my house and the school. I see eagles and river otters and no traffic. Yeah, it's a beautiful commute. It's a beautiful place to live. It is also hard to live here. We get cut off from the valley for significant portions of time unless you have a four-wheel-drive vehicle and chains. In the mountains there's often big storms that will cut us off essentially from the valley and also impede our travel. I've had to drive an extra 50 miles to school because we have a small landslide between here and the school. On [Route] 101, for about a year, a year and a half, we had lost the use of the tunnel, and that cuts off the communities. That had a very big impact because going around is a very significant haul. Sometimes we're cut off from the rest of the country.

The students, they don't get traffic. Can't even imagine traffic. Our kids driving in Portland just freaks the living daylights out of me. They've had no city driving experience whatsoever. I can't even imagine them on one of the highway overpasses in Portland where they're basically driving up in the air.

How do you think the isolation affects students and faculty?

I've always said that here you can't be picky about your friends; [it's so small], you don't have that many people to choose from. But there's also a group of kids from all walks of life who are bound together because they are the only kids in their grade that really care about academics. And they became tight friends.

I actually just had this fascinating conversation with a group of boys at lunch the other day, one of whom was lamenting not having close friendships at school. And he said, "I have my online friends who I can be close to and a few childhood friends from my school where I moved from who I'm close to, but I've no one in this building who I feel like I can have a more-than-shallow conversation with."

There are some issues here with screen addiction, with drug use, with innumerable societal issues that are going to have to be addressed in our community at some point soon because these aren't going away. And neither is marijuana; it's been legalized. And so, how do we live in this brave new world where a kid can go, "I'm just going to look at my phone instead of at you during this class period, because I don't have any interest in getting a passing grade or participating in any way, shape, or form." I mean, it's a weird world out there, Mark. I always tell the kids they're engaged in the ultimate scientific experiment to see what will happen to humanity if we let them look at little screens all day. I guess our challenge is to create engaging enough work that's important and pertinent enough to the kids that they forget they have these [devices].

I think the number of students who are college-bound is around 25 percent. I wouldn't be surprised to find that number slipping a bit because we've had such a drop in college enrollment in the last two years.*

I talked to my assistant who graduated in 2014 [and] did exchanges when she was in college. She went to England and was a copy editor at a publishing house in England for a year. She's had all of these wonderful experiences and then came back. She's living with her grandmother and taking care of her now. She said that college was a hard transition. It was difficult to go out into the world and to be around so many people constantly; it was just overwhelming and over-stimulating.

One of the other things I struggle with is the turnover. It's hard, and I think that's just going to get harder and harder for schools. I don't know what we're going to do, Mark. We currently have, I think it's three open positions at the high school that we can't fill. One of them a business teacher, one of them an advanced math teacher, and one of them a world languages teacher. We would take anyone who speaks any other language.

One of the reasons there are fewer and fewer people that want to go into education now is because it is getting harder and harder to go into education, and it is less rewarding. And with COVID out there, I mean, okay, here's one thing that's been driving my compatriots crazy lately. The Oregon Department of Education has its offices still closed and everyone is telecommuting. No one is in their

---

* During the pandemic.

offices. And yet their policies dictate that every single one of us teachers is in our buildings with a bunch of kids every day.

I supervise 15 to 18 middle schoolers at lunch every day, depending on whether I'm in the cafeteria, or I'm up in a classroom with one class of kids. That's a lot of potential for me to get exposed to a fairly significant dose of COVID, you know? And so, if you personally have one of the trillion preexisting conditions, is this a job that you can want to pursue? If I had diabetes, I don't think I would be here.

What is hard is knowing I'm exposing [my husband] Sam. He works from home because he has some unknown immune system issues that we've never been able to get diagnosed. And so we actually lived apart for four and a half months last year while I was forced to be in person at school starting in January of last year by our superintendent. He does not like teachers working from home. He was not into it.

And yet you seem to love your work.

I believe libraries are important things in schools. My library friends are always frustrated with me because I'm not a traditional librarian. I have a very wide definition of what libraries are because I look at them through history. I think they are not just about books. It's easy to say a library is about books. But what a library is about is leveling the playing field for all people and providing resources that the common people cannot afford to have themselves. That is the origin of libraries; it is about information and bringing learning and information to the people.

I'm a voracious reader who loves books with a passion and loves nothing more than finding the perfect book for the kid. You know, that's my ideal world. But of late, I've gotten more and more into robotics, programming, 3D modeling, and introducing kids to those worlds. I have two maker spaces* that I'm roughly in charge of now. I run 3D printers. We have nine between the high school and the middle school.

I don't quite think that people really have the level of respect they should for [libraries], these institutions that have had such an impact on our society and have such an amazing history. I mean, I'm actually pretty proud of the American

---

* A workspace in a school or library with tools, technology, and materials that allow people to explore an idea and complete a project.

people. I feel like there's a lot of pretty interesting creativity, invention, innovation that comes from us. Part of it is we do attract talent from the rest of the world. But part of it is we grow at least some of that talent. We have a society that appreciates that, that likes innovation, that likes change, that likes solving problems. I can't help but think that libraries have had a role in that, historically, and I think most libraries should have maker spaces. I would be surprised in 10 years if you find a library that doesn't have one. They're very much about innovation, invention, creativity, all the good stuff.

I always call the library the heart of the school. I tell the kids this when they come down that this desk is called the circulation desk. If blood doesn't pump through your body, bad things happen. And if books don't go through the circulation desk, bad things happen. It's the heart of the school. And if we don't keep kids' ideas and thoughts moving through this space, if we don't make this a rich and inviting space where kids want to be, if we don't make this a place where ideas are transmitted, where kids learn, if we don't say that learning is the focus of our school, foundationally, that a love of learning is what we want every kid to have, we are doing them a disservice. I think this *opportunity* to learn should be a hallowed thing.

"I have a voice again."
TRACEY LYNN NANCE

She is a fellow with the National Network of State Teachers of the Year, and a Voices for Honest Education Fellow. "In response to harmful legislation happening across the country, my job is specifically to advocate for student-affirming practices and honesty in education. We do that by reaching out to policymakers by writing op-eds, by running social media campaigns, and by educating other teachers and the general public about honest education and what's really happening in classrooms."

She did her training at the University of Chicago and taught in Chicago Public Schools, then moved to Georgia and was later named Georgia's Teacher of the Year two years in a row. She has two daughters, ages 8 and 11.

When I moved back to Atlanta, [where I'd grown up], I really felt strongly about teaching at a school in the neighborhood where I had lived. And I wanted my own kids to have a more grounded, real experience. Our real world is diverse, and you have to learn how to get along with different types of people. I want them to have those early formative experiences with diversity the same way that I did because I think it made me a better adult later on.

So I called up literally the nearest elementary school and said, "Hi, I'm a teacher relocating to Atlanta, my hometown. Do you have any positions?" And they said, "Can you be here in 30 minutes?" "Sure." I walked over there, and I had the job within 30 minutes.

I believe in public education. When Christopher Rufo*—you know, the orchestrator of the critical race theory boogeyman—explicitly states that his goal is to dismantle public education, I'm not sure why people aren't believing him. We can't let it happen because we know exactly which groups and which students are going to fall by the wayside.

Quite honestly, the chief of staff for the Georgia state superintendent took me to lunch and told me, after Georgia passed a resolution [to block CRT in public schools], that critical race theory is a paper tiger. The board said, "You guys are freaking out for no reason. It's just a statement of belief. It's a resolution. It's not law." And here we are little more than a year later, and it's codified law and teachers all across my state are struggling with how to teach their standards and not step on one of these divisive [landmines].

A "divisive concept ban" lists out nine terms that we're essentially supposed to be wary of. The very first tenet declares that neither our state nor our country are inherently racist nor is any individual. An educator would have to be very careful about calling any event or group or person racist. So, if I call the KKK "racist," someone might get upset . . . because there are "many good people on both sides," as "45" would say. (Laughs.) Another one: we're not allowed to talk about controversial topics in class. And, oh, you're also . . . this one is really, really important and they lean on it heavily: you're not allowed to teach or say anything that might make a white child feel guilty because of the color of their skin. That could be any child, but it does mention white privilege specifically. The truth is, you cannot legislate feelings and no teacher aims to inspire guilt. Teachers, and 86 percent of parents, believe learning from our country's complex history with racism is important to preparing kids for the future.

Further, teachers are not allowed to participate in any professional training or anything that asks them to explore their own identity. And furthermore, we can't do that with students. They have attacked the term "social emotional learn-

---

* A conservative activist and senior fellow at the Manhattan Institute.

ing," saying that its equity and inclusion components promote critical race theory and is just the backdoor in, so they have dismantled that in my state. We now have to call it "well-being and connectedness" in many districts.

I was State Teacher of the Year during this shift. I had two terms, and during the first term, everything was *merry*, Mark! They loved me. My platform was on teacher impact and educational equity. They were requesting me all across the state. The Department of Ed. commissioned me to design a workshop for their school for their superintendents and principals across the state on monitoring social emotional learning, and culturally responsive teaching in the classroom.

A year passes. COVID starts; summer of racial unrest; Perdue* is about to battle Kemp† out in the upcoming primaries. And so, there's tensions there for who can be the most extreme. And now we have Christopher Rufo and Trump attacking critical race theory on Fox News. It's the perfect storm.

And then [it was in the midst of this that] my supervisor says, "Tracey, we need you to be Teacher of the Year for another year. You're doing all this work with race and equity anyway; we want you to continue on."

Then it all gets very messy, and politicky. Perdue actually found a Power-Point that I made for a workshop and said, "Look! Kemp and Superintendent Woods are promoting critical race theory, and Tracey is the one that gave this PowerPoint, and it's on the Department of Education's website." So the state superintendent actually took down my presentation and put out a note that said, "I did not authorize this PowerPoint" because it referred to SEL—social emotional learning—and culturally responsive teaching. Basically, there was race involved, and because of that, they said it was promoting critical race theory, and that just goes back to people's confusion about what CRT even is. It is an academic theory used to examine racism in laws and is found in college and graduate-level courses. K–12 teachers just want to teach kids to be respectful and kind to one another.

Teachers are confused about what to do. I think our biggest concern is self-censorship. Because educators are afraid, right? We don't want to lose our jobs. Most of us have children. And we don't want to upset parents. Quite the contrary. Teachers want parent input and partnership. We're on the same team. We're in it for the kids. And I think it's such a shame that children have been put

---

* U.S. Senator David Perdue from Georgia.

† Brian Kemp, governor of Georgia, 2019–.

into the middle of this cultural war, in the middle of politics. It's not fair to them, and it's definitely not fair to educators.

During my state term, I traveled part time and gave speeches at conferences, and the other half of the time I was an instructional coach and interventionist at my school. As a result of having this role for two years, including through COVID, through the critical race theory ban resolution, through all these things, my platform became elevated. And I saw that I have a voice once again, a little bit of privilege that other people might not have. My teaching experience and acknowledgements give my voice a lot of credibility. And now I want to use that to elevate others.

We see and hear a lot about silencing and even retaliating against voices like yours. Do you feel that knocking on your door?

Oh, my goodness, right after the critical race theory ban in June of 2021, I received a good bit of backlash, actually. In fact, the chief of staff for the state superintendent called me and asked me to call the chair of the school state board and apologize for my remarks on a radio show.

Did you did you make the apology?

I did not. I continued speaking. I spoke on NPR on *Political Rewind* as well as *Closer Look* and Chicago's *Windy City Live*.

Are you afraid?

I fear for our kids the most. I fear for kids that don't necessarily look like my daughters. I want all kids to go into a classroom and to truly be seen. Seen, not only for their academic abilities, but also for their personalities and their emotions and all of the possibilities that are out there for their lives. I want kids to have exposure to those possibilities so that they can see so many different paths and choose the one that fits them best. I want classrooms to be a place where kids can discuss our history honestly. I think that we can still be patriotic teachers, while at the same time acknowledging where we've fallen short of the American dream. Allowing students to wrestle with primary sources and true events that happened in our country in community with one another builds understanding and develops important critical thinking skills.

What are you seeing as the impact of what you've just described?

Teachers are leaving in droves. My friends, teachers who are very seasoned, new teachers, and teachers that I had trained who I just *knew* were going stick to it, have *left*. Instructional coaches have *left*, my Teacher of the Year supervisor has *left* over the politics. The new supervisor in that role told our new State Teacher of the Year that this person is not to use the word *equity*. Yep. They didn't write it down because heaven forbid someone find that, right? Which is interesting because at the same time, they want this person to be competitive at a national level.

It used to break my heart when I saw teachers sharing online about leaving [the profession]. I'm like, "No, don't promote that idea. We don't want educators to leave." And now, after everything that's happened, I have to understand. I get it. I left the classroom because of the opportunity that I have to [use my voice], but a lot of educators are leaving because they feel they have no choice. They're out of money. They're out of time. Teachers are being villainized at a national, very public level.

At the beginning of the pandemic, we were "superheroes" and parents couldn't believe how we did this all day. And then a couple of months later, we're being called lazy and "wanting to stay at home in our pajamas." And now Governor DeSantis in Florida said that he is "underwhelmed" by teachers coming out of teacher prep programs, and therefore you should not need a college degree to teach, and he will further be bringing in veterans, police officers, and firefighters to teach, and that really undermines the value of an education.

What do your daughters think of what you do?

They love having a teacher mom. It was really fun teaching in the same school with them. Sometimes they don't understand when I start getting into the bans and whatnot and the legislation piece, but they know that mom is writing to Senator Warnock and, today, Mom is going to be speaking with Bill Nigut again on NPR. And they get really excited that I'm able to share my voice. They miss me being at their school, though. I get it. They always ask me when I'm coming back to their school. And the truth is, I don't know.

I have over 1,500 books in my personal classroom library. I have my own guided reading table, the kidney-shaped table? I have my own bookcases. I have all of it, and it's in a storage unit that costs me $175 every month. It's been there for the past three years.

"I am their wildest dreams."

DR. N'KIA CAMPBELL

She is a school district administrator in the Office of Academic Initiatives in a small South Carolina town. "Our student population is about 27 percent African American, 32 percent Hispanic, and then 41 percent Caucasian. So we are a majority minority district, Black and Brown students. I feel our demographics are changing, but our mental models aren't changing with the people that we serve. We still have the Black-white mentality."

She is 46 years old and has a daughter in sixth grade.

This is my 25th year in education. I'm a native of [this town] and I come from a family of educators. I knew when I was in fifth grade that I wanted to be a teacher. I taught fourth and fifth grade, but I did not stay in the classroom long. Went into administration very young; I was an assistant principal at 25, a principal at 30, and at the district office at 33. So I sprinted through my career. In this last lap of my career, I'm kind of pacing myself now, because I realize at the district level, you're not a decision maker, you're an influencer for the decision maker. I feel like it's important for people like me to be in these positions as well. It's not just being an African American southern woman; it's bringing different experiences to the table.

I'm going to show you something; I'll be right back. (She leaves the Zoom frame briefly and returns with an enlarged black-and-white photo.) So this is a picture of my sixth-generation grandmother, Mama Jane, who was born in slavery in Parris Island, which is one of the military bases. They think that she was born in the early 1850s. This picture was always in my great-grandmother's house, but I didn't really know the significance behind it. I now carry this picture with me in every position that I hold because I don't want to lose sight of how far our family, how far we've come. I am the first in my family to receive an education doctorate. (She points to individuals in the photo.) My great-grandmother had a third-grade education; she was born in 1896. And this is her great-grandmother. She always talked about being kind to people, having wisdom. I just believe that those spirits are in me. And so, I am their wildest dreams. And I'm excited to be a part of such legacy.

Why did you go into administration after such a short time as a teacher?

I used to work at McDonald's as a high school student. I got my check, and it was $608 for two weeks. And when I worked two weeks as a teacher, I made $646. I looked at the check from McDonald's along with the check that I got for teaching, and I said, "There's something wrong about this." I was like, "Alright, in order for you to do things and impact people, the classroom may not be the place." So I started thinking about administration.

How are the politics of these times affecting your work?

There's a new policy responding to CRT [critical race theory] without responding to it. You know how you can read a whole passage and be like, "Okay, what *is* this? What's the meaning?" It talks about people feeling uncomfortable about race and gender and all this stuff. It says that if at any point people feel uncomfortable, then you cannot use funding—federal, state, local.

Anytime you ask the state to interpret this policy, no one calls you back. Nobody. And you don't want to put your funding at risk. I have a meeting at 11:30 this morning* because there are people in our community that think we're disguising our professional development by calling it SEL [social emotional learning] and not CRT. They're saying it's a violation of the policy.

I think that the question that you asked is a part of what I wrestle with at night. I feel like I'm not doing enough. But I feel like if I do anything more, I'll derail what we've done so far. We're trying not to dismantle the work that we've done to support underserved populations within our district. We serve all kids, but we know that certain communities need that special attention. And some people see that as critical race theory. I don't know another way to say it. I know we can do more, but I feel like if I move any faster or do any more, those three steps forward will result in 20 steps back.

Right now, there's an undercurrent about changing history. This African American history conference that we did last year in the community was about untold stories. We had descendants of enslaved people in this area share their stories, from one-room schoolhouses to segregated schools to integrated schools. And I'll share this with you really quick. My mom and dad were high school sweethearts, and they were the last class in our county to attend a segregated school in the 1970s. That's the only experience that they knew. I was born in '76, and in 1970 they were still in segregated schools. Our county is under a desegregation agreement with OCR [Office of Civil Rights] because we were one of the last counties in South Carolina to voluntarily integrate.

* We began our conversation at 10:30 a.m.

I used to be a hearing officer. And I would say we saw probably about 10 to 12 hearings a week. And 80 to 90 percent of those hearings were Black boys. These are discipline hearings, so kids who violated the student code of conduct are recommended for either expulsion or alternative placement. And it breaks my heart when you see a certain subgroup, regardless of what it is, and there's not a balance that represents the student population that you're serving. That's a systems failure. And we are part of the problem. So that will bother me.

What gives you the most hope?

My daughter. I think we have this window of opportunity to mold and to create the leaders of the future. Sometimes [in my work] I feel my window is closing. And then when I see my daughter, I see that *her* window of opportunity is there. Naomi has this magnetic personality, she's so different than I am. And I realize kids like her, and the work that she's doing in her community, will help to change mindsets. So that gives me hope. She's 11, and she's a community activist. She wrote to the mayor like three times because they were cutting down too many trees. She didn't like that. She won the Martin Luther King [Jr.] essay contest in January. She started a STEM morning group for girls because she said girls need to be in STEM. She gives me hope.

Now I'm on a countdown to retirement. Here, let me show you real quick because this is my little joke. (She displays an app on her phone that is counting down the days until her retirement.) I have 1,403 days left. People are like, "What are you going to do after that, N'kia?"

So let me give you the premise of what I'm about to say. I lost my mom four months ago. She fought cancer for the second time, and she lost her battle after 15 months. I've been away from her in physical form for four months, and she's my best friend. So it just kind of solidified that I want to retire because I want to live life, and I feel like I'm limited on my creativity and ability to speak freely in a public setting or in this setting. I love my superintendent. I think he's awesome. I think he's creative. He was a needed leader for me in the time that he came, but I have to live life. I just feel like I was created to do more than what I'm doing sitting in this seat. I don't want to be disrespectful to him or his vision or put our district in jeopardy because I may want to do something a different way.

So, all that is to say I just want to come out of education. I just want to do something different. I may connect the dots back to education, but at this moment, I want to go into. . . . I want to become an esthetician. I just want to do that work: wellness, skincare, beauty. So I'll be going back to learn to be an esthetician. Because I think I'm cute too! (She throws herself back in her chair and laughs freely.)

"A routine job."
LAWRENCE BROOKS

He started his career as an elementary school custodian in 1993. "My oldest sister, she's deceased now, but she actually got me hired at McDonald's when I turned 16. I started off flipping hamburgers, and I worked my way up into management. I worked for McDonald's for about 14 years. Then, she says, 'The Board of Education is hiring, would you like to go apply?' We drove there together. I applied for a porter position, which is in the lunchroom, and I also applied for custodial. She applied for the lunchroom manager. I got hired in '93, and I haven't looked back since."

We talk on the phone while he sits in his car in a White Castle parking lot where he's just picked up his lunch. He is 62 years old, works at a public middle school in a large midwestern city, and is approaching retirement.

I basically do the same thing every day. What I've learned as a custodian is that you develop a system, a system in terms of what you do first, what you do second, what you do third. The more organized that you are, the easier the job is. Sometimes there's some additional things that are thrown into the scenario and it throws you off, but it's really just kind of a routine job. I'll start at 6 a.m. mopping the hallway floors down and then vacuuming rugs, getting some things set up for today, like the breakfast table or something like that, unlocking all the doors. And then, eventually, some of the staff people come in. But it's just a regular routine. When you're doing something so long, it becomes like a second nature. I've been doing it so long, I would say I've become a professional at it by now. I have a slogan: "I work smart; I don't work hard."

I kind of knew quite a [few] of the Mexican boys at the first school where I worked. Some of them, I watched them grow up from pre-K and kindergarten. Some of them, if they end up in gangs, I could still walk through the community and be safe because of how I interact and my personality. I would see some of them when they were in the gang—13, 14 years old. Even when [they're] in high school, if they see me on the street, they still refer to me as Mr. Brooks, you know.

They may strike up a conversation. "You still at the same school, Mr. Brooks?" They see me as like a friendly police officer or something, like Mr. Friendly, you know.

When you see kids that you know getting involved in gangs, do you try to steer them in another direction?

No, I don't see that as my role. Now, being a Christian man, I do mentor young teenagers and young men tied to my church. I may say something to them. You know: "Why don't you get a good education? The gang? That's not a good thing to do." But in terms of having lengthy conversations with them, I don't get into that.

I would say a certain amount of boys who I probably have known may have lost their lives [to violence]. It's hard to know because when they get older, like when they're high school age or they're out of high school, they lose contact with me, in terms of I don't see them anymore. If I see a young boy that I knew from fifth grade, and he's 22 years old now, he might recognize me, but I may not recognize him because of his aging, if you get my point.

How does it affect you when students are lost to violence?

It affects me greatly. I have four daughters and one son, but he's in prison right now for something that he did in self-defense. He's my only son. I used to be involved in the prison ministry early on when I was in church, but I don't do that anymore. But anytime, it doesn't matter what nationality a person is, if their life is cut short, it's going to affect us emotionally, personally, you know, because we're human.

How was your work affected by the pandemic?

When you get to how [the] board of education handled COVID-19 and the cleaning and the staffing, I mean, in terms of how they handled it overall, it's horrible. It really is because it's really . . . discriminating, to bring a harsher word. Certain people within the school, like teachers, the teacher's aides, principals, I guess social workers and nurses, they pretty much did the quarantine thing according to the CDC, and what was expected. But to me, in terms of how they handled it with the lunchroom people and custodians and engineers, it was a joke, because it was not handled properly.

Do you feel there was less care?

(Softly:) Pretty much. Pretty much. And then, with all the procedures of cleaning behind COVID-19, they were supposed to be paying us additional funds because it's dangerous. I just don't know if they did anything in the right order in that realm, if I can put it briefly.

Was the union able to help you?

The union is who they are. I think the union barely handles grievances and situations that we deal with on a day-to-day basis.

Much less something as huge as a pandemic?

Right. That's pretty much it. Yeah.

What was it like to go to work during that time?

There was a kind of a whole different atmosphere in the school because it was mostly just the staff people being in the building and keeping it clean and organized. With the absence of children, it's just a different type of environment. Working those COVID years—well, we're still in COVID-19—it was kind of all lonesome, you know? It's kind of like how, when the kids are very loud and then they leave out of the lunchroom and suddenly it's all quiet. Normally, we look for those peaceful moments. But those kids being absent from that environment, it really kind of got lonely, you know, for me personally. It's good to see kids and to see them smile and interact. And so, it was kind of heartbreaking for me. But it's what I got to do, you know, as a custodial worker. I just have to kind of roll with the punches.

What do you like most about this work, Mr. Brooks?

I like being around people. I like my coworkers. I'm a very good lead custodial worker. We have good times together, we break bread together, we retreat over the summer. And the first Friday of the month, my parents and I would pay for all the meals for me and my coworkers. And then the next Friday would be the next person, and the next Friday would be the next. So we kind of rotated throughout the whole summer. And, I mean, I've never really worked with a staff of people that were not good to work with. I've had excellent camaraderie with the staff at schools.

Are you happy your sister told you about that job opening in the school system 30 years ago?

Yes, I am. I really am. Because my mom and dad taught us as kids whatever work that you do, give your best. Doesn't matter what you do, but just do your best. And go to work on time. Don't cheat and just do what you're supposed to do. And hopefully you will succeed as long as you honor God. All this, whatever I do, a lot of who I am ultimately stems from God.

I had started at McDonald's flipping hamburgers, and when I say I'm an ambitious person, it's in a positive sense where I wasn't just going to settle for flipping hamburgers the whole time. I worked my way up into management there. But there was a great, great desire within me to excel. And that's wherever I've worked. McDonald's was 14 years, and the board of education has been 30. All the ups and downs and the changes—I just I tell people, I'm kind of like a duck. You know, when the water falls on the back of a duck it just drops down to the ground.

COMMUNITY

"A community that does not include all of its members is not a community at all."
MICAH FIALKA-FELDMAN

He is the outreach coordinator for students with disabilities and a teaching assistant at Syracuse University. He self-identifies as a person with an intellectual disability. "I can't read and write the same way as my friends, but I have technology that helps me. Like, I talk to Siri on my Apple Watch, and it will print it out on the screen. It will read to me, too."

He is 38 years old and long has been an advocate for people with disabilities, fighting for disability justice and inclusion. He is among the first wave of adults with an intellectual disability to attend college. He frequently speaks at conferences and universities across the country. In 2014, then-president Obama appointed him to the President's Committee for People with Intellectual Disabilities.

The following is a blending of two interviews, seven years apart.

The way I got this job is I spoke at the Syracuse University in 2011 at a big special-ed conference. And then I spent like a week and a half here, and I met colleagues and people that are friends of mine still. I asked, "Can I, like, move here and start working at the university?" I just thought, I love living in Michigan; I lived there my whole life but I just thought of trying something new.

They asked me to send an email to the dean of education. And then I sent him a letter, and I just explained why I felt Syracuse would be a good place for me. They've been doing work in inclusion for the last couple of years and have fought for it since 1975.

Did the position exist before you wrote to them?

No. I think they started it.

For you?

Yeah. I help people learn about the program. And I've been a teaching assistant, too, for ten years. I help teach a special-ed class. I also help teach a disability studies class. I read papers. I help talk to students. I meet with my teacher team every Monday. I read articles for class. I talk to students. I take attendance for the class. I talk to students, and I help them when they have questions. [On the first day] I tell them who I am and what I do.

What do you say?

"I'm Micah. I'm 38 years old. I used to live in like, Michigan, and I moved to Syracuse in 2012. And I go around and speak at many conferences." Since COVID it's been kind of quiet, but I like it quiet.

What is your primary message when you speak at conferences?

I try to get people to understand that people with disabilities have a voice and can share their voice.

What kinds of questions do they ask?

Sometimes people are just amazed of what I have done; they're quiet, but sometimes they have questions. I hear, "Wow, you can do all this?" I said, "Yeah, I can. Like, it hasn't been easy, but I have done it."

Why do you think they're surprised?

I think this is probably because they haven't met someone with a disability before, maybe.

Are you surprised by what you can do?

(Laughs.) Yeah. Sometimes I am. Like, I am a little surprised, but I have learned how to advocate for myself. [I tell them about when I had to fight for the right to live in a dorm at Oakland, where I went to college.]

Can you tell me what happened there?

Yeah. I was going to school at Oakland University. When I went in to pay tuition, they said I could live in the dorm, and I applied, and they took my money. Then the vice president, who's a very nice vice president, she just said no, I couldn't live in the dorm because one of their policies they came up with was that I had to be toward a major, toward a degree. But I was paying the same amount of money as anyone else and taking 12 credits. They said I could live in the dorm, but then said no. So I set up a meeting with the vice president all on my own. I tried to tell her that I was very capable, and I traveled a lot, and I was very capable of living in the dorm. They said no.

Did they give a reason?

Yeah, they kind of gave a couple reasons. They were kind of not reasons that I believed. They said I wouldn't know how to leave during a fire drill and that friends in the dorms wouldn't know how to be friends with me and stuff.

How did you respond to that?

I was upset and sad, because I probably have more friends than the vice president and most of the people that work at the university.

So, they had a wrong idea about you?

Yeah. I kind of took the next step of trying to go to my school's board of trustees, and I tried to explain to them that I was very capable. I thought because they were the board of trustees, I thought they would overturn the ruling, but no, they followed what the vice president said. My housing case took two years. I was living with my friend some of the time, in his apartment, then I was living at home some of the time.

In my lifetime, I never thought I would have a lawyer, but I had a lawyer. He was a great lawyer, and he and I learned a lot. It was through the Michigan Protection [&] Advocacy.* It's an agency that helps people who have disabilities. It doesn't cost money. They work through the state. I was questioned for five hours in a room. There was their lawyer and then there was a lawyer that they kind of hired from some big law firm.

It sounds like their argument was that you did not have the ability to live there.

Yeah, that was their big thing. Every month we would go to the board of trustees, and we would meet. Meet them and try to explain to them. Many people came and spoke at the meetings saying I can do stuff. We got notes sent to them saying that I was capable of living there, and we hoped that they would make the decision then. It was in 2008 that we went back to the board. We thought they would overturn the ruling, but they followed what the school said. I told them I could live there as a test and try it out and see how it goes. Things like that. But no.

So, you actually had to go to trial.

Yeah. It was like a last resort. I was hoping that they would just move on and be happy and say okay.

Were you nervous about it?

No, I wasn't nervous. I knew that I was on the right side. I knew that I was very capable of living in the dorm. The decision was made January of 2010. I was in Florida on vacation. Out with my family and seeing my grandma. It was cool that I found out with my grandma. I got a phone call. It was my lawyer. He said, "I just heard that you won." I said, "Oh, that's cool." He explained what we had to do. Things like that. We were worried that they were going to try to appeal. They *kind* of appealed, but they didn't win the appeal somehow during the appeal process. It was cool, spending the first night there, but I had to fight for two years just to live in a small little dorm room. (Laughs.)

Why do you think the school fought so hard against your request?

Why I think they fought so hard is because they were trying to show that they were right. But I'm not really sure why they fought so hard. I was capable of living in the dorm, I think. They wasted tons of cash and money on that. After I

* Has since been renamed Disability Rights Michigan.

graduated, before I left, I gave the vice president a poster, my famous quote I like: "A community that does not accept all of its members is not a community at all," and I do like that quote a lot.

Do you feel like you're on a mission with the work you do today?

(Laughs.) No, no, no. I don't think so.

When you give talks and work with Syracuse students, what's the main thing you want people to understand about people with disabilities?

I want them to know that people who have disabilities have dreams and can believe in their dreams. I want them to know that people with disabilities have a voice and have people that advocate for them and people to help them to have a voice, and that they can share their thoughts and share anything they want to share.

You sound very fair and very open-minded to me.

It's just how I've grown up.

What does it mean to you to have a disability?

It just means I can do a lot of great stuff, and I can meet some great people, and yeah.

People might think of it as a limitation, but I don't think you see it as a limitation.

No, I don't. Yeah, no, I don't.

"*Rewired, not retired.*"
NONIE JOYCE

She is board president of a food bank and community resource center in a small town south of Tucson, Arizona, not far from the U.S.-Mexico border. "I had worked in corporate settings; I was very much a businessperson, and I ended up becoming involved in the human resources area, what they call the 'people department.' Then I started my own business in organizational development and individual leadership coaching. When [my husband and I] moved to Arizona, I got involved in the food bank because of the church that we attend. I volunteered to be there for 90 days. That was nine years ago. And here we are, here we are. It's a volunteer job, but it's pretty

much a full-time volunteer job."
    She is 74 years old.

I'd been very involved with this church for some time working with immigrants—organizing searches in the desert, providing water, providing food. We're about 30 miles from the border, and we're directly north of Nogales, which is one of the ports of entry. If people are out there at their wits' end, we help them get help or in touch with the Border Patrol—if that's what they want. That work was very much my mission for a long period of time.

And then a couple of things happened, simultaneously. The church decided that they wanted to do some research on social needs in the community, and it was revealed that even though on the surface this is a very prosperous community—just 5 or 6 percent poverty—there's a lot of poverty in the rural areas that surround the more densely populated parts of the community.

So that research was revealed, and at the same time, the regional food bank approached us to open a very small pantry. We started in a closet in 2009, with only two or three households coming a week. Our volunteers read novels during the day because nobody was ever coming. Then, over the last 13 years, there's been 20 to 30 percent growth each year, and about two weeks ago, we had 380 households come for food. During the pandemic we were serving up to 500 families a week, but we're back to a somewhat more reasonable number, although numbers are increasing again.

Our county was pretty rigorous around closing down businesses for a period of time [during the pandemic], and so there was a precipitous loss of jobs. People stopped going out and hospitality was extremely hard hit. People left the health care field because of the fear of being infected. The economy here, like much of the rest of the country, really suffered, so there was a huge spike in unemployment. Obviously, the stimulus dollars helped, and our numbers started to come down.

But because we've gone back to more "normal," whatever that might be, people have lost the childcare tax credit that was put into place for about six months. They have lost supplemental food stamps, or SNAP benefits, because those were cut back. Now there's lots of unemployment, and with those benefits being pulled away and with inflation, people are really struggling for food.

Food banks have traditionally said to people that "this is a way for you to free up some cash so that you can keep some stability in other parts of your life." One out of eight people in our area fall below the federal poverty level, and one out of four lives below self-sufficiency. So that means about 20,000 people in our community routinely have to choose between "Am I going to buy food or am I going to pay that medical bill?"

I think we're finding we now have more stressed people coming into the food bank; their fuses are shorter. The volunteers' fuses are shorter, too, for that matter, because so much has gone on in the last few years. And people are rocky. They really are rocky.

That is why we also work with our community members to help them become more stable and to have more financial security. This helps people in the long run. Food is an urgent need, but we also help people even more with programs that support their long-term plans. Everyone has a hope, maybe a dream. And we want to become a place that works for all our residents.

What do you say to people who see what you do as a "handout" and/or assume it will be taken advantage of?

Most people who come in to work here understand that there are lots of people who need food, and so they'll say, "Take as much as you want." If we catch [someone taking advantage], we tell them they may not come back or that we will be monitoring them closely. But my theory is that you're always going to have 5 percent, maybe 10 percent of people who are malingerers, but the great majority of people are absolutely solid. And then you have some people who have so much integrity that they won't take anything that they don't think they deserve. People will say, "Well, I'll take this, but I want to leave some for other people." They don't have to be policed.

You're distributing free food to people in need. To some that gesture can appear to put you in a position "above them," as a benefactor. Do you struggle with that?

Absolutely. And it's something we're struggling with right now because there's a great deal of need in the rural areas. We're applying for a mobile service vehicle, but what we don't want to do is to swoop in as "do-gooders." We instead want to collaborate with community-based organizations to learn more from them what they need. The phenomenon you're talking about can never be avoided completely. So what we have to do is work together with them, talk to them, listen, try to respond.

We also have to debunk those who say, "They gotta pull themselves up by their bootstraps." In order to have bootstraps, you have to have boots!

Do you see your work impacted by current political rhetoric?

I certainly see the impact on myself and those I interact with. Let me give you an example. The incorporated town that's nearest to us has elected, over a number of years, to give us money so that we could go out and buy food for our clients. Well, the regional food bank made the decision to put $50,000 into a campaign to pay people at least $15 an hour to work. And when our closest town got wind of that—it's a conservative town, lots of defense industry employees, border patrol, law enforcement—when the town council got wind of that, they cut off any money to that food bank. We do not contribute to any causes that are perceived as political, even though as individuals we may support that cause. Our donors give money to us for food, not advocacy.

As far as the impact of political rhetoric on our clients, a number of them do not speak English. Some of them are legal, some of them are certainly not; they're undocumented. And frankly, people who are in that situation are really living from day to day and aren't necessarily imbued with the political rhetoric on either side, as we might be, because they've got other priorities. But I think [the rhetoric] certainly sets the tone in the community.

Every time we have someone come from Washington, DC, if he or she is a Republican, they don't come to our county, because we tend to have a fairly humane approach to immigration and such issues. They go to the county next door where there's an extremely outspoken sheriff who is always talking about crime on the border, and always talking about smugglers. Yes, there are smugglers, there's no question, but he really doesn't want to see *anybody* come into this country. He'd be perfectly happy to see all of them sent back to wherever they came from. I think it really *is* political rhetoric, and it does frame how people elsewhere in the state see us, as they tend to be more conservative. So it's a very interesting place, frustrating as it can be sometimes, but a very interesting place.

But, you know what? All that being said, I am happier in what I'm doing right now than I ever have been from a professional standpoint. I think it's because we have the support of the community, and the people that I'm privileged to work with really feel dedicated to a mission.

I'm never bored because I don't allow myself to get bored, but if I had stayed home during many of those years when I technically retired, I would probably have gone crazy. I do like challenges, and I like living on the edge of nervousness while doing new things. I've told people that I go from exhilaration to exhaustion. I'm always kind of teetering between "Oh, yeah, this is great. I feel *so* good," and the next day: "Oh, god. I've gotta do *this*!" But you know, I think if I didn't have that, I wouldn't be as fired up as I am.

What's it going to be like when it comes time to walk away from this work? Do you think about that?

I do. I'll be 75 in August. When we moved here, I was sort of thinking about retiring. Well, that surely didn't happen. One of my friends calls it being "rewired, not retired." I'm definitely rewired. I think about it, and I don't know that I'll ever stop doing something that engages my mind. On the other hand, I do want to spend more time with our grandkids. So yes, I think about it. I think about it a lot, but I know I'm a person who needs to keep busy. I haven't resolved it, yet. I'll probably be dialing down over time so that there's a better balance. But it's . . . it's a challenge.

"Baseball is still an escape."
CHARLEY FRANK

He is executive director of the Cincinnati Reds Community Fund, now in his 20th season with the Reds.

The fun part about this job for me is that Cincinnati Reds baseball is probably my very earliest memory, being at Crosley Field.* And I remember when I was 5 years old, going with my father and grandfather to the 1970 World Series with the Orioles at Riverfront Stadium.† My grandfather was a season ticket holder for 50-plus years, and I had the great good fortune of attending 20 or 30 games a year with him and getting to know all the people in our section of seats and feeling that sense of community and being knowledgeable about baseball as a young kid, learning the language, and then being able to talk the game.

What a formative part of my upbringing and what a positive, enjoyable memory. The great luck that I had cutting my teeth on the 1970s Big Red

---

* Home to the Reds from 1912 to 1970.

† Home to the Reds from 1970 to 2002.

Machine with Pete Rose and [Johnny] Bench and [Joe] Morgan and [Tony] Pérez and [George] Foster and [Ken] Griffey—these great, compelling, interesting, winning teams that lifted Cincinnati well beyond its class, put Cincinnati on the map.

So all of these rivers converge for me at this stage in my life, this early memory and interest and passion that I've maintained regardless of where I've lived and now being part of that organization, charged with taking the brand and doing the community work to connect the region. Just remembering the enormous sense of pride and connection that I felt, which has been a blessing and a curse.

Why a curse?

I've always taken the outcomes of this team, this franchise, so personally, so much to heart, even as an adult. So much of my memories, my life's timeline gets connected to what was happening with the Reds' fortunes in a given year.

I've very intentionally not infected my children with all that. They both played and enjoyed baseball and softball recreationally, and enjoy coming to a few games a year, but they are more interested in the community aspect of my work than they are the baseball.

We [the Community Fund] are one of two nonprofit arms of the Reds. We are the very intentional youth baseball/softball educational community arm of the Reds. And I'll tell you, Mark, when I started, the youth development piece of this was a nice-to-have, but now almost 20 years later we have a sport with an aging audience, and a game that is expensive and complicated to play. And it's not being taught in every household the way it was when I was growing up generations ago. There aren't enough kids playing the game.

That's a crime because baseball and softball are the equalizer. You don't have to be the biggest, the fastest, the strongest. If you know the game, if you know the nuances of the game, if you know how to play the game and you're undersized or oversized, you can contribute. You can earn a high school varsity letter; you can put yourself in a conversation for college scholarship. There's so much humility and character built into it. So we think there's so much value in teaching the game and keeping kids playing the game and not diminish teamwork.

Why do you think the audience for baseball is diminishing?

There's so many reasons. One of the obvious reasons is the technology era that we live in and the [need for] instant gratification. Baseball is not as conducive to that. Games can go on for hours. I worked in the NBA and there were 41 home games, and they were indoors and they are about two hours and 30 minutes, two hours and 40 minutes. It was all very consistent, predictable.

What I loved about the game [of baseball] growing up was the conversation about the game, the history of the game, the fact that the statistics from the 1920s were still relevant in the 1980s, 1990s. I love the feel of the game and the ebb and flow of the game. That worked in the '70s and '80s and '90s. And as the century has turned, and as people started to move faster, expect more instant gratification, baseball has struggled.

I think that because it really is a language to learn, it's something that requires adults, loving adults, to teach the nuance, to teach the love of the game, almost like a language. And with the preponderance of single-parent households over the last handful of decades, it's harder and harder for those families to teach the game. There are much bigger priorities. And life's a lot faster and a lot harder, harsher. There's a gentleness and a deliberate nature to baseball that's harder to find in everyday life.

I live near a youth ball field about half a mile away, and I walk my dogs past it. I've been involved in helping to renovate those fields. Our organization underwrites a lot of expenses for the teams that play on it. I'll always be excited when the weather's good enough for those teams to be out there playing. It's the pitcher trying to throw strikes, and it's the catcher trying to catch strikes. And if you're a young kid, it's hard not looking at youth football and basketball and seeing something where they're going to get a steadier dose of action. I just think there's some inherent challenges in the game that we try to overcome through creativity and connection.

When we started [the fund], we had one key program that was called our Reds Rookie Success League that we ran at a couple different locations in Cincinnati, trying to get younger kids introduced to the game, and then we began underwriting expenses. What began for three organizations with nine individual age-group teams back in 2005 is now over 500 teams a year. So we began by identifying what are the barriers for baseball and softball? It's funding for underserved teams. It's the condition of the ball fields. It's finding adequate coaches. And it's really having the ability to improve their game and learn the game on a year-round basis. Those were the original guideposts that we had when talking to a lot of leaders in the city. I'm always really moved by the fact that that's still our mantra today. The other big undertaking was we built an urban youth academy [providing] year-round training for underserved kids. We raised close to $8 million to build it.

One of the things I really treasure these days is being able to be part of the apparatus that breaks down the barriers in an era where there's so many of those barriers to allowing people in. The more and more and more money that gets poured into pro sports, the distance between the fans and those pedestals just grows by the minute, so breaking down those barriers and really allowing people to feel like they're a part of it—that's something that is really rewarding. Because sports is a common language, I think it may still be one of those last bastions that, at least to some extent, can avoid that deep divide.

"What do we need to hold on to so that we don't lose ourselves?"

REV. ERIK CHRISTENSEN

He is pastor of St. Luke's Lutheran Church in Chicago. Prior to that, he had worked as a youth advocate and community organizer with and for runaway, homeless, and street-dependent youth.

We are seated near the center aisle of St. Luke's sanctuary. Our voices echo in the empty hall.

Before I came to St. Luke's, they had just passed their centennial, and there had been a very intentional conversation about, will this ministry continue? They were receiving advice from representatives of the national church body who'd conducted a feasibility assessment for redevelopment at this site. The advice the church was getting was, essentially, "It's been a good run. You've had a century of ministry in this neighborhood. That's nothing to be ashamed of. We can help you kind of have a good death."

Half of the people who were here at that time thought that that was wise, and about half disagreed. And when they put it to a vote, those who wanted to continue won the vote by a margin, a very thin one.

At the time they were looking for a pastor to come and lead them, I was looking for a congregation, and both of us were having trouble for a variety of reasons. My own situation was that I had finished my seminary education and my internship, but I had been removed from the ELCA's [Evangelical Lutheran Church of America] candidacy process for being openly gay. Our denomination would change its policy about LGBT people serving in ministry, later.

Meanwhile, this congregation was struggling to find a pastor. They got a postcard in the mail one day from this organization saying, "Would you be open to looking at LGBT candidates in your next call process?" And they responded, "Well, nobody wants to be our pastor and nobody seems to want these [LGBT] pastors. You know, maybe there's a fit here."

When I arrived, the congregation was about 12 members in their 60s, 70s, and 80s.

There's something about that number 12 that I can't put my finger on.

(Laughs.) Yes, we've talked about how 12 is a good number to start with. We have about 120 members now, up from 12. Our average worship attendance on a Sunday morning might float between 50 and 75.

How much of your personal measure of success is connected to the numbers?

Well, the question of how you connect success to numbers is so tricky because growth is positive, but not all growth is sustainable. Do I want our congregation to grow? Yeah, I want it to grow in trust and in deepening commitment to one another and to the needs of our neighbors, and I want that to be done in a way that's transparent and honest and attractive enough that other people say, "I've wanted that, too. I'm going to go check them out." That kind of growth is great.

But if growth just means a count of how many people come on a Sunday morning, and does the money that they give allow us to continue to do what we've always done, I'm not interested in that kind of growth because so quickly that kind of growth becomes about justifying what we've always done as the end toward which we should always be moving. That kind of growth sucks out of the room the impetus to ask the question "What's needed now?"

As we've grown, the local regional Chicago expression of our church, and the national church, said they wanted to support us in that. They said, "You'll get a grant for the next three years, and there will be pretty severe step-downs each year. Let's see what kind of growth that grant gives you. With that amount of time, can you come to a place of self-sufficiency?" This property has about a half a million dollars in deferred maintenance.

We continued to grow, and that [financial] support continued to decline, and the question was, "Are we going to get to the place where we're able to sustain this before the support runs out?" By early 2014, we could tell we weren't going to get there. Then we had to ask ourselves, so what does that mean? Does that mean we failed because we didn't "get there"?

We started a listening campaign, kind of used some of those community organizing tools, sitting down with people one-on-one and then in small groups and then in town halls, asking the question, "What makes us, us?" And not, "What makes us a church?" or "What makes us Lutheran?" We wanted to know, what are the distinctive marks of who *we* are? And as we look at this change in front of us, what do we need to hold on to so that we don't lose ourselves?

We saw themes bubbling up as we looked at all these interviews with all these people. They were saying, "This is a congregation that's open to everybody regardless of their station in life. So whatever we do next, it better express that value." And they said that "the things that we say and do on Sunday morning shape what we say and do as a congregation in the public square throughout the week."

What they did not say was "We worship in this beautiful room." It was like a loud silence, you know? I mean, the room did come up. People were saying things like, "It's a beautiful room, I love it. But we could be us somewhere else." Just two weeks ago, we took a vote. The issue was whether or not the congregation would authorize our council, our board of directors, to list this property for sale. What drove the timing on that vote was the unsustainability of our assets and the burden of this property.

Do you think you could find that it's even possible to be more authentically "who you are" without this building?

(Pause. Laughs.) You know, the temptation is to answer that question "Yes." Like, yes, if we step forward into this new reality where we realign our assets around this conversation about values, we could be more who we are, we could be truer to who we are. I think there's a huge temptation to say that the answer to that is yes. What I'd rather say is, we *have been* who we are here. We weren't any less ourselves here.

The council said, "What do you want us to look at? Do you want us to go explore what it would look like to sell our property? Do you want us to explore what it would look like for us to reduce our staff? We serve on behalf of you, so what do you want us to be exploring for you?" And we did a nonbinding vote. Over 90 percent of the congregation said, "Give us options around selling."

Where will you go?

I don't know. I don't know. And so, in that environment of unknowing, there's a real draw to a firm answer. People would love me to say, "Okay folks, here's where we're headed." I've heard people say, "How can we vote on leaving the building when we haven't been given a compelling vision of where we're headed next?" I believe that any attempt right now to offer that vision is really just kind of an illusion masquerading as a certainty.

Do ever think about what the last service here will be like?

In this space? Yeah, I do think about what a leave-taking from this space would look like. I remember when I was in ninth grade, my family sold my childhood home. It was a huge house on a block full of little bungalows. We were a family of four in a really big house. It took a lot of work maintaining this beautiful old house. Then at some point, as I was moving into high school and my sister was moving into junior high, they could see the empty nest coming and realized we have way too much house. The sensible thing to do is to move to a smaller house.

But it was so painful. For all of us, I think. This was the house where I'd had my first pet dog. This was the house where my adopted sister, who came from Thailand, had first experienced snow. How could we still be us when all those memories are wrapped up in this place? I remember, I wrote a letter to the people who bought our house. (Long pause. His eyes tear.)

I think I chose to share that memory because, as a professional, there's a desire to frame things in terms of profit and loss and bottom lines and making the wise choice. In some contexts, you would just look at [our congregation's situation] and say, "Do we buy or do we sell? What's good for the bottom line? What's good for the shareholder?"

But when I think about the woman who has brought her grandchildren to Christmas Eve worship here for the last 30 years, I can't approach this leave-taking like it's just a matter of what's best for the bottom line. We all struggle with that desire to be practical, the desire to be efficient. I remember what it was like to be a little boy leaving my home and thinking, strangers are going to be in this house. You know? Strangers are going to be in *my* house. I don't even remember what was in the letter I left them. I think it just said something like, "I loved this house, please take care of it."

We can love a place, and our emotional connections to those places are important because important things happened there, but don't confuse those emotions with a sense of ultimacy, that this is the only place that those things can happen. I loved that house. I wept when we left. And then we had a good life somewhere else, right?

Is there an object from this church that you'd like to take with you when you go?

We have this biblical story of Moses leading the people through the wilderness and the Ark of the Covenant, and there's the question of what goes in the Ark. This is where we put the tablets of the Ten Commandments, and the things that remind us, as we move through a foreign landscape, of who we are. So I think part of what goes in the Ark for us are these conversations that we had about: Who are we? What makes us, us, and what has to continue in order for us not to lose ourselves in the wilderness? Yeah, so I think those conversations and those statements of memory and of value, those have to go with us.

What about for you, personally? Is there a little "souvenir" you'll take?

I want one good picture, like the good, old-time photos where everybody stood out in front of the church so you captured that moment in time. You can say, "This is who we were in 2015, and this was our home."

Postscript: Not long after this conversation, he and his congregation moved into a small storefront space. They did take that photo on the last day at St. Luke's.

"Our first Sunday in the new space was All Saints' Sunday. When we began singing the first hymn, people spontaneously broke out into four-part harmony, which had always been more challenging in the larger space because singing in harmony requires being able to hear the people around you. If you're 70 people scattered across a giant room, it's hard. But once we were in this tiny space, and people could hear each other, they just started harmonizing naturally, and people started crying, having this experience of hearing one another for the first time."

"You just have to keep pushing forward."
MONA WALKER

She is a deputy chief of police for a large suburban community, population 80,000, "that is extremely diverse. You have everyone from every walk of life—different socioeconomic statuses, different levels of education; we have poor, we have filthy rich, just a very diverse community. There are gangs and drugs here. I think a lot of our shootings are because of gang-related beefs. There is a drug problem. Our town kinda is a hub for a lot of the drug movement that's coming to the city and out of the city. So those continue to be huge challenges, especially in our Black and Brown communities."

She and her wife were "high school sweethearts" and just celebrated their 25th high school reunion. They have three children.

I serve in Field Operations. So, I'm one of three deputy chiefs. Basically, a deputy chief is second in command to the chief of police. The three of us, we all have our own divisions, or bureaus, if you want to call them. Field Operations is the largest division among the three. I'm in charge of all of patrol operations, so all the officers you see in uniform out on the street, that's what I'm responsible for. I also supervise our traffic bureau, our community policing bureau, and also under my purview, our police chaplains, our field training program, our animal warden, our canine unit, etcetera. It is—yeah, a lot. It's mainly my guys and girls that are out there. They're the ones that are first responding. They're the ones that are involved in all the community events.

This community is unique. You can have a group of neighbors that are complaining about an oak tree being cut down. And then that same day, you can have a community in an uproar because one of their teenagers was shot and killed. I mean, that's just how disparate that community is, very different sets of problems in different areas. But everyone's problem is a huge priority. And so, I think, with that you have to have a police force that is very flexible and able to adapt quickly on a dime with who they're dealing with and what the issue is.

I always tell people that 90 percent of the time I love my job. I believe in its purpose. I believe in our purpose-first society. I really do love my job. I've been given some incredible opportunities throughout the years. But that 10 percent, that 10 percent. That is not appealing; it has been really rough. You know, seeing things that you're not used to seeing, the trauma that you are exposed to trying to help a situation and then not really being successful with it. Some of the internal conflict, especially that I deal with within my own agency, these are the things that weigh heavy on my heart. And they're the things that I hang on to, unfortunately. It takes a tremendous amount of self-awareness to be able to self-check myself and make sure to remember that "Hey, this is what you signed up for; you've got thick skin; you know how to deal with these problems; you just have to keep pushing forward." It's a reminder that I've had to give to myself so many times over the years.

You still have to keep reminding yourself.

Yeah, you do. It's kind of like an internal dialogue. When I feel down about something that I've experienced, or I feel like something's wrong, or I feel sad about something that I might have been involved in, there's just a constant reminder, the internal dialogue: "If not you, then who?"

I very much feel like the profession is a calling, you know, it's a calling for service. And I very much feel like those that are in law enforcement are kind of the chosen ones, you know? We signed up for this, we know what we're getting ourselves into. So the dialogue sounds like that, you know, "Hey, you're a chosen one, you you you. You have to do a job; you have to get it done. And if not you, who's gonna do it?" Somebody's got to be strong and take care of it. It's kind of like the military. It's just this call to public service.

I see camaraderie and cohesiveness, but there's a lot of internal turmoil, too, that a lot of people don't talk about. They don't want to be honest about it. The competition that happens inside of police departments, the backstabbing, the not allowing people to recover from their mistakes, things like that. The internal conflict is what weighs heavy on my heart all the time. And I've seen it on many different levels with many different people. And that part is sometimes the part that eats me up; it can be very, very challenging. It can be overwhelming at times.

Right now, one of our biggest challenges is our city council. We had all those protests [after the killing of George Floyd], and then in addition to the protests, every Sunday, a group would come in front of the police department, and they would write horrible things on our building, on our sidewalk, and they would shut down the street. We asked how city council wanted to deal with this. "Do you want us to make arrests?" But nobody would give us an answer. And so, we were very hesitant to arrest because there was this balance of protecting [the protestors'] First

Amendment as well. They painted "Defund the Police" right in front of our police department. And [because of the council's not responding to us] that paint was left there for months. It was finally removed.

We're having trouble retaining our staff, both at the police department and across the city because of city council. [Our staff] has been very vocal about "I'm leaving to go to a place where the city supports me, where they acknowledge me, where they value me as a police officer." And it's sad, because I fear that we are going to continue losing people to other agencies where there's not all the racial tension and where there's more political support.

How did you feel when you first saw video of the killing of George Floyd?

I was pretty disgusted by it. In my mind, this is absolutely a police officer killing someone. There is no reason why any officer should be kneeling on anybody for that length of time. Then I was *more* disgusted when we learned that there were two or three other officers on scene that were holding people back and just allowing this to happen.

I can say with extreme confidence that something like that would never happen at my agency; we are just trained better. We wouldn't allow that. I mean, we wouldn't—if somebody was kneeling on somebody because they were taking them into custody, that person would be kneeling on that person for about 30 seconds to begin the handcuffs, and then we'd be off your back.

So pretty disgusted by that; very sad about it. This is why Black and Brown communities have trusting issues with the police, and being a minority myself, it's important for me that we have good relationships with our minority communities. I know that *disgusted* is a strong word, but that's how I felt. And then to find out they were responding there because it was for allegedly passing a counterfeit bill. I mean, is this . . . is this . . . where we're at?

We have to understand that when George Floyd—and I'm not diminishing his death by any means—but his death was a moment in time, and moments in time, they cause revolutions. And the issue is the larger system. We're just a tiny piece of that, but we're the easy ones to target and blame. I think one of the easiest ways I can put this is that the people who make up the laws aren't the ones that have to enforce them. We don't really get a say in a lot of that. For me, from a leadership standpoint, it's being able to see the big picture, and being able to look at all the parts that are impacting a larger system. So when we talk about

George Floyd, I think to myself, when all those riots and civil unrest and looting, when all of that happened, they're not really, in my mind, in my personal opinion, they're not protesting what happened to George Floyd. The people that are doing that are upset about the criminal justice system as a whole and how it has largely been unfair to people of color. But try telling that to a new officer who's just trying to do their job and can't understand that concept. It really does require big-picture thinking and looking at things from multi-levels, which is difficult to do. It's difficult to do.

Sometimes you get to a scene where there might have been a shooting, and everybody comes out; suddenly all these people that never exit their houses, now they're all coming out. And I don't know if they're being nosy or if they're trying to be helpful, but it very much oftentimes feels like we're being targeted, or that they're watching us with a watchful eye.

I can remember one specific incident where we responded to a shots-fired, and there were three people that were shot. And these were young, I mean, they were teenagers. And two of them were dead when we arrived, dead on this stoop. And the other one that was shot made it all the way inside to the residence. This happened about a block and a half north of the high school, and it happened in broad daylight. So you can imagine how many people were flooding the area because they wanted to know what the heck was going on. All these mothers came by because they wanted to know if it was their son. I mean, it was a complete cluster.

And naturally, one of the first things we do right away is to try to secure the scene and contain a perimeter so that we can keep people kind of far away. But during that incident, I remember where a female came out, I didn't know her, but I recognized her from the community. She said to me and to one of the detectives as we were putting up the crime scene tape, she said, "This is *your* fault because you guys are never out here." That's not the first time I have gotten a remark or a comment like that from somebody of the community. When they say things like that, it's very hurtful. It's very hurtful. Hearing comments like that are always very disheartening. This happened probably four years ago, and I remember that very vividly. I can tell you exactly what she was wearing because that comment, really, it was a knife to my heart. It was a knife to my heart to hear that, you know, so things like that stick out.

How much of your job do you take home with you, emotionally?

I take it all home. Oh, I take it all home. So, I'm married; I have a wife and three kids, and my wife works part time. I don't think I can do this job without her. She has an incredible gift of just listening to me complain. I get upset about things, and she doesn't try to make things better, because she knows she can't. But she has an incredible ear and oftentimes she might give some advice or say, you know, "Well, maybe you could have done this, maybe you could have done that differently." But she is who I complain to. I try very hard not to complain at work because that can really bring a level of toxicity to the police department. And I have always been taught you never complained down the chain of command. You can complain up the chain of command, but don't complain down the chain of command. Well, now that I'm almost at the very top of the chain of command, I don't want to complain to my boss because he has a lot that he's dealing with. So why am I going to complain to him? He doesn't want to hear it anyway. I bring it all home—bad calls, things that I've seen, the turmoil in the department that I told you about—I bring it all home.

What does your wife do for a living?

She used to be a hairstylist, but she had the kids, she had all three. When we had our first kid, we decided, "Well, somebody's gotta stay home and take care of the baby." And it sure wasn't going to be me because I love my job too much. So she stayed home. And she really has been a stay-at-home mom, full time. I really think that she's one of the reasons why I'm still somewhat sane.

"You can see such beauty and then such pain."
JAIME SAUNDERS

She has been president and CEO at United Way of Greater Rochester and the Finger Lakes for three years. Previously, she was CEO at a domestic violence center.
We talk on Zoom almost a year after the start of the pandemic. She calls in from her office and is the only one there. This reminds her of the day United Way of Greater Rochester had received a $20 million grant from MacKenzie Scott. Jaime had been instructed to be alone in her office when she took the call.

And I couldn't tell anybody, not my board, not my staff. I did take spousal privilege, though, because I walked out of my home office—which was a dining table—at 7 o'clock at night crying. I told John about it, and then I said, "I think this is either one of the greatest moments of my career, or I am being punked."

This had been a hard year. We had raised $35.1 million, and yet I was a million in debt because, operationally, most of the money coming in goes out to serve our community. And I can't cut any more. We're a small organization really; well, 100 staff. So it's been a really hard year, and the community's needs and pain is so high. We were having some hard conversations at the board level, and then for $20 million to fall from the sky was just unbelievable. Unbelievable.

Our community in Rochester is one of the worst in terms of childhood poverty; more kids live in poverty than not. We have one of the most segregated communities in the nation. Our upstate region is the home of Frederick Douglass, Susan B. Anthony, and Harriet Tubman; we have social justice through our bones and in our DNA, but we're doing terribly. That doesn't just happen, so we have to ask ourselves, how and why is our community doing so much worse compared to others? And how can we figure out how to make that better? Those are hard conversations and take deep reflection, but that's what drives me.

Racial injustice has been highlighted in the disparities around COVID. Black and Brown communities have higher death rates and less access to care. And then [there was] Daniel Prude, a gentleman who was having a mental health episode and was handcuffed naked in the street by the police here in Rochester while it was snowing. He died a few days later. You might have seen him [on the news]. The incident was videotaped and much unrest in our community followed.

I had thought I was a good ally, and I thought I understood the complexities of racial injustice and racism, but I have been humbled by how much more I need to learn. So the work is raw, hard, and humbling. And I'm committed to learning and learning and learning ways where someone who looks like me, and is in the seat that I'm in, can make room for others, lift others, and make impactful change within the areas that I can impact.

It sounds like you look at these issues and what's ahead, or may be ahead, and ask, "What's United Way's and what's my role in that?"

Yep, that's exactly right. And so, we try to take that view, primarily in the human service space, where we anticipate . . . we are seeing estimates between 30 to 40 percent of nonprofits will close. Unfortunately, many of those are arts or neighborhood-based smaller organizations, typically Black-led or by a person of color. They're smaller and under-resourced. What if what we're seeing is that solvency will be hard for the nonprofit sector in the next 18 months? What is our collective role to make sure that there's a softer landing, because the services and the needs don't go down? If anything, they're going up. So how do we get in front of that? What is our role?

You know, they call it a "K" recovery; you've probably heard that term. Those who make $64,000 and above are doing okay through COVID so far, and those that are not, like in the service industry, are really plummeting. And so, the poor are even poorer, and the rich are richer. Philanthropy is okay on the high net worth, but on the everyday philanthropy, the hit is going to happen in this next year as the stimulus dollars, the rent and mortgage moratoriums go away. It's going to be a very difficult year . . . *and I am an optimist!* But the harsh reality is this year will be extraordinarily difficult. And next year.

Do you ever feel emotionally overwhelmed by this work?

When I was working with victims of domestic violence, there were times I'd come home, and I would talk to my husband—without saying names because of confidentiality—to try to process some of the really hard days. One of those hard days was when we had a case where a woman was tied up to a furnace, and the boyfriend starved her for three days and was beating her child. Just horrible, egregious acts. And my husband, I remember one night, was doing dishes, and he just let a plate drop. He said, "Could you not tell me that stuff anymore? It's too haunting."

And I realized you start to build up a veneer a little bit when you witness trauma after trauma after trauma. You don't want to lose your own humanity in that. So how do you balance being open and *having* your humanity and not developing too hard of a shell so that you can be there to meaningfully support that mother and child? How do you balance those two?

When I think of my hardest days, there's an exercise where you try to find what motivates you or calms you, and I have an image of a 6-year-old girl from our shelter. When I think of what she lived through—I mean, that girl has more strength and grit, so she's my inspiration. She deserves as much as my child, as much as any other child. And so, I *can't* be tired. You know? It doesn't make sense. It is too much of a privilege to be able to be tired. That girl inspires me.

But there are days where there's so much pain, and you still have to find that light. That's where I feel so fortunate to work at the United Way, particularly when I'm in the middle of so much of the pain that you hear about and see. I'm in a position to receive from these amazing philanthropists—I mean, a company just gave us $5 million and said, "We believe in your work, go and help a whole lot of people." It's just extraordinary that you can see such beauty and then such pain and that we're in the middle of the two.

What is this job teaching you about yourself?

What I'm learning about myself professionally and personally are probably two different answers. Professionally, I have learned to show more of my human side. I think as leaders, you're trained, particularly in business school and even general readings, that people get unsteady if you show cracks, and you're supposed to have the answers so people will rely on you.

I've tried to show vulnerability as a strength. And so, to my staff, I will say, "The George Floyd and Daniel Prude [killings] really brought me to my knees," and I'll explain why. My showing that side has surprised me how much it's meant to people. I didn't realize how much people were *watching* me for cues, especially, I think, in a Zoom environment. They're trying to read your body language, your words. And I'm trying to find the right balance of how to be the kind of leader they need me to be, but in an authentic way.

And then on the personal side, I'm always mindful that it's hard on my family, and it's got to be even more difficult for others. You've heard the iceberg analogy in social work, right? You only can see what's visible and there's so much more happening in people's lives and battles that they're fighting that you can't see. I just try to have more grace and patience and love for, well, for everybody, personally and professionally.

"It's better for everyone."
BETTY BOGG

She is the executive director of Connections for the Homeless in a large, multicultural community. The mission of Connections for the Homeless, which was founded in

1984 in a church basement, is to "serve and catalyze our community to end home-lessness one person at a time." She has worked in homeless services for 30 years.

My getting into this work was all accidental serendipity, but it fit with my inner drive to fix things. My dad was an alcoholic, and that puts a person in the position of having to fix things all the time and make things work better and organize things and structures and systems. That's a big thing that not-for-profits often need. People come to work [in nonprofits] because they're passionate in their heart, but they don't know how to run payroll or keep the lights on or not get sued for something. So there's a role for folks who can have this back-office impact and a mindset around systems thinking and structure.

Probably everybody who doesn't work in homeless services has, at one point, thought that people who are homeless have done dumb things or they've made mistakes and that that's why they're where they are.

That it's their own fault?

Sure, that it's their own fault. There's this sort of American puritan idea that peo-ple need to earn their stuff and pull themselves up by their bootstraps. But people are homeless for all kinds of reasons. They come from all backgrounds, all walks of life. They are particularly impacted by generational poverty and structural racism. So, of course, people of color are disproportionately impacted by home-lessness and poverty, but it literally can happen to anyone.

Thirty years into this work, one of the things that I love the most about Connec-tions is the organizational buy-in to not treat people who have experienced homeless-ness as "the other," as people who have failed, and we're going to shake our fingers at them and tell them how to do it right. "You've made bad decisions, that's why you're where you're at, and I make good decisions and that's why I've got all this stuff."

For us it's a real partnership where we work with our participants to help them find housing and remain housed or ideally keep them from losing their housing in the first place. So what really appeals to me now as I've grown older is that the true sense of partnership is respect. (Pauses.) I get on my soapbox, so forgive me if I'm waxing a little bit about this.

That's why we're here.

I get up out of bed every morning because I can go to my office and can run into somebody for whom we ended their homelessness. I can remember when they were sleeping outside my office with their head down on a table, then getting up, taking a shower, and going to work as a crossing guard, and now that person is living in a house and living their best life in their retirement years. It's frickin' amazing. But this work can also be heartbreaking. We lose people to heart disease and overdose and suicide . . . and hopelessness, right? I mean, we have these really strong relationships, so it's heartbreaking when we lose somebody, so I've got to have something to hang on to so I don't despair all the time.

Our staff beats themselves up. They're like, "If I had just called this guy, or if I had just checked up on him." I have to remind them every time someone dies that they died knowing that we cared about them. (Pauses.) I'm sorry. I get choked up thinking about this. It is such a gift for people who have lived through really, really horrible times that they had someone who cared about them at the end. We go to their memorial services, or we have a memorial service for them. And even that sadness is a place of gratitude for me.

One of the things that I hear most from people who are homeless is the profound isolation that occurs when they're living on the street. They're viewed as dangerous, dirty, sick. People don't make eye contact with them. Their humanity gets eroded by this constant isolation. And there can be that finger wagging and shaming and denigration of their dignity. When they come to us, they are sometimes ready to be abused, like they're just waiting for us to do something terrible to them because they're accustomed to that. So people are very protective of themselves and their history and their information.

Let's say you've been sleeping in a forest preserve for 18 years. You don't just walk into our drop-in and say, "Here's everything you need to know about me to get me into a house." People are guarded and difficult to engage. With severe mental health issues and symptoms, they can be especially hard to engage, and our job is to engage them. So we have to find every possible way of doing that.

There's these three big tenets that we work with. One is "housing first," which means we put people into housing and *then* we can talk to them about the things that are impacting them negatively. That changed the way practitioners of homeless services viewed the people that we work with. They're not mistakes to be fixed, but people with real strengths. Give them the opportunity to heal and to breathe and eat and have a door and a bed and a bathroom—things that we take for granted—*then* we can start talking to them about the negative impacts their coping mechanisms are having on them.

Another tenet is called harm reduction. We talk to people all the time about what they're doing and how they could reduce the harm to themselves, so that could be coping with drug use or alcohol use. It could be doing sex work, so how can we give you safer sex supplies? Can we give you a number to call if you're being trafficked?

It seems uniquely American, how offended we are by people in poverty: they are lazy, they are bad. In India, when you give money to someone who's begging, that's seen as a gift [to you]. They're giving you the gift and the opportunity to do something good. In America, we are just deeply offended by [panhandling] and that it's not really working: "You're not working hard enough."

I get asked this question all the time: "What's the right way to handle [a panhandler]?" There's no one-size-fits-all on this. Except for: that's a human being. Panhandlers are not getting their needs met, and that's why they're panhandling. It's dangerous. It's hot, it's cold, it's trapped. You know, it's terrible. One of the things that I think we tell ourselves when someone's asking for money is if I give them that money, they're going to do something I don't approve of. And my response to that is, if you need to control what people do with their money, you should not give it to panhandlers. Just like my employer doesn't get to tell me what to do with my money. I can do whatever I want to with my money. You've got to be fine with that. If you're giving your money to a panhandler, they might use it to buy drugs. Or they might use it to buy toilet paper that they can trade for sleeping on someone's couch tonight. They might buy a hotel room for a night. Human beings need money to survive here.

But I do want to make sure I'm clear that panhandling and homelessness are not the same thing. They can overlap, but it's not my mission to end panhandling. It's to end homelessness, but if we gave panhandlers a place to live and a secure source of income and their needs were met, why would they be standing on a street corner or at a highway off-ramp when it's 115 degrees? Why would they?

I think one of the most toxic perceptions that I hear, even from people who are good-hearted, is: "I worked really hard for my money, and if *I* can do it, so can they." This could be coming from a white person who has no recognition that, yes, you worked hard, sure you worked hard, but do you think you work harder than, like, a garbage man? That's a really hard job that you're not willing to do for the money that it pays. Right? It makes my stomach flip a little bit when I hear that from a really well-off white person without their saying, "Yes, I've benefited from a system that rewards people that look like me." That's just kind of out of their consciousness. And to me, it seems like those folks just need to have a reason why they can keep all their stuff and other people can't have any of it. It's because they worked hard and so they deserve it, and those other people didn't work hard so they don't deserve it.

The mortgage tax deduction, that's the biggest institutional giveaway that there is. It gives breaks to people who already own houses. So we're going to prioritize *their* comfort over the comfort of people who are in need? All this cultural stuff is really hard to shake.

And what is infuriating to me about that "if you just worked harder" thing is that I can guarantee you nobody's working harder than those folks. Nobody who runs a hedge fund is working harder than a guy who's driving Uber and washing dishes and is a school crossing guard, and his wife is cleaning houses. This is *not* a work ethic issue. But this is how we value people.

The homeless problem is not [Connections'] problem. It's the community's problem. Connections is a way for us to help the community solve this problem. We're kind of the scaffolding by which that gets done, but it doesn't get done if the community doesn't want it to be done. It's better for everybody. If there's not a tent city, it's better for everybody. If people are employed in good jobs that make them feel fulfilled, it's better for everybody. If all kids get a good education, it's good for all. You don't have to feel altruistic, like it's a giveaway; you're doing it for yourself because your community is better when everyone is living up to their full potential. And we're the mechanism sometimes by which that gets done, but we're not leading the charge, even though people definitely want us to be.

We need to pivot toward making and talking about policy [to prevent problems] and not just solutions to fixing things that have already become a problem. Let's go after the cause.

"The sense that we're all here for each other."
DEBORAH REED

*She is an independent bookstore owner and novelist. Her store, Cloud and Leaf,
sits two blocks from the Pacific Ocean in Manzanita, Oregon, a small coastal town,
population 675. She has set two of her novels in that town.*

Manzanita is a gem of a town, and when people are here, part of the experience of
either living here or visiting here is to visit Cloud and Leaf Bookstore. Although
this bookstore is near the beach, I don't sell a lot of beach reads. When I bought
the store from the previous owner, one of the things she said to me was that every
independent bookstore has its own personality. Each one carries its own collection of books that's either representative of the community or of the owner or
both. As it turns out, I was a good fit to take over the store because she and I had
a very similar sensibility about how to curate the store and what to fill it with.
And that is really the key: it is a curation.

If I was in a very different town, it probably wouldn't work to have a literature and translation section, like I do. I probably wouldn't be selling as much
poetry as I do, but people come in and they feel that they're in a kind of a different place, a—I don't know—a little bit of an elevated place. There's an element
of sophistication to the literature. There's no romance section. There's no horror
section. If people do come in and ask, "Do you have any romance?" I just say,
"Well, the store is small, and I can't accommodate everything."

It *is* a small store. It is curated, though, to the point where there's a lot of
obscure things and also plenty of commercial fiction and nonfiction from the
bestseller list and all of that. But I think what so many people enjoy about it
are these strange little curations. I get things from small presses and that sort of
thing. They're like these finds that people, when they discover them, they're just
thrilled. They come back because they always find something unusual. That's part
of the personality of the store that was started by the previous owner, and I sort
of jumped into the flow and carried on with it.

The only things I've changed are I painted the inside all white because it used
to be orange, and so it's way brighter now. I put Turkish rugs in there, so it feels
very homey. I put in an electric fireplace that gives it an element of a nice cozy
atmosphere. But no coffee bar, no. They can go next door for the coffee. I've also
expanded certain things. I've literally doubled the poetry section.

The other thing that I've done is to prevent, in some ways, the rancor of political conversations. In a small store, people start talking to each other and there are different political beliefs. It could go downhill fast, so I created just one shelf, the top shelf, in the nonfiction section for politics. Those kinds of books used to be on that table when you first come in, and I've moved them all to the back. If you want a book on politics, you can find it back there. I also didn't want to have nonfiction books facing out with all of this ugliness on the front. Like, I carry Bob Woodward's book, *Rage*, but it's got this aggressive picture of Trump on the front. I just think that people come into the bookstore, in large part, to get away from that.

When you come to Manzanita, you're surrounded by the natural world. You've got the beach on one side, and you've got the state park on the other. There's nothing else. It's not a place to come to be entertained. I think people come here to get away from entertainment and . . . madness. It's a place of contemplation. So I carry a lot of books on things like insects and eels and trees. *The Soul of an Octopus* [by Sy Montgomery] is a very big seller. It's all of these books taking the natural world and reflecting back to us our place in it. I think there's a strong element of disconnecting [from everything else] and then reconnecting with some kind of "higher self," if you will. I don't want to sound too lofty, but I do think that that's how people feel when they come here; they feel like their better self.

It's old-fashioned, I guess, at this point, but it's all about a real, human, in-person experience that I think people are starved for. A bookstore like mine opens up the opportunity for someone to say, "Oh, I've never heard of this book. Can you tell me about it?" That's not going to happen at a chain store. It's not going to happen on Amazon. So, on the one hand, we have a smaller slice of the pie, but I think you can use that to open up the minds of people who wouldn't otherwise be exposed to certain works if they only ever shopped at Barnes & Noble. It's a little bit like junk television where if that's all they've ever seen, then people keep tuning in because that's all they know. And therefore, the networks are like, "Well, this sells, so that's what we'll keep offering." It feeds off of itself. I think a main reason why independent bookstores are so crucial to communities is they reflect a whole different aspect of who we are.

If the population of Manzanita and your clientele changed, would you change the bookstore and its inventory?

Wow. (Pause.) I don't know. I don't know. The population would have to change so drastically. Like I said earlier, the bookstore is part of the experience of being in this place, so if an element of that shifted . . . I don't know. I think I might end up with a smaller clientele if I did this, maybe, but I can't see myself spending my days recommending books that I, myself, wouldn't read. That would be a hard, an ethical problem for me.

How did the pandemic affect your business?

I did not anticipate anything like what actually happened and continues to happen. My store has been really busy this past year [during the pandemic]. I'm almost embarrassed to say that. People are very sequestered out here with their books and are reading like crazy. And people were being laid off from their jobs, so they were home with nothing to do. They also want to make sure that they support the bookstore so that it is always there forever more, you know. They were buying gift certificates and buying books just for the heck of it. All of these things were happening at the same time.

I am heartbroken and filled with survivor's guilt when I see what is happening with other bookstores. I mean, every week there are articles about bookstores shutting down or under the threat of shutting down. And, god, I don't know how I got so lucky, but it's quite something.

I think the bookstore, which was always a place of solace and contemplation and chitchat and catching up with each other, became even more important once we could open again. People couldn't travel or go anywhere else, so they could come into the bookstore and feel a sense of peace and normalcy, and they could leave with these recommended gems in their hands and go off into the world and have these experiences with books they couldn't otherwise have. I would say it's a combination of all of those things that has really gotten us through. Everybody is so supportive of each other. I hate to call that "old-fashioned" because I think it should be the future.

And that's our whole town, too. We have a hardware store where it might as well be 1950. You go in there and you shoot the breeze with the guys about nails and hammers. We've got MacGregor's Whiskey Bar where you go in there, and they'll just talk and talk and talk to you about all kinds of whiskey and local gossip. I mean, you name it. It's like everything in town has that same kind of personal connection, the sense that we're all here for each other.

I can't believe that while the world is, you know, a dumpster fire out there, what I am seeing in my little corner of the world is very different. It's very hopeful. So, yeah, back to your question. If things were to change, I don't know what I would do. I have a hard time believing that things would change that much because everyone here just loves it the way it is so much, but things do change.

POSTSCRIPT: *Since the time of our conversation, she sold the store to another writer and editor and moved to Berlin, where she is working on her eighth novel.*

HEALTH AND SAFETY

"The full complexity of a situation."
KEVIN BLACKBURN

He is 36 years old and has worked in emergency services for 20 years, first as a firefighter and paramedic in Connecticut, and now as a patrol and SWAT officer in South Carolina for the past five years.

The area that I work is a poor area on the outskirts of [a large city]. I would say it's probably 50 percent white, 50 percent Black. I'd say it's fifty-fifty fairly poor. I feel like a lot has changed since I've been a police officer for the last four and a half, five years. There's been a lot of large-scale issues. COVID changed a lot of the day-to-day of what we did when it was at its peak, and the civil unrest that we had, particularly last year, intertwined with COVID, I guess was another fairly significant thing that we had to work through, especially on the SWAT team.

I would say that the sentiment of a lot of the police officers is there's now much more a sense that—I don't want to say lack of support—but maybe there's kind of a little bit of a concern we have that even when we're doing the right thing, we're still being maligned. I think that that has made us, as a group—I hate to say negative—but when I was a paramedic, I could go to a call that has an adverse outcome, say somebody was in a horrible car accident, and even though I would do everything that I could do for them, the outcome still might not be desirable. And people would recognize, "Hey, Kevin worked really hard; Kevin did the best he could in a complex situation. He tried his best, it just didn't have a great outcome. It wasn't for poor intentions or lack of effort."

But in law enforcement, I sometimes feel, especially the last couple years, that even when we do the best we can in these real-time, complex situations, that if the outcome or the *perception* of the situation is negative, then we are faulted, right, wrong, or indifferent. And that makes it that much harder. You're in a position where, realistically, you have to deal with that type of stuff. It's what you have to do to do this job. But mentally, that's the constant—I don't like to say *fear*, but there's this constant feeling in the back of your mind where you always have to worry about so much more, I feel, than I did even three or four years ago. And maybe that's just my perception of it because I haven't been a police officer for 20 years. Police officers I know pretty well, though, who've been police officers for a long time say that the last few years have been much harder than earlier in their careers.

When you talk about a negative perception of your work, who are you saying has that negative impression? The press, the community?

I've wondered that, too. In my day-to-day, I go to a lot of calls. I would say that for the majority of them, statistically, people are pretty fair, pretty realistic, pretty objective about what we're doing, especially if I explain the legality of this situation. I think part of the problem stems from there not being a lot of awareness of the realities of police work. A lot of people's perception of it is based on the media or a TV show. It's not based on any sort of a real understanding of the practical realities of what we're legally allowed to do in terms of things like searches, anything like that.

I think that there's also—I hate to say media as a whole—but I think sometimes the media doesn't necessarily cover things as objectively as they could. A lot of the time, the people that I deal with day-to-day and know, and I don't get that sense of vindictiveness or hostility from them. But then, like, I was driving down the road maybe a month ago, and people were just yelling, *screaming* at me, calling me a terrorist, all this other stuff. It's hard to gauge the source of it. And you don't necessarily see it with a large percentage of the population. But I do see it regularly enough that it makes me feel, like I said, kind of, in the back of my mind, always worried.

The thing about police work that I've noticed even more than fire and EMT is that when things go wrong, when situations develop or happen, they happen so fast. Everything will seem to be okay, the situation will seem to be resolving or under control, and then things will just go so bad so fast. And I think that's one of the realities of being a police officer. But it does make you kind of always aware of—I'm not just talking about public sentiment, or the way that individuals interact with us, I'm speaking more generally about situations where people start fighting you and things like that. So you always have this awareness in the back of your mind, almost this pessimism that something is about to go wrong, because so many times that we are on these calls, dealing with whatever the situation is, things do go wrong.

How much of that feeling of "something about to go wrong" is necessary alertness and mental preparation and how much, do you think, is actually detrimental? Can that feeling get the better of you?

They talk about the dangers of hypervigilance and the kind of toll that can take on your body. But I also think that you *have* to have that level of awareness and vigilance as a police officer. It keeps you on your toes. I think, frankly, what we deal with a lot of times *is* negative, so by default, you know, you're always so worried about getting attacked or some sort of viral video coming out. That's the other thing I try to remind myself of: I'm dealing with the negative side of a lot of these things much more than the positive side. I want to make sure I don't lose perspective and just start assuming more negatively than I should, but when you're tired, and you've gone to 20 calls over a night shift, and everybody's yelling and screaming at you every call you go to and you're backed up on paperwork, it's . . . it's hard. It's hard not to get out of the car and be in a bad mood, sometimes.

I think a large part of this is due to larger, like, societal issues. I mean, juveniles without any sort of role models or structure or discipline or father figures, whatever it is. I mean, we see that all the time, you know. I had a—god, I think he was like, 10 years old, a couple weeks ago. He was causing a scene in a Walmart, and he was running away from his grandmother. She called 911 [and said he was actually missing], so we got involved. But [it turns out] she didn't feel comfortable handling his behavior. Obviously, this is more of a parenting situation than a police situation. It's not a law enforcement situation. You don't want a 10-year-old to think negatively of the police for no reason, so we were very nice to him, reached out to him, tried to establish rapport with him. And all he did was curse at us. Ten years old, cursing at us, you know?

And that's not on the police. That's on everything that's led up to the point where a 10-year-old feels comfortable acting like that in Walmart. I mean, that's societal. But while we were dealing with this, people's cameras were out watching us dealing with this 10-year-old. And again, you're always fearing that the perception of it, the viral video, is going to be, you know, "Police arrest 10-year-old" or "Police manhandle a 10-year-old" or whatever. That headline would be completely untrue.

Ultimately, nothing happened; everything worked out. Grandma got the kid in the car, and they left. But I mean, it just, it wears on you. How do you go to that stuff for years? You've got to remind yourself, like I was saying, to be objective, not just tunnel vision on all the negativity.

How were you affected by the Derek Chauvin murder trial?

I did not watch the trial. Me watching it and paying close attention to it obviously doesn't change the outcome of anything. I feel like, in my day-to-day work, I'm invested in being a police officer. I believe in it; I think a lot of what we do is very valuable. But there's a lot of strife that goes along with that, you know? There's a lot of challenges. I do care about law enforcement; I care about its reputation; I care about the people that we interact with, the citizens, but I don't want to be off duty and watching something that's going to make me feel like I'm at work, so I just, I didn't want to watch it.

I don't really want to go down a rabbit hole with my opinions about it, but I would not have done what he [Derek Chauvin] did. I mean, I know that's easy to say. But I don't think that he—in my personal opinion—said to himself, "I want to kill George Floyd." I think he handled it wrongly. I think there was better things that could have been done. I'm not defending his behavior at all. But there is a lot of misunderstanding from the general public sometimes about the complexities of some of these situations. When you're in them, it's hard sometimes not to get tunnel vision. And I'm not defending him, but I felt like the public thought that he was intentionally trying to kill this guy. I think that even though his behavior was wrong, and not defendable, I don't think that that was the intent of Chauvin. From what I could see.

I've been in lots of situations where you're trying to manage so much and watch so much. I think that's what the public doesn't necessarily understand. There's a lot of moving parts to this, much more than just "I'm going to kneel on this guy until he dies."

I do think there's kind of a general lumping together of all police that wasn't really fair to us [in a totally different city]. You can see, sometimes people, just the way they look at you, you know that you're being judged, and that gets old. I can understand that you can't change people's perceptions. People have the right to their opinions, but at the same time, it's like, if you are accused of something you didn't do, you feel wronged. That's my perception of it. It's hard sometimes to not feel a little bit betrayed.

Unfortunately, a lot of times when we have shootings, especially in apartment complexes or whatnot and other types of situations, they attract crowds, and often we're fairly short-staffed. A lot of times, especially in the initial response to an incident, we only have one, two, maybe three officers for the first few minutes. And, I mean, there's times when you do have large numbers of people, you're outnumbered, you're in a crowd that's hostile to you. It does happen fairly regularly.

I got called a couple years ago to a shooting incident on the other side of the city that stemmed from an earlier shootout between gang members of rival gangs. There was a funeral [for one of the members] and after the funeral, they had a get-together in this neighborhood. And then another shooting, which I believe was also gang-related. It attracted hundreds of people, hundreds, and they were all upset to begin with because of the funeral. Officers from all over the city and the ambulance were called. I mean, the ambulance could barely get through. I don't even know if they could render care on scene because of the crowds, the pushing, the everything else.

You're concerned about yourself, you're concerned about the other officers, you're concerned about the people, the citizens who are not involved who just live in the neighborhood. And even the people who *are* involved, you know, you don't want this stuff to escalate.

There's a lot of these situations that unless you've been in it, it's easy to make a judgment based on what you see on the news or in the media or, you know, a Facebook video, but it doesn't necessarily capture the full complexity of a situation. And it's, yeah, I guess that's what I'm saying.

"Move with a purpose."
JACK VICTOR

He is a wildland firefighter for the U.S. Forest Service. ("I want to be clear that I'm not talking to you in my official capacity working for the Forest Service. These are my own views.") He is 38 years old and lives in Arizona.

I had worked in politics for nine years, but I don't think I ever really wanted a career in politics or government necessarily. I've just always been interested in challenges and interesting work. It was fulfilling work for me to a point, until I decided to do something different.

I made a [career] jump late in my life. I was 29 years old. I guess I wouldn't call that "late in life," but as far as wildland firefighters go, that's pretty late.

There's a lot of different resources that respond to wildland fires. The Hotshot crews are the most experienced, they're the most trained and are the most fit. Many, many people consider Hotshotting to be the hardest job in the world. They respond to the highest risk because they have the qualifications and the fitness to succeed in those situations.

There's no such thing as an average day, but if I were to try to distill an average day, it would involve waking up at anywhere between 4:30 and 5:30 a.m., putting your boots on your feet, having a cup of coffee, maybe eating a burrito that was delivered to you or more than likely eating an MRE, the military rations. You start to build what's called a fire line, which is simply removing any flammable material from the path that the fire is traveling. You're using chainsaws to fell the trees that are in the way, or you create a trench. Usually, you're on a mountainside. You're high up in elevation, and you need to dig a deep trench so that debris and embers can't roll down the mountainside. You do that all day until the sun goes down. And if the fire is cooperating with you, you can go to bed. But if it's not cooperating, you don't go to bed. You just keep on going.

The job is rigorous. It's anywhere from 14 to 21 days deployed to any location in the United States, usually high up on a mountain, and you work for 16 hours. And then you sleep typically where you finished working. And then you continue the next day. And up until recently you got two days off. Can you do that for six months straight?

You are constantly hiking into or flying into or driving into situations that seem impossible to deal with. Just imagine hiking into a dark forest with high trees in the middle of the night. You can't see where the fire is. But you can hear it, and you can smell it. You don't know how fast it's moving. You don't know what fuel it's burning in. And you don't know what you're going to do once you get there.

What is the role of fear in your work?

Fear plays a role, yeah. I *hope.* Fear comes in by understanding the history of the tragedies that have occurred in wildland fire. There's been hundreds and hundreds and hundreds of people that have died fighting fire, so you try to understand the situations that those tragedies occurred in. So then when you see them in real life, it doesn't mean you stop what you're doing, but instead a calculation occurs, and you try to listen to that fear and say, "What's it telling me? Is it telling me to back off, is it telling me I need to mitigate something? Is it overcoming me in a way that I'm not going to be productive?" I think fear's role is to simply check in with yourself and the decisions you're making. It's an instinct that we have. It's natural, and it should be analyzed when we're feeling it.

I think that more than being afraid of fire or falling trees or whatever, though, what I've been most afraid of in those situations is whether or not I'm going to have the fitness to deal with what we're about to engage in. This feels like running marathons every day. And you're wondering, "If things get out of control, will I have the fitness to escape, to outrun the fire that's on my tail?" When we train, we train with that in the back of our minds. So: "Move with a purpose." That means we're going as fast as we possibly can. And there can be a point in time when you can't go as fast as you want, and you need to drop your backpack. Your backpack is anywhere from 45 to 65 pounds. Or your chainsaw, your chainsaw is 20-something pounds.

But I really find it important to impress on you that there's also long periods of non-activity. It's feast or famine a lot because the conditions have to be right to be engaged in the way I just described. If the conditions are not right, you can be sitting on that fire line for days and days and days, waiting for the right opportunities to engage. And that can be just as difficult.

I think experienced firefighters eventually get very comfortable with it because it's great to have your downtime. When you don't have that downtime, it's going to be really intense for you. But newer folks, they got into this job for a reason. They wanted to be up against the fire's flames. They want to be feeling heroic. They want to be engaged in adventure, so just waiting around is not in their DNA. That's not something that they're okay with, but that changes over time. Once you've gotten your butt kicked enough, you take the waiting very happily.

What we're seeing now, with climate change, is that there are no longer seasonal fires. It's all year, now. And that's not mostly California. It's starting to be in other places like the Southwest, year-round fire seasons.

The firefighters that are retiring today, those people fought maybe three to four, what we call "campaign fires" in their career. Huge, catastrophic, 100-acre fires. A 100-acre fire is not even something to acknowledge these days. We're talking about hundreds of thousands of acres, and we're talking about these happening all year round in states where they didn't even happen in the past. So the firefighters that are retiring today, they're just shocked because the current wildland firefighter, the current Hotshot is fighting massive, mega blazes. And that's every fire that they go out to as opposed to a few throughout their entire career. So, it's drastic; it means drastic changes.

Is it the new normal?

I mean, I hate that. I wouldn't want to ever use that language because we shouldn't accept it as the new normal, but it *is* what's happening. Climate change is worsening. And at the same time, humanity is building further and further into the wildlands. The problem has grown, but the workforce hasn't grown, so there is the same workforce for quite a bit more work, and more dangerous and risky work. And to make matters worse, the benefits and pay for the wildland firefighter have remained stagnant for a long, long time.

I could take my qualifications and I could take my experience, and I could go to a municipal fire department or county or a state fire department and make double what I make now. And I can have a lot less risk, and I can stay home more, and I can have a much, much better quality of life. So over the past decade, we've seen a massive amount of resignation. Wildland firefighters, federal wildland firefighters are resigning. The risk isn't worth the reward. There's less of us to do the job and there's more fire. So the mental health burden has become a crisis. There's more suicide deaths in wildland firefighting than line-of-duty deaths. It's because of the mental health burden that's placed on the wildland firefighter. There's a lot of PTSD, you know? You're in high-risk situations and your brain is constantly in the fight-or-flight mode. And once [you get home], your brain doesn't shut off the fight-or-flight mode. A lot of people struggle with that, and they have substance abuse issues. I've seen a lot of people affected.

I'd love to retire from wildland fire, someday, but [the situation] makes it impossible. I don't know if you know this. I've been doing this for almost 10 years, and I make $16 an hour. And I'm a crew boss, a qualified crew boss. There's people that have been doing it for 30 years who make $22 an hour. So where we're at today is most fast-food workers at quality fast-food restaurants make more money than we do per hour. So I'd find it almost impossible to have enough money in a retirement account after 20 years to do this for a living, and we all are in that position. We're all trying to figure it out because it's not sustainable.

Is there resentment?

There's massive resentment. People love this job, and they have tons of pride, but they can't understand why the agency heads and the lawmakers have not responded to our needs.

It's about making sure the public knows what a wildland firefighter is, and once they do know and they learn that you get paid $16 an hour, they're ashamed of their government. They know people's houses are saved because they see it on the news. They put up a banner saying, "Thank you, firefighters." But I don't think most people have any idea the difference between a structural firefighter who sits in a station all day and responds to medical calls and maybe three to five fires a year and a person that's on intense wildfires in a remote area, away from their family, being paid for only the hours that they're working, not the hours that they're away. Minimum wage. Not many people know that.

You know, back in the day, it was different. The economy was different. The pay actually was still okay. Twenty years ago, $15 an hour wasn't that bad. So it's that the economy and the wage increases just have not kept up. Back then, wildland fire wasn't a huge issue. Firefighters that are retiring today, their primary job wasn't fire. Their primary job was being in the woods doing, you know, fuel reduction, cutting down trees, building trails, and then they went in a fire a couple times a season. So the pay was never designed to be for like 24-hour-a-day, full-gear first responders, it wasn't designed for that. But it didn't change, it never changed.

All things considered, are there elements to this work that you find fun?

Yeah! It's all really fun. It's all incredibly fun and the sense of camaraderie is interesting. You're doing really, really hard things, and the people that choose this line of work, that's what they're into. They're into testing themselves. They're into accomplishing really big things. The fitness side of it at first is what you're stoked on because you're just destroying yourself every day. And for a lot of people, that is extremely therapeutic. You find a lot of people that find relief and escape doing ultra-marathons or really hard days out. Even though the pay is terrible they do get paid to do that and to forget about your life's problems for a period of time. That's powerful. It's really, really powerful. I know a lot of people that had suffered from addiction and all sorts of issues who have cured themselves doing this kind of work. So yeah, it's incredibly fun when you're engaged in the exciting aspects of it, for sure.

"It just comes down to, I have a job to do."
ALEX HILLIARD

He has been a firefighter in New York City for 17 years. He is married to Meghan Hilliard (p. 105), an ER nurse. They have two young daughters.

I wanted to be a firefighter since I was 5. My grandfather was a very well-respected dentist in Milwaukee. He always viewed firemen like these lazy guys that sat around the firehouse watching TV, sitting in their recliners. And he kind of thought, "Listen, you can do better than be a fireman." My uncle Mike was an oral maxillofacial surgeon. My mom was a nurse. My uncle Steve is a surgeon. My grandma was a nurse. So you know, my grandfather was just kind of like, "Listen, you're in a medical family; you can do better." And I was like, "Well, no, I want to be a fireman."

When I was just about 14 years old, my principal's husband was a lieutenant in the fire department that served our area. She was able to set up a ride-along for me and my grandfather. He was able to sit and talk to the paramedics and to the firemen. And we left that day with him being like, "No, you absolutely can be a fireman. Now I realize that it is not just sitting in the recliner."

I work in a specialized unit that covers parts of Manhattan and the Bronx and have a little bit extra training. We are in the SOC [Special Operations Command] community and are trained in advanced firefighter removal. We get extra training in high-angle rescue—so ropes, confined space, trench, auto extrication. My company is an engine company, but we also have the tools to begin any sort of specialized rescue. Not to sound too, like, on a high horse, but the squads and the rescues are kind of the last stop. We're like the Navy SEALs, if you will, of the fire department. The chiefs will look to us to fill in some gaps and right some wrongs. Without sounding too pretentious, if we can't get it done, it's probably not getting done.

You sound very proud of what you do.

I *am* proud of what I do. Like I say, I've been interested in the fire department since I was 5, and now I'm on the New York City Fire Department. We are what a lot of people strive to be. We go to a lot of fires, and we go to a lot of crazy incidents, and we're in the mix of things. I've watched a lot of videos. We call them "buff videos," the documentaries. And now I'm working alongside some of these guys and being taught by some of the guys that were in some of these documentaries. And it's very humbling. I'm honored. There are days when I will just say like, "I can't believe I'm here. I can't believe I'm walking up to a scene as a member of this squad."

You joined the force six years after the 9/11 terrorist attack. What did that day look like to you as someone who was soon going to be one of those firefighters?

My passion for the fire service and for wanting to be a fireman was super strong pre-9/11. And to be completely honest with you, 9/11 didn't change that in any way. I would do nothing different than those guys did. I would be charging in there just like they did to put the fire out. New York City firemen are some of the best in the country and the best in the world, really. We know that we have a job to do, and I can't, in good faith, take an oath to protect the citizens and visitors and property and life of the city of New York and then look at a building and say, "Oh, I'm not going in there." I absolutely would just grab my tools, my equipment, and respond as though it was a house fire. It's our job, you know, and it's what we sign up for.

Firefighting is a dangerous profession. You're the guy running into buildings while other people are running out. It's just kind of what we do. You know, quite frankly, as morbid as it sounds, anytime I go to work I know that could be my last time for a multitude of reasons. Cowardly terrorists crashing into beautiful buildings in the city of New York is not going to stop me from doing my job.

What role does fear play in your work?

Quite honestly, probably not as much of a role as it should, you know? I don't think I'm invincible, that's for sure. Fires are scary, but it's kind of like what we trained for. I think if I really feared what I was doing, I wouldn't be as good at my job as I hope that I am. You can't do a job well, if you fear fire. Yeah, of course I fear how unpredictable it is, sometimes you don't know what's gonna go on, you don't know what's in buildings. But it doesn't impact the job that I have to do. I have a position to get to, I have a task to complete, and I'm going to attempt to do that to the best of my ability.

You meet people in an extreme situation in their lives. How does that affect you personally?

So, I try super—(His daughter trots across the Zoom screen.)—Hey, I like your jammies there! There's definitely no way to be completely absolved of any emotion. I try really hard to treat every person we come in contact with for the most part like they're a member of my family. But I try super hard to not get too caught up in the people that we deal with.

I remember one time, a motorcyclist got into an accident with a semitruck, and the driver of the motorcycle, he had his head run over by the rear tires of the semi. It literally, like, shot his brain about six or eight feet from his head. There was a passenger on that motorcycle, and she was completely unscathed. I remember bringing her to the hospital and taking her to the emergency room to run tests and take X-rays, etcetera.

I remember getting into the emergency room and the ER attending was asking like, questions that were completely irrelevant to this woman's care. "Is this the girlfriend? But he's got a wedding ring?" You know, whatever. She wanted this crazy backstory, and I was like, "Listen, this woman was on a motorcycle where the driver was killed by a semi. Can we focus on this? The Jerry Springer version is not at all important."

So.... (Sighs.) I try super hard, and it's probably to a fault. I will probably have some sort of massive mental breakdown in 30 years, but I try very hard to be compassionate to those that need compassion, but to just kind of keep it as, you know, business, as work, as a job.

But anything involving kids, especially now having children, myself... I think about my girls, and I would jump in front of 8,000 bullets for them. They hold a special place in any first responder's heart. If you talk to any first responder in this country who is worth anything, they will tell you any call involving a kid gets their blood pumping a little bit more. I don't want this to sound bad because we do move fast, regardless, right? We take every call, no matter who it is or what it is, serious. But there's a different level when it's a kid. A lot of guys in this profession—nurses, doctors, firemen, EMTs, paramedics—they have children. And so those scenes are definitely way more hyped up. It's just the way of EMS.

You sound like someone who relishes challenges.

Yeah, probably to a fault. I challenge myself to be an extremely competent fireman. I want to have the respect of my peers in the fire service. Your reputation is built on how you perform and the challenges that you're willing to face and how you perform within those challenges. These challenges are what kinda shape you, and they shape your reputation. You could have a great reputation for 20 years and then do one completely ridiculous thing and wreck that. Some guys don't care, but some guys really do care. I'm definitely one of those guys. It's like to a fault, to where I just care so much about how I'm perceived by the men.

I like stuff to be genuine. I don't want, when God forbid, if I pass away in a fire, I don't want guys coming up to [my wife] Meghan like, "Oh, he was a great fireman" if I wasn't, which is a morbid and bizarre and weird thing to say. But I guess it's just a little bit how I'm wired. I don't care about other reputations that I have or what people think about me in other ways. But if it were to happen that I did not fare so well in a fire, I hope to have a good reputation amongst the men. Maybe I'm not the nicest guy or whatever. But, you know, I want to be well respected with my fireground work ethic.

"These moments of quiet and grace."
MEGHAN HILLIARD

She is a nurse and director of emergency services. She is 37 years old and has two daughters; one is 8 and the other is 21 months. She has been a nurse in Connecticut for 15 years. Her husband, Alex Hilliard, is a firefighter and a paramedic in New York City (p. 102).

I am a nurse by trade, but my job is I'm a regional director of emergency services. I oversee the operations of three different emergency departments. I have one that is in a unique suburban community, almost a farming community, but it's also in a town that at one point in time was the heroin capital of the world. It's a very poor socioeconomic area. I also oversee a freestanding ED [emergency department], and then I oversee a Level 3 trauma center that serves a community that is all hustle and bustle; it's near large casinos and whatnot.

Emergency medicine is something you either really love or you really hate. There's no gray space in between. Either you are energized by and love the fact that you have no idea what's about to happen all day long, or you can't bear it. I love the unexpectedness. I never, ever have the same day twice. Ever. I also love that you have to sort of be knowledgeable about everything, right? I have the pleasure of taking care of the full gamut of humanity. I get to help take care of, at the same time, sometimes in the same room, little bitty babies and people's *babcias*. It's Polish for grandma. The hospital I first trained in had a very high Polish population. I don't think that there's anything that I genuinely dislike about emergency medicine.

Any nurse will tell you that there are days that eat away at pieces of your soul. And it's because you really care about the patients, and you care about the work that you're doing. But then you have these other sensational moments where you get to tell someone that they're pregnant or give somebody other unexpectedly good news, or you get to really connect with a patient.

Like, for example, I took care of this gentleman that was—we call them a "friendly face" or a "frequent flyer," someone that comes to the ED kind of regularly. He reminded me very much of my dad. He had a lot of the same sort of physical illnesses that my dad did, but my dad lived across the country from me before he passed. And so, I used to go in and sit with and take care of that man. It felt a little bit like I was connecting with the nurse who was taking care of my dad out there. Like if I take extra good care of this guy, I know there's a nurse out there who is going to take extra good care of my dad. It sounds so sappy, but the best nurses do come from that place of "I just really value the work that I do."

And the days that "eat away at pieces of your soul"?

I can remember every child that I ever cared for that died. I can remember every single one of them. And each story is more sad than the previous one. A mom falls asleep in the bathtub with the baby, or Mom had drugs in the diaper bag and the baby got into it. And then, in the room next door, you have a woman that's been trying to get pregnant for years and just can't. And it just eats away at your soul, these pieces of sadness and inhumanity in the world.

I can remember being in a room with this parent that was crying and crying. And I remember coming out of that room and then going into the room of another patient who had been waiting for me for quite some time. And the parent in that room yelled at me: "My son has a fever, and he has been waiting, and you haven't come in with the Motrin you promised!" Just dressed me down. And I remember thinking, "You just don't even know how lucky you are. The parent in the room next door has just lost her whole world. And you're yelling at me about Motrin."

But you don't get to feel that. And you don't get to say that, because that parent is also experiencing what *she* thinks is an emergency, right? Like they think their child with a fever is the most important thing in the world, and she doesn't know the tragedy in the room next door. So you don't get to lash out, and you don't get to snark, and you just smile and you apologize and you go get the Motrin, and you tend to her child with a smile on your face. It can be really hard. It can be hard to fluidly move from one room to the next and not carry the sadness of the first room into the room next to it.

We just stuff it down because you just have to keep moving. Most of us don't talk about it with our own families because our families don't understand. I am lucky, though, to be married to a fireman who is also a paramedic by trade, and he very much understands the things that I see and do on a day-to-day basis.

Have you found ways of coping with the strong feelings stirred by this job?

Oftentimes, us nurses and staff, we go out after work and have dinner together. You have some drinks and you just blow off some steam and you laugh a little bit. You try to find some humor somewhere else so that you can just kind of keep moving past the sad things that happen.

Sometimes there's dark humor, too, that helps. Sounds terrible, but . . . there is a little bit of giggling that occurs, and it is in no way meant as any disrespect for the patient or their family or the seriousness of the situation. It is a coping mechanism. Like, we use a machine to help with compressions so that we can free up a staff member. It's called the LUCAS, and it physically does the compressions for you. But when you use it on somebody who is, for all intents and purposes, dead, their arms, if you've not secured them right, they sort of flap up and down a little bit like *Weekend at Bernie's*. Or the arm kind of drops down off the side of the stretcher and maybe brushes a nurse's leg. There's a little bit of giggling that happens there. To the layperson on the outside looking in, it probably looks insensitive, and it looks unkind, and it looks un-compassionate, but sometimes it's the way you make it through the day.

These are the same nurses, though, that when the time comes to "call it" and you pronounce the time of death, will take a moment of silence, and they stand there with that family. For as much as there can be some silliness, when time of death is called, there is a level of grace that is applied. Oftentimes, we ask families to leave for 10 to 15 minutes while we're cleaning the patient up so that we make them look the very best that we can for those loved ones. Before families come back in, you remove anything you can, like if there's blood or vomit or anything like that, you clean them up. We will remove their valuables to make sure that patient's rings and things go home with their loved ones. We bag up their clothing. We make sure that we put a gown on the patient.

We go to the blanket warmer and put warm blankets on them. Not for the patient, but for the family, right? Because no one wants to come in and feel like their loved one is cold. It's sad enough without adding the coldness to it. We put a pillow under the patient's head. And again, this is a dead person. They don't care if they have a pillow or if they're warm, but I'm about to walk their loved ones in. Sometimes I'm walking a wife in who has been married to this man for 60 years. And I don't want her to remember her husband in this sterile room in such a sad way. So you put a pillow under their head. You tuck the shroud in a way so that they can't see it because no one wants to think of their loved one in a bag zipped up. So you tuck it under the sheets so that the family can't see it. It's not a careless process. The people that do it, take it seriously. So, for all of the inappropriate humor, there are these still and quiet moments of grace.

And then, there's a whole process of getting someone to the morgue that most people don't know about. There's some standard work. You have to check the patient's name band. You have to make sure that you put a tag that has their name on it on the patient's toe so the people in the funeral home know who this person is. It is a bizarre feeling to tie something to somebody's toe and know that this person has died. Most people don't know what it's like to put a body in a shroud and zip that up. It is a very surreal moment. There's a finality there, and sometimes the nurses' eyes well up. The best techs that I learned from before I was a nurse, instilled in us that this is a sacred moment, the end of somebody's life, and you are zipping them up to move on to their next place in their afterlife.

I had the parent of a young child who died, and when she finally had to leave, she said, "I just don't want my baby to be alone" while waiting transport. I promised her, "I will hold your baby until it is time." I walked around the trauma room holding this passed infant, keeping my promise, right? That was the promise I made: that this baby wouldn't be cold and alone.

So, you carry this baby around with you in this room. And you cry a little bit because of the sadness of the whole thing. And you feel bad for the family and for yourself, and everything just feels so broken in the world right then. And then zipping a child in a shroud is . . . very hard. It's not a careless process, you know?

When the family leaves, there is this quiet moment where the nurses in the room. . . . There's just sort of a deep exhale, of. . . . (She exhales slowly.) And it's a moment of like, "That's . . . *sad.*" It sounds so plain to just say "that's sad," but it is a feeling that kind of sits on you a little while. Like: "Yeah, that was really . . . sad." (Exhales.) And then we'll call transport or security, and they come and they take the patient through the hospital to the morgue.

You almost have to be hardwired to be able to feel the good stronger than you feel the sad. When you have good moments, when you have wonderful moments, you just have to hold onto them so tight so that the sad ones don't hurt as badly. Some days that's easy and some days it's not. Some days you cry in the break room, and some days you get in the car, and you think, "I just can't do this anymore." Other days you think, "Gosh, I can't do anything *but* this. I can't imagine *not* doing this every day."

I think that if you stop having the days where you think, "Wow, that was really hard," or "Wow, that really didn't feel good at all," then maybe it's time to move on because part of being a nurse is being able to *feel* the sadness. It's what makes nursing such a different profession, right? Because so much of it is about being compassionate and empathetic and about caring about strangers. I mean, it's *complete strangers* you care about. I think when you lose that, when you lose that sense, it's probably not the field for you anymore.

"If I'm at work and there's a crisis going on, I know the rules."
MARY CAROL RACELIS

She is a clinical nurse specialist in the Department of Surgical, Neuro, Musculoskeletal, and Rehab Nursing. She has been a nurse for 35 years and an advanced practice clinical nurse specialist for the past 12 years. "I love the hospital environment. My father was a physician, and my mom was a nurse. My parents were divorced, so the time I spent with my dad would be on Sundays, and he would say, 'Go on rounds with me, and then we'll go to the zoo.' I liked seeing him interact with patients. I liked the dynamic setting. When I decided on nursing, my dad said, 'Come on, you can do better than that. You can be a doctor.' He was a really hard worker, and I saw up close the demands of being a small-town physician. I said, 'But, Dad, I would like to have some quality of life.'"

We talk twice via Zoom during the first Thanksgiving weekend of the pandemic.

In this role, you *have* to have self-awareness, and I would say, for myself, that has gone on steroids in the COVID storm. I've had to make sure that I'm a step ahead in building resilience. And if I'm not *feeling* that, what do I need to do to *get* it? Because I have to be there for staff who are actually doing a far harder job than I am and getting more exposure to the stressors of COVID in the direct front lines. I need to stay aware, sensitive, understand what they're going through, but I can't allow myself to [feel the same that they feel] or I won't be there to support them.

Caring for others in times of need and vulnerability is part of what draws us to health care; however, caregiver sensitivity over time can lead to moral distress. So I would say COVID has provided practice in that balance between sensitivity and not crossing the line. You need to think, "What do I need to do to *action-ize*?" I think that's a made-up word, but I like to use it. Taking steps towards action and solving problems helps limit risk of moral distress.

We had known it was coming. It was two weeks planning: How are we going to train the nurses for PPE, personal protective equipment, donning and doffing, and the system work? Normally, I work with two elective surgical units, patients who were having orthopedic procedures or spine procedures or plastic surgery or other elective surgery. Then, on a Friday in March, we flipped from that to a COVID unit—and those nurses changed their specialty on a dime, within two days. We probably started with an empty unit on Friday night and by Saturday night we were full, caring for 32 patients with COVID-19. And then a second unit filled within a week after that.

I'm so grateful I have 35 years of experience to pull from. There have been other times as a clinical nurse specialist that I experienced what I now know from reading is called "compression complexity." It's like this force you feel when workflows and patient types change rapidly. It's sort of chaos, but it's not chaos in the sense of people not being cared for and not following hospital rules. It's this anxiety and fear that needs to be managed. If I had tracked what I did as a clinical nurse specialist in the first four days, it was 100 percent answering questions, problem solving, and fear management. The most intense fear management I had ever experienced. It's not like people were freaking out, but you could *feel* the fear. I would have conversation after conversation, putting things in context.

Clinician fear is a sort of poison to safe patient care, so fear management became a primary function of my role. Many factors were coming together leading to this human response that was way bigger than "fear of a communicable disease." Every day clinicians care for TB, hep C, HIV. But this fear of COVID-19 was layers of fears from many contributing factors such as the unknowns about how the virus was transmitted, and PPE resource uncertainty. Dispelling myths from outside media and the president [Trump] was a big one. Also, identifying individual clinician vulnerability status. Clinicians living with vulnerable loved ones, for example. Additionally, volume of patients and changing rules exceeded the ability for institutional communication at times to reach front lines; this all added to a boiling point feeling.

When signs of fear—verbal or nonverbal—were detected in clinicians, it required one-to-one supportive conversations. I remember being hoarse at the end of each day from so much talking, problem solving, and getting to the root of clinician concerns. In the cases where clinicians were fearful for loved ones, they moved into hotel rooms provided by the hospital and the city, which is an example of how we tackled challenges one by one.

There were a couple of nurses floating to our unit that I felt had some of the biggest problems with fear, and I would sit them down and say, "Let me just share with you what I think you're going through." And I shared with them about when I became a new nurse in the late '80s. I hadn't really learned much about HIV in school, and suddenly my unit was 100 percent patients with various stages of HIV. If a clinician had accidentally stuck themselves with a needle back then, it could be far worse than contracting COVID. So I talked about some of the things that helped me during that time. I felt like the wise old lady. (Laughs.) It made me realize my age difference.

Our leadership team went from what I'd say was a strong team to a high-functioning team. The things that were low-level problems before COVID, the things that you're like, "Yeah, that's kind of a problem, we have to fix that someday," they were now like *on fire*. Clinicians who had elderly parents that were just barely living on their own before, it was now a crisis outside of work. People who maybe had health issues of their own or had somebody they were caring for at home, now had to take off work to care for them full time. So the layers and level of crisis management blew my socks off, actually.

We developed a document we called the "COVID Toolkit." We knew that we couldn't have clinicians stay too long at this level of uncertainty. The usual details of practice were blown out of the water. Like, how do nurses do what they do when they now only see their patients *half* the amount of time they had been seeing them before? Because they were told to limit the amount of time in the room, which was *opposite* of what we used to tell nurses: "Round hourly, round more often, if you can." And now it was more like, "Do good care, but see your patients four times in a 12-hour shift." That magnitude of change was mind-boggling.

If you are enjoying what you're doing and the people you work with, and you feel like you're making a difference, you can put up with a lot. The nurses' days were hard, you know, donning PPE before they'd go into rooms and doffing when they leave. It's a lot of extra work. I got tired just looking at them. It was like watching somebody swim with weights on their ankles.

What worries you most right now?

I think of the people out in the world who aren't wearing masks, the people who aren't socially distancing. I think that part is hard for me, knowing that they will contribute to the next surge we know is coming. I've always felt, even from the beginning, more vulnerable *outside* of work. People would say, "Oh, Mary Carol, thank you for going to work!" I'm like, "No, no. You don't need to thank me for that. Thank me for going into the grocery store. This is where I start to get a little nervous because people are closer to me, and they're wearing their mask with their nose out." That's actually where I've felt fear. It's been in grocery stores. I never felt that in a COVID-positive patient room wearing protection. It's always been true for me that if I was in a trauma situation outside of work, I don't function half as well as I do at work. If I'm at work and there's a crisis going on, I know the rules, I know where everything is.

How does it affect you when you see people being careless about masking and social distancing?

(Pauses. Her eyes tear.) It keeps bringing me to tears out of a frustration. And at this point, probably fatigue. I really do see nurses who have PTSD and some leaders who are on Lexapro who were not on Lexapro, before. We all wear thin, and I think I feel like I'm a mama bird to the nurses. We just hired two nurses and they had some traumatic experiences where they worked before, which didn't necessarily have all the resources we had. And one nurse said, just last week, "You mean, there's a chance we could care for COVID [patients]?" I said yes. She said, "I just need to be honest. If I hear the word COVID, I will be taking disability. I will not, I cannot come in." And she got teary, and we sat and talked. But this is classic PTSD, and she hasn't worked through it. She told me some of the situations that she had been in, and my heart really felt for her.

How have national politics impacted your work?

If the leader is not speaking with clarity and to science and consistent with what other people are saying, they're causing more chaos and more commotion that *ab-so-lutely* translates to the earthquake that is happening in the hospital, around the hospital, and in our communities. There's just no doubt in my mind. When there is a crisis going on, if the person in charge is creating more chaos, it is adding insult to injury. There's no doubt in my mind that it's created a far-reaching negative impact for us. You know, I'm more of a compartmentalizer when it comes to politics, but I'm going to just tell you, my personal. . . . That Saturday when the presidential election was called [for Joe Biden], the tears just flowed. My husband and I, we just hugged each other. The feeling of "It's over. Maybe we can see clearly now."

POSTSCRIPT: *Two years later, Mary Carol emailed: "During Fall 2021, I found the Kenny Rogers lyrics playing in my head: 'Know when to hold 'em, know when to fold 'em.' Like many, after two years striving to meet the demands of the pandemic work environment—long work hours, constant shifts in priorities/resources, and* *the nursing shortage in the inpatient hospital environment, I made a professional change, jumping off the hamster wheel, and shifting to meet a personal and professional goal I had pondered for five years."*

A year from now she will graduate from the Doctor of Nursing Practice Transformational Systems Leadership program. "I took a dramatic salary reduction to make this change; however, I feel healthier and can focus more on family—aging parents and children too."

"You need to be careful."
ALICE WHYTE

"Before I was a COVID case investigator for New York City Health and Hospitals, I was a graduate student. I had gone back to school for a master's degree in social work. I have two teenage daughters; one now is in college, and the other one's about to go. I was mostly at home; I wasn't working. And then I decided during COVID that I needed some money. And I needed some purpose because I was just really feeling down from what was going on around me.

"As soon as I heard about the COVID contact tracing opportunity, I was like, 'I think that's perfect for me, and I think I would be really good at it,' because of all the social work skills I had."

We talk on Zoom nine months into the pandemic.

You must be very busy.

We are slammed. And right now, we're using the most abbreviated script we've ever used. We have gone from what is typically a 35-minute interview to a 15-minute interview because of the volume of cases. That started, maybe four days ago? Well, with this Omicron variant. And it's hit New York, I think, a bit earlier than the rest of the country.

The way we start the interview, we ask them about symptoms. And then the next thing is about close contacts. We go through a bit of information to clarify the definition of a "close contact," which has also evolved over time. And so, we lay that out. And then we go through a very systematic process where I ask about people's household contacts. And then I ask about people who came into the house to provide services, then it moves into "Is there anybody else you haven't told me about?" The natural answer to that question is no.

You need to be careful. The script actually tells us to say, "Is there anybody you haven't told me about?" I'm never going to ask somebody that because it puts them on the defensive. I can say, "Is there anybody we haven't discussed yet?" We are supposed to follow a script, but at the same time, if you don't put in your own judgment and your own understanding of the people that you're speaking to, you're not going to elicit the same kind of trust, you're not going to come off as a person who cares. You're going to come off as a person just doing a job. I think it's so important that they feel like they're talking to someone who cares about their safety.

There are some situations where I know that it's not going to be an okay question to ask that question, and I will forego the question for the sake of the rest of the questions I need to ask. Quite often, people are doing these interviews with their spouse in the room. So there's definitely a risk that they're not going to give us a full disclosure of all their contacts. But, if nothing else, hopefully, the education that I give them about what they need to do will at least be conveyed to that contact. I know that could be the end [of the conversation] if I asked that question to a family that may seem like they're, you know, a traditional household or from certain backgrounds, like an observant Muslim family. So I might let that one go. I want to be sure that I'm taking into consideration that person's. . . . I want to be respectful, essentially.

Were you nervous when you made your first call?

I was so nervous. I was incredibly nervous. I was afraid that I could mess up. I think there's always some degree of adrenaline that flows before every single phone call, at least there is for me, because every time you call, you don't know what you're going to get.

I had a call where I had somebody who couldn't breathe, and I had to call 911 and stay on the phone with that person. She was a woman who had young kids and didn't want to leave them alone, so she didn't want to call an ambulance and go to the hospital because she was so afraid of what would happen to her kids. And I'm doing this call through a Bengali interpreter and trying to figure out if I can get the woman to agree to let me call an ambulance for her. And she finally did agree. It did work out, but the thing is, I never got to find out like, was she okay? I wanted to know that she was okay. It's hard to let it go right there. But that's the end of my role, and I'm done.

[Because of the politics around COVID] I've had people just *scream* at me about "this COVID thing," is the phrase that they use. People will definitely be angry, angry and hostile. I try and say, "I'm just really talking to you about your health right now, and I'd like to offer you some information and some services." For those people who seem hostile in that sort of political way, I typically will not mention the contact tracing until we are able to get further into the call. But really, if they're truly hostile, they will typically just hang up and hang up angrily.

We've definitely noticed patterns of where, geographically, people are not going to be happy with us. You can kind of draw a blue and red map of the five boroughs of New York City, and that pretty much aligns with where we're going to find the most hostility. And that's hard because you don't want to [be biased about] somebody for having a certain zip code and assume that they're likely to treat me hostilely, but that has proven to be true. And that's unfortunate.

But I love young people in their 20s because they'll just roll through their social life with me. They're like, "I went to this bar with these 15 people and then. . . ." They'll just lay it all out. I'm like, "Thank you, this is great."

Sometimes, you have situations where you're talking to people who are in the hospital and if they're well enough to talk, they usually want to talk because they're lonely. There are a lot of elderly people, too, who are alone in the city. And those are sad situations; a lot of them don't have other people that are coming by to see them because they can't [with hospital protocols].

I'm learning that every person that I contact has a story, and that I'm in a position where I can make something that's really scary, a little less so. I feel like it's a powerful position, and I take it really seriously. I think I learned that I'm able to take in each person fresh and give them every chance I possibly can to get through this in the least painful way possible. I think I've always known that I was an empathetic person, but I think I've learned that I'm more [so] than I even knew. They want us to work as much overtime as we're willing. But I can't do it. I can't. I don't have anything left. I have to take my time off.

What will you do when COVID gets under control?

I'll definitely go and get a full-time position as a social worker. But I have to figure out how long I stay with this versus moving to the next thing. It doesn't feel like COVID is going to end anytime soon. But I do think, for my own mental health, it might be time to hand over the reins to somebody else. When the right job comes about for me, I'll definitely go.

POSTSCRIPT: *Nine months after this conversation she reports in an email that she is now employed as a social worker in a hospital. She resigned from the contact tracer position to accept that job about a month before the COVID tracing program ended.*

"That's what we're here to do."
GEN. JEAN FRANKLIN

She is a one-star brigadier general in the Air National Guard and the U.S. Air Force. She and her husband, a recently retired pilot, and their three children, ages 10, 15, and 17, live in a small town in Maryland. She is 46 years old and has been in the military for 24 years.

What we are looking for are threats to national security, and determining how we can defend against massive attacks against the U.S. critical infrastructure in, for example, cyberspace. Our number one focus and priority is national defense. That's what we're here to do. Defend the nation.

My husband flew C-130s during the wars, both Afghanistan and Iraq, delivering cargo and personnel to forward operating bases. I was involved in both [wars] from an intelligence collection perspective. I was running operations, intelligence operations in both of those wars, and in other theaters around the globe.

I was active-duty Air Force for 14 years and an intelligence officer for 12 of those 14 years. I had a couple of different roles when the wars kicked off. When I was stationed in Europe, I was what was called a command briefer, the intelligence briefer for the four-star general who oversaw the U.S. air forces in Europe. It was my responsibility every day, twice a day, to brief him on major events and major muscle movements that could have a potential impact in Europe. I later joined the then-brand-new organization called Cyber Command working directly for the four-star general as a special projects officer and a speechwriter. I did two years on active duty in cyber operations and then I decided for a multitude of reasons to separate from active duty and was heavily recruited by the Air National Guard to come join the guard [which is where I am now].

I never thought that I could make it to a one star, so when I pinned on, it was a moment of surrealism and quiet reflection and . . . awe. It took many months to settle into the concept that I was a general officer now. Obviously, the responsibility that you feel is much heavier. You're suddenly in a fishbowl where you constantly feel like everybody is watching you and observing how you handle certain situations. I'm very mindful of that. I'm also very mindful of the responsibility that I shoulder in the sense of not only taking care of my airmen, but I also understand that at this time there's just a small number of female general officers across all the services.

When I took command of my wing here, I was the first female wing commander. I'm also the first non-pilot to command that wing, but everybody was making a big deal out of "she's the first female; she's the first female." And they kept wanting *me* to make a big deal out of it, too. I remember saying to this female two-star, I said, "I really wish people would stop saying that. I think it's more of an accomplishment that I'm the first non-pilot to command this flying wing."

And she said, "I understand what you're trying to say and that *you* might not want to focus on it, but there are younger females, and it is very important to *them*. You need to remember that no matter what *you're* feeling about it, it is important to someone." That really stuck with me. Now, being a good role model and making sure that the younger generation [of women] sees you *can* do it is really important to me.

How were you initially received by your those in your command?

There's a requirement when you take command of an organization in the military, that within six months to a year you do a climate survey to get a sense of what the climate is in your command. I did my climate survey and in general, across the wing—you're talking almost 1,600 airmen—there weren't a lot of comments about male/female this or that. There were a few that were concerning, though. And that was interesting, because as I stepped back, I realized this wasn't necessarily an attack against *me*, it was an attack against a gender and an attack against what somebody perceived as being out of the norm. I think one of the comments was about "this woke society" and the impact that it's having. It's important to say, though, that it was a tiny population that said this, but we have to be able to address what's going on because it *is* there. Sometimes I think people just want to understand why things are happening the way they are.

I've found there's a dichotomy between how the older generations in the military feel about the way that we used to do things versus this cultural revolution that's happened probably over the past 10 years with this newer, younger generation that's coming in. It's about how people view the world and how they view their place and what they should and shouldn't know. As a Gen Xer myself, we were the latchkey kids, and especially those of us in the military—and I don't want to generalize—but the majority of us, we get our marching orders and we do it. But millennials in particular and these Gen Zs, they want to know *why*. And so, I think we have to adapt to them just as they need to adapt to us in this work environment.

In your positions, past and present, I imagine you are privy to a lot of alarming information that most of us are not. How does knowing what you know about our national security affect you personally?

Oh gosh. It's been 24 years now that I've been in military service, and yeah, it gets tough, especially when I was younger. My first assignment after I came out of intel school was over in Germany, so that's where I was when the September 11 attacks happened. After that, for probably five to seven years, I stopped watching the news quite a bit. I mean, the news has a job to do and there's always those frustrations when [you want to say] "that's not the truth" or "that's not what really is going on" but we can't talk about it. Those were always difficult times, especially in the war in Iraq and the war in Afghanistan when we're in full-fledge combat operations. You always get worried about your family and everybody, but you can't talk about what you do. That gets frustrating. You tend to isolate a little bit, I think, at least I did, when people bring up those topics. I just kind of get up and walk away from the table because I couldn't get pulled into any of these conversations at that time. That was my self-preservation many years ago. But it's definitely gotten better.

Now that I'm in a more senior leadership role, I'm not real deep in the information on the intelligence side anymore. So now, of course, I do watch a variety of news organizations and news channels, just to piecemeal everything that I can together. That's just part of how I was trained, right? Don't take one particular piece of information at face value. You have to have multiple sources to be able to get a good clear picture. If you want to get a really good picture of what's happening and not just from U.S. news sources, world news organizations do a great job and sometimes they do a really outstanding job of reporting what's happening in the U.S. without all the other commentary that comes into it.

What do your kids think of what their parents do?

I think they think it's pretty cool that Mom's a general. [Before their dad retired] they liked to tease that Mom outranks Dad. (Laughs.) They kind of know what I do, but I don't think they fully understand, truly. I don't really talk about intel operations or cyber operations. We'll have some conversations around the dinner table about national and world events and what that means, especially with the older two who are starting to get to dive into history and current events and a little bit of the political science side of things.

We talk about U.S. history, especially when they're talking in school about the wars that my husband and I were involved in. We talk about what they're learning versus what *our* viewpoint of that war was because it's very different. I think every military member has a different viewpoint [from that of civilians] as to what actually happened in those wars versus what's been written in the history books.

One of the things that I always say to people, especially during the wars, was that there's probably no greater community of people that don't want to go to war than the military. I was stationed at the Pentagon for a bit and all the protesters were outside obviously exercising their constitutional right to protest. And my thought process was always the same: you're protesting in the wrong location. *We* don't decide to go to war. In fact, the military loves our country, they want to protect our country, and—this is just me; I should not be speaking for the rest of the military—but my personal opinion is you've got people that are willing to lay down their lives in defense of our nation. I really don't want to have to do that, but I will. That's what we've been asked to do, so we do it, and we give everything to it.

In 24 years, you've served under how many different presidents?

Well, I came in under President Clinton, and then in 2000, Bush Jr., and then from Bush to Obama, and Obama to Trump, Trump to Biden.

How is your work different under different administrations?

I'm not going to comment. I am apolitical. It's not my job. My job is to support and defend the Constitution and to follow the lawful orders of those appointed over me, to take care of my airmen, and conduct our mission. That's it.

Someday, when you're retired, I'd love to talk to you about that.

(Laughs.) Oh, yes, absolutely. That would be great.

What has this work taught you about yourself?

I am much more resilient than I ever understood. I grew up in a great community. I didn't have a lot of the hardships that I think a lot of people around the country have had, so I never was really tested. I never really understood how resilient you can or can't be. I learned that there are things that I never thought that I could do that I can do.

Resiliency was not a term that I would have known growing up, but looking back, I'm like, "Wow, I'm such a different person than I was then" because [in this work] you're faced with some really grave challenges and some really great challenges and are having to step up. I'm so thankful to the military and to the Air Force for giving me the opportunities that they've given me, for seeing something in me that I certainly didn't see. I'm a girl from a small town, and it's crazy to think of the things I've gotten to see, the things I've gotten to do from this job. It's been pretty awesome.

I am surprised at how this whole thing has come down. I'm grateful. I am proud. Were there frustrations? Yes, yes. Disappointments? Yes. Were there moments where I was ready to give up? Of course. I mean, just last week! You get overwhelmed and you're like, "Oh gosh, why am I doing this? Why am I putting myself through this?"

What's your answer to that?

Because I love it. There's a sense of pride to know that you're doing something for the betterment of our nation. And I know it may sound cliché, but I do really love this country. And I love what we stand for, and anything that I can do to help protect it and make it better . . . right? That's ultimately what it's about at the end of the day. I couldn't imagine doing anything else.

I've said this to my husband multiple times: "I'm struggling with what to do when I grow up." You know? When the military time is over, what do I want to be when I grow up? I just don't know yet.

"That little girl in India."
SHIWANI GUPTA

She is a manager on the Trust and Safety team at Google. She lives in San Francisco, is 37 years old, and has two children. We spoke on Zoom.

I was not born or raised here. I am from India. I come from a 150,000-people small town, which is predominantly an agrarian society. If you were to go there, you could treat your eyes to expansive fields of wheat, enjoy the smell of the first rain on scorched earth, and experience the joyful sight of cows happily ambling on the road. The daily milk supply is stable-to-table. Our vendor milked the cow in front of me and on some lucky days also gave us a glass full of milk to drink. Women cooked with wood and dung. Those were my beginnings.

We didn't have a computer at home. All we could do was go to a lab at school and have access to the computer for a class period of the day, which meant education was primarily happening through books. So when I had to write papers or do assignments I had to go to the library, find a book, and somehow sift through all the information for hours or sometimes days. (Laughs.) It was a very tedious process, right?

Then Google was becoming more widely known, and I got to see the impact of that company on my life. I could now search for and sift through the world's information very quickly. I was inspired to think about the lofty mission of the company: "To organize the world's information and make it universally accessible and useful." And I thought, "Wow, I would love to work for a company like that."

At that time, after I graduated from college, working at Google was just a dream. Like I said, I was born in a small town in India, and I'm a girl. This meant higher education was not a given for me. While the dream was always at the back of my head, it wasn't a reality in any way. Then, when I moved to a much larger city to work in the finance industry, I came across a Google job and decided to apply. It happened to be a Trust and Safety role, and it happened to be that some of my skills, my computer science engineering background, and my problem solving were very relevant to the job. Because Trust and Safety was still a relatively new function at that time, the approach was quite open: "Yes, we need people who can solve problems. We need people who can be creative. We need people who can be enthusiastic, and they don't necessarily need to be people who have a background in the Trust and Safety field." After multiple rounds of interviews I was hired by Google. I was working at my dream company!

The mission of Trust and Safety is to help all users, including kids, senior people, students, or whoever it is that is using products on the internet, from YouTube to Search, have a safe and enriching experience.

I can explain to you what we do in a metaphoric way. If you go to a big public event, many things are happening. The event is organized by the organizers, but the performers and audience could be many people coming from different backgrounds. The organizers are responsible for the physical security of everybody attending and also responsible for their mental security so that nobody is harassing anybody, saying bad things, or doing harm. In a nutshell they try to help people have an enjoyable and enriching experience. That's *our* duty, too, across products which serve billions of people around the world—to help people who are watching the "performances" [in our case, content] stay safe and have an enjoyable and enriching experience.

The way you do that is a combination of two things: Firstly, you apply technology to the problem of identifying content at scale that violates the products' specific content guidelines. Secondly, you use human expertise for the more nuanced abuse patterns. You say, "Hey, machine, I'm going to give you some training and define some parameters for you to apply to the problem of knowing that certain kinds of content do not meet my guidelines." There's no one silver bullet because content that does not meet guidelines can have many different guises. The goal is to make sure that you're able to scale it up, and the scaling comes from machines and algorithms being able to say, "I know this pattern. I'm going to apply this pattern to any similar new content I see."

But sometimes machines don't know; content is so complex. There could be very drastic things happening in the world such as people getting killed in the Russia-Ukraine war. There could be video footage on the platform that could be very disturbing to people. But if a journalist has included the footage, not for the purpose of just having disturbing content, but for informing the world, then certain products may decide to allow that content based on their guidelines.

All content platforms go through this dilemma of where to draw the line of content that is acceptable versus what is not. Once they define that line, they try to implement it and then hope most of the distinction can be made by machines. But the dilemmas facing the world will change, there will be new types of content, and the machines won't know how to apply that line to the new content, or maybe the line will need to be shifted. So constantly there is a need for human expertise to understand what the new trends are.

I lead the Trust and Safety team for one such area. My job is to build and implement multi-quarter roadmaps of investment areas like policy changes, machine effectiveness, quality improvements, user experience improvements, trust assessment of new features, etcetera, which when combined together create not only a safe experience but also an inspiring experience for users of today and future users of tomorrow.

But it can be difficult work because one is overexposed to the negative side of the world. When bad things happen anywhere in the world or bad actors reinvent abuse techniques, they inadvertently show up on the platforms in different ways and we act as the first line of defense for our users.

I salute all the Trust and Safety professionals around the world who take on this difficult task of putting the world's safety first, which sometimes can disbalance your well-being in unexpected ways. Fortunately, the company I work for puts in a lot of effort and focus on well-being, but the reality of being overexposed to the negative side of the world is something I have to actively acknowledge and manage. We have access to mental health resources and strong team support that makes this aspect manageable.

Would it be over-romanticizing your story to say that when you were in India sifting through pages of books to write your school papers, that Google kind of introduced you to the rest of the world from the computer screen in your small town in India?

I had multiple introductions to the world, and I think the biggest one was in college when I went for an internship to Serbia. I was definitely the first girl, most likely even the first person in the history of my town to take that leap of faith. But, you're right. I think you could romanticize it and say that Google introduced me to the world.

My dad was a professor, and he was always the person giving me the dream. He would tell me, "You can be the CEO of Pepsi one day," or whatever else he had read in newspapers, saying, "That is the dream I give my daughter." My mom worked in the irrigation department of the government. I told you that was an agrarian town. Still is. She is very hardworking. So, I think if I were to analyze myself, I'm a mix of those two. I'm very hardworking, persistent, but

I'm also fearless and not scared to have dreams. Did I have this exact dream? No. But I always was, and I still am, motivated by the dreams which my father created for me in the sense that I want to do something so that the world can remember me as a positive influence. And that has taken many forms through multiple years, but I think that little girl in India was always very fearless to try out different things.

So, in the eyes of that little girl, this, what I am doing now, was a dream— it's still a dream. And now that little girl often says, "Good job, Shiwani. You're on track." She's not judging me all the time, but sometimes she's strict: "You can do better." But most of the time, she's cheerful and expresses, "I'm happy with where you are."

PART TWO:

"THIS BRAVE NEW WORLD"

"We're in This In-Between Place"

"There's a lot of 'shoot-the-messenger.'"
MATTHEW HEISHMAN

He is the manager at a big-box retail store pharmacy. He started with them in 1999 as an intern. "I had finished two years at the college of pharmacy and was looking for some summer cash. I got on as an intern for what I thought would be a part-time summer thing. And here I am now, 22 years later, almost, with the same company.

"I'm just a no-judgment human being. I'm extremely liberal, I'm gay, and my partner and I have been together 21 years now in an open relationship. I don't know every customer's story. I don't know their business. So, unless someone is asking for something that is just illegal or harmful, it's not my place to make a judgment."

We talk on Zoom.

I had known I wanted to do something medical with my life, but I don't really remember how the pharmacy thing came about. I don't have medical people in my family. I think my mom was the first person to go to college, and I was the second. I come from a long line of folks who mostly do manual labor and blue-collar jobs.

Now I feel like this is the thing I'm supposed to do, but I don't love the direction the profession has gone. Back in the early to mid-2000s, I was considered an all-star in central Kentucky for Walmart because my pharmacy grew very quickly. When I took over, we were filling 300 prescriptions a day. And when I left six years later, we were filling 650 to 700 prescriptions a day. That made me a "success." (Laughs.)

We're still stuck in the '90s and the 2000s, where the more prescriptions you fill, the more money you make. So then it became "Okay, we can add immunizations, not just flu shots every year," and now we give pneumonia vaccines, we have a shingles vaccine, the tetanus vaccine. Right now, I have a long weekend calm before the storm of the [first COVID-19] vaccine arrival and a lot for us to do. There's a whole range of vaccines that I think, from the business side, became an additional source of income. As the reimbursement from insurance companies for prescriptions has continued to get worse and worse and worse, it was also a way that we could show that we're more than pill counters. We are clinically trained. I have a doctorate degree, a doctor of pharmacology.

Our technicians are so much better trained and so much more skilled than they were 15 or 20 years ago. They could do most of the dispensing activities and do them well and do them safely and free me up to be using my brain and my knowledge more clinically rather than handling the pill bottles. I feel like myself and most of the folks in my profession have the ability to deal with more of the clinical, but we don't have that authority. So we're stuck in this purgatory of being beyond just counting and dispensing of pills, but not fully able to use our training. We're in this in-between place.

My ideal job would be to have a little booth out in front of the pharmacy, out on the floor in the over-the-counter drug area where I could have a computer out there. I'd just be out there answering questions, whether it's over-the-counter drug questions or to give counsel on a medication. The space I work in is very small, so I'd like to be outside that box, out front where I can just deal with people. I would feel confident—if I was allowed to by law—adjusting medications for blood pressure, diabetes, for treating high cholesterol, things like that, but we're not there yet, for the most part.

There is certainly a push, though, within our profession to show that we are clinical, that we are not just dispensing prescriptions. We have a term now, "MTM"—Medication Therapy Management—where we are reminding folks, "Hey, you need to refill this blood pressure medication. Do you know your blood pressure medication doesn't help if you don't take it every day?" Or "You got a three-month supply of medication four months ago, and you still have some left. Are you having side effects from it? Is it too expensive? If it is too expensive, we can reach out to the doctor about that and try to find something that would be less expensive."

So we are this neat link between patients and prescribers, and between patients and insurance companies, who dominate what's covered and what's not. Right now, the fight is to get reimbursed, to get paid for our knowledge, to get paid for more than just shooting prescriptions out the door.

Most folks call what we do "retail pharmacy." Your Walgreens, CVS. We call it "community pharmacy," because a retail pharmacy puts focus on the dollars part of it. But regardless of what you call it, the fact is it's a business, no matter how large or small, and the business side of life is very difficult. In our case, we purchase drugs from a source and then an insurance company tells us how much they're going to pay us for it. That's a bad business model because insurance companies continue to lower their reimbursement. For probably a fourth or a third of the prescriptions I send out every day, I get reimbursed less than what we pay for the medication to stock it.

There are these things, they're called PBMs—Pharmacy Benefit Managers— that sprang up in the '90s and 2000s. For companies like Blue Cross Blue Shield, Aetna, Cigna, these big insurance companies, they handle the pharmacy portion of the program, and they have become the dominant financial force. They determine what drugs are worth, and they determine how much a pharmacy gets reimbursed for it. That is not a great model for the business of pharmacy.

I recently picked up a prescription, and the pharmacist apologized to me for the price. Do you ever feel the need to do that?

All the time, all the time. It's been that way for years. I had an insured patient come in Tuesday who is on a weekly injectable medication for diabetes. Her co-pay was $845 for a one-month supply. This is what they call a high-deductible plan, where, for the first year, you have to pay out of pocket. So, yes. It's almost an art to not give someone a heart attack when they're picking up a medication. That is an absurd number, and those absurd numbers are for *insured* people, you know. It's a system that really has never worked for everyone and continues to not work for everyone.

But you try to find a way to help. Like, okay, it costs this much, but there are a lot of these brand name drugs where the manufacturer puts out some coupon cards that can help absorb some of the costs. Or you can approach it like: "This one is really expensive. We can reach out to your doctor because there's a couple of other options." There are ways to try to soften the blow. You have a number of folks who are shocked when something *isn't* a fortune. (Laughs.) They come to the pharmacy expecting, you know, 75, 80, 100 dollars for something. And if it's $15, they're elated! I feel like I'm king of the world! But mostly, it's a lot of just having to agree with them. "Yes, you're right, it is a lot of money." If you have someone who is sick or not feeling well, they may be a little more prone to anger directed at me. You know, there's a lot of "shoot the messenger."

I think I've always been an empathetic, understanding, sympathetic person. But when I did my own round of cancer and cancer treatments, I got a lot better perspective on the people I deal with every day and what they're up against. That was a really good lesson in life: how to be an even better professional, how to take even better care of people and to try to be a little more patient and a little more understanding if they maybe aren't in the best of moods.

You've been conducting drive-through COVID tests, and when you return to work next week, you said, you're going to begin administering the vaccine. How else has the pandemic affected your work and life?

My best-friend-slash-more-than-a-best-friend is a flight attendant. He has incredible energy and has created a life around a career that allows him to travel the country, travel the world whenever, wherever he wants. And that suddenly stopped. He lives four or five blocks away from me, and it's been wonderful having him here much more. Instead of seeing him once a month, now it's been twice a week.

I've always felt that I have this rigid, planned schedule of work where I have to ask for time off at least six weeks ahead of time while he has this crazy, change-able, spontaneous life. But with the pandemic, he and the rest of the world had to come into my lane of traffic, the right lane, the slow lane. The whole world slowed down to where I didn't feel like everything and everyone was flying past me. I've always lived life in the right lane of the expressway. Slow and steady wins the race. I think that part of me is a little bit of a grounding influence for my best friend because we're so opposite. He's that crazy, wild, life of the party, and I'm more shy and quiet until I know people. Part of him wants to be happy with some stillness and some quiet, but he can never quite achieve that.

And now we have the vaccine, and we'll be going back to where the people in my life will be going warp speed again, and I'm still going to be plodding along, still in my lane, still in my planned-out rigid schedule. The frenzy of returning is already happening. He can see it when he's at the airport. There's more and more people there.

I'm glad, of course, that we have the vaccine. Of course, I am. But here is what makes that a quandary for me: in my job, I'm going to be giving people the vaccine that is going to help everyone achieve warp speed again, a speed that I really don't want the world to go back to. It's going to be incredibly too fast for me. But in my work, I am going to help make that happen.

POSTSCRIPT: *Several months after our conversation, he saw an ad for a position as the director of pharmacy services at a hospital. He interviewed and got the* job. "I had thought I would be at [that store] forever. My partner said, 'You've been really unhappy,' and so did all my friends. And I understood that I had been a very unhappy person. I informed my boss that I was leaving. I'd made my decision. I felt like a different person."

"Oh, it's great to have these problems again."
MOLLIE HERMAN

She is a 36-year-old events administrator and an American citizen who lives with her partner in Oaxaca, Mexico. They travel often both in their work and for pleasure. We talk shortly after she was able to return to working outdoor events for the first time since the pandemic started.

I work for a company which is one of the premier environmental waste management companies for [public] events in North America. I've worked for them for about 13 years. In the event industry, we always use this term, "many hats." My technical title is "administration and asset recovery," which is keeping track of all the things that we have to remember. I organize a lot of back-end data because a huge part of the event world is advancing. So everything from, we need this many chairs at this event, we need this many credentials, we need to feed this many people to figuring out where they're going to stay, how these kids are going to get there. . . .

It's kind of like the circus, that's the easiest way to explain it—or the army, just because of its completeness; it's its own world. It's like a lifestyle; it's not just a job. It's not a 9-to-5, it's an entire community of people who are like touring bands. So when COVID happened, I was just blindsided. I didn't just lose my job, I lost the community I've lived in. It's definitely refreshing to be back now. The first event we did was Fourth of July weekend. It was this festival in Pennsylvania that's pretty small called the Peach Music Festival. It's kind of like a jam band, old hippie kind of thing. They had Les Claypool.

I remember it felt incredibly comforting to be back in the network and to be around my tour work family, to be around these people that I've spent so much of my life with and with whom we do so much creating. It's great to be back with all these people who love this work. We're like, "Oh, it's great to have these problems again! Great to be frustrated by the same things again!" I find myself much more relaxed, to be honest.

In some ways, it felt like we had been in the unsafe place the whole time we were away, and *now* we were coming back to the safe place. It felt better in a lot of ways to be in this place. And it still does. I think possibly also the fact that we're outdoors helps a lot. And then obviously, you know, the spirit needs to be enhanced and the arts do that. And coming together and collaborating and building these little mini cities for the goodness of people does that. It's also like, for many of us, we were missing the routine that we had built and established. For many people coming back to that provided more calm.

But it was really interesting. I do staffing, and some other people, they just had become . . . different. They had embraced different parts of themselves during that time away, so they came back thinking that this world would change with them. And they were just, maybe, prioritizing their personal time more now and not wanting necessarily to be on a team in this capacity anymore. So there was definitely kind of this effect happening of people coming to work and then realizing, "Actually, I don't want to be around all these people."

Some people were more apt to want more personal time, say, or "I don't want to share a room, anymore." People were much more demanding about their needs. And sometimes those needs were not going to get met, you know. We had to say, "No, you're not going to get your own room." And "We're not gonna give you a $10-an-hour raise." But I think that sense of advocating for oneself has come out.

You seem to see a connection between the pandemic, the pause in the work, and their changed attitude toward work and what they now expect from it.

Yeah, I think part of it was the language that was coming out of the media. There was so much stuff around self-help and self-care and advocacy. I think that definitely is something that everyone's seeing on Instagram, like, "I'm gonna make my own thing!" I remember someone saying, "But I can't pay my rent off of this." Well, maybe this isn't for you, then. Or maybe you want to change your lifestyle to match what you're trying to achieve.

Do you feel like you've matured through this?

Yeah, totally. I think about my life and the larger picture more, now. I have a greater understanding of how unique the work that I'm doing is and the role that I get to play. I mean, I've been doing this work since I was like 20. And it has grown and changed and morphed in different ways. I knew I had a specific kind of skill set, and I was aware of the possibilities and the potential of the work. I had been in this like, mode of do, do, do, work, work, work, and always trying to plan out farther ahead. And maybe being almost disappointed often by things [that don't work out as planned]. And now I've seen myself just . . . relax about it. And so, now the idea that some things don't happen the way we expected is incredibly comfortable.

I would imagine that the Mollie who now returns to work is met, in a way, by the pre-pandemic Mollie. Returning to that familiar work, do you see in higher relief the contrast between the two Mollies?

Oh, yeah. I had been on this pace at home. I was cruisin'. I was Zoomin'. And then we started coming back to events. I went from "I have a garden I hang out in" to "Okay, I'm going to work, cool," to "Oh my god! How are we moving at this fast pace?" For so many of us we were like, "I'm in a rocket ship!" I mean, we were asked to go back to production from zero to way-too-fast. And so, yes, I *could* see myself at that before time, and there's definitely a lot of comparison, even still, between what I used to be able to do and what I can do now. Now I'm definitely finding that I'm much more lax about things for a number of reasons. It's hard to keep that pace that had already been established. To me the wisdom of the experience is like, "Oh, yeah, I shouldn't be doing things *that* way anymore." (Laughs.) I'm finding that maybe it was just too much. Now I'm like, "Whatever, I can lose jobs, I can change careers, like whatever." But if I'm trying to run to catch up with my younger self, that's probably . . . (laughs) not a good idea.

It sounds like you're gaining an—

—An appreciation for and some *laissez-faire* about life. Now I'm like, "Yeah, we'll wait that out. It's ok." I recently was getting semitrucks to meet us at one event to load equipment to take it somewhere else. And normally, I try to do that stuff super far in advance, like four weeks. And then the other day, it was 36 hours! (Laughs.) I was like, "It's gonna work out." I've learned how much the world of outside events just like, keeps moving, and it's so intense, and especially with logistics and production and all that, we are just such a little blip in it. We're just going to get picked up and moved along.

I mean, I love this work; I'll probably expand upon it at some point—in the same field, or maybe not. But definitely, taking a break from work was just the best. I would have *never* said that before.

"It's what you know, and it's what you do."
JOEL GREENO

He is a dairy farmer. We talk at the kitchen table in his farmhouse on a cold and foggy November morning. His youngest daughter, a preschooler, sits on the couch and watches us for a while. Joel's wife, who works in the district office of Walmart, is in the living room watching television. Their daughter Anna divides her time between her mother's lap and her father's. Their second daughter, Abby, age 7, is in school. Joel is 47 years old.

Tell you about Kendall, Wisconsin? Wow. Big question. Hard to believe that Kendall used to be a big railroad town. Now, today, there's hardly a business left running. There probably wouldn't be anything if, in the last few months, a smoke shop and a gun shop hadn't come to town. Otherwise, the grocery store's closed, the hardware store is closed, the drugstore is closed, the clothing store is closed. That all started in the last 15, 20 years. It's been the biggest exodus, and you could probably almost target it exactly to the farm crisis of the '80s.

I mean, our towns are done for, because all the farms that supported those towns don't even exist anymore. There's nobody to go to those towns to keep the businesses going. You have one centralized office where all the money has to end up. Now our feed co-ops have merged, and so their headquarters are 100 miles away. And so, farmers go to their local mill and spend money, but it doesn't stay there anymore. It ends up at a headquarters somewhere. So, I mean, it really is a vacuum cleaner effect. The money, the life, has been sucked out of rural America from our farms all the way through our towns.

We lost 50 percent of our nation's farms through the '80s, just extreme financial pressure. Friends and I watch the obituaries. Almost certain, in cases where they're saying, "died unexpectedly," a lot of times [we] are finding out it's suicide.

I grew up here in Kendall. My family has farmed here in Monroe County since 1872. Mostly farming, but part of the family tradition was construction work, so doing brick and block and stonework. My grandpa used to blast stone and quarry it and move stone to the job site. Build barn walls, house basements, you know, whatever needed to be, just by quarrying stone. And I can remember watching him work. Stone went together for him like Lego blocks do for kids.

I can remember my dad had bought a farm and the barn had collapsed, and we cleaned it up, and we were pushing the old stone walls back into place, and there was one wall that had totally collapsed. So we were rebuilding that from stone, and I was watching Grandpa work, and I can remember Grandpa turning around and saying, "Boy? You can always mix more mud or carry more stone, but you can't stand still." And just turned around and went back to work. And Dad said, "Don't worry, he's that way with everybody." (Laughs.)

I suppose that's some of where the work ethic came from, and you know, part of the love of farming. The family's always known hard work. It's what you been doing, it's what you know, it's what you're comfortable with. Dad's farms were just up the road here a ways. Growing up I just was always in the barn doing stuff. I remember Mom telling a story. Farms are inspected by health inspectors, and the health inspector had been to the farm, and he said, "That crib in the milk house has got to go. That can't be in there." She says, "Okay, that's fine. When will I see you, tomorrow?" He says, "What do you mean, tomorrow?" "Well, if the crib's not here, then you're coming to babysit."

So, I as a baby was going to the barn. The crib was in the milk house at the barn since Mom was doing chores. We were right there, too. I know Dad said that he was milking cows at age 5 by hand. And the only person faster at milking a cow was his mother, and he would make his brother so mad and stuff 'cause they could never keep up. I probably started milking cows at 11, and that was probably the first break Dad—I know Dad had went 17 straight years and never missed milking his cows twice a day every day in that stretch.

It's what you know, and it's what you do. That's what you get in your mind. I know all of us, I think almost everyone, my cousins and everything, the profession their dads were in, that's the line they went down. I had uncles that had went more to hogs and beef, and so their sons, my cousins, went more down those lines.

My mom and dad's 29th "anniversary present" was a farm foreclosure. It's not really a present to be told you're being foreclosed on and to have the sheriff's department deliver those papers. Had never really seen a lot of emotion out of Dad, certainly never seen him cry. So I was getting in my truck to go that day, and he was like, he says, "I don't think you should go." I said, "I need to go; I'm going." Seen Dad cry for the first time. He says, "You know I'm going to lose the farm."

And their 30th wedding "anniversary present" was a sheriff's auction on the courthouse steps. It's really hard to believe that your entire life can be sold in five minutes at the courthouse. People were saying, "Well, your family's going to have to make this right." Like we did something wrong. I was totally shocked by that.

It's an internal defense mechanism. There's every reason for them to know that they could be in the same boat, but they put you down just to distance themselves from you. I mean, the phone stops ringing; nobody comes to see you anymore; you go to town and everybody walks away. It's really hard to put that into perspective, but you lose so much more than the farm. It's your dignity, it's your respect, but also it's the fact that you don't have any friends anymore because no one will associate with you. And people don't think it can be that bad and that blatant, but it really is. You got nothing. Mom and Dad literally went and got all new friends. You wouldn't think it.

[In 1990, three years before his parents lost their farm, Joel bought a 160-acre dairy farm of his own.]

I had some surgery last December and ended up, couldn't milk cows for months, so had to hire it done. My dad and sister and a guy from town did chores for me till I healed up from surgery. I had 48 cows. But just, you know, circumstances. You lose a cow here and there, you sell a cow here and there. But ended up, I had sold my bull just so nobody got hurt while I was laid up, and so I ended up with cows and heifers that weren't pregnant. And so, my milk flow had dropped low enough that it was getting tough to keep up with bills; and equipment breakdowns were next to impossible to deal with 'cause there just wasn't the cash flow.

My wife and I, there was a lot of months and months of just kind of back and forth trying to decide what to do. This is probably the case on most farms, you know? The guys are out there doing the work and the wives are left stuck at the house with the checkbook, trying to figure out how to make it work. And there's a lot of months it's really tough. There are just a lot of tough days and a lot of tough months, and just comes that time when you have to decide whether you want to or not. Just for family reasons and whatnot, we decided that it was time to let go and sell the cows and look for work.

Three trucks came. Abby and Anna were watching the cows being loaded down. And the second truck driver told Abby, says "You're sad, aren't you?" She just shrugged her shoulders. He says, "You know how I can tell?" She shrugged her shoulders again. He said, "I can see the tears in your eyes." And she just lost it. And so then Anna hugs Abby and then *she* loses it. Well, then the truck driver feels bad, so he goes to his truck and gets them each a dollar, and I mean, it's like, now *I'm* a wreck. Where's *my* dollar? (Laughs.) Gee whiz. But it was tough. It was tough. My wife videotaped it, the cows loaded out. The girls crying in the road as the three trucks pulled away. It's just tough. I mean, it's like family.

Anna [the youngest] hadn't been to the barn a lot. She had actually probably only been going to the barn a few weeks before we sold the cows. That first time in the barn, it was just. . . . It's hard to even describe. Abby had been to the barn a lot with me. Pretty comfortable with the cows. [So she took Anna] up front; there's all these great big 1,200-pound Holstein cows looking down the manger like, what's going on here? Who are these two? Abby's like, "Okay, Anna. Let's look at the cows." So Anna took Abby's hand, and they walked down in front of the one row of cows and come back, and they got to the end, and Abby said, "What you think?" And Anna Marie says, "Do again." So they turned around and made that walk back down again, all those big cows looking at them.

And I mean, it's priceless. What do you say and that? You have that joy of a father, your kids starting to make that connection with the cows, and even now they'll say, "Let's go milk, Dad." You know? What do you say? It's tough and that. I mean, family history. Your legacy. So many things. Hard to put into words. Just so many thoughts and feelings about all the things I didn't get to complete. I felt like I'd let down every family and person still trying to milk cows today. I was the last one that was farming full time and still in the dairy business.

I still own the land and actually rent one of Dad's old places back from the owner there and that, so that's tough every time I go. You look at the house and you look at the barn and see all of Grandpa's stonework and cement block work, and there's just that little bit of awkward hesitation and stuff. But you know, they're good people that live there and stuff. Done wonderful things in fixing stuff up and that. But just, it's hard to let all that go.

POSTSCRIPT: Not long after we talked, Joel took a job at a factory. "You take a farmer and put him in a really loud concrete building, you know, not the the environment you would like. But I need work, and it's a good job and a good company."

He is now divorced, he says in an email. "One of the casualties of the farm crisis."

"It's absolutely imperative to create change."
VANESSA SHERIDAN

She has her own consulting business, "and it's going really well." She does consulting, training, and speaking for business organizations about transgender and LGBTQ awareness.

I knew I was different when I was two or three. I really did. I grew up in a fundamentalist Southern Baptist home in the South. You didn't talk about being trans. That wasn't something that people understood or were even willing to discuss. And so, I didn't really address these kinds of issues on a meaningful level until I was into adulthood.

But it was interesting; as a kid, part of me wanted to be a Disney princess and part of me wanted to be a pro football quarterback. And it depended on which day you got me. I always had a fairly fertile imagination, and I did a lot of reading as a kid. My mind was always filled with infinite possibilities as to what I could be when I grew up. But I gotta tell you, I never really had a plan for what I wanted to be. I just kind of fell into this work that I do. There was no master plan.

When I first started doing public outreach, it was quite unique. This was 30 years ago, and hardly anybody was doing that, so to have an out, trans person who was speaking and doing things to raise awareness was a pretty strange and different kind of thing. I wasn't the only one doing it, but I was one of the only ones. It was just something I felt called to do. I saw a need, and I tried to help meet it. And that's why I got started. I just tried to make smart decisions and go with it.

I'm very fortunate because I've spent those 30 years building up some credibility in the business community and in the trans community, and I get a lot of referrals. Pretty much all of the work that I do is based on recommendations from people. For example, right now, I'm working with several major organizations like Pfizer Manufacturing, H&M—the international clothing retailer—and I'm working with Marriott on their international organization.

What I'm learning is that the global business community has recognized that LGBTQ inclusion, and maybe more specifically, trans inclusion, is really a business imperative. And because of that, organizations need to be equipped with the information and the resources and the tools that they need to make that be successful. And that's where I come in. I try to encourage them to create opportunities in which trans people and business organizations can come together for mutual benefit.

I think it's the smart, successful businesses that are getting on board with trans awareness in particular. For example, in the year 2000, there were only three Fortune 500 companies that included gender identity as a protected class in their organizations, and today it's well over 75 percent of the Fortune 500. That's a significant shift in a relatively short amount of time.

Businesses, at least for-profit businesses, exist exactly for that reason: to make a profit. And if I can give them some sort of competitive advantage or benefit in that regard, they're going to jump on that. At the end of the day, they're going to be asking the questions that businesses always ask: "What's in it for me? How am I going to benefit from this? How is this going to impact the stockholders, the bottom line?" I try to focus on the competitive advantages. If you can enhance your organizational culture, that's going to improve everything. It's going to improve teamwork, it's going to improve production, it's going to impact your bottom line in a positive way. That's going to make your stockholders happy, that's going to improve your PR in the community and within your industry. And if they don't, then they're cutting their own throat, frankly, and putting themselves behind their competition. I tell them that, too.

Do you face pushback or negativity?

When I first started out, I might have gone in with both guns blazing and said, "Okay, we need to start firing this person and do this, and that, and the other." And now I've kind of learned to take it easy. I think I come across as pretty non-threatening to people. It's more like, "Let's look at the bigger picture, and let's try to do what's in the best interests of the organization as well as the individuals." I always just assume good intentions, and so far that's played out pretty well.

By the time they've been [at my presentation] for a few minutes, they realize I'm not going to, you know, attack them or infect them with some sort of disease or something. I tell them being transgender is not communicable. You can't catch it like a cold just because you're in the room with me.

I'll often touch on the whole bathroom bill thing that states have tried to pass across the country. I'll tell them it's really kind of a tempest in a teapot. For example, in 2018, I was able to go to the U.S. State Department in Washington and do trainings for State Department employees. I'm standing on stage in the Dean Acheson Auditorium in the State Department building, and I told them, I said, "I don't know if you're going to throw me out of here or arrest me or what, but I'm going to tell you the truth about something. More U.S. congressmen have been arrested for public misconduct in restrooms than transgender people." And it's true. They got it. They all laughed. I breathed a sigh of relief.

Do you consider what you do as activism?

It's not necessarily overt activism. I think what I do is more like coming in through the side door. Being an activist means pushing some sort of agenda, and my agenda is always to simply raise awareness. Change often happens first in the workplace, and because that's true, I feel like I can be a catalyst for that kind of social change. I'm passionately political on a personal level, but I try to avoid bringing politics into the work I do with my clients. I focus on how, if you enhance your organizational culture, it's going to improve teamwork, it's going to improve production, it's going to impact your bottom line in a positive way. And the more awareness you raise, the better a society becomes for people who are misunderstood or oppressed, like the trans community.

One of the things that we're learning is that there is a pretty large contingent of non-binary people in this country who use they/them pronouns. That's particularly true for Gen-Xers, Gen Y, and Gen Z. So business organizations need to be aware that if they want to enhance their recruiting and retention, for example, they need to be aware of the pronoun thing because young talent is not going to work in an organization that doesn't understand or respect their pronoun usage.

To me, it's simply a matter of a becoming aware of the fact that this is real, and this is becoming more and more prominent throughout society. And we need to practice because it doesn't come naturally. We're all conditioned, we're socialized to use certain pronouns. We also need to recognize that we're going to make mistakes, and it's okay to make an honest mistake. It's *not* okay to keep making the same mistake over and over and over again. I talk a lot about that with people who say, "Well, what if I make a mistake, and I use the wrong pronoun?" Well, apologize and then move on. And then don't use the wrong pronoun anymore. It's a process and processes take time; they have to unfold, they don't happen instantaneously.

Now, shifting over into the personal level, I'm a very political person. I like to think I'm a progressive. I am all about dragging everybody kicking and screaming into the 21st century and making progress as a society. I think the political implications of that are huge. I take that very seriously. I vote accordingly; I think accordingly; I interact with people accordingly. But I don't talk about politics when I do my presentations, or when I work with organizations because, frankly, I don't want to muddy the waters. The waters are murky enough already. We don't need to make them worse. What it's going to do is polarize the audience, and you're going to get diminishing returns. And so, I just simply don't go there.

What worries you most?

When I read the news about what happens to trans people across the country. When I hear about the murders of trans people; when I hear about the legislation people are passing or trying to pass. And it's all due to misunderstandings, ignorance, or lack of awareness. And that's why I feel so motivated to be an educator about these issues. I think it's absolutely imperative to create change, and the only way you create change is to educate people and to inform people and make them aware. That's why the work I do is so meaningful to me; it gives me the opportunity to do just that.

Now having said all that, let me just say this: I think we live in interesting times politically. And I have no idea what the future holds. But I would certainly like to see us continue to be a progressive country and society rather than a regressive one. I've really got no interest in going back to the 1950s when trans people had to be in the closet, and when we were considered mentally disordered, that kind of thing. And so, I'm focusing on trying to bring progressive values to the work that I do without using political language to do it. It's kind of walking a tightrope in a certain way. But I'm very much aware that I'm on that tightrope, and I pay close attention to it. And I really try not to fall off. So far, I've been pretty successful with that.

I feel so fortunate to have ended up where I am, particularly in relation to where I first started out as a young kid from a Southern Baptist home—a really strict, fundamentalist Southern Baptist home. To end up doing what I do is fairly remarkable, I think, in certain ways. And I feel lucky to have kind of come out of that particular environment into the one that I'm in now.

"I write a lot of stuff nobody reads."
ANDREW GOLDSTEIN

He is a lawyer who practices in the area of intellectual property and information technology.

"Since law school, I've worked at just two firms. I know people who, every three, four, or five years move to a different firm, but I've just had the two. If I'm happy in the situation, I'll stick with it. I'm a barnacle. I just kind of attach myself, and you have to pry me off."

He is 62 years old.

I'm not a litigator. I don't go to court. I deal with what people would call corporate stuff. I deal with M&A—mergers and acquisitions—deals where there's intellectual property involved, corporate deals, one company buying another, one company selling itself, things like that. I've been involved in that a bunch this morning.

I also help clients out with trademarks and copyrights. I handle a lot of licensing work like software licensing, any kind of technology licensing; you know, those things that you click on to agree to use software or whatever that nobody reads? I write those things. For example, I write the rules that govern the sweepstakes. You know: only one entry per person and it has to have this hashtag on it and we'll do a random drawing and here's the prizes, worth X dollars.

Do you consider writing those rules to be creative work?

I always tell my clients I try to stay out of creative stuff because they're the creative ones, and I'm just a simple country IP lawyer.

Do you enjoy doing that fine print work?

On a scale of things, no. But it gets the bills paid, I guess is what I would say.

Is there a word limit?

Oh, hell no. There's been some movements, legislatively, to make those types of documents, like website terms of use and privacy policies, to make them in plain English. There has been some movement towards that. But nothing's official. I just shovel in whatever I think is appropriate.

Turn your recorder off for a moment. No, I'm kidding. I never read them, myself. I mean, the way I look at it is, for a guy like me and a guy like you, they're nonnegotiable. You take it or leave it. And if you want to use the stuff, you've got to click on it.

I like when I'm involved in sweepstakes contests. Sweepstakes you may be familiar with are McDonald's Monopoly or Scratch and Win games. Those are fun—sometimes. You get some crazy schemes going on. It's more stuff that I write that nobody reads, the rules. Yeah—I do a lot of unfulfilling things. I write a lot of stuff that nobody reads.

But if something goes awry, or some spit hits the fan, then they come into play. That actually happened with the pandemic. I had worked with a couple of clients who had active contests going on when the pandemic hit, and they're like, "Well, now what do we do? Nobody's out buying the product." And so we went back to look at the rules and luckily, with the foresight or skill or whatever you want to call it that I have, I had put in there that if there's what we call a *force majeure* event, an act of God type of thing, we can cancel or alter the game, and that's what happened in a couple of actual incidences.

I also deal with recording contracts and things like talent contracts. Actually, I represented John Wayne Gacy* once. Yeah, now that's a story. I was at a different firm then, a big major firm, and they had been appointed to handle his death row appeal. They were working with him, and Gacy asked, "Hey, do you have anybody who can help me with an HBO deal?" HBO wanted to get his life story and do a movie on it. And that was me. So I ended up working with him. I never met him; we just corresponded back and forth. It was interesting, his letterhead—yes, he had letterhead in prison—his letterhead said, "Execute justice dot-dot-dot. Not people dot-dot-dot." It wasn't as—well, I mean, it was creepy, but not as creepy as you'd think.

Particularly in the area of intellectual property, what is the impact of constant and rapid changes in technology?

I just read something a couple of days ago that patents have to be originally filed by individuals, and that an AI program cannot be listed as an inventor of a patent. This is wild stuff. There was a ruling just the other day. It's constantly developing and changing. The same thing had happened with copyrights. If a monkey takes a picture of a candle, it can't copyright it; has to be a human.

* A notorious serial killer and sex offender who murdered at least 33 young men and boys between 1967 and 1978. He was executed in 1994.

It's new and different stuff that's going on, but most generally, you're apply-ing existing principles to it. Which is interesting. It's basically the same rules but applied to different technology.

When the pandemic hit, I was counseling clients a lot about Zoom because of music rights. For instance, aerobics teachers. The way music licensing works is an aerobics teacher goes to the local rec center and puts on his or her boom box and plays songs. And technically, supposedly, the rec center has a license with either ASCAP* or BMI† or one of the other performing rights organizations, so that every time they play a song there, they pay a fee to ASCAP or BMI that gets divided up with the artists.

Now, in the pandemic, you've got the same aerobics instructor sitting in their home or their apartment, playing the music and doing their aerobics and they aren't covered by an ASCAP or BMI license from the venue. And ASCAP and BMI and the others are going after some people for their Zoom performances and saying, "Look, you've got to sign up and pay us a fee." Zoom did affect things in that way. So I was counseling some clients and sending out client alerts about these kinds of things.

How has the nature of work and the nature of a workplace changed for you?

I think this notion of a dedicated office space will likely disappear. It's going to be more like—are you familiar with the term *hoteling*? Consulting firms like Arthur Andersen, Accenture, etcetera, had been doing this for a while when their consul-tants were on the road. You don't have a set office. You've got a rolling file box, a file cabinet that you have your stuff in. You say, "Hey, I'm coming into the office next Tuesday," and they'll assign a phone in the office with your extension num-ber, and you'll be in that office that day. You roll your file cabinet in there. And the Tuesday after that, you may be in a different office. I believe that concept is going to really take flight. I expect my firm to go into something like that, frankly, at some point. It's been a trend for a couple of decades with the consulting firms. And I'm pretty sure that's where a lot of places will be going, particularly these days with the whole WeWork type of environment that's kind of like that. I think that's going to be part of the future.

---

* American Society of Composers, Authors, and Publishers.
† Broadcast Music, Inc.

Do you feel like you are adjusting well to all these changes, professionally?

Well, yeah. I was positioned to adjust, to pivot to it. I was already used to working from home, so it wasn't that much of a change—all these Zoom and Microsoft Teams and whatever the heck I have to adapt to for the next person I was talking to. But I adapted to it quite well. Just a ring light and a camera and I'm off to the races.

"What if this is the new normal?"
ANN BINES

She is a nurse manager at an acute in-patient rehabilitative facility. "My complete title is MS, RN, CCRN. Worked hard for those initials, you know?" It is 7:30 p.m. on a Tuesday night. "I just got home from work about a half hour ago, wolfed down some dinner, and here I am. I don't mind doing this with you, though. You're allowing me to put off my piano practicing for another hour."

We talk on Zoom nine months into the pandemic.

We deal with a patient population that has suffered a significant trauma to their brain, whether it be from a motor vehicle accident, flipping over the handlebars of their bike, skiing into a tree, whatever it may be. Patients come to us a lot of times with a lot of personality changes that go along with the brain injury. So re-socializing them is a very important component of their therapy. Teaching them how to interact with people, how to be socially appropriate again.

Our unit is a 30-bed unit, and normally the hallways would be filled with patients and families interacting with each other, interacting with their therapist, interacting with their staff. We really encourage patients and families not to sequester in their rooms, so they can become part of the environment because that is such an important component of the rehab process. Before March 2020 [the start of the pandemic lockdown], the unit was full of people interacting all the time and therapies were being done in the hallway. It was just a place of bustling human energy.

Now—I don't know how else to phrase it—it's become a ghost town. Family visits are limited. We can only have one designated family member visit a patient for up to 14 days, and then they can change to another designated visitor for 14 days. The family member has to be masked the entire time, and they have to stay in the patient's room. They can't go to therapy sessions with the patient. They can't participate in therapy sessions with the patient unless the therapy is done in the room, but very little of our therapy is appropriate to be done in the room. They can't walk the patients around the hall. They can't interact with other patients' family members, which was a huge opportunity for families who had been through a very traumatic event to interact with each other and to support each other. Therapy can't take place in the public spaces anymore, and in the dining rooms everything is very, very spread out. So it's very segregated. It's very isolating. Yeah, it's like a ghost town. It's a very different environment.

You have to put on goggles. You have to put on a mask. You have to put on a face shield, and I think anytime someone comes into your room in full infectious disease garb—gloves and gowns and a face shield—it's like really. . . . Human touch is so very, very important when you're talking about creating a healing environment and a positive environment, and all these restrictions and the garb puts up another layer of barriers.

When you work with new and student nurses, does it worry you that they're learning this profession via Zoom now?

Immensely. I think that we're not going to feel the impact of this absence probably for another year or a year and a half. The people that are graduating now, they've had the opportunity to have clinical experiences. It's the group that's going to be graduating and coming out in a year and a half, two years that I'm very, very worried about. It's different when you do a procedure on a mannequin or in a simulated environment than when you do it in reality. There's no substitute for learning how to communicate with a patient, how to communicate with a family member. You can do all the role-playing you want, you can be in all the simulation labs you want, and do mock emergencies and mock scenarios, but there's absolutely no substitute for doing it in real life. There's just no comparison.

One of the things that is hardest for a new graduate nurse coming into this environment is not just the care and the technical skills that you learn and master, but it's prioritization, it's time management. I have X amount of time. I have this much to do, how do I prioritize and get done what's needed to be done and still maintain my sanity? Also, delegation. And clinical judgment.

Every time you come up against a situation that is part of the learning curve, it makes you a more efficient and effective practitioner, and that doesn't happen in a sim lab.

I think what everyone is hoping is that we will, first and foremost, get the vaccine and this will be over so we can pick up some of the slack and make up for lost time with students' [in-hospital] experiences. If that doesn't happen, we're going to have to, as a profession, develop some other way to allow students these experiences. There's just no way that you can turn out a nursing student who has never set foot in a hospital or seen a patient; same for a PT student who's never felt a bone or felt a muscle move. You just can't. So we're going to have to figure it out. We lobbied very, very, very heavily to continue to allow clinical nursing students into the environment.

I think that the initial reaction was kind of a knee-jerk reaction and one of fear on the part of hospitals saying, "No, no, no, they can't come in." And also on the part of the schools saying, "No, no, no, they can't go in." But what if this is the new normal? If this *is* the new normal, we're going to have to find a way to work this out *within* that new normal.

I look forward to this being all behind us and our environment being what it used to be: the positive, therapeutic milieu that we were able to create for these patients and their families. That's probably the biggest thing. I don't know if we'll ever get there again or if we will get to some semblance of that type of positive therapeutic environment, or how long it's going take to get back there. I do think it is going to change the way that we practice medicine, nursing, and the way a hospital environment—well, *every* environment—is set up.

Given where I am in my career, I may not be around to see it. So I just hope that we define our new norm quickly and *get there* because this is an opportunity for change. It's why I became a nurse. I'm a bridge.

POSTSCRIPT: *Ten months after our initial conversation, she wrote in an email: "Three 'retirement dates' have come and gone since we talked. I am still working. I felt I could not leave. The pandemic has changed a lot in health care: the way we deliver it and the people who deliver it. The people are becoming less available, and so here I still am."*

"THE BOSS OF ME"

"Nobody tells me what to do."
DEBBIE LESSIN

She is 68 years old and has been a tax CPA in private practice for 38 years. She is also an author and entrepreneur whose books, website, and speaking engagements focus on maintaining work-life balance. Her business card reads "The brains of an accountant with the soul of an artist."

I haven't looked for new clients in over 10 years. I have a very stable, steady base of clients. I'm lucky that I have that. I don't have to continually try to reinvent myself in building the practice because I'm more at the end than I am the beginning or the middle, and more thinking how to get out than anything else. I'm single. Never been married; don't have kids. But does my life have to all be about work? No, it does not.

I was in the public accounting and corporate world '76 to '84. Two and a half years in accounting and then I was in the corporate world for five years. I just knew I didn't want to be one of them. I had gotten to a level where I could go to the corporate dining room—when they still had some of those things. I was not even 30 years old, so it seemed kind of cool. But I knew I didn't want my boss's job, even though, when she left and went into operations, I could have had that. I just wanted to know that I *could* have had her job. I just didn't want her time.

I had been doing a little bit [as a CPA] on the side before I went off on my own when I was 29 going on 30. My thought process at that point in time was, well, I can try this; what's the worst that can happen? I can always find another job because I have a sparkling resume—and I *do* have a sparkling resume.

Now I have office space that is walking distance from the house, which is nice. I can't work from home because I'm still a paper whore. I don't care what people do with all this stuff on the computer. I need to touch it, feel it, look at it. But I will not allow [that paperwork] in my house because I'm about work-life balance. That's one of the reasons I hated the pandemic: working from home. I suppose that I could have worked at the office because I work by myself, but I didn't want to meet clients there. I'm a good girl. I'm a rule follower. They said don't go to work.

I will be honest with you. Most of my client work is not in person. I don't really meet with my clients; I find that to be a waste of time and money because you sit and meet with somebody, and you go, "Uh-huh, uh-huh, uh-huh." But until I analyze the information, I'm not answering their questions correctly. So the majority of my work is really done on my own. At one point, I think I had two full-time people and several part-time people. But then, probably 28 years ago, I downsized it to where I'm back to just me. "Just me" couldn't make me happier.

I think the thing I enjoy most at this point is I can look back at how I created my own life. I mean, I take very good care of myself, even during tax season. My family knows not to talk to me during tax season. If everybody's afraid of me during tax season, so be it, right? I work very hard. I stick to my three days a week. I don't check work email if I'm not at work. I don't call in. I gave people my cell phone during the pandemic, because [giving them] my home phone was worse. Now I've told them, delete that number; I have a work number; call me there. There were different concessions when everyone was dealing with a pandemic. But, you know, I'm sorry, there is no such thing as an income tax emergency.

There are times I just hate, *hate* the business. Well, I'm very methodical in how I work. I'm the boss of me; nobody tells me how to do it. I have a hat and a T-shirt that say "Boss Lady." I don't like being told what to do. I just tell myself what to do. And clearly, you have to have a level of discipline, which I have.

If I had to do this every day, though, I would hate it. I mean, it's not necessarily fun. Well, it's work. But sometimes I look at it as a puzzle, and it's putting the puzzle pieces together. Most of my clients, a lot of them are self-employed. So there's some creativity and deductions and things there. And others of them maybe have rental property, or now people have been doing things like refinancing, putting three houses together. That's not all tax deductible, so you've got to figure some of this out. I just think it's a matter of attitude. I look at it as a working-with-people thing.

I have clearly carved out my own life, including how I manage my business, how I manage my work schedule, how true to it I stay. I don't work on Saturdays until at least the second week after February 15. We're talking at most eight Saturdays [a year]; I can do eight Saturdays. That's pretty good. And then, you know what? Then I'll treat myself. So I'll have a massage on Wednesday night, and I'll go get my hair done on Thursday night. So I have enough things during the course of the week to balance out the work to give me energy to get up and do it again the next day, because I worked very hard pretty much from March 1 to April 15. And then I cut it off cold.

I don't view anyone as my competition. I don't need competition. I don't care. I'm not looking for new clients. If somebody isn't happy with my services, move on. Business has been steady, even though I've had an attitude of trying to wind it down and work a little less for some years. I'll take a few new ones if it's like a friend or family member that's desperate, but I'm not taking somebody new who comes to me now that hasn't filed their taxes for, you know, four years. "Can you help me?" "No, I cannot."

How do you imagine your retirement?

The thing is, I'm not sure that doing this isn't good for my brain. Right? I can't see doing nothing. Maybe volunteer, but I don't know what organization I'd want to volunteer for. I don't necessarily have enough people to travel with. I don't know the answer to that question. And I don't think I need to know the answer to the question. As long as my brain is functioning, and I can still do it without hating it, it's okay.

"I like controlling my own environment."
DREW MCMANUS

"What is my job title? (Laughs.) Well, it depends on what element that we're talking about. The bulk of my revenue, let's call it, comes from technology. The newest, if you want to call it 'product' that we've launched, is a full CRM [customer relationship management] database and ticketing system for the nonprofit arts and culture industry. But for about 12 years, I've also run a web development agency that builds websites. "When I fill out my taxes? I just say I'm a small business owner."
He is 51 years old.

I grew up in what would now be defined as a radical, fundamental Christian, independent Baptist home. That mindset does have a very strong self-reliance element built into it. And that is now a benefit because you were always taught that you can't rely on anyone but yourself; you have to make your own opportunities, so to speak, and everyone's always against you. Now, that last part is obviously wrong. And there's a whole bunch of other stuff that I'm aggressively against these days, but one of the benefits that did come from that was this degree of continuous pushing.

I define who I am as a person by what I do. And I know that's not healthy and good for all people. But it is for me because it's what drives me to do what I do. And because of that, I think I've been more willing to take larger risks and explore areas that were new because that also fascinates me. I don't have a degree in business; I don't have a degree in programming. I do have a degree in tuba performance. I thought that was what I was destined to be. (Laughs.) But I was fortunate enough to know early on that I was not going to get a job as a tuba player.

I like learning and growing and doing something different and new. When I was in my early 20s, I decided to go in this direction. It wasn't just the level of control [that appealed to me], there was a real financial benefit to it, as opposed to moving into a traditional career path where you're just going to be an employee of another organization.

For the longest time, I've just been an LLC, and actually this last year, we converted it to an S corp. I have enough employees now, and I technically pay myself a salary. When you're a sole proprietor as an LLC, you don't have to pay yourself a salary; you just take whatever money comes in from the business, and you can transfer that into your account and the IRS is perfectly fine with that. But we've had to change that up because the business has grown enough to that point where we can't do that and not expect an audit at some point.

It's next to impossible to be a small business owner and not get audited at some point in time. You know, there's the whole traditional concept of the American dream as being your own boss, but it is nothing like the picture that, at least in my generation, was projected. You *are* the one who gets to make the decisions, but it's harder to file your taxes, it's more expensive to file your taxes, and you're *gonna* get audited. It's just a fact of life. It's harder to get things like home loans and car loans. That's the reality of owning your own business in this country now.

But if there's not that agitation, I get a little panicky, to a degree. In the business field, complacency can lead to all kinds of errors. In personal growth, too, it can also lead to similar sorts of errors and oversight. I think we get a little too complacent and boring the older we get.

Are you seeing indications of complacency?

In myself? Yeah, yeah. I'm glad I'm not single. My wife has been a remarkable benefit being a sanity check and a reality check, too, when I do push too hard. Or if I do start to get a little lazy and compliant with things. I think we've both been that role for each other in our careers. We both pushed ourselves to be more and better, but also trying to be realistic about it so that we don't harm ourselves. If anything, I'm probably far more guilty of pushing too hard than being complacent. I'd be curious to see what she would say.

We haven't been on vacation for years; we really want to vacation. When I was growing up, we were very poor, so vacations just never happened. I didn't grow up in a culture of vacations. I mean, there was time off, but you just stayed home. My wife grew up in a very different family; they were fortunate that her father worked for the airlines, and they could actually travel, they could just hop on a plane and go to a beach for a day and come back. And so, it was a very different culture, and that's something we both know influenced us, I hope positively, in terms of the need for doing more vacations and taking self-care seriously. But also being able to weather the times when that's not an option.

You have a staff of about seven. As their boss, do you think about setting an example for them in terms of taking vacations and self-care?

I have never met any of my employees face-to-face. I've never been in a situation where I had a group of employees that are together in a single brick-and-mortar kind of environment, so it's a very different discussion, actually, about the kind of example that you set because you don't have the day-to-day face time with your employees. There are no lunch breaks that are shared, nothing like that. The time that we get together and engage is on Zoom meetings; we have weekly stand-up meetings. And then I communicate regularly with employees over Slack all day long. But even then, it is still mostly business-oriented. I do make a concerted effort to try to inject at least some personal communication into those. I ask how their day is going, find out what their hobbies are so that it isn't just purely, you know, one-dimensional. But past that, it's on the tech side.

It's been a learning experience for me to figure out what these folks need for inspiration or guidance or *mentorships*—that's the big word. The 20-to-30-something sector are looking for some sort of mentorship opportunity. And even my seniormost engineer is 29. I'm having conversations with him about making sure that he does more day-to-day team meetings and Zoom than I do to make sure that he's available for mentorship opportunities because I hear from those employees that the reason they work here is to work with this guy. He's got a great reputation. I need to make sure that he's following through on that. In some ways, I guess for me, though, mentorship is sort of passive transfer.

You've been a professional for 30 years. Do you ever long for something you've never known: a traditional work environment?

I don't think it's anything I've ever aspired or longed for. I like being in my office [at home] with my cats. I like controlling my environment. It allows me to be productive. I still can't wrap my head around how people spend time commuting every single day. That's time that you could either sleep in and be better rested or have more work time and not rush yourself on all these things that can be done instead of going from point A to point B, especially if you don't *really* need to be at point B to begin with.

Nonprofits in particular have always had what I consider an extraordinarily unhealthy attitude towards remote working, like a visceral aggressive resistance to it, but the pandemic forced it on them. In my work environment pre-pandemic and pandemic, nothing changed. We were okay, we were already home anyway. I am glad to see employers start to realize the benefit of that. It does have problems though because those 20-somethings are still looking for mentorship; you still have to find ways to have those "here's the way things used to work" conversations that you'd have in the break room or over coffee. Email is so dead now. Nobody in my company. . . . The only time we email each other is if we have to forward something we've received from somewhere else.

My wife, she's a professional violinist,* and her studio and office is basically on the other side of that wall behind me. We communicate more in the day through Facebook chat, which is our personal—I actually hadn't thought of it this way before—but we have our own like operating policy. She doesn't use email or texts to communicate with me because she knows that's disruptive to my other communications flow. We've agreed Facebook Messenger is how we communicate best personally with one another even though we're literally one room away from each other.

Do you ever find yourself wishing that you continued with the tuba?

No, I don't. I think I would have been remarkably unhappy if I went into that career. I would have to say I was lucky that I actually got a job that paid a living wage, which I wouldn't have done if I played the tuba. It's so limiting and narrow. And I think I

* Holly Mulcahy, p. 333.

would have ultimately been bored, frustrated, had a drinking problem. (Laughs.) I don't know. It just wouldn't have been enough to be engaging for a lifetime.

You used the words limiting and narrow. Does that mean that you feel that what you're doing is unlimited and broad?

I think so. That's one of the wonderful things about software development: it is a giant open field. There's new opportunities that open up decade to decade, and I can include more and more types of services either as default functionality for the system, or I could work with a company that provides that and offer more of a seamless integration of their service in a way that doesn't exist now. There's just no end to this stuff. There's many directions you can go. It's like a choose-your-own-adventure kind of book that is constantly being updated. You know, it's not boring.

"I want to be the rescuer."
STEVEN BISHOP

He is an insurance agency owner. "I focus on home, life, and auto. My business is a franchise of an independent insurance agency. I had been with [a large, well-known agency] for about eight years. The difference between that and what I do now is that you just had the one company, and you had to play by all their rules, you had to be the spokesperson for them to all these different customers. And you didn't really own the customer in any sort of way. I wanted to have access to more insurance companies who are more willing to take on different kinds of people, so about a year ago, I switched to do this opportunity."

The insurance world is very discriminatory. I mean legally discriminatory. They discriminate based on various factors and so some of them are very specific in the things that they discriminate against. That's going to be, for example, credit history, whether you own a home, I mean, all these different factors, right? How many miles you drive a year. They'll discriminate against you if you drive a lot, and you'll get a higher rate as a result. Where you live is going to be another factor, too. Every insurance company factors that in; some of them factor it in more than others. So that's where, in my mind anyway, it becomes more than just a rating factor, it becomes more of a "We don't want this person because they live in that area" factor.

It sounds like that doesn't settle well with you.

That doesn't settle well with me at all. Some of the companies do it less than others, but they all have a similar approach. There are some newer ones that are coming out that are trying to be more transparent. They're trying to be more inclusive there, but it's a business. And it's always been built on using these factors to rate price and to rate eligibility.

I think it probably was heightened in the pandemic because you had people who were in a very high-pressure situation where they're definitely feeling financially stretched. One of the real frustrations I had was that although the company that I used to work for tried to make some changes during this time, in my mind, they seemed to be more about optics. It was so they could say, "Oh, we gave everybody all these discounts and look at us! We're making a difference in the community! We're trying to help people because they're in this crisis."

If you fast forward another year to after the pandemic, now they're removing those discounts, and they're sending people to collections. Some of the other companies pause [payments], saying, "Okay, you can't make your monthly payments this month, so we'll pause on that, and we're not going to cancel your policy, we're just going to let it accumulate." And then, you fast forward four or five months, the same person who couldn't pay their one-month bill can't pay us for six months now, so then that bill doesn't get paid and it gets sent to collections. And now they're out on the hook for $600. Whereas, if it had been in a previous situation, they probably would have only been on the hook for $60 in collections.

So having four, five, six conversations every day with customers who are financially impacted really didn't sit well with me. I feel like insurance is supposed to be a tool to help people help protect their finances from things that are unexpected, right? So, a car crash or a fire, all these different things. I find that people who need insurance the most are these people who live paycheck to paycheck, who have a hard time holding a job. And if something happens, they're not going to be able to just pay out the three or four thousand dollars. They need the insurance.

But the issue that you consistently run up against when you sell insurance every day is that for those same people who need it the most, it costs the most. And so this person who's living paycheck to paycheck, who has bad credit, who, maybe they've gone in and out of policies lapsing because they can't afford to keep it up, now, if they want insurance, they have to pay three or four hundred dollars a month. Whereas the person who is well off, who has good credit, who lives in a more desirable area, that person is going to pay a fraction of that cost.

And they, more than likely, could handle some of these financial pressures that may come up. That was the constant frustration for me, seeing and having conversations with people who I know need the insurance the most, but who almost always have a really, really hard time finding a policy that they actually could pay for consistently, like every month.

That was one of the primary impetuses for me wanting to be able to help them with their insurance, regardless of whether they own a home, regardless of whether they have good credit, that kind of thing. Most of the insurance companies that I partner with now are built for homeowners, but then there's a larger percentage of them as well that are for everyone.

The thing I can do now is I can be a resource for people, for everyone, you know? I can try to make sure they're getting a fair price; I can try to make sure they're not getting taken advantage of. The reason why I've partnered with these particular independent agencies, to be a franchise of them, is because they have similar views. They have a similar approach. They want to be able to offer something for everyone.

You sound like you're approaching this work from a place of great empathy. Did you always have your sights on a career in insurance?

I went through a season where I wanted to be a pastor. And that's what I went to school for. I did my graduate program and then did a 180 and got into insurance.

I do think there is something pastoral about the way you describe your approach to selling insurance.

When I was looking into pastoral ministry, I really wanted to help care for people's spiritual needs. And now I've sort of shifted. I really want to focus more on their financial needs. But I think it's part of the reason that I probably have more of a challenge in this role, because I probably go pretty high on the empathy scale, almost to the point where it can really emotionally impact me more than it would probably emotionally impact other people. And so, that's just part of my personality that I've started to realize over the last few years: that I can only take so much, I can only internalize so much before it's just not a healthy situation. I think I probably, over the last couple of years, have been more—*traumatized* is probably too harsh of a word or too intense a word—but I've probably, over the last several years, been feeling this more acutely, and it's now become more of a conviction for me.

I've done a pretty high volume of business in the past, especially when I was [in my previous job] where I did a lot more, and so to have back-to-back-to-back-to-back calls with people where you say, "Nope, not eligible; nope, nope, not eligible." Having to be someone who has to deliver that information to people is probably what I find the hardest for me, emotionally. I don't want to be the bearer of bad news; I want to be the helpful person, I want to be the rescuer.

Is this the job that you'd like to retire from someday?

(Pauses.) I don't know. Yeah, I'm not sure. I think so. I sort of set it up that way. I actually hope *not* to retire. (Laughs.) But when I think about some of the struggles I've had over the last few years, if something similar to what happened recently [with the pandemic] were to happen four or five years from now with a similar emotional impact, I don't know how I would respond to that. That probably would be the only thing that would make a change in my thinking about retirement.

I was listening to the radio, and the DJ made this comment that the weekdays are for what you do, and weekends are for who you are. And I was wondering, as I was thinking about this, how many people are like me and think it's really important to have a meaningful job, a job that feels like it's significant, that's actually making a difference in the world.

"Not have the future of someone else on my back."
MICAH COHEN

"I'm a truck driver. I have my own business, which is a construction and trucking company. I do short-haul runs. I'm working locally, about 100 miles out from my house, so I come back home every night. Hauling logs, wood, timber. I take pretty much all of that to the paper mills. I do two or three hauls a day. This is my niche, right here."

He is 26 years old and lives in Columbia, South Carolina. He has a 3-month-old son. Until two years ago, he was an elementary school teacher.

Why did you choose to be a teacher first?

I knew that deep down I wanted to help people, but I just didn't know in which way I wanted to do that. I wanted to go into the military, but God spoke to me one day and said not to go that way.

So, what's the next best thing? I was like, well, education. That's an awesome career where you can impact the youth and leave your impression on kids in a positive way. Someday, I thought, I'm going to be a teacher. I stumbled upon a program that was grooming me to be a teacher, an African American role model in the schools. I'm like, "Oh, yeah, I can really do this. This is great." That program was really a big help for me because it taught me to grow as a man, as a Black male and [showed me] the importance of having that presence in the classroom. Because, to be honest, I don't really think I had it when I was in school.

I'm from a small town in South Carolina and basically it's just pretty chill. I mean, I grew up riding dirt bikes, hunting, fishing, you know, just going outside. The school I went to was majority white, to be honest; well, or half and half. I guess I really didn't have too many Black friends growing up like that. But I think I had a pretty good experience.

The school where I first taught was just completely different. It's in the heart of uptown Charlotte, so it's more, I guess you'd call it urban. And it was like something I'd never experienced before. I've never really seen poverty until I got there. I'm like, "Man, some of these students here, these families are hurting for real." I had no idea. You know, seeing the struggle, I tell you, to give the students homework and stuff like that, and they just don't do it. Their parents are working 12-hour jobs and are gone before they leave for school, and they're gone when they come home. So there's no one to help them on their homework. It's easy to fall behind like that. [Another reason they might not do the homework is] they're not grasping onto the subjects as fast as what they need to. And that's understandable because some students need extra help and more time, but the way the curriculum is, they try to rush everything and there's no way possible to even teach them thoroughly the way you want to. It was just a struggle.

They wasn't built like me. I was nurtured growing up. You know, I had a different upbringing. Some of those students, I felt, were raised on survival, just trying to get by. Unfortunately, that's how things play out sometimes.

[He was an "end of the year" teacher, meaning his contract only went till the end of the year, and he wasn't renewed. He had trouble finding a new teaching position. Over the summer he worked as a pipe fitter, "underground, putting in water pipes, sewer pipes, because I had to keep some money coming through. You know, as a teacher, over the summer you got to figure something out." He finally was hired on

the spot at a school near where he lived.]

That school was difficult, too, but I'm going to say more from an administrative demand type of situation. What I mean by that, it wasn't so much from students, they were just regular students. They were 95 percent Hispanic. I'm not trying to discredit the Black students from the previous school. I was just trying to make a statement that they were a little bit rough. But from an administrative standpoint, it was tough because you're basically trying to meet unreal expectations every day. They're like, "Okay, Cohen, we gotta get this student's reading level up to here. Alright? We want [this student] to be at a four or a five at the end of the year."

I'm sitting there thinking, "Now, come on. It's possible, but he didn't even pass the third grade, but he's in the fourth grade, and you tell me he needs to get to a five. It might take a little bit more time." They struggled a little bit with their reading skills. It puts stress on you as a teacher. It's like, "Wow, I'm trying the best I can, but you just kind of harangue me, you know, telling me I need to do this, need to do this, need to do this." But it just makes you sit down and think, like, who's making the curriculum here? This curriculum is just a cookie cutter. One size fits all, and it really misses the point that the district is so diverse; every school isn't the same. Students all learn differently.

But what I will say about that is I know I struggled as a student back in elementary school. And one day, recently, I looked at my end exam scores when I was in like, fifth grade. I just had never looked at them. I opened it up, and I had gotten proficient in history, and everything else was below average. I mean, I just didn't know what to think at that time. I'm like, "Oh my gosh, I've been failing this whole time and had no idea." I thought I was doing good. I knew I wasn't doing the best, but I mean, I thought I was doing okay. I was like, "Well, I passed fourth grade and I'm going to pass fifth grade and I'm going to sixth, so I must be doing something right."

Why wouldn't *you think that?*

Right? Why wouldn't I think that? They never said anything. I thought I was good.

How did you get into trucking?

After a while, [teaching] becomes overbearing because, I don't know, I'm not gonna lie; it was a little hard to wake up every morning to go to that job. And it wasn't the kids, it was the stress of the job, and the pressure that you get from the administration to do this, to do this, to do this. It just became too much. It came to that breaking point where I was like, "You know what, there has to be better out there. There has to be more money out there. There has to be jobs that are a little bit easier."

I was just so frustrated with everything. I was like, "What business can I work for myself, not have to listen to anyone no more, not follow anymore of you guys' rules, where I can go to right now with little overhead and make more money to pay my student loans?" That's my goal. I just want to make enough money to pay my student loans and live comfortably because I'm in so much debt. I owe so much; I owe $70,000.

Then I thought of trucking. My dad was running a dump truck when I was in college, and I really want to do that. I remember I was sitting in class one day, and I was like, "Alright, guys, go ahead and read for the next five minutes." And meanwhile, I was on my computer on auction websites, bidding on trucks. That was probably October. I knew then. I was like, "Yeah, yeah, this teaching is a great profession. So wonderful, such an admirable, admirable profession, but it's not sustainable."

So I bid on my first truck, and I won the bid, got that truck, shipped it all the way from Missouri, and that's when I started my journey with one truck. I just love the freedom of being able to be my own boss and also build financial awareness and generational wealth, because I want my own kids to turn out better than what I did, of course. I mean, my life, my upbringing was pretty cool, but there's always room for improvement, and I want my kids to have it a little bit better than what I had it. So generational wealth is really important, especially in the Black community, because to be honest, we don't really have it.

I always used to say this: the worst day in trucking is better than the best day teaching. Just to me personally. Like, I really enjoyed it. I was really passionate about it. But now, I can wake up every day and be like, "Man, I'm going to go get this load. I'm going to get it because I *want* to go get it because I want to make money." I'm saying it's what *I* want to do. It's just the freedom to just do that. It was like, "Wow, I don't have to worry about the future of someone else on my back."

I've done a lot of jobs in my life, and I can say I love this. I mean, it's good money, too. And if I want to take a day off work, I can.

When you're driving those 100-mile runs, do you ever think back to your teaching days?

Oh, yeah. I think about it probably every day. While I'm driving, I think about [how] we'd be going to lunch right about now. I'd probably be watching the kids and chilling with them, you know, sharing the good moments. I think about it all the time. But then again, as I'm driving, I also start to think, "Wow, I'm glad I'm not doing that anymore!" So it's like I have those good [memories], and it's like, "Huh." But then, "Oh, well."

"My eyes are trained to see the broom handles in the forest."
AMANDA LEE LAZORCHACK

She crafts handmade brooms near Kansas City. We talk on Zoom. She is seated in the studio she built with her own hands in her backyard. "This is a very special place. I'm very, very proud of it. I think anybody can build anything. I'm not a professional house framer. I'm not a professional woodworker. But I know how to read, and I know how to research, and I know how to ask for help. I think I built it in about eight weeks. So I'm out here really, really screaming to people: 'You can do the things you want to do!'"

I'm enamored by brooms. I think they're amazing and beautiful; they're aesthetically pleasing. I love the intersection between domesticity and our tools. I love the intersection between utility and beauty. I love functional art. The broom is so easy to forget about. Nobody talks about their broom, so they're an easy way to open up a ridiculous conversation.

I grew up on the East Coast in a small rural town named Clarksburg, Maryland. (Laughs.) That's ok, *nobody* knows where that is. It's just north of DC. My parents have always done a lot of things. When I was growing up, my mother managed and waitressed at a strip club. My dad was a chimney sweep and a general contractor. Now they work at and manage a hobby racetrack.

Later in my life, I was a migrant farm worker all over the country. I harvested blueberries in Cherryfield, Maine; I did beet harvest for many years up in North Dakota and Montana. I harvested apples in Washington, detasseled corn in Iowa. That was how I sang for my supper. It was a wild experience. I did that for a decade. A lot of it I look back on and love and cherish, but the work is hard and grueling and nasty and you're mostly dirty and you're also mostly homeless and you're living in your truck, but that was a chosen lifestyle. We weren't homeless because we had to be homeless. We chose to be migrant workers. Our crews were ragtag, and we were young, and our bodies were still really strong. I learned a deep respect for how hard agriculture work is, and how important it is, and what it really takes to bring food to someone's table. And so now, when I look at this fiber (she holds up a hen's wing whisk broom she made), I know that it has a deep history, and it's traveled in large part many miles to get to me. It's about understanding that the story is larger than me or this bundle.

How do you make a broom?

With aches and pains in your hands and your wrists and your shoulders. (Laughs.) *That's* how you make it.

I go to the Ozarks to harvest broom handles. It's the closest beautiful place. I have some really good friends down there, I'm familiar with the area, and it's just incredibly beautiful. What I'm looking for are hardwood saplings. Some people just go pick up sticks off the ground; usually they're broken branches. It is important to me to be able to stand behind my work with a 100 percent lifetime guarantee. I can't guarantee a broken dead branch from the ground.

My eyes are trained to see the broom handles in the forest, but it's also important for me to be able to turn that off and not see the forest as a place of commodity, but a place of communion.

When did you turn your interest in broom-making into a money-making venture?

I wanted to be damn sure that what I was making was quality. I wanted to be sure that it wouldn't fall apart, I wanted to make sure that I could stand behind my work. And I wouldn't say I'm a perfectionist per se, but I didn't want to be an amateur craft maker. I wanted to know that what I was doing was as good a quality as my skill could get at that time. And that took a few years.

And then I guess I just decided, well heck, what do I have to lose? My skill, I feel, is really solid, and I'm ready to offer it to the world. So I went full time as a broom maker . . . smack-dab in the middle of COVID. Mostly mail-order stuff, and then as mask mandates became more regular and vaccinations started to happen—this was probably a year after the actual lockdown—the market started to come back around, and I did some wholesale work. Now I make a steady income. This is my only job.

I've known artists who struggle with pricing their work at its true worth. Is that hard for you?

This is not the first time in my life that I have, you know, hustled or made a thing for money. I've had different experiences with the conversation I have to have with myself about value, and it can get tricky, it can get muddy. It's a conversation that the craft makers that I know have over and over again. My mentor gave me some incredible advice. Probably the best advice I've ever been given about money for craft ever. He said, "Please do not undervalue your work. When you undervalue your work, you undervalue everyone else's work. That does a very large disservice to the art community."

As a craftsperson, no one is paying my bills; *I'm* paying my bills. I'm my own product manager. I'm my own advertising manager. I'm my own accountant, secretary, *and* I'm my own craftsperson. So it's a lot of roles. I think I'm good at wearing a lot of different hats, and I think that the time and the labor and the reverence and the love and the quality of what I make is . . . I would say probably worth more than what I charge for it. And so, learning to balance the reality of an art with what the market will bear is interesting.

Being a market artist, though, is not sustainable for me. It's really harsh on my body to pump out that much inventory. And then to sweat in the sun every Saturday and Sunday at a market, you know? And that's not to say that I'm above hard work. That is to say that I want to organize my time in a way that feels more sustainable to me. And also, I have to leave room to be out on my boat as much as possible.

I think a lot of the ideas and maybe personal feelings that I have about work at large were formed by Kahlil Gibran. There's a series of historic poems he wrote, and the piece about work* that's most striking to me ends with (reads aloud): "You have been told also that life is darkness, and in your weariness, you echo what was said by the weary. And I say that life is indeed darkness save when there is urge, and all urge is blind save when there is knowledge, and all knowledge is vain save when there is work, and all work is empty save when there is love."

Just reading it gives me like, full-body goosebumps. The idea that perhaps

---

* In *The Prophet*.

when we work, we really do bind ourselves to our project or our vision or our community or our loved ones or the earth around us. And I think to be connected to those things offers us what I perceive to be a better, a healthier perspective and maybe a more joyful experience.

It sounds cliché, but think how much of our life goes back to our parents. Oh my gosh, I watched my parents really struggle. And they worked so hard. Blood, sweat, and tears, and bloody knuckles. I watched the middle-class American dream absolutely fail them, without a doubt, absolutely fail them. And that informs a lot of decisions that I make in the world.

If you didn't have to work to "put food on the table," would you be making brooms?

(Laughs.) Probably. I have this note on my window that says, "Act in accordance with your first nature." And then a second note under that that says, "What the hell *is* your first nature?"

"To build something new and exciting."
SHAHARA BYFORD

She graduated with a civil engineering degree from Purdue University and started on the operational side of construction as a project manager. She was at Pepper Construction for about twelve and a half years, then was recruited by Power Construction to establish an HR department. "I sat as a part of the senior leadership team and grew it. By the time I left, I had 13 direct reports. We really grew that and worked hand-in-hand with our president and CEO in terms of running a business and staying true to our culture and who we are."

Although she was offered ownership in the company, she left Power on good terms to found her own company.

She has three children—a 13-year-old and 11-year-old twins.

My dad was a crane operator in the steel mill. My mom was a high school counselor. They both had 35-, 40-year-long careers at the same establishments. They were both very passionate about what they did. They worked their career, and they received a pension at the end of the day. You just didn't change jobs, right? You didn't up and leave opportunities within a company. That just wasn't how their generation approached the work.

So, my leaving a good position to pursue a passion, I think they felt a little bit of . . . fear? I don't know if that's the right word, but I think it was more of a desire to understand [my decision] and make sure that I had really thought through why I was leaving a good job and why I was doing it.

What did *compel you to do it?*

Somebody told me you look at your career in thirds. The first third, you're really trying to learn everything you can; you're very green and trying to absorb the information. The second part of your career, you're trying to advance and climb that corporate ladder. What do you want to do? Where do you want to go and how quickly can you get there? The third part of your career is about leaving a legacy. What does that want to look like? What do you want to be remembered for? And how can you truly make that impact?

I've been very fortunate for the first two parts. And so, as I looked at that third part of my career, the question was: where can I have the biggest impact as a female and a minority in the construction industry? Although I had been able to do so much at Power, which is now a billion-dollar company and the largest general contractor in Chicago, I felt that I might be able to do more to create opportunities for females and minorities in the industry if I wasn't under that umbrella. They were very supportive and encouraging [about my choice to leave].

The industry is shifting but has a long way to go, so does our society as a whole, right? So I'm always trying to be intentional. My husband is going to continue doing his own job; he is not going to be a part of this business. I want it to stand alone, so we've also been very intentional in terms of the financing of the business. The ownership of the business is 100 percent in my name so that I truly can represent a female- and minority-owned business.

I don't know that this will happen in my lifetime, but my hope is that down the road there won't be goals on projects where you have to provide so-much percentage to minority businesses or to women-owned businesses. There will be more equity throughout the contracts that are being awarded so that it no longer needs to be tracked because it has finally become a very diverse pool of corporations that are working on these projects.

So it becomes the norm.

So it becomes the norm, correct. I also believe I'm going to have an opportunity,

both from that side, the corporate side, to impact and to help teach others and
to prove that a female minority company as a start-up can be successful and can
get repeat work *because of the work that you do*, not because you're a minority or
because you're a female.

I want to be able to help people who don't have 20-plus years of relationships in
the industry to truly have the opportunity to be able to teach and mentor so that our
industry is more diverse from both the trade and craft side of things, as well as the
ownership side of things.

I spoke to a young woman who is a welder. She discovered welding while she was
incarcerated and found she was really good at it and that she loves doing it. She said
she wished her high school had exposed her to career possibilities like that and hadn't
always been pushing college exclusively.*

It's interesting, when we started a venture at Power for getting into the schools
and talking to students about our field, we had a lot of pushback. It was really
difficult actually. We'd call and say, "We're a construction company; we want to
come in and to talk to the students." And they'd say, "No, sorry. We are focused
on the college prep and getting kids into college." We'd say, "Most of our project
managers went down a construction management path or an engineering path.
Those are the people that we want." And they're like, "Oh, I guess I didn't even
realize."

I would be remiss if we went into the schools and talked about college
opportunities and didn't let students know that if they choose not to go to
college or decide after they go to college that it's not a great fit for them, there's
still a really financially lucrative career and a sense of pride that you can have in
construction, whether you go the college route or choose not to.

I feel like construction is very much about working with a team of people,
which has always been a focus for me—that team environment to build something new and exciting and tangible, something you can look at it at the end of
the day and say, "I was a part of that. I had a piece in that." I think that there's
a real sense of pride that goes along with that. And I think that's true from the
project managers to the carpenters and laborers that are on those projects. They
can look at [what they built] and at the quality of work. They put their heart and
soul into their jobs, their craft, whatever that might be. And at the end of the day,

* Jordan Coley, p. 249.

it all comes together—all these parts and pieces for this beautiful building or this huge highway that connects these two different parts of the country. I think that for a lot of people who go into construction, being able to look back at something you did helps to remind you of all of the relationships you built while you worked on it and the ups and the downs and that you worked through them all and you came out on top. And now there's this really beautiful structure that is the result of all of that hard work.

There's something they do called a Topping-Off Party, often on steel frame jobs. You get all the way to the top of the job and there's that last piece of steel that goes in place. And often everybody who's out at the job signs that piece of steel, and then it becomes a part of that building. Then the bricks go on the front and the drywall goes up and the paint goes up and you never see it again, but those people who were a part of it, they know it's there and it is a part of that building forever. So that is very much a part of the industry. It's an accomplishment for everybody who's out there that they've made it to the top, and this is the last piece of steel, and now they can go on with finishing the building. It's something that I think a lot of people take to heart. You really take a sense of pride on that day. It's a turning point in the job because it is no longer about how are we going to get to the top. You've made it to the top and now it is about building everything out from within. I've worked with people who like to say, "I like being able to shape the skyline," to say, "I was part of that."

I was once at a meeting for an institution that was just starting a new building project. Ground had just been broken. And at this meeting, the president said, "I'm pleased to report that what was once just an idea is now a hole in the ground."

I love that! That's fantastic. Fantastic. Yes. Well, that's the promise of what's to come, right?

"Feeling at home."
DENISE LOWELL

She is the owner of a small boutique for fine furniture, accessories, and pianos.
*   We talk on Zoom. She is in the showroom she designed and built herself on the lower floor of her home in a suburb of a large midwestern city.*

We all have a sob story. The good, the bad, the turbulent times, and the great triumphs and all of that. I've had some tough times in my life, and you know, there's still a lot that I battle.

Are there ways those battles and turbulent times have helped lead you to where you are professionally, today?

They really have, actually. I have all these kind of old-school values that I was brought up on, like a very hard work ethic. I worked through years of very, very crippling depression. And it made me the better person. It made me a hard worker, and I am grateful for it. Some people say I work too much. (Laughs.) But the reality is, work is good. You know? Work is good. I grew up in a very old-school, traditional, conservative way. I hold a lot of those values still.

It's interesting how my boutique came out of this. I actually had been planning on doing a small project [an addition] on the back of the house. But I ended up having some issues with the city, and they declined permits and stuff like that. And I realized, well, guess what, my sales skills are still there. These things that I've learned [about business] over the years in regards to the paperwork, moral decisions, ethical decisions, how to interact with people, you know, the correct handshake and how to do it, all these sorts of things. It's all kind of formulated into a "calculated harmony," to use a musical term. And I also have a skill set from the interior design background to make nice vignettes and tableaus and settings [to display my furniture] that can help people envision the piece that they might want to buy in their *own* home, because they're seeing it in an ambient home environment. So I'm working my boutique out of my home, and it's been an excellent move.

One level of the house, now, is designated as the boutique. I put about $10,000 into my own remodeling here. And I've done all the work. If I hired a contractor, it would have cost probably a couple more zeros.

So you built it with your own hands?

Yes. (Carrying her laptop, she gives me a Zoom tour.) So you can see the trim work, the crown molding, the archway to this entire fireplace wall with the built-ins and all the lighting. I always have accent walls. I did all the paneling everywhere. I take aesthetics very seriously.

Everything that you see is for sale and potentially can be part of your home. I've had people who come in and buy an entire room of stuff—the chandelier, the rug, the sofa, the tables, the chairs, and the cocktail table, the accessories. They say, "I just like it. I'm going to do it exactly how you have it. I want your wall color, too."

There's so many people who are shopping online now, at Wayfair, or whatever it might be, for even the nice, higher-end stuff, like the stuff I carry. You know, Marge Carson or whatever. But they can't envision it in their own home because the space [where they're shopping] doesn't feel like home. When you go to a large warehouse, a place that has a large assortment of pianos, you can't get any sense of scale. This room here, it's deceptive. It is 10 by 14, and that gives you room for a six-foot grand, a sofa, and a chair, and so people can imagine a six-foot grand in their house. What it really comes down to is being able to let people see and envision what you have, and what they want, as their own.

It's like having a friend, if you will, and that's really the goal, to not have a situation where clients feel like, "Oh my gosh, it's another salesperson, this is just going to be torture!" Buying a car is a nightmare in my opinion, and I want to be the exact opposite of that. And that's one thing that I pride myself on. That's what I always feel is so important. I want people to feel comfortable.

You know, obviously, I'm transgender. There was a client over the other day, a lady and her child, and the child actually said to the mom, she said, "Mommy, is that a boy or a girl?" In the business setting, I have a basic response: "I'm transgender. And if you have any questions, feel free to ask." The mother kind of paused. And then I interjected because I felt that I didn't want to create—I didn't want there to be any discomfort in the pause. Like I said, I want people to be comfortable.

You mentioned earlier the "correct" handshake as an important part of doing business. Do you think that your handshake changed as you changed?

"Growing into my identity," that's the correct way of saying that. Because it's not a change. It's becoming yourself, really, growing into yourself. But yes, my handshake actually is different. In fact, I thought of this the other day. Years and years ago, before transition, mine was the typical, nice, firm handshake. It was attentive. It was not necessarily domineering, but it was, "Hey, I am here, I'm present." It was really about being able to show that you are capable and have the aptitude. Yes, my handshake has changed. Now, it's much more.... It's inviting, it's more delicate, it's an embracing, if you will, like, "Welcome. Welcome. Come sit down, feel comfortable." It establishes a welcoming environment, not necessarily a sales environment. And that's the difference between my business and if you shop at X, Y, or Z where people expect a salesman or saleswoman to say, "Alright, what can I do for you?" For me, it's "Sit down, have a cup of coffee, let me get you something." And it usually always ends up with me playing a piano [for them]; people always listen to the piano.

I guess really what it all boils down to is that I've learned through my time on Earth so far, that it's really all about making people feel comfortable and doing the best you can. And that's what I do for my clientele: I make people feel comfortable. And feel at home.

POSTSCRIPT: *One year after this conversation, due to increasing debt and being "cheated by several clients," she closed her furniture boutique.*

"If I had an apartment, I would feel obligated to live in it."
ERIC BOGEL

He is 30 years old, currently living in Denver, Colorado. We talk on Zoom. "How do I identify myself professionally? Ho boy. I'm interested in a lot of things, right? Right now, I'm just doing a lot of street performing. I'm hoping to branch off more to doing circus education, but I guess you could say I'm a mover, a shaker, a day maker. At least I try to be, anyway. Does that answer it?"

Before I got my RV, I used to live in my car. That's where I am now. A 1999 Isuzu Trooper. I don't know if you can see, but I took the back seat out and put a mattress in there. I'm parked across from a Panera to draw on their Wi-Fi for this call. It sounds silly, but I guess I don't actually think of my work as a hustle; you do it because you love it. And, I guess, because you need to eat, right? It more than just feeds your wallet; it feeds your soul and creativity to go out and find ways to survive. Everyone does different things to eat. That's what it's all about.

The way street performing started for me was my brother, who I lived with when I was in New York working as a dog walker, said he wanted to go to Europe. And I said, "Yeah, okay, I'm in." We were there for about three months, and I went to this park every day, and there was all these jugglers there. I would juggle with them and hang out and was getting to be friends with them. And then they were like, "You should work the traffic lights. We'll show you."

So I went with them one day. Well, what they do is when you're in your car driving and you come to a red light and you're sitting there for about a minute and a half, they run out into the crosswalk, yell and scream, get your attention, throw their clubs up, spin around, do the bit. I think I made, I don't know, like 27, 28 euro in under an hour. And I was like, "Wow, I'm making money." You don't need much for food or beer in Barcelona, so it was like, "Oh, I got money for food, I'm good."

Then we went to Majorca because it's a very touristy town. Flights are cheap, only 30 euros. I made a few hundred euro there and a bunch of friends. And I said, "Wow, this is a *thing*!" So that's when taking my juggling and turning it from a hobby into a skill that is profitable became a thing for me.

I don't want to sound egotistical or anything, but I average, *average* about $110 an hour out here. I'll probably work like 20 to 25 hours a week, or sometimes I won't because I worked a great week the week before. I like to treat it like a job, honestly. I don't work 40 hours a week, but I really don't need to.

I would wake up, I'd hit the traffic light for about two and a half hours. Then I'd go to a park where there was a building where I found an outdoor outlet on the outside of it, and I would charge my phone there and whatever else I had to charge, and just kinda hang out and maybe juggle the park a little bit, maybe read a book. Denver is a legal state, and I do enjoy marijuana. I'd get a little stoned, relax, and then try and go back to the traffic light around 5-ish or 4:30, maybe, when it wasn't so hot, and juggle for another couple hours. So, that was that. And then I make myself some dinner. I had a little Coleman thing, a little stove thing that I take back to that park and make some dinner there.

I have a Planet Fitness membership, so I will go shower there, use the restroom, though it's been trickier in a pandemic. I go into a Safeway, which is like the grocery store here, to get my yogurt in the morning or my apple and then use their facilities. But that park that I mentioned, there's porta-potties. At night, if you can't wait until 6 a.m., when the Safeway opens, you can drive yourself to the porta-potty quick. I mean, there's mild inconveniences, but there's always a workaround. Always a workaround.

Once I had some money saved up, I bought an RV for a great price, which I now live in. So now I have a bathroom in it, so I'm good in that regard. A lot of my friends are like, "Why don't you get an apartment? You make enough money to get an apartment." I don't know. I guess I'm just kinda used to making things work in a way that's less conventional. I also like the idea of not being tied down somewhere and being able to kind of go. If I had an apartment, I would feel obligated to live in it.

If I drove up to your red light, what would I see?

I could show you if you want. I got my clubs right here. I can pop out into this parking lot. (He leaves the vehicle with three brightly colored clubs in one hand and props his phone up against a tire with the other.) Alright, here we go. So I'd run out, and I'd go, "Hey, hey, ho, ho, and welcome to the traffic light show! *Bienvenidos a la espectáculo de semáforo!*" (He performs his routine, throwing the clubs high in the air. He spins, catches them behind his back, and ends by catching one club between the other two. Then he bows with a flourish.) *Thank you!* My Venmo is Juggle Struggle. (Returns to the car.)

I have a shirt that's got "Juggle Struggle" on it. (Holds up a white T-shirt with the name printed with a Magic Marker.) But then someone actually pulled up one time and was like, "What's your shirt size?" And I was like, "I'm working my way to a medium." And later she came to the traffic light and had printed my Venmo, @JuggleStruggle, out on shirts for me. I was like, "Oh my god! It's great." For every person who gives me the finger or yells, "Hey, get a real job!" there's 50 more that roll down the window and say, "That was the coolest thing ever!"

It's a little silly how well I do out here. I'm building a future for myself now in a really cool way.

Do you have health insurance?

I'll be honest. I am uninsured. And it's something I should look into getting. I mean, as far as if something bad were to happen in traffic, it's not as dangerous as it sounds. I'm pretty safe with it. I guess as safe as one can be. I got a ski pass this season. I've been having so much fun learning to ski. And *that's* where I'm like, "Ooh, I should have some health insurance because this can go poorly quickly."

Would you like to be doing this when you're 50?

You know, that's the question, right? I don't know. I guess it's tricky because it's tricky for me to even think of myself as 50. Can I be running out in the traffic for those bills at 50 years old? I mean, if my legs allow it, maybe, but also, do I want children, do I not? I don't know. Maybe. I like the idea of having three young ones to teach all the things that I feel like I missed out on when I was at that age. And to give them the opportunities that I forsook. These are questions that, once you hit 30, you're like, "Wow, I got to start whittling them down, get some answers."

I've been thinking about getting into—it's called flare bartending, where the bartenders flip the bottles and balance them on their elbows. It's just a real showy way to make a drink, and I have all the basic skills. Those flair bartenders clean up when they do private events or even Vegas; they get tipped out big. So that's something that maybe I'd like to work towards for more of a career aspect of it.

I'm feeling more hopeful towards a future. I'm thinking about saving up money to try and buy some property. I already live out of an RV, so it'd be cool if I were to get some property to put the RV on and start a thing there. But this is down the road, Mark. I'm just starting to dream. I'm just starting to dream. But I don't know. I feel good about it all.

I might be looking to leave Denver sometime this summer, but I'm not sure where it will be. I just made a reservation at a campsite in Yosemite for August. I did that so that now I know I'm going to be in California in August. So that's one thing that's settled.

"This Is the United States of America"

"If anyone can do it, moms can."
JOSINA MORITA

She has been commissioner at the Metropolitan Water Reclamation District [MWRC] for five years. At the time we talk, she is running for Cook County Board in the 13th District of Chicago.

"I got my master's in urban planning. That's planning physical environments. There's a whole field of how they are used to segregate, used to isolate, used to contain different communities. I'm Japanese American and Chinese American; my Japanese side moved to Chicago out of the internment camps, and back then Chicago was very Black and white, and they didn't know what to do with us. So they literally put us as a buffer between Black and white communities on the South Side."

We talk on Zoom. Behind her are several large, exuberantly abstract drawings by her young children. "That's their genius art," she says when I ask about the art-work. "They're colorful and make me happy."

I have a 2-year-old and a 3-and-a-half-year-old at home. I've been a community organizer and worked in the nonprofit sector for almost 20 years now focusing on race and public policy issues. I also chair the statewide Asian American Caucus and chair the country's first Mama's Caucus, a caucus of elected moms with school-aged kids.

I founded it along with five other elected moms here in Illinois because a lot of us had different struggles. For example, I was denied maternity leave when I was at MWRD, others had babies while they were campaigning or while they were in office and faced a lot of different challenges. We just started talking to each other, and we said we need a caucus to bring people together and advocate for making things better for not just elected moms, but moms across the state. We also talked about the recession and how hard it hit moms. As policymakers, we talked about how are we trying to pass policies that make it easier for moms to get back in the workforce? But I would say, when it comes to actually working on legislation, there's been a number of challenges.

We're all working moms who are elected officials, so it's been hard to find time. All of us were up for election this year, so that added another set of challenges. Also, we're one of the few bipartisan caucuses in the state, and that makes it *really* hard because we have very right-wing Republicans in our caucus, so finding points of agreement, well, it's challenging. But we always say, if anybody can do it, moms can.

Do the caucus members on the other side of the aisle believe that, too?

I think that we did when we first started, but as politics comes into play, people's personal campaigns come into play, and it gets harder to separate what you would like to do as a mom versus [what you would like to do in] your political career. One member was running for lieutenant governor on the Republican side. It's hard to do bipartisan when you're running in a very polarized political time.

It's interesting because when we first started we did a survey of moms across the state about what we should be working on. I was expecting things around choice, affordable childcare, living wages, support money for small businesses for women. But we were getting all kinds of stuff from anti-choice to "protect my daughter from these gender-neutral bathrooms." I mean, it was the whole spectrum. If you think about who moms are, we really are everybody and that's both an asset and a challenge.

Do you like campaigning?

"Like" is a hard word in this context. (Laughs.) But I think it's worth it to have the ability to make change. Do I love knocking on doors and asking people for money and getting yelled at by people? No. Do I think it's worth my doing at this particular time to work for the things that I want to get done? Yes.

When you're in politics, people say whatever they want to you. I came from nonprofit which was very PC. But when I was campaigning, I was *"ching chong,"* I was asked whether I spoke English, and there was a lot of sexual harassment on top of that, very racialized sexual harassment. An elected official told me that he had never tasted "chink pussy." These are things that I had never experienced before. I don't want to say you "take it"; you *absorb* some of that really overt racism and sexism because you know you're here for a reason. For me, it also comes with the responsibility of like, "Okay, so I'm the first Asian American; how am I using my platform?" I'm not just an elected official, I'm an Asian American elected official that's trying to build Asian American political power in the state. I'm a water reclamation commissioner, but I also chair the statewide caucus, and I've been able to build a broader political strategy where we've grown from zero members to nine in just five years. We just won 19 out of 22 primaries across the state of Illinois. That's my *why*, right?

I grew up very much in an activist family, both of my parents were civil rights activists, and I always said it was something I would never do.

They met at UC Berkeley in the '60s during the Third World [Liberation Front] strikes [in 1968] and the fight for Asian American studies. My dad's been an activist writer all of his life. He was the founder of *Colorlines* magazine and also authored an antiwar newspaper for a number of years called *War Times*. My mom started with the Filipino farmworkers in central California as a public health worker, worked at a community clinic and then at my high school as the nurse for a number of years. Now she's a volunteer first responder. She worked [Hurricane] Katrina, she worked Ground Zero. She's worked the California fires. Even though I said social justice activism was something I wouldn't do, here I am doing it.

I think my resistance to it when I was younger was a little bit more complicated than just kind of a [teenage] rebellious thing. It's also, my parents were really busy. I grew up sitting under the table at meetings instead of at birthday parties and those kinds of things. I didn't have the same kind of childhood that a lot of my friends had. I think there's oftentimes that sense of resentment, and that sense that it's a choice they made lifestyle-wise.

Now, with *me* being a mom, I have to make a choice about how to balance politics and ambition and making change and being in the community with being home and being with my kids and protecting them from the public life, especially in these really aggressive political times.

Did your experience as a child, for better or worse, teach you anything about balancing work and life?

I don't know if I've learned how to balance, but I think I've learned to appreciate the challenge. I've learned that it wasn't as black and white as I had thought, right? It wasn't my parents choosing me versus the movement. They were doing the movement work *for* me. And I think that that's how I view my own work, too. I'm doing this political work and public service for my kids.

At some point, I might say, like, "Okay, this is not my lifelong career. I was here to help like a startup, and then I'll hand it over." I don't see myself. . . . I'm not a lifer. As my kids get older, it may be harder for me to find this balance [if I stay in this position].

I also think—just to be frank—I can't afford to be a public servant my whole life and be able to send my kids to college. I took a pay cut when I left nonprofit, that's how bad it is. As my kids get older, I have to think about going back to a career where I can make enough money to send them to college.

What is the example you'd like to set for your children?

My kids are Asian American and African American. I want to instill in them being proud of who they are, and the idea of doing something that is about more than just yourself. There is a responsibility to the next generation. I think it's also about leading with some integrity and some grace in the middle of all of the madness. It's about how you deal with the public scrutiny but knowing who you are and feeling like you can stand by every choice that you've made and everything that you say. And doing the hard work. I hope that they see that I do the hard work to try to make things better and really focused on coalition building and being thoughtful about how policy is going to impact people. I want my kids to lead with knowing who they are and what they're passionate about and not just, you know, making money, but leaving something better behind.

"There was a lot of fear."
DAPHNE QUERY

She has been an immigration attorney in private practice in Miami for 18 years. "I always knew that I wanted to be a lawyer. That started happening very young. I had worked in volunteer legal services. I was not doing immigration for them, but we were doing some public outreach, and when I was speaking to different people, immigration was always the primary concern anytime you speak to anyone needing legal services at a low cost. Because if I don't have a status, I can't get a job; if I don't have a status, I can't get health care; if I don't have a status, my kids can't go to school legally. So I knew that that's the work I wanted to do."

Right now, the most challenging cases that we're getting are people coming to the border trying to come in but getting sent back to Mexico to wait. We've seen in the last few months—I don't know if this is really good to say—but I feel almost like the discrimination starts at the border. I see a lot of Venezuelans. I don't know if it's because our government has made a formal acknowledgment of the situation in Venezuela that they've been granted temporary protective status. But then some of our clients, families from Nicaragua, which is facing problems, too, which our government is aware of, are *not* being allowed to pass through. So I feel like the challenges start before the person is even given an opportunity to explain their request for asylum protection.

A lot of times what people are suffering [in their home country], as terrible as it might be, doesn't fit the legal requirements here for asylum. You have people who have abandoned their homes, are coming over the border with children, and they can't get a work permit for a year. That's a challenge now, because it used to be just six months, but now they have to wait a year to get a work permit. They're waiting for an opportunity to hear their court case. What's happening is court is being postponed, and we have people who aren't scheduled till next year or the following, so a lot of people are in limbo. But they tell me they prefer to be in limbo here than in the dangerous conditions at home. It's not that people are complaining. It's just that it is challenging, and the laws change under different administrations.

One big change, when Trump was president, was that domestic violence wasn't a basis anymore for applying for asylum. That affected a lot of people, and women in particular, from certain Central American countries. Also, the government restricted the use of saying that you're threatened by a gang. In the past that would have allowed you to apply for asylum. And more and more, a lot more people are being put into orders of supervision, meaning they get a deportation order, they appeal it, their appeal gets denied, and now they have to present themselves every year. The fear is that at that appointment they can detain you and deport you. So you have people living in constant fear every year, that it might be the time that they're going to put an ankle bracelet on or [be] detained to be sent back.

There was a lot of fear, mostly because of the ICE memorandum expanding who was considered an enforcement priority. Under Obama, it was "let's focus on criminals and people who might pose a threat." Whereas under the Trump administration, pretty much everyone was seen as a threat. If you're driving without a driver's license and you get stopped, that might have been a ticket before, whereas now it's reason to be detained and put into removal proceedings. So there was a lot more fear, understandably, that just doing day-to-day things could put you at risk for being detained and deported.

I saw in my experience that—and I don't want this to sound bad, but it's the truth, at least in my experience—the immigrants feared and respected United States more [under Trump] than they have under other administrations. Sometimes, during Obama, you'd get someone saying, "But citizenship is easy because Obama really, really likes immigrants. It's going to be so easy, so why should we hire an attorney?" Okay, whatever. And then under Trump: "No, no, no, no, no. I have to get this right. I need to be represented." Sometimes I feel like there are certain groups maybe that see the United States as weak and generous. And sometimes we *are* very generous. And there are some laws that I do think *could* be harder. I think if you're married to a citizen and you have children, it should be much easier. But it's not. Then you might have somebody else who committed a crime, and there's a ton of waivers in that particular case because under different administrations there are different priorities. But Trump was frightening for people. I think that some of the laws are really unfair.

There's a lot of delays now, so a lot of people are very upset. They're not getting their work permits or not getting driver's licenses, there's a lot of confusion, and the courts are closed [because of COVID].

Do you consider the work you do to be, in part, activism?

When we get a denial of an appeal, we can petition to the 11th circuit, and if we get a decision that's published, that becomes law, so that helps. That's an "impact litigation." When you get a good case, and you get an audience with the 11th circuit, and you get your argument won, it can be very beneficial to a lot of people.

We had a case, it was an asylum case from Colombia. The woman had traveled back and forth many times. The judge in Miami denied her application for asylum because he said that her travels undermined her saying she was afraid. "Why would you keep going back if you were afraid?" At that time, the laws and asylum were really, really against us in this circuit. There was even one case, there, that said the FARC* guerrillas shot and missed, so that wasn't persecution, but they did approve for asylum. They overturned the denial from the Board of Immigration Appeals. I remember the judge saying it's like a soldier that goes back to war; they can't always be afraid, but it doesn't mean that they're not facing any danger. So that was impact, and I would say our activism.

Another time, we had a case of a lady, she was an attorney in Colombia who worked with the FBI to bring some people to extradition here. And the government attorney was trying to say that she was a terrorist because in her affidavit, she said that she gave the FARC guerrilla a soda. The government tried to argue that her providing them with the soda was giving them material support. We had to argue that she was not a terrorist because she gave the FARC guerrilla a soda. (Laughs.) I thought it was ridiculous. And it was so frustrating. And this is immigration law; your clients don't have a lot of money. At least in our case, we're not charging them hourly. We're not getting paid so much more for having to do ridiculous briefs and keep going back to court. So it's not that lucrative, I guess you could say, compared to other areas [of law]. In the end, we won. But was it really that necessary to get an expert witness—who's actually now in jail for money laundering in Venezuela—to testify on her behalf? This was before he was arrested and jailed, of course.

Miami is very, very different, so you get exposure to things that you may not get somewhere else.

Do such cases affect you personally?

* The Revolutionary Armed Forces of Colombia—People's Army (Spanish: Fuerzas Armadas Revolucionarias de Colombia).

They do. Especially because these are people that you see every day. My sister lives in the Keys, and her best friend's husband is someone who has to wait the five years. I know him, I know the children. They know that I'm doing my best, but at the same time, it's like, every time I go in [to meet with them], it's heart-wrenching. It does get depressing. And I know a lot of people, even some judges, who have quit under the last administration and changed jobs.

What keeps you going?

Because this is all I've ever done. . . .

"It's a story that needs to be told."

DR. LAWRENCE TAYLOR

"The reason I came back up here to the Midwest from Mississippi. . . . Everyone tells me it's a story that needs to be told. It's a story that you would not believe. I had PTSD for about 10 years; I couldn't talk about it. I had left Chicago, where I had a good practice, and moved to Mississippi. I was there four or five years, and I was run out. If you don't mind indulging me, I'd be glad to tell you the story."

He is 67 years old and is a foot and ankle surgeon with over 38 years of experience.

I had been practicing in Chicago and was very successful for about five years, and then managed care came in and pretty much decimated my practice. I had a buddy who I had done my residency with. He had gone to Mississippi about three or four years prior. Matter of fact, he had wanted me to join him when he initially went down. I thought he was joking. I said, "You know what? When I look at the map of the United States, and my eyes get right around Mississippi, I don't see a state. All I see is a black hole."

The third time Mike called and asked me to come down, that's when I was starting to feel the changes in my Chicago practice because of managed care. The landscape was changing, and I said, "Okay, Mike, I'm coming." I had never been down there in my life. When I told my dad I was going down, he warned me, but I was kind of in a panic because my practice was being swept out from under me.

The plan to work with Mike ultimately didn't work out. But I went down to Mississippi to visit another buddy and spent three or four days down there. There was no board-certified podiatrist in the entire state of Mississippi except one. So I decided I was going to do this on my own.

It was very difficult to get established. We had to fight for privileges in the hospitals. We put up a lighted sign outside of our office; apparently that was a no-no. We started hearing grumblings about that. And so, this little, tiny sniping at us started almost immediately, and that continued.

I got to know everybody [in the state senate] because I ended up being a lobbyist, although I had no idea that's what I was doing. But when I look back, I was lobbying for podiatry because the Podiatry Act, which was dictating what we could do in our practice, was very, very archaic and limited. It wasn't specifically spelled out in the law, so I was trying to get the law changed. All along the way, I was making enemies, and I didn't know it.

A state senator I'd met there comes to me one day, and he says, "Dr. Taylor, I need to tell you something. These people not only want to put you out of business, they want to put you in jail." I said, "*Jail?* You have to commit a crime to go to jail. How can they just put me in jail?" He said, "They know everything about you. They know where you live. They know you drive a BMW. They know everything about you. So you need to watch your back."

I was puzzled by this and a little bit frightened at the same time. Two weeks later, my front girl, working the front office, came to me: "Dr. Taylor, there's a lawyer on the phone, wants to talk to you." I get on the phone, and he says, "I'm an attorney, here. I want to meet you. My office is right down the street from you. How about lunch today?" So I went down and met him for lunch, real nice affable gentleman.

He says, (affecting a southern accent) "I just want to get right to it. The reason you have so much trouble here is because you're Black, you're articulate, you're good at what you do. They don't know what to do with you. As a matter of fact, I hear them talking about you all the time. So what I would do if I were you is I would sue because what they're doing to you ain't nothing but discrimination. And I can help you."

And I'm saying to myself, first of all, who *are* these people? And why are they after me? I left that meeting, went back to my office, and I pondered the whole thing. And I thought: You know what? I'm not even bothering anybody. Can you imagine if I go on the offensive and sue these people? I thought, I can't do that. What I have to do is protect myself the best way I know how. In my practice, I dotted every *i* and crossed every *t* because I knew what the government was doing to doctors there at this time. They were putting a lot of them in jail for Medicare fraud. We did everything we could to make sure we were always in compliance.

Then I got a letter in the mail, said Medicare was no longer paying my claims. That would be like $250,000. They said, "We're not paying your claim because we're doing a review." And then one day I was in my office. I had just treated a patient. I walked out of the room, and there were four gentlemen in suits. They flashed their badges. And one of them said, "Are you Dr. Taylor?" I said, "Something tells me I wish I wasn't right now." And they said they're with the FBI, "and we have a warrant to search your office." So they spent the entire day taking files, computers, everything. And my young lady up front, she told me, "They been trying to take the appointment book!" I said, "Sheila, this is the FBI; they can do anything they want. Just give it to them."

I called my brother who is an attorney, right away. He said, "You have to get a lawyer." He contacted an attorney down to Mississippi. I get a call from that attorney who says we need to meet. Okay. And by the way, every time you talk to one of those attorneys in a case like this, you have to write a big check. Thank God my mother had taught me to save my money.

I gave him the whole story. He says, "I'll take on your case." A couple of days later, he calls me, and he says, "Lawrence, I have bad news for you. You've been indicted." It was a 45-count indictment for Medicare fraud. We have a conference call. It was me, my Mississippi attorney—who, by this time, has an assistant attorney—and there was a paralegal, and my attorney from back home, are all on the conference call. So the attorney in Minneapolis says to my Mississippi lawyer, "Look, why don't you go to this U.S. attorney, tell him to drop these bogus charges, and tell him Dr. Taylor will leave the state of Mississippi."

The Mississippi attorney was a woman named Katie, and after the conference call, she was over in the corner, just bawling her eyes out. I walked over to her, and I said, "Katie, that sounds like a good idea to me. What's the matter?" And she said, "You just don't understand. I was born and raised in Mississippi. And the thought of them running another Black man out of Mississippi is more than I can stand."

The paralegal comes up to me, and she says, "You know, Dr. Taylor, Katie's a good lawyer. And she can really help you with your case, but every time she hears your name, she starts to cry." Come to find that [her family name] was a long-history name. Her father was in the KKK and she grew up around that, and she hated it.

By this time my office was shut down. And then the bankers come to visit me. They said, "We understand you have some trouble, Dr. Taylor, so we're here because we're going to call your loan." They wanted me to pay my bank loan back. I looked at them, and said, "I'm not paying you anything. I have lawyers to pay." And they said, "That the way it is?" I said, "That's the way it is." They got up, walked out; I never heard from them again.

Was there evidence of fraud?

No. When the FBI searched my office, they didn't know I had a hard copy of every single patient record. They took the computers, but they didn't take the patient files, so I had a record. There were 45 patients that they had picked who swore that I had cheated Medicare and committed Medicare fraud. So I found all 45 patients in my paper medical records: written, documented evidence that disproved the theory of the indictment. So I took it to my attorney, and he looked through it all. And he said, "Oh my god, this is great." So he takes it over to the U.S. attorney, and they dropped the indictment.

Indicted me again. This time 25 counts. So I did the same thing. I'm sitting in my office all night long going through papers. Same thing. Dropped the charges. And it happened *a third time*. They indicted me *again*. Ten counts. At this point, my attorney says to me, "Dr. Taylor, I've been practicing for 25 years. This is all I do. And I have never seen anybody indicted twice, let alone three times."

One day, I ran into my office manager, who I had not talked to in a few months. She said, "Christmas Eve, the FBI came to my house. They said they wanted me to testify against you. And I told them, 'The things you want me to say against Dr. Taylor means I would have to lie because he didn't do that.' And they said, 'You're not going to cooperate?' And I said, 'I'm just not going to lie.'" So they indicted her, too. So I had to pay for her attorney; wrote a check for $30,000. Now I'm paying like three or four attorneys.

I never left my house except to go to the store. I never came out at night. People were throwing liquor bottles in my yard. There was this car, this mysterious car, that was parked outside of my house all the time. My doorbell would ring, 2 or 3 in the morning.

They came to me with a couple of proposals. One was that I plead guilty to one count of Medicare fraud and go to jail for five years and pay a fine. My attorney said, "Look, Dr. Taylor isn't pleading guilty to anything. So just get ready to go to trial."

I was going to sell my house because I decided to just get out of Mississippi. But I had to get permission. They had put a lien on my house, the government did. I got permission to leave, and I moved north and stayed with my brother and his family.

I had a trial date in March. I go back to Mississippi. I told my dad not to come down. I had put my family through enough. That was the hardest thing, what it put my family through. Came a point, I just made up my mind that I'm going to jail in Mississippi. I get down there on Friday night. I go to my attorney's office Saturday morning. The trial was to start Monday. My attorney says, "They want to cop a deal." It was actually something that my other attorney had suggested weeks ago, but they had turned it down. He said, "They want your corporation to plead guilty to one count of Medicare fraud. All the charges against you personally will be dropped. You will have no record. Your corporation will be kicked out of Medicare for five years. And your corporation has to pay a fine of $250,000." I thought back to sitting in that courtroom early on in this process thinking to myself, how many Black people have sat right here in this courtroom who they put in jail or sentenced to death?

I said, "Okay, I'll do it." My corporation, which was now not a functioning entity except that it was still on file with the state, was still registered with the state as a corporation, pled guilty, and I was off the hook, personally. So, it was over. I paid the money. I paid the bank loans. All the money I saved over the years. I sold my house and made about $80,000 on that, which the government had a lien on. So that went towards paying the fine.

I got in my car, and I drove back north. Then I had to rebuild my life. I was 50 years old. At 50 I had nothing. No money, no home of my own, no real income, and an uncertain future. Somehow with the help of my family and God's grace, I was able to rebuild my life and finally got a secure job.

I had a patient come in, a Black guy, and we were talking. He said he was from Mississippi. And I said, just in passing, "Oh, I was in Mississippi for a while." He said, "I *knew* I knew your name! Man, I can't believe you got out of Mississippi. They were having meetings about you. They were going to kill you. I can't believe you got out of there." And he's shaking my hand. "I'm so glad you got out of there."

After I had lived there for six months, I had a ritual every morning. I'd go into the bathroom to get ready, brush my teeth and shave. I'd look in the mirror, and I would say, "This is the United States of America. This is the United States of America. This is the *United States of America.*" I felt like I was in a different country. I had to *convince* myself that I was in America.

POSTSCRIPT: *"I'm doing well, now. Minneapolis is a great city. I love it. You can make it here. But—I'll always speak from the Black perspective—there are no perfect places for us to live, anywhere. Look at George Floyd. I tell you, with each breath I take, the older I get, the more painful it becomes. I used to think that life would get better in this country, that one day. . . . But now, to see all that come crashing down, you know? (Pauses.) I'm sorry. (He turns the camera away for a few moments and weeps audibly.) I cry too easily these days. To see things getting worse.*

"Again, speaking from a Black perspective, George Floyd's is not a new story. It's an old story, but there's a whole group of people who are now hearing the story for the first time because it's affecting them."

"Cultures are never easy to change."
VISHAVJIT SINGH

He is a storyteller, performance artist, writer, cartoonist, and public speaker focusing on diversity, inclusion, and equity. Two months before our second of two conversations, he assumed a full-time position at the New York City Fire Department as a manager in the Office of Diversity and Inclusion. What follows is a melding of the two conversations.

I was always a minority. Even [growing up] in India, we're an ethnic minority. I came back to the U.S. [for college], and people have no idea what Sikhs are. They see my turban, long hair, and they just presume I'm ultra-religious. People are calling me names on the street every day, laughing in my face. They call me "genie" and "raghead." I have lived with stereotypes about turbans and bearded people in India and in the U.S. That's always been part of my life. So I struggled a lot. I have even survived a genocidal massacre of Sikhs in 1984 when I was living in Delhi.

I had an existential crisis in my sophomore year of college in Santa Barbara. I'm like, "I don't want to stand out. I want to fit in." So I cut my hair, took off my turban, cut off my beard. It was a very difficult decision. I had never cut my unshorn, waist-length hair until I was 20 years old. I knew it was a profound thing to give up an identity, the only identity I knew, the identity that marked me as a young boy who could be killed on the streets of Delhi. My parents could have easily said, "Let's just cut our hair." They didn't do that. They were not a religious family, but they had a connection to this identity, and they said, "No, we're not going to cut our hair or take off our turbans. Even if it means we may not escape death." So I knew what this meant.

I remember after I did it, walking down the street and people were not staring at me. It was magic! I thought, "Wow, this is what it means to be invisible. This is what it means when nobody's looking at you." In that sense, it was like, "Oh, okay, this is good. I'm not marked for being 'other' in a negative way."

Did you like the way you looked?

You know, I did. I was like, "Hey, I look good. I look better." That sense of vanity was there that I'm a better-looking man now.

As we speak now, you are wearing a turban and have a beard again.

August 2001, for the first time in 10 years, I put on my turban again because my hair had grown long enough to put in a bun. I put a turban back on not knowing what was going to happen a month later. My life would be turned upside down again on September the 11th, 2001. I did not leave my home for two weeks. I did not feel safe.

Did you consider cutting your beard and taking off your turban again?

Actually, there are many Sikhs who did take off turbans and cut their hair, shaved off beards. I did not. And the reason was I'd fallen in love with my Sikh faith. But 9/11 was one of the events, like 1984 in Delhi, that totally uprooted my life and put me in a spot where I'm like, "Whoa, okay, what do I do now? I am in an existential crisis. I don't know who I am or how I fit in."

In New York City, I've had verbal abuse over the years, and that verbal abuse has come from not only white people, it's also come from Black men, from Hispanic men and teenagers. I think people saw me, and they defined themselves as more American in relation to me, who looks to them as very un-American, somebody who just *cannot* be American.

President Trump did give license to people to be more open about racism.

That's what's happening to [U.S. representative] Ilhan [Omar] and others. We have members of Congress who are very open about their bias and prejudice, and they are just . . . saying it. And they have an audience that's listening to them. And so that is now all out in the open. So, has [this hostility] really gone up? To a certain extent, yes. But I think in large part, it's just gotten a license to resurface itself.

You had been effectively raising your voice against this in performances, workshops, and through your cartoons. Now you have this new position in the Office of Diversity and Inclusion at the FDNY.

It's a department that is working to not only diversify the department but also trying to change the processes *by which* you diversify and create a more inclusive space in any institution. What is interesting about this—I mean, one can guess this, but fire departments in general across the United States are not very diverse, but especially in the big cities. A lot of times they do not reflect the city's demographic breakdown, and New York City is no exception. It's slowly changing, but our workforce, especially the uniform workforce, the firefighting workforce, is very, very white and mostly men. Our police force, by the way, in contrast, is almost half non-white. They have also made a lot of changes. There have been many efforts across the U.S., but especially here in New York City, to really have the workforce reflect the city's diversity that the people deserve. So what happened is, in 2014 a lawsuit comes out claiming discrimination. Our last mayor settled for $98 million and as part of that settlement this department was formed. We have to, for example, change our recruitment practices, change the test and how we reach out on a lot of different things. So I am coming in at a time when the Office of Diversity and Inclusion itself is in transition. It's in the process of getting a new leader. So it is, itself, learning what are some of the needs, what are some of the resistance points within the institution to how we change and how much we change?

It's an exciting time. I've met some really amazing people. I felt really a warm embrace from everyone, top leadership to others. And I'm learning; cultures are never easy to change. So I'm working with our team to get a feel for the culture and capture some of the stories that exist. There's always stories in an institution, so I want to capture some of the stories but also create space for new stories.

I come in as a storyteller, as a visual artist and performance artist to capture those stories, create a space for the stories, but also create a space for saying, "Hey, what we have done is a combination of the good and bad like society at large in many ways. Our mission is not changing. But how do we create space for a more inclusive and diverse family and keep that mission going?" So, it's a challenge.

The FDNY is an over-150-year-old institution; it goes back into the 1800s. And I think from the early days, it was a department that was mostly white men, European men who were serving. I keep hearing stories of people who are serving whose fathers, grandfathers, and great-grandfathers served, so it runs in families. People serve with a lot of pride. This department has a low attrition rate. Once they get in, they don't leave because they love the job they do.

Does that mean that it's inherently racist? What I would say is, it's like many other systems in America. There is a systemic bias in the system that has been recognized as part of this lawsuit and the settlement, so systemic solutions and changes are being made.

One big component is how do we create a truly inclusive space [which would make people want to work there]? You can diversify a space, but that doesn't mean you're making it inclusive, right? That's the challenge a lot of places have: we've hired this many women and people of color, but how do you make it inclusive [once they're in there]?

Somebody who [is thinking of applying for a position] sees this, rightfully, as a department that's very white and mostly male, so why would they want to go in there? I'll use another example. We have even fewer women than African Americans. The numbers are very low across all of these groups—Asian Americans, women, Hispanic Americans. And so, there are some common challenges to how we open up and invite members of these different groups in.

What is very much at the heart of the lawsuit and the settlement is, do people coming in feel welcome? Have there been challenges for African American firefighters who are coming in and finding they're the only ones serving in a firehouse? I have spoken to a few of them in the last two months as part of my work and some of them have told me, "Listen, Vishavjit, yes, challenges exist. I personally have not been harassed that much, but yes, there are challenges because you have to make efforts to fit into an existing culture as opposed to that existing culture creating the space for you to be who you are."

What about when you yourself came in? Have you been able to "be who you are"?

It's interesting you ask that. It's still kind of a work in progress. I think on the civilian side people probably know more about who Sikhs are, but I think on the uniform side—I've always wondered, what do people think of me? Do they see me as somebody who is not American? I don't know.

As I said, I actually have been very warmly received across the board, but the question is, does everybody who sees me, do they see me as somebody who happens to be a member of the Sikh family, part of the American family? I don't know. I really don't know. And so, the other question that comes out for me is about religious diversity, which is also lacking in many other institutions, but especially here.

One of the things that I've taken upon myself is to work towards more religious diversity as well. So I'll be building bridges between the Sikh community in New York City, which is one of the largest Sikh communities in the U.S., and the fire department. It's a two-way street, right? Both need to know each other. I want Sikhs to consider the fire department as a career opportunity, and also for the Sikh community to learn about fire prevention measures.

I am going to build some of those bridges in the coming months and next year at our Sikh Day Parade, which is one of the largest Sikh Day parades in the U.S. I'm going to make sure there's fire department trucks there. The few Sikh employees—civilian, EMS, and fire—will be there. I will be there. I'm going to be building and working across bridges, and yes, creating that awareness that there is ignorance everywhere. And how do we create awareness?

People are asking me, "How can we help you?" So I think that gives me hope that we can certainly talk about hard things, and we can hopefully bring about change. I'm mindful that it might take a few years for some of those changes to become apparent, but we are going to lay the foundation for those changes to happen.

"A fresh start."
JOBI CATES

She is executive director and founder of Restore Justice Illinois, a "statewide criminal justice reform organization focused on long-term incarceration and its impact on individuals, families, and communities." It "utilizes its resources to engage in direct legislative advocacy at the state level." *

* From their website: restorejusticeillinois.org.

If it's okay with you, I'll share a tiny bit of my personal story first because, well, because I think it's part of the story. I actually got sober 14 years ago on November 9. And when I got sober, I found myself living a life that I couldn't really live. About two weeks before my last drink, at my very lowest, I accepted a position as VP of development at a large nonprofit. I had a big office, managing a staff of about 12, I think. Crazy hours, high expectations. For the two years before that, I was consulting for the Bill & Melinda Gates Foundation half-time and a number of other high-profile clients in the nonprofit world. I guess I was sort of a nonprofit mercenary.

There were defining characteristics of my drunken self—or of my ego driving the bus. I liked jobs where I got paid well, even though they had to be nonprofits, so I'd look good, so I looked altruistic. But I needed to get paid better than other people, have a nicer office, a better title. And these needed to be fancy enough that my parents would acknowledge that [my job] was important. I wanted them to be proud of me.

I needed a fresh start. I found a job raising money, which is a skill I have, at a place called Human Rights Watch. I did that for about seven years. But in the first year, I was introduced to a thing that I didn't know happened in the world—and I thought I knew everything! What I found out when I got this job was that it was possible in our country—not only possible, but that it happened with more frequency than you would like to think—that a child could be given a [prison] sentence of life without parole, life without the possibility of ever getting out, basically a sentence of death in prison. A 15-year-old, 16-year-old. And I couldn't believe that. I found myself really drawn to the people I met who were working on this issue, the lawyers and ultimately the family members of people serving life sentences for things that they did when they were kids.

What drew you to them?

Anger. I think my blood is like 60 percent righteous indignation. I have to concede that. As long as it's not too *self*-righteous. At the time, it was more an intellectual anger. But I can tell you exactly when it transitioned from being intellectual anger to being personal anger. I started going to meetings of a coalition that had convened at the Children and Family Justice Center at Northwestern law school. And in 2008, they asked, "How many kids do we have in Illinois serving these sentences?" Well, we have 103. And 103 is way too many, right? But it's also a manageable number from the point of view of finding them and finding their parents and finding their loved ones. So they raised some money, and they found the family members, and they invited them to come to the office and talk about their kids.

I found myself at a table sitting next to a woman named Joan whose son is still in prison right now. And at the time, Joan had never been around other family members who had lost a loved one to incarceration. I got to be with Joan as part of her journey. I got to watch her and her husband, who's a retired Chicago police officer, of all things, wrestle with being isolated in dealing with this awful thing. As I got more involved, Joan became a bigger part of my life. And then, at the very end of 2012, I went and visited her son, Carl, which was my first prison visit. I think from the day I walked into the prison and met Carl, it was pretty clear to me that this was what I was going to do with the gifts that I had been given earlier in my career and in my life.

I was afraid, walking into a maximum-security prison the first time. Prisons are way worse than anyone thinks. Prisons are 1,000 times worse than has ever been depicted on television, ever. I went to Menard [Correctional Center], which is in Chester, Illinois, about an hour and 15 minutes south of St. Louis, in the middle of nowhere. The visitor parking is literally as far away from the entrance as physically possible on this plot of land. You couldn't have made it harder for a mom to see her kids. And there's a gun trained on you the whole time, right?

This is really what got me and what I think changed [the course of] my life. The guy I was going there to see, Carl, he would be, by Illinois legal standards, considered the worst of the worst. And if all you knew about Carl was that he was convicted of a double homicide, and then if somebody told you he'd killed two little girls, 13-year-old girls, the person you'd conjure in your mind when you hear those words is so hateful. And so awful. And you can't imagine what kind of a monster could do this.

So, I walk into a room. I see Carl, and he makes immediate eye contact with me. He puts his hands out, and he goes, "Hey, you're in prison!" You're allowed to get up for a minute, and he gave me a big hug. The person who sat down in front of me was not what I had imagined. He was a selfless, compassionate, funny, interesting human being.

He's been there since he was 15. He had gone out on a December morning in 1995, and he never came home. He was part of group of kids who were stupid and reckless, and as a result of their actions, those girls lost their lives. Carl and five other boys went to prison, four of them for life. It's tragic. And I know [the girls'] names. (Sighs deeply.) You know? The girls' names are Jane and Anna. I say their names when I talk about Carl's case. I think about them, and I think about their families, but the horror that has happened to [the other kids and their families] and to Carl and his family has not brought the girls back. And it will never bring them back.

A very wise woman said something to me years later. Her sister had been murdered, and she had started off believing that the only thing that would balance the scales for the murder of her sister was the murderer's life in prison, his never getting out. But over about a decade, she had come to believe that the only thing that would ever fill the gap for the loss of her sister would be her sister's killer's redemption. That was her journey. That was her path.

Carl doesn't still belong there [27 years later]. He's not that same person anymore. That first visit was enough for me. I'm in. What do I do? Where do I sign up?

So, I founded [Restore Justice Illinois] in 2014. We exist to roll back the laws, most of which were passed between 1978 and a few years ago that cause extreme sentences for people who did that stuff when they were young. So we try to prevent those people today from getting life sentences. That is a true restoration: restoring opportunities for relief. What I've learned is [the system] doesn't actually care about rehabilitating at all.

When you say "restore justice" it implies there was a time when there was justice. Is that what you mean?

I came up with the name, but it's funny, I kind of disagree with it now. I don't think we've ever had justice in this country. So when people ask me now, what does "restore justice" mean, I don't say it means going back to [the past]. I say it means we would like to restore the *concept* of justice to be something owned by communities and by people and not by a merciless and racist system. I didn't know that in 2014.

What I am most proud of is the first bill that we worked on that passed in 2015. It was a tiny little bill, which was so funny because it was so hard. We bled on this thing. I mean, tears and fights and anger and a million trips to Springfield and people pulling their hair out, and knockdown drag-out fights.

[The way it works] in the state of Illinois is, if you're charged with a certain offense, you are automatically transferred to adult court. So your age is not relevant. In terms of which courtroom you're in, your *offense* is what's relevant. And once you're in adult court, as a juvenile, you are subject to 100 percent of the same jail time [as adults]. It's just insane what went into getting [the bill] signed. And all it did, prospectively, is it gave back to judges the ability, when a child was sent to their courtroom as an adult, to consider their age, and in fact, *has* to consider their age in sentencing them, and cannot give a mandatory life sentence. That part was already the case, but because Illinois has the most severe "gun enhancements," [meaning] gun penalties, in the nation by an order of magnitude, they build life sentences with gun penalties, and they just make them out of the air. In Illinois, if you're a kid, and you're involved in a shooting and the person dies, the mandatory minimum for the murder is 20 years. And the mandatory add-on for the gun is 25. So if you were that kid and you stabbed someone in the heart with a knife, your sentence will be 20 years. If you shoot from across the street, your sentence is 45.

The little provision we got in that we're so proud of allows a judge, for an under 18-year-old, to waive that 25 years. That kind of changed things. But we bled on this shit, we bled on it.

How do you and your colleagues help each other not get destroyed by your own response to what you see and experience?

Yeah, it's tough. It's tough. And there are good times and bad times. So it's the little things like getting visitations expanded from five a month to seven, which we did. Every time someone's released, every time someone has a year anniversary out of prison, every time one of our guys gets the permission to do something magnificent, we have to stop, and we have to love that moment. That's how we do it.

Here's another example. This happened today. So, I was at lunch with my son when the Rittenhouse decision* came down. And I got a text from a woman. Her son had been incarcerated for almost 30 years. He came home a year and a half ago.

This is what I got from her, today. (Reads the text from her phone.) "Hi Jobi, I am just doing a well-being check. I know you heard about the verdict of Rittenhouse. And in your mind, you're trying to put together our boys and how they handle their situation. Not all of them were guilty. God help us all to

---

* Kyle Rittenhouse was 17 years old at the time he shot three protesters, killing two, during civil unrest in Kenosha, Wisconsin. He was found not guilty on November 19, 2021.

suppress our emotions. Because God's got this. [Rittenhouse] is not free. There will be a price of a different kind. Be blessed. You're doing a great job, anyway, for the justice of young people. Take a few minutes to relax and have a hot drink of coffee or tea."

I don't need anything else. That's my MacArthur genius award right there.

POSTSCRIPT: *In an email, Jobi tells me that Carl was released five months after this conversation.*

"It's not a surprise to me that it's a fight."
CHESA BOUDIN

He worked as a San Francisco deputy public defender and was assigned to represent indigent criminal defendants and provide them with legal defense. In 2019, he ran for district attorney and spent much of that year on the campaign trail. He served as D.A. until he was recalled from office by the voters in the middle of 2022.

"I'm currently in between jobs. I'm mostly taking care of my 14-month-old son at the moment."

He is 42 years old.

I never set out to have a career that would simply earn a living for me and my family. I mean, obviously that's basic and baseline. And if you're lucky enough to do that, then I think you start thinking about higher order things, like careers that are fulfilling intellectually, that have an impact, a positive impact on the world and the people around you.

I have a lot of lawyers in the family. And many of the people in our social network who I look up to and admire and who I see making an impact on the world are people who had legal training. So I felt there was a certain value in the contribution you could make through the law. Running for public office is a big decision, not just for the individual but for the entire family. It was something I had to talk through with my parents and with my then-fiancée. Obviously, it had vast implications in terms of sacrificing income while I was on the campaign trail, exposing myself to a level of public scrutiny, and [I knew the job would require] being on call 24/7. That's a very big commitment. So I thought deeply and had some important conversations with my family to be able to make that decision.

Were they on board about this from the start?

Well, I think everybody close to me expressed concerns about the impact on my life and the level of attacks that I would endure because politics in this moment in American history is extremely toxic and dishonest. And also, there was my family background and what people would say about me as someone with parents who had been incarcerated my entire life. My biological parents, Kathy [Boudin] and David [Gilbert],* were incarcerated from the time I was 14 months old. My mom didn't get released until I had finished college. My dad only got out last year. I was raised by my adoptive parents [Bill Ayers and Bernardine Dohrn], and I consider all four of them as my parents. They were all fodder for the police union attacks because of their political histories.†

There was also the fact that I had spent much of my career at that point as a public defender, and now I was running to be the district attorney. It's not the most common path or profile for someone seeking the office of district attorney, and I think people correctly and accurately predicted that there would be vicious attacks from the police union, for example. And indeed, in the final weeks of my campaign, the San Francisco police union spent more than $750,000 in really very violent and dishonest attacks on TV and over email and direct mail trying to prevent me from getting elected.

I think the general public might wonder why anyone would want to put themself through that.

I think you're right; most people don't want to be involved in running for office for a whole slew of reasons. It comes at a tremendous cost—both individual sacrifice and broader collective sacrifice for the family. And the nature of the attacks that every elected official or candidate for office endures is a major deterrent for many people. But it was worth it for me, in part because I'm so deeply passionate about the work we were doing, and because I've experienced, personally and professionally my entire life, the failings of this country's approach to criminal justice. I wanted to play a leadership role in solving those problems.

* Boudin and Gilbert, Weather Underground members, were convicted of the murders of two police officers and a security guard during the 1981 Brink's robbery in Rockland County, New York. Their son, Chesa, was a toddler at the time his mother was sentenced to 20 years to life and his father to 75 years to life. Boudin was freed in 2003 and Gilbert in 2021.

† Ayers and Dohrn were cofounders of the Weather Underground.

It was a very steep learning curve. I'd spent most of my career as a practicing criminal lawyer in San Francisco's Hall of Justice. I knew the system intimately. I knew the players. I had tried many cases against the lawyers in the district attorney's office and in front of the judges in the superior court. I was intimately aware of some of the bottlenecks and some of the real deficiencies around technology and around court capacity. And yet, when I took over the [district attorney's] office, there were lots of things that I was surprised by, like [the level of resistance] and how difficult it was to solve even some of the most obvious problems.

It was extremely frustrating to me when we couldn't even get cases to move forward in court because the courts were so backlogged and so shut down due to COVID and other factors, that we had victims who would reach out to me and say, "I've been waiting for five years, six years, eight years, and my case still hasn't gone to trial." And, of course, I was only in office two and a half years total, so I hadn't been the D.A. the entire time those old cases were languishing, and yet I wanted very much to move forward to give them closure and due process. But it wasn't entirely up to me. We had a sheriff's department that was a bottleneck. We had a superior court that was also a bottleneck. We had all these issues that were out of my control and sometimes resulted in folks understandably being very frustrated with the system, and it was hard for me to not be able to solve those problems.

And yet, in the two and a half years that I was district attorney, we made tremendous progress in addressing and solving and advancing solutions to problems that affect not just San Franciscans, but people across this country. And we had an impact on more lives and a bigger impact than I've probably had in any other two-and-a-half-year period of my life.

But I think, for me, the hardest losses were in situations where I felt that the outcome was really unfair, when I had clients who were being railroaded by the system, when I had judges who made rulings that were designed to coerce a guilty plea or to direct the verdict for the jury, or when we had expert witnesses that misrepresented factual science to secure a particular outcome. I think those sorts of scenarios were always extremely frustrating because it wasn't just a matter of what the outcome was. It was a question of the process, and as a lawyer, process matters. I wanted to ensure, even if we were going to lose a case, that we had a fair fight and that my clients had a fair opportunity.

As district attorney, I made mistakes, our office made mistakes. On day one,

I inherited more than 5,000 open criminal cases. We filed more than 10,000 new criminal cases during the time I was in office. Inevitably, we made mistakes. We tried to learn from them. We tried to put in place systems that prevented mistakes from being made in the future. We tried to do training that minimized the mistakes our staff made. And, politically, there's lots of things that I would have done differently. But I don't actually think any of those things would have made a difference in terms of the outcome of the recall.

Right-wing billionaires pumped more money into the recall than has ever been spent in any attack campaign in San Francisco history. They spent more than $9 million. The people who are donating millions of dollars don't care about the office functioning well. They don't care about respecting the will of the voters or democracy. They care about being able to buy the people in power and own them. And that's exactly what they did.

I also think we witnessed in the country an unprecedented pendulum swing in 2020 when there was a national consensus that we needed criminal justice reform, that we needed to do a better job protecting Black lives and holding police who use excessive force accountable. Within six months to a year of George Floyd's murder, we saw what was really the largest national protest movement in this country's history not only disappear, but get replaced by a huge and powerful right-wing backlash in which local news media coverage was dominated by reporting on crime in the San Francisco Bay area. Pretty much every story about crime put my name in the headlines, even in cases where police had not made an arrest, where there was no opportunity for my office to hold someone accountable. It became clickbait, and so inevitably voters started to associate me or criminal justice reform with their perceptions about rising crime. And when people feel scared, when they feel unsafe in their homes and their communities, of course they're going to vote for change. In reality, during the two and a half years I was in office, overall crime fell by 20 percent as compared to two and a half years before.

The city, in many ways, needed a scapegoat. And I became that scapegoat.

How do you keep from becoming cynical about this work you obviously care about? Or do you?

Well, everything worth doing is worth fighting for. If it were easy, it would have been done long ago. So it's not a surprise to me that it's a fight. It's not a surprise to me that there are obstacles, that there are folks who are cynical or opportunistic in undermining democracy; we know that's happening around the world. These are fights that I signed up for when I decided to run. And I know we have a lot of work ahead of us.

You said you are now mostly spending time with your son. How is that going?

It's going well. Earlier in our conversation I talked about the steep learning curves and the challenges and the surprises when I started as a public defender, and when I was on the campaign trail for the first time, and when I became a district attorney. I think the same thing can definitely be said about parenting. It is challenging. It is difficult. It is rewarding. It is a steep learning curve. And I'm tremendously lucky to have a healthy, fun-loving son who is teaching me how to be a good parent as he goes through the world learning himself.

How long do you anticipate doing this?

I don't know. I have a lot of job offers, but I made a commitment to my family that I would focus on family and on parenting, at least to the end of this year. So that's been my focus. And then sometime early next year, I assume that I'll go back to more traditional legal work of some kind.

And another learning curve.

Yeah, indeed.

VOICE

"I help people fight for more."
JULIA FRIEDMAN

She is an organizer at Service Employees International Union (SEIU). She is 51 years old, "which in union organizing years is like 99." She works primarily with hospitals and nursing home workers.

 "I'm just so horrified by the prospect of this conversation with you! (Laughs.) Why? At the end of an election, workers have gone through a very profoundly intense experience with me. They had become their best selves and faced a lot of really hard things, including the big fear about getting fired. They don't know much about me,

and they don't know my last name half the time, and that's how it should be, because
it ain't about me. [Eugene V.] Debs used to talk about, 'if you follow some Moses into
the promised land, you're going to follow somebody else out.'"

She has two children, ages 6 and 12.

People who do purposeful work, there's always a discussion about who we are
and why we do the work. Right? And the answer to that is always evolving. What
I've noticed about people who survive in justice work generally is that we tend to
come from one of two places. We come from either a whole lot of love or some
pretty deep anger. If you don't marry those two, then you can't stick in the work.
The people who start off with "[I'm in this because] my mom cleaned floors for
a living"—that doesn't work. They burn out and burn up because they are so full
of rage. Too many things in the process of trying to form unions only reminds
you of how laws are written by people with money who aren't part of the working
class. So I think something happens where it just doesn't last.

And then the "love" folks: if their love of humanity doesn't increase by doing
this work, if it doesn't grow enough to encompass deep rage about capitalism and
what it does to people, what it does to our collective imaginations, what it means
about the possibilities for us to evolve, to live, to do something other than survive
. . . those folks go on to do something else. So you have to marry the two, the
anger and the love.

I do think that if you have a certain kind of political orientation and you're
up to something, the "good trouble" that John Lewis talked about, then I literally
can't go anywhere else [with it]. This work is all I can do. To *not* do it would burn
me up. *This* doesn't burn me up. Right? It feeds me. But I do think it is the case
for a lot of people in the world we live in that they don't have a place to do something about [what is wrong]. And so, at least here in my work, I get to *try*, I get to
try with some other folks who want to *do* something.

Do you find there are people who go into this work and see themselves as folk heroes?

A hundred percent. It's a pet peeve of mine. I have no patience for it. When people romanticize about the working class, I'm always like, have you *met* a worker?

We are talking, today, on the heels of a success that you and your colleagues just had,
and you sound energized by the work you do. What if we were talking the day after
something major had crumbled?

Listen. SEIU likes to say, "When we fight, we win." But for me it's more like, "When we *don't* fight, we *definitely* don't win." That's more true to me because we *don't* always win when we fight. My job is to create opportunities for folks to try to do a thing and to push them to make a choice around what they want to do with their lives. I really do see myself as planting the seeds for something different. And longer-term.

My job is not to coach, to cheerlead, to cajole, to convince, but it's to lead workers into struggle so that they understand coming out of that that they have the power *now*. Even when I've been in situations that are not successful, the workers who are most connected to it, while devastated, at least still have some understanding that we *tried*. If I've done my own work well, they think, "Well, I guess we needed to get more folks," or whatever it is. But we *tried*.

You cannot be good at this work if you are conflict averse. I'm wired a weird way. I kind of enjoy it. I have gotten on the wrong side of people as a result of that, but that's maybe the most important thing, if there was just one thing. But wait, maybe the *first* most important thing is *believing in the work,* not just the working class, but in humanity and humans and what we're about and what we can be like and those kinds of things. If you *do* believe in those things, then, for me, respect requires telling the truth. It means saying, "I'm gonna tell you the 20 things you're going to have to do to win. And if you don't want to come to the meetings, and you don't want to put your name on that piece of paper because you're scared that you're going to get fired, then I promise you, you won't get *anything.*"

How long do you think you can keep doing this?

You know what? I fell in love with this work when I was 27 years old. I was so happy to find a place that made sense for me in my life. I have, a couple of times, tried to find other things to do because you get tired, you know? But nothing scratches that same itch. I don't know what else I would do honestly. Even when I was on maternity leave, I needed to constantly be in touch with organizers to hear about what their campaigns were and how they were thinking about it and to be engaged with those people.

Do your children understand what you do for a living?

I do not know how to answer that. The older one [age 12] does; the younger one [age 6] would probably just say I help people fight for more. I actually think that their biggest learning happened one time when I was in the car with them. This was during a school strike. I drove around a corner and all of a sudden, this bus drives up with the scabs on it. And I *lost my mind*! There was *no one* blocking that bus or causing any trouble. The scabs were just walking in like they didn't have a care in the world.

And I pulled over, and jumped out, and I was like, "*What the hell?* You people should be ashamed!" Because I can't help myself. I had barely stopped the car. I just like jumped out of the car because I couldn't believe that no one was causing trouble for these people who are taking those jobs and making it that much harder for the workers to win and who, by the way, are getting paid more to *break* that strike than it would cost to settle that strike. It's outrageous. Like, do you have *no* conscience? I know someone who says that scabs get paid a lot because souls are expensive to buy.

I got back in the car, and I was crying I was so angry. I explained to my kids why I was so upset. Of course, I'm always going to get upset about something like that, and I just did not care that the kids were in the back seat and saw what I did. I don't know exactly what that episode taught my kids, but something important.

"I felt the weight of the moment."
DR. A. D. CARSON

He is a performance artist and an associate professor of hip-hop and the Global South in the department of music at the University of Virginia in Charlottesville. He received his PhD in rhetoric, communication, and information design at Clemson University.

"My dissertation was a rap album and digital archive titled Owning My Masters: The Rhetoric of Rhymes and Revolutions. *The work that I do now is to offer rap music and other hip-hop cultural products as ways we can think about some of the pressing issues that permeate society, like race, injustice, incarceration, abolition, equity, inclusion, what our ancestors say, how we tell histories, what does the land say, and what does knowledge production mean?*

"All of those things are embedded in what we know hip-hop and lots of other Black cultural practices have been doing for a long time. But [I want] to bring them into this academic enterprise."

I had arrived [at Clemson] to start my PhD program on a Wednesday, and the

Saturday of that week was when the jury came back in the George Zimmerman trial for his murder of Trayvon Martin and was found not guilty. Thinking about the world as the classroom, there was no way that I could separate my arriving in Clemson from my attention to this trial about this wild "stand your ground" defense of George Zimmerman which is contingent upon casting Trayvon Martin as guilty of his own murder, rather than it being a trial of George Zimmerman. What we were hearing was why Trayvon Martin deserved to die.

Those kinds of events, from 2013 forward, are very present for me and mark the memories that I have now of the things that I was reading in my [doctoral] program about histories of rhetoric, histories of philosophy, and literary cannon formation. So all of these things are swirling around with this collective work that we are doing of memorializing and thinking about what Black life means to America, for America, and the *utility* of Black bodies as opposed to the *valuing* of Black life. They can't be separated in my mind. I think that if the doctoral program did anything for me, it helped me understand the necessity of seeing all of the things that happen in my life as a part of the project of building knowledge, of producing knowledge, rather than thinking about it as something that only happens within the walls of a classroom.

And then in August of 2017, the Friday right after I graduated was when the white nationalist folks came to Charlottesville [where I was about to begin teaching], and they had a rally around the [Robert E.] Lee statue with tiki torches. So these national events happened in my front yard.

When I was offered the position here at UVA, they said, "Well, what would you need in order to be successful in this job?" And I said that I think we need a rap lab; we need a place where the students come and figure shit out. Where they just come, and they can be wrong, they can be loud, they can be with each other, but they need to have access to it, a place that is both [physically] open to them, but also open to them being able to have conversations with folks in the community, particularly the hip-hop communities, that are here. So we want it to be a space *at* the university, but maybe not *like* the university where, when you come into the room, it's easy to forget that you're at Thomas Jefferson's university. We want to put graffiti up on the walls, we want to put a rap booth in there, we want to have drum machines and samplers and a projector, like media stations; we want to be able to have whatever you might need in order to try to ask these questions and work on these problems. And, most importantly, where you don't have to have the "right perspective," so to speak. Once you come in, you don't have to have that figured out in order to get started.

The seats are on wheels so we can move around, and it can be reconfigured in all kinds of different ways. The students who are in my classes, and the ones with whom I do independent study, all have 24-hour access to the lab. They can come anytime. And that's important because people work differently, and especially music-making people. There are plenty of times where I've had an idea in the middle of the night and then just started working it out by making some music about it. I want students to be able to have that as well.

The world informs what we are doing. And so, while we're thinking about the books that are being read over a particular course, we've also got to be mindful of the fact that *12 Years a Slave* was in the theaters, and that was the same semester of the Zimmerman trial, and that was the same semester that *Fruitvale Station* came out, and Kendrick Lamar's "Good Kid, M.A.A.D City" is also playing, and Jordan Davis was killed by Michael Dunn. What's happening in the classroom is happening in the context of a world where all of these things are going on. And we don't separate those things out. Our "textbooks" are all of these things.

How was your raising these questions received when you first started?

Not as generously or graciously as I would have liked. But I shouldn't have been surprised. My first faculty meetings were folks on the faculty saying, "Well, how do we talk to our students about what just happened a couple of weeks ago?" [Meaning, the white nationalist rally.] And my thinking was, I surely hope that my colleagues don't put our students of color in the position of having to explain what it felt like to be traumatized as incoming or returning students to this place.

For me, the impact was, I have to make sure, not just for myself but also for my colleagues, that we are creating an environment for all of our students to have understandings of what it means to be doing what we do in what I'm sure will be the long shadow of what just happened. And then to create an environment where whatever it is the students want to talk about and what they feel free to share and what they feel free to make is the kind of thing that we are going to be doing. We can't ignore it, but we also can't put the onus on them to be the folks who are doing the job that *we're* here to do.

I felt the weight of the moment. I can't lie and say that there weren't times where I felt—maybe, for the first 15, 18 months, here—like just overwhelmed, really overwhelmed at what it means to be me, what it means to be me living in America, in Charlottesville. And considering what my students must be feeling, what my neighbors must be feeling, all of these different things.

One of the great things that happened this semester is that in my grad seminar, there were five students, and there were also lots of undergraduate students who were really interested. The grad class is called The Black Voice, and we're trying to explore a history of listening practices in America. We think of race as a sort of a visual phenomenon, but we have to understand it as both visual and sonic. We've constructed ways of hearing race, even though we know race to not be a biological fact. So, what does it mean for someone to, quote/unquote, "sound Black?" And that gets really, really tricky because *sounding Black* isn't really a thing, except that when we say sounding Black, folks kind of understand, even if very loosely, what that might mean.

Undergrads are really fascinated with that. But also, sometimes they maybe feel ill-equipped, because it's like, "I don't have the language to describe what it means." So, when the classes are going on, because other students have access, undergrads can come in and they can work while we're having the seminar, and they can participate in the conversations with the graduate students. Or they can just come and listen and watch.

I feel really good about the direction that these things have been going and the directions that I've been pulled into because of the kind of work and the kind of support and the kind of resources that exist in a space like this at this moment.

I feel proud of what has been created with my students and with my colleagues and the kinds of interactions that we've had and the ways that's influenced the stuff that is being considered as my academic output now, the albums and the videos and the writing I've done that try to help facilitate these kinds of things for audiences. I'm not standing in front of students—or on Zoom—addressing them directly, but making music and making art that is representative of the kind of scholarship that I think I should be doing with them and that people might be able to tune into and then ask themselves questions and ask others questions, and then maybe also respond, too, with other kinds of art or other kinds of responses that *they* want to make. Because I feel there's a lot more work to be done.

"Yeah, we're here, we are here."
RORRI BURTON

She is a freelance American Sign Language interpreter in Los Angeles. "During the past couple of months, I have been interpreting the coronavirus briefings out here."

I sometimes think the way I interpret is more generally understandable because of how I learned ASL. I learned ASL from Black people when I was growing up on the South Side of Chicago. So, my ASL—I wouldn't call it "Black ASL," but it's more akin to that than it is for most other interpreters. My interpreting and my signing, in general, tends to include more general gestures than a lot of interpreters who trained and went to school for this, who have their degree in this or whatever. I think I tend to be more, I believe, accessible, which has helped me be very successful despite the fact that I'm not someone who's certified or has all the letters after my name or the on-paper type qualifications. I don't have any formal training in interpreting at all. That might make you think, "Well, she's not going to be that good; she didn't even go to school for it. She doesn't have any type of certification." But I think my success has been based on the fact that I can understand and be understood by people in the community.

When I was 12, I met a little girl in church who was Deaf. Her mom started to teach me ASL, and I started to interact with the little girl and acquired the language. I already had known I wanted to be a teacher because I was a very smart kid, and I loved teaching. I had a knack for that, and also, I love languages.

So, I am very grateful of how I learned, how I came up in the community. It gave me not just the vocabulary and not just the grammatical features, it gave me the culture of the people who actually use the language and thereby it engendered in me respect and a natural love for the community. That was great, but how I came up in the Deaf community and in the interpreting community is unique.

In general, there are not, by far, enough Black interpreters in the field because they are discouraged and disenfranchised and not even invited into ASL in the first place. And then once they are there, they're discouraged from continuing. That's a huge issue. There's the standard ASL and then there's Black ASL. There are differences. That came about because of segregation when Black and white Deaf children went to different schools.

There are just so many reasons why there are too few. A lot of times the pipeline to going into an interpreter training program is to have ASL in your high school as a foreign language, and many times the high schools that have ASL as a foreign language are in the more affluent white communities. And so Black students who would be great with that just don't even get the opportunity to be exposed to it.

From what I've heard from friends in interpreter training programs, [the field] is very much white-driven, and the Black students who do join end up dropping out because of how those programs are run. The inherent racism. Black interpreters often were relegated to be church interpreters or just doing Black History Month. They weren't seen as skilled.

I sometimes work VRS [video relay services]. You would make a [video] phone call to interpret for someone who's Deaf, and a lot of times there'd be a Black Deaf caller who would pop up, and they would see me and be like, "Oh my god, a Black interpreter! Oh my god, I've been using VRS for 10 years. I've never seen a Black interpreter. Whoa, this is great!"

I remember working at one VRS center, and it was a big center. We had just four Black interpreters there. When I would tell that to other people at other centers, they'd say, "Oh my god, you have four Black interpreters out of like 50 people! That's great. I wish I was at your center. I'm the only one. I'm the only one. I'm the only one."

A lot of times I have had the experience of showing up to an assignment and people being like, (with a displeased expression on her face) "Oh." The underestimating of my abilities based on the fact that I just show up Black, it's a real thing. And it's very discouraging for a lot of Black interpreters. A lot of times Black interpreters are like, "Okay, I have to make sure that my hair is assimilated to what a white person would feel comfortable with." I've had that, too. One time I went in for a screening at an agency just so they could make sure that I had the skills to join their agency. And I passed everything with flying colors, but I had braids, and the comment was made: "Oh, your hair might be distracting to most Deaf people."

What does my hair being braided have to do with my skills as an interpreter? But Black interpreters have to keep that in mind: "Okay, I can't look too Black. I can't be too, you know, different. I have to assimilate." So there's a constant struggle.

But then with Black Lives Matter and everything that's happened, more events are now being focused on the Black community and other communities of color. Now people are like, "Oh, we need to have Black interpreters." But we're saying, "Well, you need to have *culturally competent* interpreters whose understanding matches the conversation they're interpreting."

I have gathered a group of interpreters, and I kinda formed my own fledgling agency. We provide paid services interpreting, but we interpret for Black Lives Matter events pro bono. This has been a great time. Since now everything's online [due to COVID restrictions] more Black interpreters are available. Whereas before, if you lived in rural Kansas and you wanted to host an event, where are you going to find a Black interpreter, especially if it was going to be a Black or a POC-type of event? You're not going to find any interpreter that would be suitable for that, and you'd take whoever. But now you've got access to interpreters all over the country and you can seek out specifically who you want for your event.

So now there are more opportunities for Black interpreters. Now we're being seen. It's like this blanket has been taken off of the group of us, and we're all huddled up under there, like, "Yeah, we're here, we *are* here! We've *always* been here, but you've always overlooked us. As much as we've tried to edge our way forward, we've gotten pushed back." But that's changing some now.

"He was waiting to hear my voice."
PAUL OAKLEY STOVALL

He is an actor, singer, producer, writer, and activist. He served as press advance associate for candidate Obama and later served as a media logistics coordinator and advance staff lead for First Lady Michelle Obama, representing the Obama administration across the nation and overseas.

At the time of this conversation, he had been playing George Washington in the first national tour of Hamilton: An American Musical *by Lin-Manuel Miranda. The tour had recently been halted by the pandemic. We spoke on Zoom.*

My parents were finally able to see *Hamilton* in Louisville because that was close enough to Arkansas, where they live, and my cousin, Diane, could pick them up and drive them, plus my brother lives in Louisville. My mom and cousins sat in the house seats. We got separate seats for my dad and my brother because there was a wheelchair-accessible area that was closer to the stage. My dad's eyesight is kind of going now, so he was waiting to hear my voice so he'd know I was on stage.

My entrance is when they say, "The moment you've been waiting for/ the pride of Mount Vernon/ here comes the general/ George Washington!" And then Dad hears my voice. He turned to my brother, and he went, "*What's going on?*" He didn't realize how loud he was talking. My brother was like, "Dad, be quiet. Paul's playing the president." My dad's like, "He's playing the *president*? Washington's not *Black*! My son's playing *George Washington*?" They had known nothing about the show before this, and he couldn't even comprehend that. "Yeah, Dad, he's playing the president." Then, he was just like.... (Makes a gesture with both hands like tears flowing.)

He was emotional about it?

Very, and he's not an emotional man. I'm glad I didn't find out till afterwards because it would have put me in a very emotional place. Meanwhile, my mother's having a different experience. During intermission, she's just bragging to everyone, you know. "Yes, that's my son! Uh-huh. He came out of my body. That's right. I taught him how to sing." She's just, you know, Queen Joyce.

For them, though, it was really about wanting me to be financially secure. They are African Americans from the '60s and '70s who made the migration north from Arkansas to Illinois for better jobs and opportunities. And so, they've always been dubious about me being in the arts.

After the show, I had to go out to the lobby and find them. And there was this woman and her two children. They knew who I was and came barreling toward me. The sister was not far behind. "Oh my god! Oh my god!" And the mom: "Can we get a picture? Can you sign this? Can you sign that?" And my father saw that. He *saw* that.

By now I had been on the tour for quite a while, so this type of thing, on any other day, wouldn't have had any effect on me. I often have to come around the front to meet people, do the autographs, take the pictures. I'm happy to do this. It's great. Happy to inspire the kids, and I love it. But my dad *seeing* that—I think he then began to understand, "Oh, Paul's not just up there doing plays for his own personal enjoyment. My son is contributing to the ongoing betterment of the world." I think that was an important thing for him, not just to see a musical I was in, but to see *that* in the lobby. Our relationship has been different since then.

I don't know when we'll be able to perform and tour again. I wonder what it will be like after all this, the pandemic, the Black Lives Matter movement. I sure would be fascinated to find out. Before the virus struck, we would be doing the show and come to the line in act 2 where James Madison says, "A *quid pro quo*." And it was right after the impeachment hearings. People would come to us and say, "Did Lin add that line to make it more current?" "No, what, are you kidding? That line's always been there, but it just didn't mean the same thing before." Now you have a president plotting with another president in a back room. It would get, in some cities, uproarious laughter. And then we'd be in some areas that are more Trump country, and it would get a very different reaction.

And the line, "Immigrants, we get the job done"?

Even a more different reaction because in Virginia that is a different line than it is in Chicago. Or in Fort Myers, Florida. Hearing about immigrants, there . . . it's just different. I'm not besmirching anyone; I'm just saying that some of these things land different in different parts of the country. And now, I think we're in a very different age, too. It'll be even more different. So I can't wait to see how the play will be received after all this.

How do your artistic and your political work intertwine?

They didn't intertwine until *Hamilton*. I had always either been headfirst into the arts or, to be very frank and raw with you, when things weren't working out, I looked to busy myself with something else, and my passion would always take me to activism, and I had no problem engaging with it. But as I worked more for the Obamas, I had no time to be an actor. And yet, that's when I was finding my writing voice. I thought I could be an activist through the things I was writing. (Pauses.) Wait. I think maybe I just lied to you and myself. I think that's how I started engaging with politics, it was through my *writing*. That was my way to reach the truth.

And then when *Hamilton* came along, it was almost like an anvil dropped on my head like in the old cartoons: Wait, this is a no-brainer! Here I am playing this role in this very important piece. I have a *responsibility*. So, after every show, you are met by young people who think they just want an autograph. Some of the cast would try to get out to the autographs before me so they could just zip on down the line and get out to do whatever they wanted to do. But I felt we're not just there to do an autograph. I ask every kid, "What do you want to be? What do you want to do?" And "Did you notice how Washington was a team player? Did you notice how he tried not to lose his temper, but sometimes he did, and that's okay?" If a little girl was dressed as Eliza, I'd say, "So is that the part you would like to play?" "Yeah." And I'd say, "Well, what would you think of playing Hamilton?" "Oh, I can never do that." "No? Why not?"

I have conversations with every single kid. I would be there sometimes for 45 minutes after the show. So I found my activism in activating the minds of young people to get past the fandom of *Hamilton* and really start engaging them with the ideas of it. I was about to say no one did that for me, but I don't mean it to be melancholy. I mean, as an artist, no one did that on that *level* for me.

You've asked me the question and by answering you, Mark, I'm finding out the answer: It isn't just that I care. I do care, of course I do. But we already know certain things are true about the desire to be kind and helpful and to educate a young person. But, for me, there's an inability to *not* do it, is what I'm realizing now. It's like I *have* to do it.

What about the relationship between your work and your own life?

I have to tell you that to play this particular role, being a Black man in America; a Black, gay man in America; a Black, tall, gay man in America; a Black, tall, built-strong, gay man in America; a Black, tall, built-strong, *out* gay man in America, gave me everything I needed to play George Washington.

Stick with me on this: it's not that I felt that George Washington was a Black, out gay man, or whatever, but he was six-foot-two in a time where that was seen as a giant. And he was a loner. He liked to just hang out on the horse in the tobacco field. He lost family early. We don't have all of those things in common, but we do have this thing in common: feeling outcast and different. I could bring myself and every year of my life and everything I've gone through to the role. So it's the *core* of what we share that I can bring to the theater every night.

And that's where my activism, and my life, and my art have found a place to merge. So I'm in the right show and the right role for all that. And I recognize that it won't last forever.

"What are you going to do with that sanity?"
ANDY BOROWITZ

He is a comedian and writer of political satire. His column, The Borowitz Report, which has appeared in the New Yorker *magazine for 20 years, satirizes politics and parodies news reporting. "I sometimes think of my column as kind of a verbal cartoon. The thing I like about the format is that it's, by definition, very concise. It's basically one joke. The joke is the headline. I'm not sure how many people read beyond the headline, but I really enjoy the parody element as a study of a style. I'm parroting the kind of hack-AP-reporter style."*

We talk two weeks after the midterm election of 2022 and several days after former president Donald Trump announced that he was running for a second term as president. Borowitz wrote, "Trump to Try for Historic Third Impeachment."

There is a question, a very large question that I ask all the time. Since we had gone so many centuries without ever reading the news because there was no way to do it, my question is what is obtained by reading the news? What is the point of all this because the fact of the matter is, we have no influence on 99 percent of these events, and most events have no impact on us. Watching the news on this kind of moment-to-moment basis and checking the polls and all that has no impact on the results, but it does have an impact on your nervous system.

The cable news channels will say something about how control of the House of Representatives is news that you have to know, so "start the day with us!" *Why* do I have to start the day with "the House of Representatives is under Republican control"? How does that change the way I'm going to conduct my life that day? I *don't* really need to start the day with you. I could start the day by reading a Balzac story, actually.

But I do feel that I have to stay informed, and one of the reasons why I like the news is I'm experiencing it as—I wouldn't say "entertainment," but I'm interested in it the way I read history. I'm interested in the characters. I'm interested in this unfolding story, this unfolding narrative. I don't really differentiate it from other forms of entertainment.

So, it's like news producers are showrunners for a very long TV series?

That's a very interesting comparison because I used to be a showrunner and worked in sitcoms.* One of the enjoyable aspects of the sitcom for the audience is the predictability of how characters will act. When you're watching *Cheers*, you know how Norm is going to act and how Cliff is going to act.

I actually see that what I do in the column as very much akin to that because I have a set of characters much like a sitcom. And when you're reading my column, you know how Rudy Giuliani is going to act and how Trump is going to act. So we're playing on the audience's expectations. And it's like—to get a little academic—the *commedia dell'arte* where you have different sorts of character types, right? You have like the sexy vixen, and you have the drunkard, and you have the dope. There's always a stupid character. That was Woody Harrelson on *Cheers*, and then it became Joey on *Friends*. And so, for me, it's Marjorie Taylor Greene, Lauren Boebert, Sarah Palin. . . . We seem to have a bumper crop of the dumb characters.

In the midst of all this, you have a significant platform and megaphone. How do you feel about the role and responsibility inherent in that?

I like to keep things in perspective. I only have a significant platform in that the *New Yorker* has a certain amount of credibility and is held in high esteem, both of which have nothing to do with me. I think some people are entertained by what I do, but I don't think that I've contributed to their pantheon of, like, Rachel Carson and John Hersey and the other great journalists that have written for the *New Yorker*. So I tend to keep my role in perspective.

I think that one thing I've seen with people in comedy is a dangerous overestimating of our impact on things. You can have a huge audience that laughs at what you do, and you can entertain them. But that doesn't necessarily mean you're motivating them to think a certain way about politics, or that you're changing anyone's mind. I think that I try to keep realistic about the impact that I have.

The best-case scenario for what I do is that *maybe* I am lifting some people out of despondency about current events so they may be motivated enough to be politically active. But that is a wildly optimistic scenario. I think most people, myself included, really shrink from any kind of political activism because it's really hard and boring and requires a lot of hard work.

When I went on tour 2018 to 2020, which was the absolute heart of the

---

* He cocreated, for example, the NBC sitcom *The Fresh Prince of Bel-Air*.

Trump era, I was getting the biggest audiences I'd ever had because people really needed, especially in the red states, a sense that they were not alone, that they were in a room with a couple thousand other people who felt the same way they did. And a really nice thing that some people would say was, "Thank you for your writing. You've helped keep me sane."

I would thank them and say that was very kind of them. But then I'd ask, "What are you going to do with that sanity now that you feel sane?" Okay, it was nice to laugh at Donald Trump and laugh at the news, but if that's just been palliative, then in a way we're reinforcing the current power structure. We're really kind of doing the Trumps of the world a favor because we've taken the edge off their potential harm.

I try not to sugarcoat things. I try to make things funny and satirize the news, but I try not to eliminate the element of the madness of what's going on. Essentially, I'm writing about terrifying things, and I think it's just the way my mind works. My mind is transforming these terrifying things into funny things.

One thing that I have heard as a criticism of what I do is people say, "Well, you are just preaching to the choir; you're a liberal, you're writing for a liberal magazine, and you're writing for liberals, so you're just reinforcing their point of view; you're not challenging your readers." And I say point well taken, all those things are true. But I also think there's tremendous value in preaching to the choir, because if you don't do that, then the choir gets so demoralized that they will not do any of the hard things and boring things that we need people to do in order to make the world a better place.

I guess my point in all this is that there's value in reinforcing a point of view that you think is important, even if the people you're supposedly preaching to already have that point of view. I think that just to be contrarian for the sake of being original or challenging or a renegade is a form of vanity, actually.

Have you ever felt like you've gone too far?

I've never created outrage like [Barry Blitt's "Fist Bump" *New Yorker* cover, July 21, 2008*], but there have been a couple of times when [the *New Yorker* and I] have disagreed, like when I've done something where I've made fun of voters, not politicians. Especially during the Trump years, I would do stories where I was really making fun of Trump voters. I mainly just thought they were really

* See p. 322.

dumb. I actually think now that's a very obvious take and probably not a very nuanced take, and it was coming more from a sense of anger and frustration that we've wound up in this mess. "How could we have so many stupid people in this country?"

Here's an example: I had done a story about a rabid dog that climbed onto a stage at a Tea Party event and everyone started cheering the rabid dog. It's funny, right? It is funny. It worked as satire of the Tea Party. What I've learned since then was that a lot of members of the Tea Party were super well educated. They were, as a matter of fact, much better educated about how government works, which is why the Tea Party was, to some extent, so effective in local politics. They were wrong about a lot of things, like they thought Obama was a Muslim and they were very racist, a lot of them, and there's no way around that. But they weren't dumb. So, making fun of a whole swath of voters is very reductive.

My editor at the time didn't want to run the story. He said you can't call these people idiots. And I said, "Well, why not?" And he said, "Well, we don't want the *New Yorker* to appear elitist." (Laughs.) I think the minute that a magazine decides to have a mascot with a top hat and a monocle, that ship has sailed. But I do think that the *New Yorker* hierarchy really does, on some level, think that they're speaking for the common man, which I find really charming. They're running stories about like, Guy de Maupassant and somehow think that they're the salt of the earth.

But if people think I'm sitting in New York—of course, I haven't lived there in a long time—but if there's this image of me sitting in New York in my smoking jacket taking shots at the little guy, then I'm punching down. And on that level, I totally agree. I think that's a valid point. I think, though, they were objecting to the content but for the wrong reason. They were rejecting it from a point of view of branding, which is the wrong reason. "It's gonna make us look bad." Which is hilarious, because who do you think your subscribers are? Kid Rock is going to cancel a subscription to the *New Yorker*? At the next NASCAR race everybody's going to be complaining about that issue in the *New Yorker*? He was right for the wrong reason. I'm much better off punching up, taking on the president and the government and the Supreme Court.

PART THREE:

THE PURSUIT OF HAPPINESS

"Making a Living": Six Reflections

"The dancer has been the dance."
MARILYN HALPERIN

She began her work life as a social worker, then worked at Morton Arboretum for 12 years before leaving to join a small team that was running the fledgling Chicago Shakespeare Theater as their director of education. She has worked there for the last 30 years. She is 70 years old and will retire soon.

I do think about work so much. I don't mean just my work—obviously, I think about my work a lot—but the *notion* of work and our relationship to it is so vexed. And so ambivalent. In the generation I grew up in, work was associated much more with the male than females. My father was, oh my god, he was in school probably until his late 40s. He was an MD, then he became a psychiatrist. I remember him still being in training at the Institute for Psychoanalysis. So much of my relationship with and embracing of work, I think, came from my father.

On the other side, my mother was probably born at the wrong time. [If she'd been born into] my generation, she would have been a career woman as well as having a family, but in the '40s and '50s that was a little different, right? And so, I felt from her what it was like *not* to work when one wished to work. She was a writer, and she eventually went back to work when I was about 10 years old. She became an encyclopedia editor. So my father's embodiment of training and work, and the fact that it was his life, and then my mother's longing for it, I suppose affected my relationship to work.

Could you, as a child, sense your mother's longing to work?

Yeah, absolutely. I don't know if it was as conscious when I was little, but I certainly knew that when she did go back to work, it was because she wanted and very much needed that. I understood that the choices that she had made, or the lack of choice, impacted her happiness. So, yes, I think that I did understand it, and I understood it differently as I grew older.

Did you get, from your father, a positive impression of what a work life is?

I think yes and no. Yes, in terms of how I saw how he embraced his work, how extraordinarily important it was to him and how important he was to the people he worked with. I would visit him at work; he was the head of psychiatry at the West Side VA Hospital, and some of my best days growing up were when I got to spend the day with my dad at his hospital. In my mind, he was king, you know. He was revered and adored. And I felt all of that. But the flip side of it was that he wasn't home a lot.

I went into the field [of social work] for a few years. I got very good feedback. But there was such a deep disconnect between how people saw my work, and how *I* saw my work. Deep, deep discomfort in being a beginner and a learner in a profession where we had so much impact upon other people's lives. It was really difficult, painful for me. I didn't feel like I knew enough to have that level of power and influence.

My father died right as I was graduating, and in one of our last conversations, I asked him, "When did you become comfortable in your work?" He said, "Around when I was 60." I thought, oh my god, that's a lot of years to have an impact on people. I could do a lot of damage in that time. I wanted to influence, and I wanted to help, but I didn't want to hurt. So that's why I left. That comment still has had a deep impact. It's as though he said it to me yesterday.

I've always been reflective, that's a piece I take from my upbringing; I am a reflective person. I take what I do [at the theater] so seriously. There's this beautiful, beautiful quote from William Butler Yeats: "How can we know the dancer from the dance?" I think about that a lot. Because I do see us *being* the dance that we do at work. I do see this blending of the person and the creation of the piece of work as one. And I want that dance to be an authentic one.

What do you do actively and consciously to be sure that it is authentic to your satisfaction?

Well, "to my satisfaction" is an interesting phrase because it's rarely to my satisfaction. I think that what I do is to constantly evaluate. It's just who I am. And I'm going to say that, for better and for worse, I expect it of the people I work with as well. For better and for worse, it's sort of a relentless path.

Does your pursuing this "relentless path" ever get the better of you?

I think it can be tiring. When I think of the community of work and the people who we work with, I know some people love that and thrive on that. And some people just want me to go away, like, "Enough already! We already have a really good teacher workshop here. Enough already." "We have a really great system for welcoming students. Enough already." "We have 50 job descriptions for volunteers. Why do we need to be thinking about more?" So, yeah, it is tiring. I think probably less for me because that is kind of how I roll. But not everybody wants to roll that way. As I've matured, I absolutely understand that not everybody does approach work and life that way.

When I worked at the Arboretum, the director during my first 10 years of 12 was a man who was a scientist through-and-through. He was much more comfortable with trees and woody plants and a microscope than when he was with people; it's just who he was. I loved him, and I respected him completely.

One day—this is that moment where I knew he was a father figure to me, I remember it so vividly. I might have been harping on someone who was causing me grief. I don't know. But I remember what he said. He said, "Marilyn, the most important part of what we do is this community of people. The trees are going to be here." Of course, this was before the crisis of climate change was fully upon us. But [the point was] it is this group of people who have come together to work for this period of time that matters most. I think it had even more impact because it came from him. I knew he was more comfortable with trees, more comfortable with the process of science than the process of people.

I think now about our community that we build at work here at Chicago Shakespeare Theater, and the relationships that we have matter more than what we create. And that is, to me, sort of a revolutionary idea. Whether I came to the Arboretum because I was devoted to that natural space, or I came to Chicago Shakespeare because I was devoted to Shakespeare and performance, that takes a back seat to the relationships we have to build in order to do that work. I know not everyone feels that. But for me, absolutely, the relationships and the community of people creating something together matter even more than this thing that we have committed ourselves to, which is odd and strange. But very true to me.

Why do you say it's odd?

Odd because I think we all believe that we're here to create art, or that we're here to sustain a museum of trees that we collect and study and teach people about. That we come to work to do something, we come to work to teach students, we come to work to drive a bus, we come to work to stock grocery shelves, or whatever. That's what we're paid for. That's what we talk about in terms of this interesting phrase "making a living," which is one that intrigues me so much. We make a living [doing] what the institution or the organization does, but we're also making a living, a *life*, with the people we're making that living with. I guess I say "odd" because it's not the way we tend to think about why we come to work. "Making a living." It's such an interesting phrase.

Your work clearly means a great deal to you. What's it like for you to anticipate retirement?

Well, it makes me anxious because so much of my identity—I mean, the dancer *has* been the dance. I don't know what my retirement will be. What I *do* know through a lot of self-reflection is that I will volunteer a lot because I believe in volunteerism so deeply. I see it as work, I don't see it as distinguished from work. I don't know where yet. I'll figure that out when I have a little more time. I also know that I'll be looking for some sense of community because community is so important to me. It will have to be a place where I can be with different generations. At some point, I'll be looking at places to live where I can be part of a new community that I can contribute to, that will fuel me and feed me. I don't know yet quite what that means. I'm figuring that out.

"You don't work for the money itself."
NICK MADDEN

He has spent most of his adult life working in the West Virginia coal mines. "I also worked in steel, I worked in cotton, other things, too." For 14 years he was an underground miner and for nine he worked in factories. He now works as a grassroots union organizer.

"My father wasn't around much; he was working. But he kept us in a place to live, which meant that we weren't necessarily poor. There were times when everything was short, including food till the next paycheck, but it wasn't being poor by the standards of where we were living. It was just the way it was." He is 72 years old.

My whole family worked; you worked in the coal mines or the factories. For a while, we were sort of part of the Appalachian diaspora coming north to Ohio and Michigan. Then we moved back to West Virginia. Everybody I knew worked in industrial jobs. I think my earliest assumption was that I would do that, too. But I was supposed to be the one who went to college in my family. So that got pushed into my head, that I would do something different. It was always: you're supposed to grow up and do better than your father was able to do, which was both an attack on the father and an expectation on the son.

I was raised in a trade union family. Our father was on strike sometimes, so I knew about being a unionist, I knew that workers weren't treated right. I think that was maybe the initial formation of my views. It was from stuff like the time I went to a lumberyard with my dad when I was about 12 years old. We were going to build something; I don't even remember what. We'd driven 30 miles to get there and found out they were on strike and out picketing. He got out of the car, walked over, talked with these guys for a few minutes, came back, got in the car, and we left. I said, "Well, what about the wood we were going to get?" He said, "If guys are on a picket line for their families or themselves, you don't ever cross another man's picket line."

What do you think your parents were teaching you about making a living when you were growing up?

Really not anything. I mean, not directly, except that you work and get paid to support your family. I don't remember any discussion of money. They just didn't worry about it; they wanted to feed the family and they wanted to be able to help—there were three sons—help us go to school. My perception of the role of money was and still pretty much continues to be that it's absolutely necessary to have money to feed your family and keep a roof over their heads, but you work for *those* reasons. You don't work for the money itself. The idea of getting wealthy never entered my mind.

What I worked for was having a job without having to compromise my values. I never did anything for the money, still haven't. I have never taken a job—this'll sound weird—I've never taken a job because of money or refused a job because of the money. There've been times when I had to feed my family with food stamps; I was on unemployment and so forth, and I took jobs because the survival of my family depended on it. So I worked every dirty job there is, but I've never refused a job because it didn't pay enough money. At the same time, I never took a job because it paid more than something else if I thought the job was putting me in a compromised position in terms of what I believed. I wouldn't have worked in the coal mines if I had any knowledge at the time [about its impact on] the environment, but I didn't know anything about all that stuff; the mines was just something that—it was just one of the options.

How do you think you came by this strong ethos?

I think it came from two places. One is my parents, definitely, and in different ways. My dad worked at anything he could get to support his family. My mother was a woman who was really, really smart, and never had the opportunity to do anything with that, but she passed on to us that love of knowledge. And she made sure there were books in the house, and people were talking to each other about things. So I think it comes from that home life plus a strong working-class culture.

One of the highest values that you could say about anybody in the family was "he's a worker." You took a job and you did the job and you did the job well, even if you were, like I've been doing, union organizing. When the job was right, you didn't screw off on the job, you did quality work. But you expected to be paid right and treated right and you'd go out on strike or slow down or work to rule if they didn't want to do right.

Some people think, why would you work in the mines if you weren't, you know, stupid? I worked with guys that had college degrees. People who were just totally skilled at their work and absorbed in it, who played music, produced art, were good, loving parents. Even though I disagree with the use of coal now based on what I know now, I still have to support the guys, particularly the guys who work underground. If people really want to stop the mining of coal, they need to get serious about a transition that's fair and just for miners.

Do you or your family have any particular feelings toward people in an economic class higher than yours?

I certainly did. I didn't like them. I think my father didn't, too. Basically, the "boss class." There were those who worked for a living and those who lived off the work that other people did. We're talking about the people who never got their hands dirty and walked around the plant shouting orders at people with their engineer shirts on and stuff. It's a group of people who consider themselves better than everybody because they had wealth.

But the reality was they were in that position because they had been willing to kill people in the coal mines; they were the ruling class. And I think it's gotten much worse. The level of avarice. It's *all* about the money. People don't live lives, they live lifestyles. I think it has gotten a lot worse as people spend their lives trying to mimic wealth and accumulate symbols of wealth at the cost of a sense of community that is based in mutual support and solidarity.

Were there points in your career when you really wanted to get out of coal mining?

No. I was ready to work until I retired; I just got laid off. They shut the whole mine down. We came out on midnight shift, and they were standing at the portal handing out layoff slips. We'd had some layoffs and cutbacks in the past, but we'd been told that things were pretty secure. So this was a complete surprise. We mined metallurgical coal, and essentially two things happened. One is, they basically quit producing basic steel in the United States. Most of it was coming from Europe and then eventually from China and so forth. So they weren't really producing steel like they used to, and then the use of coal for producing steel went away.

Yeah. Walked up, got a slip. People were angry. People were stunned. In the mining industry, people are used to cycles where you would get laid off and then you would get a job or eventually get called back or you'd go on strike and then come back in when the strike was over. But sort of a different thing took place when I got laid off, which is awhile back now, but it seems like yesterday. The jobs started going away and not coming back. Like we were all getting thrown away like we were of no use. It was one of the things that propelled me to be an organizer.

I think we have a culture, a society that's based on profit and money. And that makes it destructive, because its number one priority is, how do I make the most money? If that's getting rid of jobs, if that's people working unsafely, if it's ripping off money for my personal use to the point that other people can't make a living, well, okay. The gap between the top and the bottom is the result of the theft of wealth by people who are already wealthy. I think we're in an unsustainable society that needs to change. I view myself as a dyed-in-the-wool socialist because of that. I think money cannot mean society. It has to be about people.

Do you think we're going to see that change in our lifetime?

Not likely. But I see a lot of young people now getting involved. I think we just need to keep nurturing that. It's a generational struggle. People fought for a different kind of way to live for a long time. Anne Braden* said that you want to be a part of what was called in the civil rights movement "the beloved community." You want to be a part of the struggle for a better way to live. Then she said, "You won't live to see the results, but you want to be a part of it." And that's basically how you do it.

You can't have a world without struggle; struggle is essential. Without struggle, the same views and the same people will continue to rule. If we established the world we wanted at some point, somebody would need to change that, too. The struggle to make things better for folks is always there. Struggle is the way we are able to live more human lives.

"The primal desire to escape."
MARK SIWIEC

He is a 58-year-old real estate entrepreneur in Rochester, New York.

"There are 3,600 agents who sell real estate in the six-county region, and I happen to be the number one salesperson. The average agent in this region sells about $850,000 worth of real estate annually; last year, I sold $86 million. In other words, what most agents would hope to sell over a 100-year period of time, I sold in a year. I have a team of 15 people around me, and I'm getting ready to launch my own boutique brokerage that'll go live next year."

I grew up in Buffalo. My dad was a cop. He was drunk on the day that I was born. He was drunk on the day that he died 12 years ago. There was a lot of violence in the house. Just a small ranch, so there was no opportunity to escape the daily turmoil. When I was a child, we had no money, we had no ability to travel, and there was just ABC, NBC, and CBS TV [to watch]. As a result, I assumed that every city in the world was very much like Buffalo. There was a bar on every corner and across the street from that bar was a church. Very, very, very blue collar. Oh, and growing up as a gay kid in the '80s in this environment—that only added to the challenge.

My mom and my dad both graduated from high school, and, well, that was the sum total of their education. She had part-time work for a company where

---

* (1924–2006) She was a Louisville journalist, organizer, educator, and white ally of the southern civil rights movement.

she would dial the phone and ask people a series of questions so that they could secure either auto insurance or homeowner's insurance.

Despite my lower-middle-class upbringing and the fact that I wasn't raised in a household filled with educated family members, I did have one great advantage. I was fortunate that I had my mom, my aunt, and my grandmother, who every single day of my life told me that I could be and could become whatever it is that I wanted. As a result, I became convinced of the fact that, one day, I would succeed. I knew this not just cognitively but systemically. I had no better champion than my mother and, today, I'm still her pride and joy.

What do you think you learned from them about the work world?

The one thing that I've always said about my father, the only kind thing that I'm capable of expressing about my father is that he worked *doggedly*. I mean, that guy worked *hard*. And he taught *me* to work hard. In some ways he was a Willy Loman–like character. He had aspirations and a desire to become successful, but because of [the limits of] his intellectual abilities, he wasn't able to pass an exam which would have allowed him to advance and become a captain or lieutenant in the police department. You throw on top of that the drinking, and he just didn't go anywhere. He couldn't figure out how to escape. He couldn't figure out how to better his life. He would simply wake up in the morning, light up a cigarette, open his first beer, and then go to work. He knew that if he worked every single day of his life for 10, 12, 14 hours, he was able to put food on the table and provide for the family. It's right out of Arthur Miller. Actually, a novel cowritten by Arthur Miller and Upton Sinclair.

My father did get to see some of my success before he died, though, and he was very proud.

Do you know what your dad's own aspirations were?

I think that he couldn't identify a dream other than a primal desire to escape the circumstances into which he was born and the pathetic figure that he allowed himself to become. He would never admit to it, but he did understand, at some base level, who he was. I think that this was the source of so much of his disappointment and so much of his frustration.

What were your own aspirations growing up?

I was told repeatedly that the way to become successful was to become a doctor. I secured a scholarship to the U of R and I moved to Rochester at the age of 18. Cognitively, I was fortunate enough to enjoy a lucky roll of the dice, but I wasn't brought up with the discipline that would allow me to prevail in school. I did, however, graduate after four years, and then set about trying to figure out what to do with my life.

Ultimately, I secured a job with the state health department conducting HIV counseling and testing. Well, on my first day, I was told to talk to this guy who was sitting in the exam room. "Fine, what do you want me to tell him?" My supervisor said [the patient] has gonorrhea, "so you need to find everybody that he's had sex with in the preceding six weeks and tell those individuals that they've had sex with somebody who has gonorrhea. And then you'll start the process over again."

I thought, "*This* is not the dream that I had as I was growing up as a kid." After a year of doing this, I started to look around to see if I could find another path. I had no money. I was not going to go back to college, and even if I did, I didn't know what I would have wanted to study. Then I noticed that the people around me who were successful, those who were beautifully dressed and were driving nice cars, they all were selling real estate, and I figured, well, anybody with a pulse can secure a real estate license, and that's how it all started.

I just fell into a line of work that is well-suited for somebody who's insatiably social. Anybody who's successful in real estate will tell you that they're successful because they've mastered the skill of developing strong and meaningful relationships. This was the underpinning of my initial success as an agent. Thankfully, my career started to take off and I began to transition from being an agent to a team leader and, from there, the owner of a small business.

I don't know how to tap dance. I don't know how to sing. I don't know how to paint a painting, but I do find building and growing a company to be a great creative outlet for me. And I love, I *love* that. It's this really fun, cerebral exercise for me.

[In addition to my work in real estate, my partner], Duffy, who was a teacher for 35 years, and I are also involved in politics, board work, and charity events. When we first met, Duffy said, "I don't think that I can ever spend the rest of my life with somebody who is as busy as you are." I thought, "Well, let's work on getting him onto a board in New York City, so that he's going to be as busy as I am," and now he's more involved than I am! He became the co-chair of a political action committee and lobby whose responsibility was to try to secure marriage equality in the state of New York. And as a result of that, we were in and out of New York all the time and constantly meeting really interesting people—celebrities, politicians, socialites, etcetera.

The phone rings one day, and it's a friend who is a congressman in Brooklyn. His name is Chuck Schumer. "I'm running for Senate. I'm going to be coming into town. Can you help me out?" Absolutely. So I became Chuck's money guy in town during his first run.

Then, there was a guy running for state attorney general named Eliot Spitzer. We became very close with Eliot during those early years. Of course, he went on to become governor and before resigning in disgrace, Duffy had become his secretary of education.

On another occasion, we asked a very close friend, the chief of the Rochester Police Department, to run for mayor while sitting at our dining room table. He ultimately won the election and became mayor before moving on to become lieutenant governor of the state.

All of this political work tied in nicely with my day job, which helped to fuel more interesting parties that we would host, which helped to further grow our civic involvement and charitable work. The whole thing has become one circular entity. You know that adage "With privilege comes responsibility"? Well, we are fortunate to have the opportunity to give back.

Is that what drives you? Is that at the center of what you do?

No. (Laughs.) No. The center of this for so long was crawling out of the sewer that I was born into. I was terrified until probably five years ago of not having financial resources to take care of myself. It seems that the poverty and the hardships that my parents suffered through was very much a part of that which drove me. I mean, every day I would wake up and think, "I've got to succeed. I have to create a financial safety net for myself." And then, in time, it became, "Okay, I've created that safety net for myself and for Duffy." Now I have to ensure that my mom and my brother are safe. As a result of creating that security, I'm finally at peace with myself and with the world in general.

That financial security is also important because when Donald Trump or the conservative right is railing against whatever it is they're railing against or demonizing, well . . . I feel as though if things get really bad—I don't want to become too dystopian, but if this is Weimar 2024, we can pack up and we can go to Costa Rica, Belize, Canada.

Do you think about your retirement?

There was a point in time, probably 15, 20 years ago when you were negatively thought to be a workaholic if you weren't retired by the age of 65. Well, now that we live longer as human beings, you need to find meaning in your day, day in and day out. Unless you remain engaged and involved, mentally and otherwise, how do you find that meaning? People often state that the longer that you work, the shorter your life. For me, I believe just the opposite. The longer that I work, I think, the longer I'll live because I will remain engaged, cognitively and socially. Look at Jimmy Carter. What a great role model. He's 98 and still on a roof swinging a hammer!

What do you think about when you look back over your career so far in relation to where you started?

I often come back to the image of all of the Vietnamese men and women on the roof of the U.S. embassy in Saigon [during the evacuation in 1975] scrambling to secure a place on one of the departing helicopters. They're frantically grabbing onto the skids, *hoping* that they're going to be carried away to safety. I think of myself as one of the last guys to be evacuated, who just manages to grab onto the skids, and they're carried off and deposited onto the deck of our warships in the Gulf. So many are left behind while a lucky few make it out of the country alive.

I wake up every morning—(Pauses and looks away.)—I'm actually going to get choked up saying this. I wake up—(Long pause. His eyes tear.)—I don't even know why this is killing me. I wake up every morning saying, "I love my life. I really love my life. I'm so lucky. I was able to escape."

"Now I'm stuck."
KAREN GRACE

Her career has included almost 20 years of leadership in a variety of educational settings. She was laid off six months before this conversation when the company she was working for downsized by some 80 employees. She is now trying to establish her own consulting career. She is married to Michael, a small business owner. They have one daughter, Kelley, who is 6.

We talk in the kitchen of her home. It is a small duplex ("We share a wall with our neighbor") but neatly and attractively furnished. She is 40 years old.

How do I self-identify professionally? Oh boy, that's a tough one. It's funny that you ask that question because I feel so much anxiety. A lot. I think as you get older, you keep thinking, "When am I going to be in a place where I'm satisfied professionally, where things are not so stressful, so full of anxiety all the time?" It always comes down to money. It's not about the work, itself; it's always about money. But what really, I think, feeds that anxiety is my own expectations of where I thought I would be at this age, and I'm not there. Not even close. Growing up, you just had these visions of your grown-up life mirroring what your life had been as a kid. [I've read that] we are among the first generation to not do better than our parents did. I definitely feel that.

My dad was an advertiser, had always made a nice chunk of money. Four kids. All of us went to Catholic grade school, all went to college, didn't have to pay for college. Dad paid. We had a nice house. It wasn't fancy, but it was nice. I knew we were lucky back then.

What did you learn from your parents about making a living?

Nothing. Nothing about managing money, nothing about planning ahead. I mean, I learned other things, but not that practical stuff. My dad is creative. My dad is a risk-taker, or *was* a risk-taker. I don't think he's so much of a risk-taker now because he's had some real failures, financially. He's 72 and he can't not work; he can't retire; he *has* to keep working, financially.

My parents' life took a big turn for what, if I had been 10 years older at the time, I could have helped them to avoid. But they made a really bad decision. My dad was unhappy in advertising, so he chose to leave that career behind, and they opened up a retail operation. They sunk all their money into it, and it did okay at first, and then they tried a new venture, and that didn't work, and then they were stuck. They were in this cycle where they were just throwing their money into this project, and it was not succeeding, and their retirement was dwindling, but they didn't know how to get out of it. Finally, the business died, thankfully, but they were left with no retirement, nothing. So my dad started working at Home Depot.

[Last] Sunday morning, I was watching the news and not really watching it, kind of staring off. And I remember thinking to myself, I feel so insecure, financially insecure. And the phone rings, and it's my sister to tell me that my dad might be having a stroke, and I need to get to the hospital right now. I was sitting with Dad at the hospital two days ago. He was kind of staring off. I said, "You alright?" He's like, "I just feel so stuck." I thought immediately, my parents have no security, nothing. If something were to happen to my dad, I don't know what we would do. I don't know what my parents would do. Someone would have to take them in, and who could do that? Certainly not me. And so, the burden falls to the other siblings who can afford it, and then you feel like a failure. You can see the spiral, right?

I'd love to be in a place where what I bring is allowed to flourish. Where I can be so creative and innovative and in a place that draws upon all of my strengths, to take something really complex and make something happen. I would love to be able to make a difference. Be part of a place that has an identity, that's doing good work, and that has a path upon which I can navigate to something and see myself there for a long time, you know? I'm too old to be thinking, "Okay, I'll try this for five years and then I'll do something else." I think I'm past that age where it's safe. Especially because we have nothing to fall back on. There's no nest egg. It's just been paycheck to paycheck.

After I got my doctorate, I had thought, "Okay, I have a doctorate [in education] now; I'm valuable. The rest of the world can see my value." But then I was one of the many who got laid off. That was the moment where I realized, I don't know what's going to happen. I feel completely insecure. Even now, when I'm working on several consulting projects, all of the work is great, but I don't know that I could continue as a consultant and feel secure. We're still paycheck to paycheck around here. We're not any better off than we were 10 years ago. I was saying to Michael, "I feel like in order for us to see something change, we need to do something drastic, like really drastic. I really think we should sell the house. Plan a lifestyle where we live off of your income, solely on your income, and everything I do will be first to save for Kelley's college and concurrently to pay down our debt, and we do that for three years. We could live in an apartment somewhere." And he just crumbled at the idea. Because it would be so devastating. I think he said, "I would just feel like such a failure. I wouldn't know how to face people." It's a pride thing. And I understand it. But I'm much more optimistic than he is about it. I'm like, "There are some really great places we can find that don't need any work. Look around this house; everything here needs work."

It's hard for Michael. It's really hard for Michael. Because the finance side of it is so unpredictable, he's terrified about how to pay bills if the money isn't a set amount every single month. How do you manage that? I haven't paid the taxes yet; taxes are due at the end of the month. I haven't paid those yet. I don't know exactly what they're going to be, so it's going to be scary. We have this pot of money that will go away. It'll just disappear. I think he's terrified about what's next.

What does Kelley understand of what's going on?

She is aware that we struggle financially. She's not fearful. I don't think we've gone that far with her. But I think she knows that I want to move, but we can't afford it. She knows I want to sell this house; she knows I hate this house.

I'll be up in the bathroom trying to blow dry my hair, and the fuse will blow. Or there's another leak over here that we can't fix right now because it costs too much money. The central air is out. Last summer we had no air conditioning. It was 100 degrees with a humidity index of whatever for a long time and we just had to suck it up. I said, "Kelley, it's old school. Just like when I was a kid. We didn't have central air till we lived in this house." She's totally fine with that because she doesn't want to move. She likes this house. It would be a really nice teachable moment to be able to talk to her about how to weather it, but you feel so fragile, you know? You want everything to be fine. I don't want her to have to worry.

On what do you hang your hopes right now?

Well, I don't know what to say about that. I keep saying this every year. I keep saying, "This one [opportunity] is going to [work out] or that one thing is going to go my way," and then it doesn't. So rather than what I'm hopeful about, I think it's really more, what am I thankful about right now?

I'm totally reenergized by the people [I'm consulting for] who are passionate about making the world a better place, and that gives me hope. But it doesn't take away the fear or the insecurity. That's ever-present. It's always, always there. So I'm hopeful that I'll be in an organization that I admire, doing work that is meaningful. And using my skills, my best strengths to do that work, and being recognized for it. That's what I'm hopeful for. Will I find it? I don't know, I really don't know.

Is anger any part of how you feel about all this?

Oh, sure. Absolutely. Being bitter about it because you made choices based on. . . . You go to Catholic grade school, and you say you want to make the world a better place, right? So you think that the value in somebody is placed in the good work, in helping others, in making the world a better place, leaving the world a better place than when you found it.

There *is* value in it, but there's no monetary value, and I think that was for me one of the biggest disappointments. You want to do good work and be creative and help people and help yourself. Just angry about where we place our value in this country. It really pisses me off that people who are just trying to do good work, people who are trying to help make our community better, they're the first to be demonized and they're the first to get cut, and they don't get paid much. I just think that's so wrong. I don't understand how we can foster that in this country, but that's what we do.

I think the anger comes, too, when I think of the lack of guidance that I got from my parents, partly because my mom never went to college. They never had to worry about money because my dad had always made money. Nobody ever sat me down and said, "Here's how it works." Never. I've had to figure out how it works, and I figured it out way too late. I'm making up my own path, and it's way, way harder like that.

But really? I think it's really more me not having a clue. It's real easy to get angry at my parents. But the reality is, honestly? I can't just say it's my mom's fault. (Laughs.) I don't think that's fair. I think I just didn't grow up for a long time, I just didn't. I'm just angry because I didn't want to be the first generation that didn't do as well as my parents. You know? What happened was totally out of my control, but now I'm stuck here. Still stuck.

Michael comes down this morning. He sits right where you're sitting, and I'm sitting here. He said, "God, I love watching Kelley wake up." I said, "Why?" He said, "Because she'll wake up, her hair is all over the place and her eyes are little slits, and I'll say, 'How were your sleeps?' And she always says, 'Good.'"

She's always got a little smile on her face. And she sleeps like a rock, this kid. She puts her thumb in her mouth, that's it. For 10 hours she'll be completely out. And when she wakes up, she's like, "It was good. Okay, what's next?" Tail is wagging.

Michael said, "She doesn't wake up and say, 'I worried about money all night.' She wakes up and says, 'Good!' I would love to be able to sleep like that. I would just love it."

And I said, "I know. Can you imagine?"

"Battles in the middle of battles."
JERRY KING

He is 50 years old and a United Auto Workers special assigned representative to the Employee Assistance Program in Detroit.

"I had COVID this year, and so did my wife. Man, it was hard. She didn't tell me how bad it was for her. And I never told her how bad it was for me. We were at home. I didn't want to go to nobody's hospital. So I learned how to breathe within my restricted range of breathing. I didn't push. I just took multiple breaths within that shorter reach. Within about a week and a half it went back to normal.

"So we both went through that, and it's changed some of my priorities. I got to spend more time taking care of me and my family versus everybody else. Found out I gotta learn how to blend. You wind up putting so much in everything else and you don't put as much into what you need to around you. COVID made me rethink a whole lot. Her, too."

We talk via Zoom three days before Joe Biden's inauguration.

I grew up between 12th and 14th on Atkinson in Detroit. I grew up walking down 12th Street, Woodrow Wilson, and you see all of those stores that were burned out from the riots.* My grandparents live right around there, right? Right around Clairmount where the riots took place.

My mother was way over—what's the word I'm looking for? Protective. I never got it until I became an adult. It took me into my 40s to say, "Ya know, *that's* why she was like that." She grew up seeing young Black men at an impressionable age during the riots when she was 17 or whatever age she was then. She saw how they were treated. She saw the tanks coming through, she saw the fire that had been a part of that. So, to grow up right in the middle of that. And then your father, the union leader at that time, whatever was coming out of his mouth at that time, right? So it took me that to understand her a little bit, and apologize a little bit, because I always pushed back: "You're overprotecting me!" No young man wants to be raised where he doesn't know what the world's like, right? You want to know the rough and tumble because you're going to have to live in the rough and tumble. Right? But yeah, so it helped me understand that.

Just growing up in Detroit, you learn many different sides of the coin, and

---

* The Detroit Riot of 1967 between largely Black residents and the police department resulted in 43 deaths, hundreds of injuries, almost 1,000 fires, and over 7,000 arrests.

you got to find your way to where you want to be at. So, for me, it winds up being in manufacturing, but it's now more about taking all my skill sets and using them.

I am a UAW member assigned to the EAP department, the employee assistance department, civil rights department, equal application department, and new hire orientation. I came from actually two plants before I got this assignment. I started out at the Detroit Axle facility here in Detroit, and then, due to some manpower reduction—redeployment—I was fortunate enough, because of UAW, to get transferred to Warren Truck Assembly. I've never missed one day's pay. Yeah, you know, manpower reduction is a scary time.

I've been involved in quality management in both facilities. That's my background before becoming quality assurance manager. So that's kind of my background: understanding processes, procedures. My job is diversity, new hire orientation, sexual harassment prevention, the understanding of civil rights in the plants, how people can be violated, and how supervisor investigators investigate. I've had the opportunity to serve the interests of the UAW and FCA* doing new hire orientation and training and kind of playing a role trying to put some positive, guiding information into the new people coming into the system. And training them about workplace violence prevention, sexual harassment prevention, things like that.

And so, it's about caring about people, right? It's about setting up a corporate culture that meets the intent of what we need. And, to be honest, like I tell the workers coming in, these are professional relationships. You know? We forget that a lot of times. We think about friendship, think about, "Oh, she could possibly be my new boo." But that's not what we're here for, alright? We're not here for that. Things happen, that's great, but you can't let a secondary undermine your primary.

Your goal is to extract the very best out of each other, no matter what your hiccups are with each other because here you're not going to get a raise, you're not going to move up. You can win the argument, you can be the loudest person, but the leadership we're looking for is the person who takes a bad situation, a bad relationship, and turns it positive. At the end of the day, you want to go at somebody hard enough where you have a level of respect established, but once there's a level of respect established your true goal should be to flip that relationship: How can we work together and achieve common goals? How can we buffer

* Fiat Chrysler Automobiles.

the things we don't agree upon? One day, we might mature to the point where we finally see what each other is missing. Right?

The true goal is for everybody that benefits through collective bargaining to truly, truly *own* the fact that there's enough of us to take a stand, so we need the public to come out and vote with us on laws; we need people who are going to stand with us. And believe me, without them people, you can see we're losing our teeth. We're losing our teeth and we're going to need to get transplants, you know? (Laughs.) This is not a natural thing that's going to fix itself. It's going to take some pain. It's going to take some heartache. It's going to take some sacrifice of time.

Are you proud of the work that you do?

Yeah, yeah, it wakes me up every day. I am blessed to have a role where I can directly see and help people. Right? Help connect them to a thought that might help them keep their job, you know?

Is this the job you'd like to retire from some day?

You know what? I am 50 years old. I got 15 to 20 more years. If I'm in a capacity where I'm working like this, where I got my paid job, which is just taking care of the membership, doing the new hire orientation, the civil rights work, the etcetera, right? And then I got my after-hours job with the community: president of a chapter of the A. Phillip Randolph Institute,* and then there's whatever labor needs me to support. I understand that in my role, being blessed to be in a position where I can be of service to a membership at the level that I do, that my volunteerism to support labor is just as important as my 40-hours-a-week job. Because see, I'm in a role to leverage and help shape the mission of labor and who we are, our preamble, our values. And the fact that people recognize me for one role, and then when they see me in my community role, it strengthens the whole role. And that's even better.

In two days, we'll have a new president. Do you think that will impact your work?

Well, hopefully, hopefully, there's some impacts. You know what? My work is

* Founded in 1967 for African American trade unionists. It "advocates social, labor, and economic change at the state and federal level, using legal and legislative means" on the principle that "the fight for workers' rights and civil rights are inseparable."

nonpartisan, but we're particular. Particular about working-class values and making sure not just the working class, but the underserved have a voice and a pathway. You have many underserved people that might not ever have a job. And you can't turn your nose up at them and feel like they're worth less. Because some of those people were damaged by the poor decisions of a leader. Like the Flint water situation, you got kids that are going to be permanently disabled, not able to function at their best. They're the underserved, right? And they're under-served not by their own choice, but because somebody made a decision that put profit, or money, over the welfare of those human beings. And now these human beings are left with the legacy of that poor decision. Should I feel bad that some tax money's coming out of my own dollars to help support them? No, I shouldn't feel sad. I should be okay with it.

Because . . . .

Well, the simple fact that that could be me.

POSTSCRIPT: *I heard from Jerry during the United Auto Workers strike that began September 15, 2023. "It's refreshing," he said, "to have the elephants in the room discussed during bargaining: inequality influenced by financialization, corporate stock buybacks, outrageous CEO compensation. There's a problem here in America. It's time to have this important conversation."*

"How is this not a job?"
JUSTIN ROSARIO

He is a stay-at-home parent and lives in Alexandria, Virginia, where his wife, Debbie, has been working for the DEA for the last 15 years as an administrative assistant. They have a 12-year-old son.

I started being a stay-at-home parent when my son was born. He was diagnosed with autism when he was 2, so when COVID happened, it turned out to be really good that I was a stay-at-home parent. He needs a full-time person sitting next to him when he's doing virtual teaching. I work with him. He's fine with me sitting next to him. He doesn't give me a hassle about it. The person who normally sits next to him at school, they're called paraprofessionals. That is the job that I'm currently doing, myself. I redirect his attention.

In some ways he is a 12-year-old, and in other ways he's more like an 8-year-old. He didn't even start holding our hands until he was 5. He didn't want to snuggle until he was 5 or 6. Now, he's like a huge mama's boy; he loves getting hugs from Mommy. He loves sitting on her lap, which is hilarious, because now he's four inches taller than she is.

What kind of reaction do you get from people when you tell them that you are a stay-at-home dad?

I get into arguments all the time with people online. And one of the things I've had people constantly say to me when I tell them I'm a stay-at-home parent is that I'm not a (air quotes) real man. They've tried to undermine my masculinity about it. And I've always found that to be very, very funny. Because it's like, I can't think of anything that's more being a man than taking care of your kids. You know? Than being a father. The other thing I always found to be really amusing is it's like, "Why don't you get a *real* job?" I'm like, "Okay, I want you to go ask your mother or grandmother if she had a real job when she was raising you. I dare you to go say to your grandmother, 'Grandma, you didn't have a real job when you were raising my parents.' See how that works out for you." When I say that, then the conversation stops.

We actually got a lot of crap from my wife's family. I wasn't really in touch with my own family at the time, but her family gave us a lot of crap about it. They're retired. Her father was a cop. Her mother was the secretary at a factory of some sort. And I kind of forget what her stepparents did. It was so horribly stereotypical, it just made me want to cry. Like: "That's not really what a man should be doing. You should be working." I was just like, "Are you serious? Like, come on, man. We're in the 21st century. You gotta let that go."

My wife is really good at her job. She wasn't as suited to being around a screaming, crying child all day long as I was. She doesn't have the same amount of patience for it as I did. I mean, I worked in a toy store for a number of years, so I was used to having screaming children around me all the time. So it was a no-brainer for us, like why would she do that then? Because she's a woman? That's the stupidest thing in the world. She's not naturally more able to put up with it than a guy because she's female. That's not how that works.

I got less trouble from her father and her stepmother than I get from her mother and her stepfather. One Christmas, I swear to God, they got me a sweater vest. And I'm like, "What is this for?" They were like, "When you go on job interviews." *Really?* That was like, wow, I *have* a job, right? It's called raising my kids. *That's* my job. That's what I do.

"I Made That"

"That's when my heart took flight."
MELISSA JAMES-GESKA

She cofounded US Ceiling Corp with her then-husband in 2001 as a subcontracting firm, primarily working in the commercial sector of construction and specializing in drywall, insulation, metal framing, wood framing, acoustical ceilings, and air sealing. She has been president of the company since its inception.

"There is tremendous satisfaction and pride that comes from driving around the city and saying, 'I built that; I built that; I built that.' Being able to have a tangible example of the work that you've done collectively as a company is probably one of the proudest moments that you'll have."

I experience resentment and disbelief every time I go to meet someone and tell them what I do—still to this day! If I tell someone that I own a commercial contracting company, they're like, "But you're a woman." It's 2022, and I still get the same reaction, like, "Wow, that's really unique. You're a woman!" I don't see how my gender has anything to do with it. There's other times I've experienced where people said, "Oh, you're just a pass-through because this is your husband's business."

Fairly recently, three years ago, my now ex-husband left the business, and I met with someone who told me that the assumption was that when he retired, all of the capabilities would leave with him. And that clearly wasn't the case. We have more success today than we had five years ago when he was in operational control. But that's the assumption, and it's unfortunate because it's based in ignorance. It's really hurtful. I can tell you that gender discrimination is very much alive, and misogyny is very much alive.

I also have experienced a lot of hostility by having a diverse workforce, like racial epithets spray-painted on bathrooms. There were other times where I was actually asked to engage in fraudulent activity from a procurement perspective where people wanted to use my business as a pass-through venture so that they could meet the [diversity] requirements of their projects but not actually do the right thing by engaging with firms and providing actual viable opportunities.

I identify as a Black woman, but when I go into most public environments, based on the actual color of my skin, not everyone recognizes that I am Black, so oftentimes I hear the things that people say when they think they don't need a filter. So I've witnessed a lot of the racism that my older brother, who has a very dark African American complexion, does not witness because people are so politically correct and don't say the things they really think around him.

I've always tried to use my "white privilege" to call people out and to ask for change and demand change. I like when those opportunities present themselves because it's a chance for me to dig in. It's like that stubborn little girl is still within me: "I'll show you!" Sometimes I need a fire in my belly, and I kind of get it from those opportunities.

When your ex-husband left the business, did you feel a need to prove yourself?

I definitely felt the call to action to prove myself, and I think—to be vulnerable with you—I felt a tremendous amount of anxiety about my ability to do the job. He was 23 years older than me, Mark. He had 50-some-odd years of industry expertise that walked away. And yeah, I knew I could go find the answers I needed, but there were some moments of, "Oh, I'm walking on a tightrope, and there's no net beneath, and all eyes are on me."

I don't want to feel like people were looking for me to fail, but I do feel like there was an assumption that I would. I think that's one of the challenges of being a woman in a nontraditional work environment: we often feel that we have to be perfect, because anything less than perfect invalidates our existence. That's something that's very common among women that work in this industry with me. They have to be perfect at all times, because the minute they make a mistake, someone's going to turn and say, "Well, you didn't belong here anyway."

There's some [women] powerhouses that have been running construction companies for 40 years. And when I think about [a woman] running a construction business in the 1960s, it takes my breath away to think of what they faced and the courage they had because they didn't have a lot of the regulations and protections that I can turn to today. There's a lot of white male privilege in pockets of our economy, and women and people of color have just been willing to find their way. I think it's dramatically improved, but I still feel as though it's sometimes a daily struggle just to meet the microaggressions and the things that you hear and that you have to work hard to overcome or just ignore, just to keep going.

I'm the first woman and the first person of color in 134 years to serve as the chairwoman of the builders exchange here. I take that mantle very seriously. I do. I do quite a bit in the community to raise awareness for our industry from a workforce development perspective. I also started the DEI taskforce to always keep Diversity, Equity, and Inclusion at the forefront of our industry. We do a lot, really, based on three pillars: workforce development, building capacity for women and minority contracting firms, and leadership development. Because I serve on five community boards, and I'm often the only woman and the only person of color on those boards, I'm trying to do my part to increase diversity.

[In my own business] we have just shy of 100 employees. Currently 46 percent are people of color and about 27 percent of those would be considered economically disadvantaged individuals. I want to have the most diverse contracting company in the country, not just New York State but in the country.

I think the moment that I realized that there was a business case, a successful business case that could be made for diversity and for aligning my personal values and mission with the business, I think that's when my heart took flight, and the business really exponentially became more successful. I'm trying to increase the pipeline and provide the actual projects that can sustain the diversity work. Right now, I'm beholden to the award of contracts by others that may or may not have that value system. *I* want to be the one awarding the contracts with the right DNA and the right value system. That's what we're currently focused on.

It's a shame that somehow, at some time in this country's history, we lost respect for craftspersons and craftsmanship. When I was in school, we had skilled training programs that happened off-site, and there were often really cruel jokes made about the people who would leave school to go participate in the skilled trades programs. There was this very negative stigma that they were "lesser than," and that they couldn't do anything else, so they were doing that. Unfortunately, that couldn't be further from the truth. The level of skill and intelligence that it takes to actually build things so far surpasses even the college education that I received. When I think about what I was studying, and I see our people in motion and what they're able to do and build! I mean, I'm light-years behind them in those capabilities.

When we turned toward seeking education and wanting our children to have education, we somehow devalued skilled-trade work in the process. It's to the point where it's going to cause a major economic crisis because we have so few young people that respect skilled trades, and so they're not pursuing those skilled trades. You have baby boomers and such that are retiring at rapid rates, and we can't fill the funnel, and the economy is so dependent on construction projects. I mean, that's literally the lifeblood of our economy. The demand hasn't changed, but the availability of skilled workers that can do the work has dramatically changed. And so most companies are operating at a major deficit for labor, and they're at the point where they'll just take anyone, anybody will do, and you just pray for the best, and hope that you can train people.

But when you have instances where Walmart and McDonald's are offering signing bonuses and paying people $15 to $20 an hour to start with zero experience, it's really hard to solve that problem. I often joke that we need to bring *sexy* back to construction because there needs to be that desire and demand to do that work again. And we need to elevate our sense of appreciation and respect for those that do skilled work.

I'd like to think that's the vision of America that I hold in my heart in terms of creating an environment where if people are given an opportunity, they can find success, and that if they work hard, their hard work can be rewarded. We've had probably 12 employees that have had a passion to become entrepreneurs themselves, and they've started their own subcontracting firms, and guess what! They work for us. We give them business, so we've created a safe space for them to stretch their wings and assume some risk, but we help them manage the risk so that they can walk before they run.

I think the most satisfaction for me comes from looking at the lives that I've had [an] impact on and that my business has had an impact on. I've had individuals getting their citizenship working for us; we've collaborated with a local bank's first-time homebuyer's program where we watch people buy their first homes; we've had people having kids, going to college, people taking their first and only vacations. When I hear those stories, it's like, that's my *why*.

And I think *that's* what America means to me.

"Not just anybody could build that."

RAY WOLLEK

He is a carpenter who does commercial work in office buildings—"a lot of cabinets, a lot of everything from framing and drywall to doors and hardware, trim work. I rarely work outside now." He is 37 years old and recently became the father of a son. We talk on Zoom a year and a half into the pandemic.

I always say I'm a "union carpenter" because I like it to be known that I'm a union guy. I've been a union carpenter for about 18 years now. 18 years? Yeah. Since I was about 19. It means that I'm a skilled worker. I mean, I was trained at the trade school for four years. [And it means] that I have protections. I feel like I have someone in my corner as far as workers' rights go. They have good insurance. That's a plus, you know, and just knowing someone has your back. There's a brotherhood. If you go to meetings and stuff, you're a part of something bigger. And I feel it's a good thing.

I do feel unions get a bad rap sometimes. Since frickin' Reagan, man. We still get shit a lot. You know: "All you guys get paid way too much" and this and that. It's like, well, not really, if you look at wages and inflation, the cost of everything, it's not. Yeah, I feel we take heat, sometimes.

My dad, he's retired now, he was 45 years in the union. He got me into [carpentry]. He said, "You need to get a job and get out of my house." In high school I worked in car detail shops, car washes, stuff like that. My dad kind of wanted me to do something other than just working at a car dealership. He kind of saw, "You need a little more of a future here." I always worked with him through high school, doing side jobs with him. Dragging me out of bed on Saturday to help them work. It was the kick in the ass I needed.

I like working with my hands; never really liked school that much. So I guess this was the way to go. I mean, it's good benefits and stuff like that, too. I like it. I'm constantly going different places. I'm not always going into like, an office, the same place every day, so there's a change of scenery. It's nice. Some of the places I work at, I see the people, day in and day out, at the same office. It just wouldn't be for me. I think I'd be miserable. So yeah, I do enjoy what I do. I wouldn't be doing it if I was miserable. You know, it's hard work. That's what my dad said: "Hey, you're not gonna be rich. And you're gonna work hard, but you'll make a decent living." I find that to be true.

I get paid by the hour, so if the work dries up, I'm not getting paid. With the housing crash, for example, I got laid off in 2010. I was off for, I think it was two summers. I was hanging siding with a friend of mine, just getting unemployment and working for cash for him. There's always people looking to have something done.

What happens if you're injured while doing a side job like that?

Well, I'm kind of screwed. I would have to—you know, God forbid—I'd have to go to the hospital and just claim it under my own insurance. I couldn't get a workman's comp claim or anything like that.

The impact of the pandemic is kind of still in effect. Things definitely got real slow, and I think we're still feeling the effects of it. It still hasn't really recovered. You've got a lot of people working from home now, so not a lot of people are remodeling their offices. That halted that work a little bit. Unemployment was really good, though. It was close to what I had been making. I just had to be sure I kept up on my hours for insurance. That's how my insurance works. You gotta work so many hours per year and per quarter. And then that's how you keep your insurance. But [during the pandemic] they lowered the hours required for that. So I was good. I was gonna be having a baby in October, so I was really making sure I had my insurance. It worked out pretty good. The unknown really sucks but being on unemployment was really good.

We hear politicians say that when unemployment benefits are good, workers aren't going to want to go back to work.

I feel like if there was some better-paying jobs out there, people would be a little more incentivized to go to work. Right now, the low pay is unreal. But I feel also like I had a different situation because my wife was pregnant, so I was a little scared, to be honest with you, to go back to work, given the [COVID] situation.

Do you find that your profession is mostly men?

Yeah. I've only come across a few women, and they've mostly been in, like, other trades, you know? Like electricians. In my company, rarely do I see women on the job.

Do you have any thoughts on why that is?

I guess it's just the way it's always been. I don't know. I mean, it doesn't bother me. If you're qualified, though, I don't care what you are, you know?

Do you ever go home at the end of the day and think, "Man, I've got to go back and redo something I just did?"

That's constantly. Sometimes I'm my worst critic. On my way home, I think back on the day and think, "I should do that better; I gotta go back and fix that." I can't just leave it in good faith, you know? Yeah, I take pride in my work. I mean, my name's on it, not literally, but that's the way I feel about it. I don't like doing something sloppy or something I wouldn't do in my own house. I'm kind of a perfectionist. My wife kind of tells me when I'm doing [our] house, she's like, "It doesn't have to be perfect." (Laughs.) She's like, "No one else is gonna notice that." But whatever it is, *I've* got to walk by it every day and see that.

Is your father like that?

To a point, but I don't think he's as bad as me.

Do you have any desire for your son to become a carpenter? Would that mean something to you?

I don't really care what he does, as long as he makes a good living. You know what I mean? I mean, I'm definitely going to show him that aspect of things. I think it's good to learn how to do stuff with your hands. Like I said, even when I was a kid, I liked working on cars. My dad, he got a beater, a '85 Caprice or something, and we pulled the motor out of it and got a motor from a junkyard, put that in it. I think it's good to have that. It's kind of a shame, though, that . . . I feel like schools, they've kind of cut programs like that. You need a shop class; not everyone's made out to go to college, you know. I went to a Catholic school, which was more like a college prep, more geared towards college. I mean, you need shop and stuff like that. You've got to work with your hands.

You know, when I was a kid, my dad, he made our swing set. He also made a bank out of wood for my own kid—glued a bunch of blocks together, different woods, and then turned it on the lathe and make it round. You know, it's really nice. He engraved it. He made a little rattle for him, too. Stuff like that. Eventually, I'll think of something to make for him like that.

I would like to build my own house, someday, too, you know. Yeah, I think that'd be nice to sit down with an architect and draw something out. That would be cool. I mean, not for a little while, you know? Maybe I'd like to build a house to retire to.

What are you most proud of in your work?

That's a tough one. I guess I get the sense of, not just anyone could do it. You know? It takes skill, and it's a skill that *you* have. A few months ago, I put two dormers on my house with some guys, my wife's friend's husband, and my dad was helping me, too. Not just anyone could build that. To me it's a sense of pride that at this point I can do that. I go downtown, see an office building, and I think, "Hey, I worked on that." It's a sense of pride. It's nice to step back and say, "Hey, I did that." It *is* satisfying.

Studs Terkel interviewed a steel worker in the '70s named Mike Lefevre for his book Working. *And Mike said he'd like to see a building, like the Empire State, with a foot-wide strip with the names of everyone who helped build it. "Everyone should have something to point to," he said.*

Yeah. Yeah. That would be cool. That'd be awesome. To say I was part of that, you know? Yeah.

"I'm here! I'm the new welder."
JORDAN COLEY

We talk via Zoom in late November of 2020, nine months into the pandemic. She is 30 years old and has two children, ages 4 and 5.

The way I got to be a welder is I was incarcerated. I was in jail for 20 months, from August of 2016 to March of 2018. Before that I went to college in Minnesota, and I got a bachelor's degree in criminal justice with a concentration in management. I was going to go all the way; I was going to go to be a lawyer, possibly a prosecutor. Post-incarceration, though, it's hard to use your degree.

And so, I learned about welding by going to these outreach things that took place at the jail. And they talked about welding and trades. It was the first time I had ever heard about a trade in a way that wasn't dismissive. In high school, it was drilled inside of our heads that everything that we did was geared toward going to college and what your career should be. They gave you surveys and then it was like, "Okay, you should be this or this," you know? A doctor or midwife or attorney. So everything was geared towards college, but they didn't tell us that if you go to a trade school, you won't have as many student loans. If any, at all!

You get in an apprenticeship, and at 18 or 19, you're making a wage that's the same as your age. And it goes up, and by the time you're in your mid-20s, you will be debt-free with a six-figure income. So, nobody's told me that. They never told us about trades. And I never heard about it nowhere else in my life, either. My mom never did because she went to college, and of course when you go to college, it does become a legacy thing. You know: your mom went to college, your mom's mom went to college, so it becomes more like a legacy thing instead of just another option.

And so, when I learned of welding, it kind of clicked. Like, I can do that! They told us trades are more likely to overlook your background because they're more unionized, and they fight for you. So I went to welding school six months after I came home. When I graduated, I was the only woman out of three in my class who finished. And then God blessed, and I was able to get a job and keep a job welding. I've been on this job all year.

I think if we, as a country, put our money towards rehabilitation, we could build a better society. You don't have to lock people up in cages and feed them slop like pigs and say, "That's what they deserve. They should learn their lesson from that." Who has ever learned from abuse or neglect or being harped down on as the lowest person? When you are in the gutter, you start feeling like the gutter and you keep acting like the gutter. I've seen people leave Cook County Jail who had come in as innocent little people who messed up and who just really needed pushing.

Welding geared towards my creative side because I write, I draw, sometimes I write poetry. I have a big imagination. With welding, you're using really hot temperatures, and you're melting things together. And when those welds come out perfect, this is something to be proud of. You look at it as a work of art; it really is. When two pieces come together, it's supposed to look a certain way. So, when I do that, and it comes out that way, it's as if I had just wrote the best line of poetry that I've ever written. So really, I wish I had been told about welding when I was 18, right?

What was your job interview like?

That was the exciting part! I knew I was one hell of a welder.

For the interview, they put a dusty old helmet on you and tell you whatever they want you to do. They give you your gun, your welding gun, and you lay out a bead for them, and they like it or not. Maybe they'll have you weld a couple corners together to see how you do it. And other people spectate; it's like a sport, you know? Other people come in, they look, they like it, say, "Oh yeah, you got the job. Girl, you shouldn't be doing nothing else but welding." That process is really quick. That was nothing. It was the interview process that got me nervous.

They ask you, "What's your work history? How long you've been welding? How long ago did you graduate? What are you certified in?" Because there are different types of welding techniques and materials. They ask, "What made you go into welding?" I tell people—I leave out the incarceration part—I tell people most of the time that my degree from Minnesota wouldn't have paid me as much as welding. And that the debt that my degree cost—$72,000—versus my welding certificate being free. So, money talks. People definitely understand that.

Do you remember your very first day at work?

Yeah, I remember it! I was happy, had my gear, everything, walked in. I'm like, "I'm here! I'm the new welder." And the man greeted me. He was like, "You know, I've been asking for them to send me a woman welder for a long time." And I was like, "Really?" He was like, "Yeah, because women are better welders. You guys have an eye and a steady hand and you get the job done."

Now, sometimes he will come through and show other people, like, "Look what she does. I don't even have to check on her." And so, I remember that feeling on that first day when he was basically *happy* to have me there. Like, "I've been asking for a woman for *months*." And I was like, "I'm supposed to be here!"

I was at work for a while in the beginning of the pandemic, but when we had to stay at home, shelter in place, the daycare closed. My two children were at home. I have a son who is 5 and a daughter who is 4, so I had to be at home. My mom, she worked for the state of Illinois, so she still had to go into the office, and then my children would be at home. So I guess you could say I had to quit, but they didn't fire me or lay me off. It was like, "Come back when you can." When the school was opening back up around May, that's when I was able to go back to work.

Were you eager to get back?

Yeah, man, but I think for the wrong reason. I think we have been tricked into believing that we are useful because we have a job versus being a mother at home. But I was useful at *home*, you know? I got to spend more time with my children. Mind you, I was previously incarcerated, so that was two and a half years away from them, so there was much-needed bonding time to do, as well. They got used to me being home. They would tell me, "Mom, don't go to work. I like it when you're here."

I wish our country was more geared towards raising good human beings instead of workhorses, because then a mom could be paid and financed to stay at home and raise these good human beings. Because how do you expect me to raise good humans? I work all day, and then how much time do I really get to spend with them? If I work eight hours, and they sleep eight hours, what am I supposed to do? How am I supposed to teach them things with just the little bit of time that I can squeeze out before bedtime? So, yeah, I was only eager to go back to work, with this disguise that I'm now "useful" again because I'm busy again. But that time at home, that was precious.

POSTSCRIPT: *"I am actually in social services now," she later says in an email. "I am a program coordinator for a program that helps felons get back into the workforce."*

"From Point A to Point B"

"We're all in this together."
LYNDSEY FOLGER

She has been a flight attendant for a major airline since 1989. "At that time, we still had smoking on board, if you can believe that. But I took the job knowing that it was soon going nonsmoking, that it was already in the works. When I started, we had height and weight requirements. I had to be weighed in; it was still a part of our life. And if you were within a certain weight, you could weigh in just once a year. But if you had problems, you'd have to weigh in twice a year, or sometimes three times a year. The height requirement I could understand, but the weight was definitely about aesthetics. You can't get away with that, now, of course."

When I first started, I remember flying the same route a couple months in a row. And this older gentleman would come on each time. He said, "Now, I know you young girls don't understand this because you just started, but back when I was flying, I always brought gifts for the stewardesses." So every time, he would bring us little gifts, like a Kleenex holder or something sweet. But he's from back in the time in the '70s, where that's what you did. You brought gifts for the crew members, and they were all female flight attendants. But, nowadays, that just doesn't happen.

Back in the day—I don't know if the word is that it was *classier*—but you just respected that this was a privilege to be able to get on an aircraft and go somewhere far away or even close within a short amount of time. And if there was more . . . just respect, now, that this is a really great opportunity. I think air travel has become a given for people, so they just expect certain things. And, to some extent, it is what the airlines [have] put out there as [what people can expect]. So, I get that as well. But I think sometimes when something becomes commonplace, we lose that respect. I always want all of us, me included, to not take things for granted.

I have been all over the world. I've been very, very lucky and blessed to do many wonderful things with my company. But with that, I always try and remind myself how truly privileged it is to be able to travel and to be able to just pick up and go. I mean, that's amazing, and not everyone in the world has that. When I was doing a lot of Europe, I would get my wines, cheeses, and chocolates from Europe. You know, why buy a beer at home when I can get better stuff and less expensive and bring it home? You just get used to that lifestyle.

People think it's all glam, and it's not, but it still truly is a very sought after job. Once you get in, you kind of get stuck in it because you just don't want to give it up. A lot of the airlines have gone through buyouts and things like that because we've gone through a lot with bankruptcies, and 9/11, and all that. We've gone through a lot in the recent years. And I'll tell you, these flight attendants who have many years and are definitely up there in age, it's really hard for them to decide to leave or not. Some leave and they're very happy, and others have regretted the decision.

(Laughs.) I've been doing this for 32 years. And counting.

Why do you laugh?

Oh, because sometimes it seems like 32 years should be a lot of seniority, but it's not in our industry. If you work in another company, say, for a large corporation for 32 years, you have a lot of seniority. But in our industry, your start date is everything. Everything revolves around your seniority date, it's how you bid what trips you're able to get. And we have flight attendants that have been flying 50-plus years because we don't have a retirement age!

What are some of the stressors for you in this work?

When you hear [in the media] about the extreme behaviors [like fighting and rudeness] that's going on, people are stressed. I mean, life has really gotten stressful in the last couple of years with the pandemic and being home and then finally saying, "Okay, let's fly now! They're opening things up!" "Now, they're closing things down." It's this constant "Yes, we can go now," "No, we can't." "Yes, this country will let us in." Then: "No, they won't." And it's hard. I think a lot of it also stems from people that are terrified of flying. I have to say flight attendants are very good at reading people, and when it gets down to the psychology of it, people that feel that they are not in control, they're usually the ones that will lash out, will have too much to drink because they're scared. But they won't tell you that. And a lot of times, in the news, you don't hear that aspect of it.

There are many variables, and flight attendants take those many variables and shove them all into this metal tube, close the door, and say, "Okay, go!" And *we're* the ones that have to deal with all that. You can say what you want, but *we* are the ones. We're being doctors, nurses, psychologists, you know, babysitters, I mean, you name it, we have to deal with it, because we're up there. Our training *has* to be good because we are faced with things that sometimes you can't anticipate. Somebody comes at you screaming or throws a tray at you, and you're like, "Oh my gosh, why did this all escalate so fast?" But it could be because that person lost their job or something else that has nothing to do with us or being in an airplane. But bottom line, we're called to deal with it; we have to, because we're the ones there.

I will say, thankfully, our training has changed a lot. We all do go through self-defense courses, and then situational awareness. When you're on the airplane, you only have access to certain items, and so you need to know how to use those in—God forbid—a situation where you need to protect yourself and others and certainly the cockpit. I mean, that is our goal: to protect the cockpit. So you need to know what you have access to instantly, if you need it. And if you have to use it, you have to use it.

When you think back prior to 9/11, airplanes would be hijacked, and we were taught to kind of comply and see how you could keep calm, keep everyone else calm, keep the hijackers calm, all that stuff. And then with 9/11, we realized, no, this *plane* can be used as a weapon. We were so heightened. Everybody was on edge. "We cannot let that happen again."

I remember where it was like, "Okay, I want to see everybody's hands." Somebody still has their hands under a blanket, and I'm like, "Nope, hands out. I want to see every hand." All of us were very conscious and very diligent about everything we were doing.

I remember I ran into a good friend of mine, and he said, "They're not going to win." I said, "No, they're not." Yes, it was scary, but I think all of us said, "You know what, no! This is our job. This is our airline. This is not going to be a weapon ever again." I feel most of us got right back into it and said, "No, this is ours. We're taking it back. They're not taking that from us." And I think passengers, especially right after that, passengers were great. They were so supportive of us. They were absolutely willing to help. And there was such camaraderie with passengers that we've never felt before or since.

Yes, things have been crazy and heightened right now. Absolutely. But truly, people are good. People do want to help other people. We just do, we really do, and it's sad to me that it doesn't get the notoriety that other things do, like the crazy situations that happen, the fights that break out, you know, that's what gets our attention in the media. But there are beautiful little moments that happen all the time, and I just wish people could see that [on the news] and could realize that [all these good things] happen all the time. And it's only out of goodwill. It's not out of, "Oh, watch what I did for someone; did you get this on video?" No, it's when somebody is struggling to lift a bag and somebody will stand up and say, "Oh, here, I'll help you." Or "I'll move my seat so you can be near your husband and children. I'm a father; I understand." I just wish that people could see *that* and know that it is there. You're talking about people from all over the world being on this plane, so we have this wonderful opportunity to all be together and realize we all want the same things. We just all want the same things in life, you know?

Just two weeks ago, I was sitting in a terminal because we had a break. And as we were getting back on the plane, this woman randomly came up, she and her husband, and said, "I just want to thank you for what you do every day. We are so grateful." And I was like, "Oh my god. Thank you so much for saying that."

People are aware of how much stress we're under right now. And I believe that people *do* know we're all in this together.

"How small the world is."
LAURA ZURCHER

She is vice president of a small freight forwarding company. "I work on ocean procurement. I also do a lot of our U.S. sea export shipments, and I manage a team. I started in this industry 20 years ago. I had graduated from St. Mary's College in South Bend, Indiana, with a political science degree. Go figure."

She is 45 years old. We talk on Zoom while she is visiting her parents for the Thanksgiving holiday during the pandemic. At this time, severe supply chain delays are having a significant impact on many businesses and industries.

The easiest way I can describe what I do is to say we are like travel agents for freight. We're the ones who help take it from point A to point B. You've seen those big steel boxes that are driving down the highway? And you've seen those big steel boxes that are on the rail cars? I move those.

We do import and export, rail, air, truck, and ocean. So, all modes of transport. If you called me because you wanted to ship your widgets to Germany, my first question to you would be how many? What is your piece count, your weight, and the dimensions of what you're sending? Are you sending one skid, or are you sending 40 skids, because it's going to determine how we're going to send them. We would also do your customs.

What you're hearing about right now on the news is how there are hundreds of. . . . Last week, I think, LA Long Beach hit a record of 111 or 115 container ships docked off the port of LA and Long Beach. Normal would be 20. And there's now 115.

If you go back to November of 2019 and you had wanted to send a 40-foot container box from Shanghai to LA it would have cost you about $1,500, give or take. Now, at the peak of this year, it's costing you about $15,000. That peak has since dropped, so maybe it's costing you about $10,000 now. That's all supply and demand.

When this all started to hit the news, I started getting text messages: "Do you see what's going on?" And I say to people, "What do you think I have been complaining about for 10 months? It's been going on since last year."

Is it because of the pandemic?

It's consumerism. First, the world shuts down for a few months. People aren't manufacturing, people aren't shipping, people aren't in the office, right? And so, the steamship lines took vessels out of rotation because there wasn't enough freight to warrant having all those vessels going. So they pulled vessels out. Well, then the manufacturing starts back up, and as that starts up the world starts to reopen. We as consumers, for the last however many months, hadn't been going out to dinner, we hadn't been going on vacation. But we *had* been redoing our kitchens. And we've been building additions to our homes, and we've been buying Amazon freight. So, instead of spending money on experiences, we bought something tangible. And so, when the economy started to come back, instead of coming back as a trickle, it just was full force because all of this backlog of all this freight that was needed. And it just went like gangbusters.

I think people [in the industry] saw it coming. I mean, that's my own personal opinion, obviously. I think people saw it coming. I think they liked the money that was coming with it. If you have a container that used to cost $1,500, and now it costs $10,000, that just perpetuates money and more money and more money. And that cost all goes back to the person who wants to know why their jeans cost more, their milk costs more, whatever product it is. I mean, you look at the price of lumber, now, and it's outrageous.

They didn't expect it to last as long as it did. Everybody kept saying, "Oh, this will just be six months." Now in the industry they're saying that this is going to continue through next year.

Are you finding ways to adjust to it now that it's been here for a while?

We have been adjusting to it every month. I mean, in the industry, we would say, "Oh, gosh, okay, I think September will be okay; I can breathe." And then October is worse. Even April and May. Now? We're almost at a standstill. Now it's at a point where truckers are saying we don't have any capacity to take any more shipments for the rest of the year.

Back in the good old days, you could have said to me that you have a container-worth of freight to pick up. And in a day or two's time I would have a container to you. Now you tell me you have a container with freight to pick up, and I tell you I hope I can get it by Christmas. Or the New Year.

What frustrates me is that it took our government this long. It's mystifying. I feel like the government—and I'm a Democrat, so I'm not, you know . . . but that's part of the frustration. I said to my colleagues this summer, "Why is no one talking about this? Why are we not seeing it in Congress? Why are we not seeing Biden step in? Why is no one talking about this?" People are finally talking about it now because of Christmas. People want their Christmas presents. But do you know when Christmas presents hit the U.S.? The summer. Peak season is July to September. That's when your Christmas presents come to the U.S. because they've got to get through customs. And now you're barking around about this at the end of October, beginning of November! You're already three, four months late to the game.

For us, it has made for some very long nights. I'm routinely working till midnight. Lately, I'm not because of the standstill that's happened. But at the peak of all of this, I was working 16-hour days. What might have taken me half a day now takes me five and a half days, because you can't find the equipment and you can't find the vessel and you can't find the trucker to do it.

How is your staff weathering this?

They are weathering it, some better than others. I think we were all exhausted. I kept saying to them, "I can't keep seeing emails from you guys at 11:30 at night. You need a break just as much as everybody needs a break." The business is always gonna be there. There's always going to be an issue, right? So you've got to take a breather. I think I've tried to convey that I'm here just as much as they are, and I'm in the weeds just as much as they are, but I'm not so much in the weeds that I'm not there to help you.

How are you weathering this, yourself?

If you talked to me in 2019, it would be a whole different story. Right now, it's a very interesting and stressful environment, but I have to tell you, I love what I do. Which maybe doesn't sound like it right now. (Laughs.)

Your work gives you an interesting vantage point. How has that impacted your worldview?

My sense of geography is so much better than I ever learned anywhere in school, even college. The amount of geography that I didn't know was astonishing to me when I first started in this industry. It really does show you how small our world is. I mean, every day I'm talking to people in Australia and China and Europe and India and the Middle East. I'm talking daily with people who are in Jordan and Iraq. All of these different regions and all of these different cultures.

And that's something to get used to. You learn that you can write the same email to three people and offend them in three different ways. Let's say, we get an email from our colleagues in India, and it's really harsh. I mean, real direct, real harsh. It might offend one of my employees. I have to explain to them a lot that they weren't writing that in an offensive or angry tone. That is just how, culturally, they do business. In India, whoever yells loudest and longest wins. And sometimes you have to "yell" back. You have to learn how to do this push and pull. I kind of celebrate it. It also has probably affected my views on religion and other cultural aspects because you learn how to be respectful of different cultures and what that means. I probably learned it without even realizing it, to be honest with you, because it's just something now that seems so ingrained in my everyday work.

It gives me sort of an understanding and a gratitude of how the world works and how different cultures work. It definitely has given me a wanderlust. I would love to be able to see all of these different places that I ship things to every day.

[Her father, whom she is visiting during the holiday, leans into the frame and tells me to ask about some of the strangest things she's shipped.]

I have shipped frozen jellyfish to Thailand from Florida. I have shipped a whole paper manufacturing mill that was disassembled and put into containers. I have shipped a water treatment plant for the U.S. government for the Army going to Djibouti in Africa. I have shipped an airplane! This is where you realize how much money some people have. I shipped a personal airplane, like a Cessna, that someone had crated.

(Laughs.) I am 45 years old, but Mom and Dad are still very proud.

"It's not a very glamorous job, but I don't mind what I do."
ROBERT KOPYSTYNSKY

He has been an over-the-road (long-distance) UPS truck driver for 17 years.

"I go from Chicago to Ontario, then down to Anaheim, California, then across to Memphis, Tennessee, and then back home. Takes four days. There's two of us in the truck. It's a team operation, and we switch every 10 and a half hours or so. One sleeps and one drives. It's got a twin bed in there. There's a curtain in between the front

part of the cab and the sleeper unit. I have six inches of memory foam on top of the mattress to try to make it easier to sleep, which, right now is very challenging. I got diagnosed with a torn rotator cuff. I don't know how it happened."

Five years before this conversation, as he neared retirement, he ran for and was elected vice president of Teamsters for the Central Region for a five-year term.

I mean, there's a lot worse things that can be done for a living. I was fortunate to land where I did in the transportation industry. Ending up with and staying with UPS was the best decision I ever made because of the wages, the benefits, the pension. Benefits are top notch, and the wages, there's a payroll progression there. When I first started there, it was two and a half years to reach full scale. Currently, it's four years and they're reassessing that now because there's such a shortage of drivers out there; everybody is scrambling for drivers. The benefits in the pension are better than anywhere else in the industry. So, you know, it was a wise choice on my part, and they're not going to go anywhere. They're definitely financially stable.

When I first applied there, they offered me a position doing package delivery. I was 50 years old when I applied, and I told him, I says, "You know, I'm 50 years old; 250 stops a day? I don't see that. That's not gonna work." And then two months later, they called me for a tractor trailer position. And I jumped on it. Yeah. It's top of the food chain.

Two hundred and fifty stops, is that what they average in a day?

In an urban area, yes. It's really pathetic, in my opinion, because of the fact that you hear time and time again, how people say, you know, "We love our UPS guy." And yet the company terrorizes them. [The drivers] can never do enough, no matter what they do, it's not enough. Everything in that truck is monitored. There's inward facing cameras. There's sensors on all the doors, there's electronic recording devices for the truck itself for how you drive it. Everything is timed. And they're always looking to get more out of those package car guys. You see them on the street, they don't waste time. Reason why is the company is busy trying to figure out how to get more out of them. I mean, how much more can you get out of them? So that's one of the reasons why I want to be involved in the [union] negotiations, because there definitely has to be limits in place. And it's not like UPS is struggling financially. Seven billion dollars net profit is huge. Nobody else in the transportation industry is anywhere near that. So they're not hurting.

But I don't mind what I do. I like to travel and especially now when the weather's good. I'm running across I-70 through the Rocky Mountains every week, and it's just a beautiful part of the country. I love going through Colorado and Utah. It's gorgeous. And I'm fortunate I got seniority, so I can pick a route like that. But a lot of people just don't want to be away from home. My wife is not a big fan of what I do. I mean, we haven't been married that long. We just got married last year in August, you know. And she's not a big fan of it. But she knows that the end is in sight.

What made you decide to run for union leadership?

I had met the people that were running against [James P.] Hoffa. I liked what they had to say. And I believed in them. So I was very active in the campaign. You know, things like when we needed petitions signed, I was active in the petitioning role. I was active in the fundraisers and whatnot.

And they came up to me one day, and they're like, "You know, we've noticed when you talk, people listen. We'd like you to be part of the slate." And I started laughing. I was like, "*Excuse* me?" (Laughs.) It was something I never considered doing. And I told him, I said, "I'll be honest with you, I really don't know anything about it. I do know what the union's about and whatnot." I mean, I was an elected union steward, but I never really ran for an office like this. The only thing I knew was if I worked harder than everybody else, my chances were pretty good.

I ended up—out of 60,000 votes—I ended up winning by a 10,000-vote margin. So my strategy turned out to be effective. Plus, the guy I was running against ended up getting indicted, anyway. You may have heard of him: John Coli. He was indicted for shaking down the film studios over there by 14th and Western. They do the shows *Chicago Fire* and *Chicago Med*. He was shaking them down for $25,000 every quarter. The IRS was investigating the owner of the studio, and he cut a deal with them. He said, "Well, what if I can give you John Coli?" John Coli had been indicted previously; he was no stranger to a grand jury. And so, they're like, "Go ahead; talk to us." So they wired him up. He'd go in there and pick up the checks and the payoffs. They indicted him on five counts of accepting gifts of value from an employer, and one count of racketeering.

Even though the indictment didn't come till after the election, I was able to beat him, and he wasn't happy about it at all. He wasn't popular with a lot of members, and people wanted change. There was a lot going on with the Central

States Pension Fund, which made it ripe for reformers to come in. It made things a lot easier for us to come in and take over.

When you took on this new role, did you discover skills you didn't previously know you had?

Yeah, you know, communicating with the members. One of the things that I've always felt is important is to be honest with people. It was kind of funny because when I was out campaigning, people would ask me to make a promise. "What can you promise us if we vote for you?" And I was like, "Well, I can't promise you this; I can't promise you that." (Laughs.)

In the back pages of the teamster magazine, they always list all the various different investigations that are going on regarding corrupt officers and whatnot. So I'd tell the members the one thing I *can* promise you is that you'll never read about me in the back pages of the teamster magazine. And they would laugh, like "We can live with that." That's something I *can* legitimately promise, but I can't tell you we're gonna get you this, or we're gonna get you that. I said, "It's called negotiations for a reason."

It's interesting, Hoffa and I don't really get along too well. I ran on an opposition reform slate against his people, and he wasn't very happy about that, but I'm not worried about his opinion that much, to be honest with you. He's been a detriment rather than an asset, to be honest with you.

I don't get typically assigned to anything by Hoffa because of the fact that, you know, we don't get along. Jim Hoffa, his background is that of a corporate lawyer. So he always—his favorite line is "We all got to try to get along." (Laughs.) And that just doesn't work in today's world. The more you give a corporation, the more they want, and the harder they're going to push. And we're seeing that across the board with all employers nowadays. I don't care what industry it is, you know, especially when you got behemoths like Amazon out there.

My five-year term is up next March, but the group that I'm associated with said that they're guaranteeing me an administrative position with the IBT [International Brotherhood of Teamsters] if they win the election. Depending on what the position is, if I'm intrigued by it, and if I like the offer, I'll accept it. I want to sit across the table from these people just once in my career.

What would that mean to you? You just got a big smile when you said that.

Yeah, I'd like to say no to them because nobody has in a long time. For the last 20-plus years Hoffa let them do whatever they want. And it's got to change. It really does. It *has* to change, you know. The company keeps on taking, and they keep on crying that "Well, if we don't get this we're gonna go bankrupt. And if we don't get that we're gonna go bankrupt." But they showed a $7 billion net profit. And they still keep on throwing this bankruptcy threat around. And every time I hear it, I laugh. I'm like, "How do you think we're going to take $7 billion away from you? Come on, let's get real here."

You know, something I've seen over the years, and it's gotten worse and worse as time has gone on, is the way employers try to bully the employees. And I like to try to stand up against that. You know? I don't think anybody should be bullied, you know what I mean? So many employees today are afraid. Like when I was working as a [union] steward, they'd talk to me [about things that happened], and I'd tell them, "You need me to file a grievance?" And they're like, "Well, I don't want a target on my back." And I just kind of laugh about it. And I was like, "Well, what do you think *I* have? I got a bigger target than anybody around here." And I mean, some of the things could have been simple wins, such as funeral leave where someone was shorted on the day. And I was like, "It's an easy fix. Give me a grievance, and I can get you paid for it." "Well, I don't want to be a target." "But you're owed the money." "Well, I don't want to be a target." Fear. The companies, see, they thrive on that.

I've never been fired by them. And I've stood up to them. I mean, I've had some pretty heated debates with them where I was literally just about nose to nose with one of the higher-ranking managers of the building I work out of. I don't care. Because I knew I was right. And there were witnesses there, so I knew things weren't gonna escalate. But I was gonna stand my ground because people need to do that nowadays. Like I say, these employers are just getting bolder and bolder.

"Capitalism is what takes the fun out of people working."
ELEANOR DELORES

She works for Amazon Logistics in a warehouse which is referred to as The Last Mile. "We get the packages out. I started as a tier one operations on the floor. Now I am a tier three; I'm also a driver trainer.

"I'm over 50. That's all I ever say, now, 'I'm over 50.'"

In the morning, you walk in and of course we have on what we call our hobo clothes. Jeans, comfortable. They want to make sure you have good solid shoes; like you couldn't wear Crocs, couldn't wear flip-flops. Women want to wear their fun gym shoes. I mean, the young girls especially tend to want to look cute at work. You punch in on the clock.

And then you get in a group—this was pre-COVID—called stand-up meetings. You stand in a circle, you get what's happening for the day while you do your stretches. You find out what the goals are, and then they remind you about certain safety things. "Remember to push your carts, don't pull them. Remember to wear your gloves." They did tell people you should stretch before you start work because it's the stretching—Well, if you don't stretch, you're not limber, and that's where you can have injuries.

You need to keep a certain pace. You have a scanner, and you attach it to your badge barcode so they can meter how fast you are going. If they need somebody to pick up the speed, they're going to say you need to pick up the speed. So if you're bringing your rate down, they say, "Okay, we'll switch it out." That way we can keep that momentum going at pretty much the speed that they want you to be at.

Does it ever become monotonous?

It all depends on who you are, let's put it that way. I'm kind of an oddball in terms of how I look at jobs. I'm kind of like the Mary Poppins. "Every job, you can make it fun." We would sing, we would dance, we'd do a groove while we're working.

Some people, though, just want to take that scan gun—because it's a big gun—and just toss it and go, "I'm outta here." So, it all depends. But yeah, it can be monotonous. Absolutely.

The whole thing is "customer obsession," they call it, making sure the customer gets their package when they want it. So if you don't have those metrics, you're going to fail, and customers are going to go elsewhere. So that's where Amazon has made themselves very successful, they keep the metrics going. I never felt abused by the metrics; kind of like, for me it was a fun way of "Okay, how can I keep improving myself?" Because I'm one of these personal best-type people, too.

What's morale like in a room like that?

Well, it goes up and down. Corporate America, unfortunately, is looking for that dollar. Capitalism is what takes the fun out of people working. And some people, they are afraid to speak up. Especially in America. You've got immigrants who are legal, working legally, but they're afraid to speak up because they don't know if they're going to lose their job.

I've been very fortunate. I came from a very strong, Polish American family, and my mother said, "You speak up. You don't be disrespectful, but you speak up, you stand up for yourself." So I'm fortunate that I always had that self-confidence, where other people, they're limited. You know, they might have like a huge family that they're supporting, and their spouse can't get a job. And for whatever reason, a lot of these Amazon positions, this is their second job, so they're just exhausted.

Have you seen in the news that Amazon workers wanted to unionize? It started in Alabama. Ultimately, [Amazon] did stop the unionization, and I found that kind of sad because by now corporations should be prepared if that's what their workers want. This isn't the 1930s. So it worries me that some of the lower level, the tier one, they're just starting, and they're trying just to make ends meet. Yes, Amazon was one of the first to bring [starting wage] up to $15 an hour. But people need to make a lot more money to really have a decent wage now to afford living in the United States. Medical costs are outrageous, and etcetera, etcetera. So it makes me sad that they feel that they're not strong enough as a company to allow a union. And that's what bothers me.

I'm in a position where I'm not afraid of Amazon. I'm not afraid of any company because they're just an entity. And yeah, they might have a bunch of lawyers, but really, you want to beat up on one person? So I'm not worried about that. But we did have protests at our warehouse, and if you look at—I think it was on Fox News and maybe CBS—you'll get a sense of what they were protesting and why they wanted to be unionized. You'll get a sense of what some of the tier one workers were going through. But they're still working there. Nobody was let go, so kudos to [Amazon]. They just didn't want the union. They were doing whatever it took to not have the union happen. And there was. . . . Well, nobody felt threatened, let's put it that way. But my intellect still says, "*Why* don't you want this? What's going on?"

Everything else they're doing, like with safety, and you do have access to free mental health counseling, that's fine. I mean, they do a lot of things. But then the businessperson in me says, "Well, you do that for CYA [cover your ass] legal reasons. Do you really care about people?" And then those who are more conservative: "Well, are we *supposed* to care about people?" And then I get into that philosophical discussion. I'm like, "Well, you don't want to throw people away." But that's what a lot of people on the floor are feeling now, that once they're done and over with you just bring another crowd in. And that's sad because that's not how I felt back in 2018. It's changing bit by bit by bit; it's changing fast.

My big thing is I would like Amazon to do one thing. Here's my big thing: Those trucks—we keep increasing the number of trucks that are on the road. Why isn't Amazon putting money towards infrastructure? I haven't seen anything about that. And I would say they might be doing it quietly, but they should be doing it widespread. They're beating up our roads with all the vans, the box trucks, the big 18-wheelers; they're huge, you see them everywhere. So, if you're going to do that, put some money into it, you know, be part of the community in that regard.

They do a lot of other things. They help during COVID; we felt very safe during COVID. So they do the right thing, in that there was free testing, we were six feet distancing. I mean, they did a lot of things to make sure, but then, as one person said, they also benefit from all of us working constantly during COVID, and people were afraid. Their online business grew because of COVID, so yeah, they helped with people who didn't have money, you know, the community food banks and things like that. But for me—it's just me—it's an optics thing. I want to see something big, like infrastructure. I want people to be paid more, and I want people to be able to not be afraid to unionize. And if that's the fear, speak up! And hear from the people why they want the union, and make those changes. What are you afraid of?

When you have a CEO and he's moving into the more creative areas of Amazon wire services, and he and his brother have Blue Horizon, the rocket going off, and they're going to take off in space together, that'd be interesting, because that'd be fun. But, you know, find out what is it that people are lacking, and then act upon it—$196 billion you're worth, oh my god, just having one of your billion dollars. Gandhi has said it, the world has enough for everybody's needs, but it doesn't have enough for everybody's greed. I'm paraphrasing it, but the need and the greed is what America is about. And it disturbs me.

God, how many times have I said, "I wish I was a billionaire"? I'd be like, "Where can we fix this? Where can we fix that?" Let's not be stupid. We know corporations and governments work hand in hand and you've got lobbyists, so let's not pretend that it's separate. It is all together. So let's fix it. Let's take care of those things, so everybody can have a decent life. The disparity is huge in this country now. I thought we learned better. What happened? And now there are some states talking about taking away child work laws. *What?* You're gonna have kids working long hours? We did that in the early 1900s.

I wish I had been in a position of power. In my belief, you have to connect with the people versus being all about the dollar. And if this is what I'm supposed to be doing, this work, the training I do, I want to help them have a better life.

But the reason I just keep going back is because I know I can make a difference. I wake up at 5 in the morning, I get to work, I don't get home sometimes till 8, and I crash, exhausted. And I do it four days a week. It's an exhausting job physically, even though I'm not lifting packages anymore like I used to. I used to lift those big heavy bags. But I go to bed exhausted going, "Oh my god, I should just quit," and then I wake up and I'm like, "No, no, no, I'm gonna go back in."

POSTSCRIPT: In an email a few months after our conversation, she says she quit. "I had had enough of the abusive mentality from management. They had lost their vision of taking care of people. Over time it just became too abusive in terms of how they kept pushing and pushing and pushing for improving the numbers. And they put a ton of money into paying lawyers to train those of us in leadership to stop any kind of unionizing. It was just sick.

"After I left, I tried very hard not to purchase anything from Amazon, but I kept thinking of all those people who needed jobs. Sigh. So I do buy some stuff from Amazon. Everything else, I go to brick-and-mortar stores again so I can interact with people. Because really, that's what it's all about. People."

After leaving Amazon, she went to bartending school and is now thoroughly enjoying being a bartender.

"I am who I am."
BRODERICK LOVE

"I am, at best, a tier one associate of Amazon, still at this point. Initially, when I started there three years ago, I was just a temp. I thought I was an actual Amazon employee, but when you first come in the door, if you're not in management, you're just a regular temp. You're on schedule, you're an employee of the company, you have a position, but you don't have any benefits. You're there, but only as a temp, meaning that they can get rid of you at any point at their discretion.

"When I first applied here, I already had preconceived notions in my mind because of all the rumors that surround Amazon. I heard, most likely from social media and the news, about employees having hardships to bear outside of work as well as coming into work and having to deal with the anxiety of work and everything that is expected of you on the clock."

His shift is from 1:05 a.m. to 11:35 a.m.

My interview for this job was very, very vague. There was the drug test and there was no personal conversation, it was done in a mass setting, like it was a group of about 20. It was just like: "This is what's going on; this is what's expected of you; this is what you'll be paid; this is when you start to get benefits." And that was it. "Any questions?"

I was originally assigned to stow, which is basically after a package has been inducted and labeled, I was the person that scanned it to its designated stow location.

Did you find that the rumors you had heard about the job were validated or contradicted?

Oh, it's all in the person. I've worked in overwhelming industries, so my stress tolerance level might be higher than someone else's. I worked at O'Hare airport way before I worked at Amazon. I used to push aircrafts off the gate. I towed them from the gate to the hardstand. I did this in all seasons of weather. And my superiors were always complaining at me, expecting more. So when it came to Amazon, I felt like my [threshold] was higher as far as how I could tolerate a lot more. So like, if a conveyor belt breaks down, oh my god, managers start losing it. If engineers can't give them an actual, factual time of when it will be repaired, it's like, *"Agh!* Okay, I gotta call my superiors and tell them what's going on." But me in that situation, I feel for the manager, but at the same time, it's not human error. That's mechanical error. I'm not going to stress out over that.

Why do you think they get so stressed about that?

I guess it's a lot of money involved. We're expected to kick out 60,000 packages for delivery in the morning. And it's a real problem when there's a mechanical issue or my truck is late. That means that now you have to take people, potentially associates or managers, away from their other job duties that were already on the schedule for the day, to now get this other work inducted and ready to be delivered. So that slows down the operation drastically. Because now it's not as many people out on the floor to build routes as fast as we were in the beginning of the day. Now they have to pay more drivers that weren't expected for deliveries that day to then deliver those late packages.

This year, we've got a lot of mandatory overtime. So when you're getting off work on your Friday, or whatever day of the week it might be, you go home, and you're getting ready to lay down and plan your weekend, and you get a notification like, "Hey, forget your plans, we need you to come to work." And that's the bottom line. And that's usually dictated by customers, in my opinion.

Based on what I've seen so far, if you want to climb the ladder, you're not gonna have to kill somebody, but you're gonna have to do some unfavorable things in the workplace. You're gonna have to be buddy-buddy with somebody that you ordinarily wouldn't be buddy-buddy with. I feel like this: I'm going to be myself in the workplace and outside the workplace. I'm not going to change my character for anybody. You know, I am who I am.

A bad day for me is basically when they don't recognize you as a person. They just say, "Hey, do this, do that, stop doing that, go over here, do this." And it's like they bounce you around all day. And no one stops to say, "Hey, I'm sorry. I know I've been yanking your chain and having you do different jobs." Nobody takes the time to say that at the end of day. They half-heartedly say, (speaks rotely) "Thank you. Appreciate your hard work today." It's like, okay.

Do you think they may have been told to say that at the end of the day?

Exactly. Yeah, that's how it comes across to me. You know, I believe everybody gets a little complacent.

What's a good day for you?

Where everybody's laughing. We're at a stow, whatever, laughing at each other and everything, you know, it's a good time. We're working hard. We're still getting the job done. You know, management might not like *how* we do things sometimes. But you know, we get it done. So, and then everybody's happy. It's good to me when the management and associates can have a good day together.

We all feel like we could be paid a lot more than what we've been paid. They're making so much money, but the little guy. . . . They actually had to negotiate to give drivers back their tips that Amazon took away from them for a while.

I believe there was an option on the app for you to tip your delivery person. And those tips went to the employee. Well, Amazon took those tips for a while. It was a shock to me when I found out. It sounds like a lot of something went on, but they gave those tips back. Like somebody sued them.

How does that make you feel as a tier one worker?

Initially, I'm frustrated. I mean, I'm like any other person: that's just disgusting. You want me to be satisfied with peanuts while you're eating and living fabulously, and we're struggling down here to survive? When you think of what they're raking in, and then they send this guy to space.

But in this capitalist society, I'm not surprised. I take it with a grain of salt, you know?

What do you wish Jeff Bezos knew about what you do?

To care more about his employees. Not just putting policies and people in place to keep an *appearance* of concern, but where your employees actually do things for their care. Not just wellness checks, but people you can call and talk to, who will say, "Are you physically healthy?" Give us something we can enjoy and speak about [when we talk about] coming to work, besides an occasional catered meal or salad party, thank you. I don't know. It feels a lot like gesture.

It doesn't feel authentic?

No, no, it's not authentic; it's not genuine. We as a company, we don't . . . there's no humanity. You know, it's like, just the necessary concern. You know, nobody really cares. I'm not looking to make anybody my best friend at work, but I want people to understand, it's not just about the job. And a lot of times management will make it seem like it's just about a job.

What would you change if you were in charge?

I would probably make it more important that management becomes familiar with their staff and associates. Rarely do they ever really find out what their employees are into. Some will come and ask you, "What do you like doing when you're at work?" You know, others won't even ask you that, they'll just ask how long we've been there, and some very vague questions. That's just very not personal, and it's always something work related. And it's not like, "Hey, are you a parent? Do you have a grandmother that you're taking care of? How's your personal life, if you don't mind talking about it?"

You know, maybe they just need somebody to care for a moment.

Do you feel like it's risky for you to talk about Amazon like this with me?

I was concerned about that initially when you asked me to do this, but at the same time, I quickly threw those worries out the window. I feel like I understand company policy and protecting the way Amazon does its thing, but I don't think anything that we're talking about is dangerous to my job.

But if this should happen to reach Bezos and it makes a dent in his understanding, I'd be proud if it cost me my job. Hey, at least it mattered somewhere.

FOOD AND SERVICE

"You need to figure it out."
CHARLIE AYERS

He is a chef, cookbook author, and restaurateur. In the '90s, he was a chef for the Grateful Dead. He was Google's employee #53 and its first chef, from its first year until 2006. When he left, his stock options were worth $40 million, which he applied to opening Calafia Café and Market A Go-Go in Palo Alto, which operated from 2009 to 2018. "Sadly, I wasn't able to compete with the nearby newly opened high-end corporate chain restaurants. I couldn't keep up."

Today, he pursues multiple passions and projects.

I'm really very blessed that I can taste things in my head, just from my past experience working with products and creating dishes. You're tasting, you're touching; there's textures and different mouth experiences and feelings with different foods. My industry is unlike many industries; I get to use all my senses in everything I do. Someone that works in the office environment, they don't use all those senses. My ex-wife used to jokingly say, "He's like Rain Man with food." My motto in the culinary industry is you never stop learning. There's something you can learn every day in the kitchen. It's just a daily occurrence.

When I first interviewed with Google, they were very small, there was only 18 people, and they were over the bicycle shop in Palo Alto. I thought,

"Wow, I don't think they're gonna make money. They're all playing. There's toys everywhere." I was very new to that culture.

The gentleman that I interviewed with ran the facilities part of things, and one of the things he told me was, "These people don't really know what they want, Charlie. They're all fresh out of college. Some of them had worked at other tech companies, and the format in the tech companies is very predictable, and they know what's going on all the time. What you need to do is something completely different that no one's ever done. What that is, I don't know, but you need to figure that out. The one advantage that you have is that we don't charge for our food. You really have a very big budget, and I'm never going to tell you how big it is, but I will tell you when you have to slow down the spending." And they never did tell me to slow down.

I had *carte blanche* to create a resort-like environment on a daily basis. I went from this very small [operation] to serving crowds of like Disneyland [proportions] on a daily basis. It's something that I adapted to and understood well.

But it took me a little bit of time to learn all this in the beginning. Larry Page* sat me down one day, and he said to me, "Do you know how much each one of these engineers makes an hour? Some of them made up to $300 an hour. So you have to understand, if I have a bunch of engineers emailing each other at work, saying, 'Where are we going out for lunch because they're serving Indian here, again?' two-thirds of that group leave for lunch. Then my productivity has gone from spiking like Kilimanjaro to flat like the plains of Illinois, because I have no work going on. And engineers, because of the way we treat them and exalt them and put them on this pedestal"—remember, this was what Larry Page was telling me at the time; he was aware of this—"they don't take one-hour lunches, they take two-, three-hour lunches. It's not so bad with one engineer or two engineers having lunch like that who make that much money, but when I have 20 or a whole team, we have nothing going on. And then when they come back, it takes them a good 45 minutes to get back into the thing they were working on."

I said, "But they work late."

He's like, "Yeah, but I want constant productivity."

After he taught me that's what he was looking for, I had to figure it out. We created a 36-week cyclical menu that [the engineers] were unaware of, and we mixed it up all the time. There was never ever a Taco Tuesday or Indian on Wednesday or fried fish on Fridays. It was mixed up enough where it was always

* Cofounder, with Sergey Brin, of Google.

exciting for them. And we never launched the menu until 10 minutes before 12 o'clock, so they never knew what they were going to eat. It became a thing where people are like, "You don't have to pay for the food at Google, and it's the best food in the Valley."

Some people are meant for the kitchen and understand the ebb and flow and the process of what needs to be done. My dad was an officer in the military, so that's where I learned to be able to not take any shit from anyone in the kitchen. I know you may have an opinion, but it's not gonna happen here, unless we're having a meeting, and we're looking for that. You can't have too many artists in the kitchen. Nothing really gets done.

So, as chef, you need to be left- and right-brained, oddly enough. [In addition to understanding food], it's understanding business, and it's understanding how people behave in business. The leaky faucet, that lightbulb that's left on, letting employees eat whatever they want, not having a standard and control, not watching everyone—all these things are money out the door. And next thing you know, the business is closed. It's understanding that employee that's the nicest to you and wants to help you the most is the one that's stealing from you. It's understanding that you need to have cameras everywhere except the restroom. It's sad, but that's how humans are.

And you've learned to be the way you are because another chef taught you that way. You have these kids that want to be chefs and be the next Charlie Trotter, and you have to let them understand that they may not get there. You may not be that famous dude that you want to be. And that's okay, as long as you are providing for yourself and your family, and you have pride in what you do. You're always trying to do better than you did the day before and not become complacent.

And that's the thing. In today's culinary world, because of TV, all the kids want to do competitions. "I have to be the best." And that's not what it's about. It's about camaraderie and helping each other and bringing each other up. It's that camaraderie thing that when you get a chance to do that, you're like, "*This* is why we do it!"

Do you mentor those young ones now coming into culinary arts?

As a side thing, I also place private chefs in very wealthy homes. It's very lucrative. I get a percentage of their annual salary. So I'm holding their hand in helping them learn that whole process. I'm calling on different chefs that have worked for me in the past, that I know will represent me well. I've got five or six of these chefs who used to work for me over the years that I can cherry pick and place them in these homes. A lot of them have [done well] because they listened to me.

I say, "The client doesn't want you talking to them. That's not why you're hired. You're just a fly on the wall. And if they engage with you, *then* you reciprocate, but never start. The most you can do is say hello. But don't do anything else, like, 'Hey, did you watch the baseball game last night?' They don't want to hear that."

It's the ones that have learned that that have done very well, where others are like, "I can't believe you had me go to that home." I'm like, "I told you the deal." Some people don't understand, and they're like, "I'm not their servant." I say, "Actually, yes, you are. You're in the hospitality industry. You're in service. This is what you do, regardless of if you like it or not."

What did you learn from your years as a personal chef for the Grateful Dead?

Ah, loyalty, loyalty. And trust. I jokingly tell people that working with the Grateful Dead is like working with the mafia. You don't ever leave them until you're dead. They'll always call in a favor. When the Grateful Dead had their 50th reunion anniversary in Chicago and then at Levi's Stadium in Santa Clara in 2015, they brought me back in, probably a month before it all started, so I could begin catering for the new band that was starting, which was Dead & Company with Bob Weir and John Mayer.

I work with them not because the management or the musicians love my food; it's that management knew they could trust me. They would say to me, "You do exactly what these musicians do. You invoke emotion and make people feel something that they've never experienced before, and they want that back again." That's what the food is.

What are you passionate about right now?

I'm working with a plant-based seafood company right now. The name of the company is Ish. We make shrimpish, crabish, salmonish. It's all plant-based. It's all vegan, kosher, halal. We want to make everyone happy. And it tastes amazing. We've done sampling to thousands of people. And then we tell them, this isn't real shrimp, or this isn't real crab. And they're completely amazed. It opens a lot of opportunity and doors for people that no longer can eat seafood or shellfish because of health conditions. Now they can enjoy that experience again, without the dangers. And you have another segment of people that because of religious reasons, they don't ever eat it. But they've always been curious. Or maybe they *do* eat it with no one knowing. You know, everyone's a secret eater. But now they can eat it in the open and feel good about it.

One of the largest seafood and fishing companies in the world is investing in this. That tells you something. This is the future.

You are *a constant learner.*

You have to be, you have to be to be good. I think that's what keeps things exciting, where you're constantly learning and being able to apply what you've learned and move forward.

"The universe has given us permission to do the best we can."
AMY MORTON

She has been a restaurateur since opening her first restaurant in Chicago's Old Town in the 1980s. As the daughter of Arnie Morton, founder of the Morton Restaurant Group and Morton's Steakhouse, and the granddaughter of restaurateur Morton C. Morton, she has worked in all phases of dining since she was 15 years old. "Though, when I was 10, I was sweeping out the construction site that would become Arnie's."

We talk on the phone the day before the first Thanksgiving of the pandemic. She sits in the front window of Found Kitchen and Social House, a restaurant she founded 10 years earlier in Evanston, a northern suburb of Chicago.

If you peeked in the window right now, you'd see me in a chair, practically laying down with my feet on the window. I've poured myself a glass of red wine for while I talk to you. Behind me is an empty restaurant, yet with people working; tables not set up for dining, but for takeout. There are about 30 bags set up for our first pickups; tomorrow we'll have about 120. We started working early this morning and are still chugging along. Our executive and our all-female management team—love that!—got everything organized. We have extra hands, we're working through this, and everybody's in a great mood, just doing their thing. Christmas carols are playing.

Doing this work is about making hard decisions quickly and retaining our capital. So that's the name of the game. We're going to lose over 60 percent of restaurants in the country by the end of this [pandemic], big and small. So, on the business side, I am whittling down every carrying cost I have. We had 120-plus employees last January. We probably have 10 now. And starting January 1, we'll have less. (Her second mobile phone rings.) Would you hold on one second?

(Into the phone:) I'm so sorry. We are a hundred percent sold out and, in fact, we had to make more because we have so many orders. I'm so, so sorry. It's the first time we've ever tried this. Please do try us for Christmas or New Year's. Thank you for supporting us. Bye.

Sorry. What that was, we decided to do two packages for Thanksgiving. Since we closed, we've been trying to do different things to keep going. We're doing this Thanksgiving To Go. We thought, "Oh, we'd love to do 100 packages." We did 262, which we're really happy about. We offered dinners for two and for six to eight. We were positive the dinners for six to eight were going to be the rage. We had only a few orders for six to eight. And 200 for two because people really are following the [CDC] rules. Thank God! Fortunately, we have Christmas and New Year's to deal with—or, no, not to *deal* with, but to be *blessed* with, right? In terms of doing major sales. So that's on the one hand.

On the other hand—this is the silver lining side—I have to be honest, this has been one of the most invigorating years of my life because as an operator—well, I should say as someone who develops concepts for a living, because I'm not just an operator, there's a million great operators who don't necessarily develop concepts—but for me, by necessity, I feel like I keep channeling my dad because every single day I *get* to, not only do I *have* to, but I *get* to come up with a new concept every day. We'll go to our farmers, we'll see what they *need* to sell and work from there. We'll do amazing, really cool anniversary dinners for people that *do* want to celebrate, or we'll start a juice bar, which is what I did in the summer. So that's been the other side of the coin.

Plus, I am . . . well, of *course*, I'm neurotic and crazy. Everybody in this business is. And truthfully, I have always had so many deep, dark worries in the past: we have a bad week; we have a bad month; we have a bad winter; we have a bad year—I mean, oh my god, what I put myself through! But this time it is the universe, and it is beyond our own individual control. And so even though I have control within what's going on at the end of the day, I just feel there's no blame, there's no guilt, there. I mean, I just feel like the universe has given us permission to do the best we can and know that we're not responsible. So there is a crazy freedom in this time.

How is your staff doing, the ones that you were not able to keep on?

Well, people are furloughed, so it means that they have a job when we reopen. People that were on insurance maintain it. Very, very few people in this industry are on it. It's usually just the management, so it's very tough. I mean, after the shutdown happened, I began to realize it would be at least through January, so we try to do everything that we can for the team. With all of our to-go orders, all the money we make in gratuity, we distribute to all of the team who aren't able to be here in the restaurant. But you know, it doesn't really even scratch the surface. But we do the best we can. And for sure this Christmas we'll either give a ham or some sort of dinner to everybody for their family.

   The hardest thing is our players. My chef at the Barn Steakhouse, who, by the way, worked with me at my very first restaurant in 1989 in Old Town, said to me twenty times, "Don't furlough my guys, furlough me because my guys *can't* get furloughed." Even though these guys have green cards and papers, the Hispanic-slash-Latino community rarely apply for unemployment because they're afraid. And these guys are the ones that are *always* working two jobs. They run from one to another, and they save for their families, and they send money home. And so that's the worst part of this. We heard, for example, that our amazing dishwasher, who we hired eight years ago coming out of homelessness, who got her first apartment she'd ever had after she started working here and just had her second grandbaby last week, she just learned this weekend she can't get any more unemployment. I mean, it is so *wrong*! But, you know what? The light at the end of the tunnel is that Trump actually lost!

I sense so much energy in you. You seem to enjoy thinking on your feet and meeting a challenge. And it sounds like this situation is allowing you to let those abilities and skills flower and grow. Is that accurate?

Ten thousand percent. The challenge has been—I mean, I'm not going to call it insurmountable because that would mean a challenge that we couldn't meet. The challenge of this, though, has been awesome. I feel like we've met it at every turn. I am the person who looks for the next challenge. I mean, the creative side is great. And the crazy thing is, in the past, I don't think I even kept my own checkbook in order, and this time around, the numbers might even be my favorite part.

You know, there's a strategy—it's not just the concept that matters, the numbers need to work. So, it's been great.

From day one of the pandemic, I believe it was the universe and continues to be the universe telling us that we are sick: "You're sick as a culture." We're sick as a world and we need to wake up, we need to slow down, and we need to take stock of who we are, and what we need as a people and as a world. And I think the reason this is not over is because we haven't learned the lesson yet. We haven't. It's promising, though, that we had so many reservations for dinner for two, as opposed to dinner for eight, so maybe people are starting to get it.

You sound very optimistic and upbeat in the face of all this. Are there things, though, that scare you and keep you up at night?

No. I already feel like I've been through all that. A couple of years ago, I had such massive anxiety and, oh my god, I just felt so responsible for *everyone*—my partners, my family; how was I going to do all these things? It seems cheesy to say, but this, what we're all going through, will be what binds this generation and all of us for the rest of our lives.

When this is over, how do you think you might be changed by it all?

I think one huge thing is—and it's something I've always said—I want to empower the people that I work with. I don't want to feel like I have to be the only one that does X, Y, and Z. And this situation has, more than anything, forced my hand at letting others do. And that might be the greatest thing I'll ever walk away with: I don't have to do it all; I have to trust people and know that people want to help. I always knew it in my head, but now I really *feel* it. I would say that is something huge that will be different. The other thing: I like to think I'm someone who doesn't take things for granted, but I know that I will be infinitely more attuned to that now. I'm thanking my lucky stars and being ever more grateful and thoughtful.

Hang on one second. (On the phone:) What's your name? Well, Jamie, let me check for you. (Calls out:) Danielle! Can Jamie Webster pick up at 6? Okay. Jamie? That would be fine. Ohhhh, thank you. Well, listen, there's not a person on the planet that has any experience with what we're all going through. So, thank you. We really appreciate you supporting us. Stay safe, and we will have your delicious meal ready for you at 6.

Okay, so sorry.

Do you have an image in your mind of what it will be like when we're all able to gather again at places like yours?

I think that it will be bustling again, but the difference will be people are going to be kinder. And I think that was the point of this whole thing.

"Why did it take a bitchy waitress to figure this out?"
SARAH WEBSTER NORTON

She was a server for 25 years before founding a nonprofit organization called Serving Those Serving, which is focused on supporting and providing mental health services to the service industry. She is 45 years old and a mother of three.

I worked everything from five-star, really exclusive stuff, to corporate places like [TGI] Fridays, to dive bars, so pretty much the whole gamut. I liked the dive bars the most. Well, because that was the management that had my back. I mean, I worked at some sketchy bars, and I've never felt safer because everybody was looking out for me there. Customers would try to walk out on their tabs, but it wouldn't work. They would try to hit on the waitresses, but they'd get ejected. They'd get too drunk, and they gotta go. At a dive bar, that's more my personality, anyway; that's more my style. I loved it. I could walk up to people and be like, "What the fuck do you want?" and they laugh, you know? I'm an actress. I was a child and young adult actress before I had kids, so I can pull it off wherever I am. But I get the best tips at dive bars, to be honest.

The abuse is rampant [in this industry]. I used to say people are coming in here for the sole purpose of abusing somebody wearing stripes.* They're coming in here because they know that if I say anything, if I stick up for myself or say anything back to them, that I will lose my job. And I've got babies, and I've got a husband I'm putting through school, so they know I can't say anything. I mean, I've been sworn at, and I've had things thrown at me. People think that we exag-

---

* "In the late '90s and early 2000s," she explains, "the servers and bartenders at TGI Fridays—coast-to-coast—had to wear red-and-white-striped shirts and suspenders with multiple pieces of 'flair.' Buttons and pins and flashing things. The worst part about working there was the 'clown' factor: 'Look at these idiots with flashing buttons and red and white stripes!' We knew we were targets for disrespect, and we were consistently let down by management."

gerate [about the abuse] but we're not. If anything, we underreport the abuse that happens to us in our industry because we're putting on a show. Putting on a show is a big part of what we do: "Don't let them see you sweat. Don't let anybody see the mess that's happening in the back of the house." We're here in the front of the house to smile and keep everybody calm. And that was something that I was always really good at. What I wasn't good at was tolerating abuse, and it created a lot of problems for me in the business.

There's one time in particular when I definitely lost my temper. That was at a bar where someone was very drunk, and I'd cut them off. I wouldn't serve them anymore, and they swung at me, missed, and I grabbed him by the scruff of his neck. And I was just about to deck him but then the bouncer saw what was happening.

That sounds like self-defense to me.

Well, you're not supposed to throttle the customers regardless, like it's kind of against the rules. (Laughs.)

Were you supported by your management?

Oh, no, not at all. No, no, I was written up, as a matter of fact. I was disciplined. And then they had to deal with me and my "attitude problem." It was me; it was my fault; I'm a loose cannon; I should know how to handle intoxicated guests, something along those lines. That's typical.

Why do you think customers feel they have license to treat you and your colleagues that way?

You know, if I had to pick one reason, I would say classism. I think there's a certain amount of homophobia, racism, all the other isms, but I think classism is the thing that we fight against the most. People say, "Why don't you go get a real job?" Oh my god! Is this not a real job? I'm raising three children, I put my husband through college and bought a house. How is this not a real job? I heard this so many times. "When are you going to do something with your life, Sarah? You're just a waitress." And I'm over here like, "I'm perfectly happy, thank you. I can take time off whenever I want and bring my kids to the pool. Can *you*?" (Laughs.) A lot of it I think is the ignorance of what it takes to be good at this business. I think it's ignorance. And I think it's prejudice against people who are serving you. It's like they think you're lower than them if you're serving them.

Do you take it personally?

Absolutely. I think we all do. It's hard not to because we take pride in what we do. It's almost always a personal attack.

I started Serving Those Serving with basically just a handful of bartenders and servers that wanted to make a difference regarding political issues in the workplace. The collective aim was to represent both employers and employees alike because a lot of times we get pitted against each other as employer versus employee. We felt that the issues that confronted us as employees also were confronting our employers. So our point was, can we please come up with a compromise that works for everybody? My point always is why would Serving Those Serving need to exist if the union was doing their job? Like, during the pandemic, workers lost health care benefits offered through the union. The reason given was dwindling contributions.

[By raising issues], I didn't realize that I was kicking kind of a hornet's nest. I didn't know. I was just speaking up from the collective attitude that my peers have. That's it. That's literally all I was doing. [The local union] was calling my jobs trying to get me fired, calling me a racist, smearing me in the media. I really got dragged pretty bad. Again, I just didn't realize that I was kicking the hornet's nest. I know a lot more now, obviously.

What we did, we looked at all the different factors that are kind of pulling at the threads of the restaurant business, all the different challenges that staff go through. Things like housing and transportation, childcare, financial, legal, immigration issues. And when we looked at that, we were like, "Well, shit, where do we start?" And what we realized was that all of our problems tied directly back to mental health. There wasn't one problem that couldn't be made better with adequate mental health resources, and so that was a real epiphany for us. That's why we're losing people to suicides and overdoses. That's why we're losing people to preventable things, is because they don't have anywhere to turn, there's no safety net. And the union's safety net is so shitty that restaurants are like, "No, thanks."

We wound up being able to hook up with an Employee Assistance Program. EAPs are really common in the rest of the workforce, but they are unheard of in the restaurant business. Nobody even knows what they are. My mom happened to have work ties with a woman who owned an EAP provider that covers almost a million employees across the whole country. She was about to sell the company, and she grandfathered us in.

We are their love mission and not their moneymaker. Our modest 2,000 or 3,000 employees that we carry through them doesn't mean much to their bottom line, but it means everything to the restaurants and bars that have access. We have about 55 restaurants right now that use us, and we keep adding new ones.

It's hilarious to me because, like, why did it take a bitchy waitress to figure this out? Where are the PhDs? Where *are* they? It kind of comes back to that thing where it's like, nobody has ever really given that sort of credibility to our industry. It's like, "Oh, it's just a transient industry. It's just people working for a year until they are done with college." Or it's a classist thing where "These are poor people that don't deserve to get benefits." I just call bullshit on all of it.

I think it's the most valuable work and one of the most valuable workforces out there and it deserves to be treated as such. And so, our message is one of dignity and strength and keeping your mental health in a place where you don't feel like you need to punch a customer. I mean, I had gotten to a point where I would be at work and somebody would walk in the door and I would just hate them just for being there. I was so sick of dealing with people.

I didn't have to work over the pandemic and there's a reason that the good Lord above decided not to put me in that situation because I think I would have lost it. I don't know how anybody got through that. I mean the absolute idiocy of the political arguments, the mask harassment, and all of that. I wept for my people every day during that time because of the abuse that they were suffering.

(Pauses. Her eyes tear.) Yeah, I get emotional all the time. It just happens. People don't see that side of it. Really ever. So that's what I'm trying to bring to light without being a depressing person. You know, I need people to understand it's hard out there. But we don't need pity. We just need support. Right? I just get rageful, the mama bear in me comes out when I see my people getting mistreated. It's real hard for me. I mean, I'd love to go around town throwing elbows, but I can't; you know, assault charges and all, and mama doesn't need those. But this work is the metaphor for throwing elbows. It's basically just, "I've got your back, you guys; my board has your back," and they know it. They know it. We're not looking for handouts, we're not looking for pity, we're not looking for any of those things. We just want to be respected. We are hell-bent on the mission that we will make things better. It's not our fault we inherited a very dysfunctional industry, but we want to leave the campground cleaner than we found it.

I don't know that I'm going to be able to change the way that society feels about my people. But I think I can change the way that my people feel about themselves.

"I Love This Work; I Just Love It"

"Having a great life, being happy, is work."
KATHERINE O. NGUYEN

She is the owner of three toy stores in Chicago, called Building Blocks, which she founded at the age of 23 in 1996. She had immigrated to America from Vietnam when she was 4.

"My grandparents were entrepreneurs, and they did very well for themselves [in Vietnam] until the Communists came and redistributed everything, but they paid for us to be smuggled out of Vietnam on a freight boat that was exporting watermelons to Thailand. That's how we left the country. I grew up in Queens, New York, in a rent-controlled apartment building in a very poor neighborhood. My mom worked in a sweatshop."

In time Katherine's parents were able to earn enough to open their own business and are doing well today.

We sit in one of Katherine's stores before business hours.

This is a very difficult business to be in. You've got people who can easily get on the internet, (mimes typing) click-click-click in their pajamas, and they don't have to get out of the house, they don't have to look for parking, they don't have to do anything except click-click-click, and they can get what they want for the best price on the internet.

How do you compete with that?

I provide something that you can't get on the internet. First of all, on the internet you can't say, "Hi. My grandson is 5, and I want to get him a building toy. He's got a baby sister, so I don't want it to have a lot of choking hazards. He already has such-and-such a set that he didn't like that much, so I don't want something similar to that." You can't really get on the internet and talk to Amazon that way. So it's the expert service, the expert knowledge of our products.

People come into my store with their children, and they're invited to play and touch and feel. It's not the type of environment where it's, "Don't touch! Keep your children by your side; make sure they don't break anything." I want them to play; I want them to touch. It'll give a mom a really good sense of "What's my kid gravitating towards? What should I get to really support them in fostering their play?"

Mostly everything I have here is very interactive, and if it requires batteries, it better have a really good reason why, because I want a lot of hands-on interaction. I want the kid to build. For instance, the puppy that you put batteries in, and it just barks and walks around? Why? But that said, I have a lot of baby toys that do require batteries, but it requires the child to press a button and see a light happen, not press a button and let it play by itself for 20 minutes.

What does your being an immigrant mean to you today?

I am really connected to that world. To that other country. I may not have any experience or memory or friends back in the old country or memories of growing up there, but I'm grateful for everything that I have. I feel like I experience life and living a lot differently than people who are not immigrants. I'm so proud and happy for that.

What did your parents teach you, implicitly or explicitly, about making a living?

Unfortunately, how important it is.

Why do you say unfortunately?

It's hard. I work really hard not to be too focused on it, and not to be scared. But I'm scared sometimes; I'm always afraid of living in poverty again. I don't think my parents talked about it, but my whole life, they've been focused on making sure that they go to work and make money. They were very attentive to it because they had to be. They had to be frugal, they had to be upset if they had to spend money on fixing a car, doing things like that. So money was always sort of like, on the foreground of their attention. So for me, it's important to keep that in perspective. I want to have more freedom around it. I try to keep that in mind a lot, not to stress out about it.

I think having a great life, being happy, is work. I don't mean "work" like a burden, but you don't just sit back and wait for that to happen for yourself. It's something that you have to pay attention to, and you're always working on, whether it's in your marriage, career, everything. It's a choice to be happy and to have a great life.

When I had my son four years ago, it was a big [wake-up call]. There's now a human being that requires you 24/7. I had been running my business [with me in charge]. Most small business owners run their business that way. Having my son was a great opportunity for me to break myself of that and to give away more responsibilities, take that plunge and hire more and pay more, expand my company in that way so that it's not so reliant on [me, me, me]. Maybe some of the things are "me" and some of the things are these other fantastic people who really can translate my passion and my commitment to serving people.

But I also wanted to connect and relate to other working moms, and I really didn't find any moms' groups or online board discussions where I felt like I fit in. There were a lot of stay-at-home moms, and there are working moms who have typical 9-to-5 jobs. I didn't really feel like I fit in either of those. So I started a group called Moms in Business, and basically it was for people who are like myself who have their own business, and they juggle family life with kids. I knew about 12 people, and I added them in this group, and we kept adding people and introducing people to people. We support each other by trying to do business with each other, providing resources, lending a sympathetic ear to "I haven't slept for three days!" to advice, all types of things like that, and now we're over 400 people strong. We're online in a Facebook group, so we can talk anytime we want, even at 3 in the morning.

I get up every day and "live to work," versus "work to live." I heard that quote from someone, and I said, "That's exactly what it's like for me. I really love it."

The other day at the airport, I was leaving for a work convention, and I said, "Have a great time!" to my 4-year-old who was going to see my mother-in-law, and he said, "You too, Mommy!" And I said, "I always do, because I love what I do for my work." And he said, "I want to work, too, at the toy store."

"I'm my own cheerleader."
JERRY MCDUFFIE

He is a car sales rep who has worked at the same suburban Toyota dealership for over 24 years. "And that's a ridiculous number. But there's still two guys in front of me on that: one is 30 years, and one is 32 years at the same place. That's very uncommon."

It's a crazy business. And a lot of times, you gotta be crazy to be in it. But I love cars. I'm actually a mechanic by trade. I had been fixing them. I used to drive a tow truck. My godfather had a limo. It just kind of snowballed. Now, when I run into somebody from high school, if I haven't seen them, and they haven't seen me on social media or something, and they say, "What are you doing?" I go, "I'm selling cars." They start laughing. And they go, "Figures."

It's a people business. Anything you're selling is a people business. You're selling clothes, you're selling phones, you're selling, you know, cabinets for their home. Everything you sell is a people business. But sales is an interesting business. Say you're a customer, you walk through the front door, you see the car, it's the color you want. You already know the price; you saw it online. You look up, you see the salesman, you're like, oh my god, here he comes. (Laughs.)

Why do you think people have that reaction?

Because they don't trust that they're not gonna be taken advantage of. You're seeing a bunch of forms you've never seen or heard of. You're hearing a bunch of terms you haven't heard before. A lot of times the guy's talking too quick. He's excited trying to make the deal. You're apprehensive. But I do it differently than a lot of people do.

How do you do it?

So, if I see you, Mark, walk through the door—Look, in my mind? There's no way I'm selling you one car. There's no way. One car? No, there's no way. You'll come back when you want the next car. If you're in the insurance business, say, you build your book of business. That's what I do.

At this point, I built [what I have]. I've checked the numbers; I am approximately 96 to 97 percent, where they've either already bought a car from me, or someone told them to see me. Yes, that is a ridiculous number. But I had to build it. I had to build that.

Yesterday, a lady, a good customer of mine, she said, "You know, I want a Lexus." And I found a perfect car for her. And I put her in that car right there. And I gotta take care of the owner's buddy tomorrow. And then I have a lady that came from the South who was on her car for 17 years. So, when I started showing her everything in the car, she was like, "Oh my god, I don't want all *that*!" (Laughs.) Well, that's all standard now. She didn't understand. So, everybody is different. Sometimes I'll take a new customer because I'm bored. I bore easy. But one thing about this job is every single customer is different. Because they're people.

One of my managers makes fun of me for it, but on your birthday, you have a card every single year from me. If I see you in a service department now—I have my mom's memory—I can walk up and say, "Hey, Mark, how's the Camry?" Not because I looked at your ticket when you came in, but because I got the memory. So, everyone has a different skill set. The guys in the shop, from the porters all the way to the manager of the service department, they buy their cars from *me*. Because, one, they know I know about cars and, two, I had to earn that trust.

What is a porter in this context?

That's the guy at the ground level in the dealership, the guy that, when you pull your car in, that's the kid, usually a teenager, early 20s, who jumps in your car and parks it for them to work it over. It's done, they're the one parking it outside. Yeah, I had that job as well.

Were you good at it?

Oh, absolutely. I got a little Starsky and Hutch in me.

When you see a couple come in, what are you assessing as you approach them? What is going through your mind?

You want to do the right thing, very first. Say hello to both [of them]. Make sure you say hello to her, too. Because it's 2022. And you'll be surprised, there's still guys [who will] only walk up to Mark and not say anything to *her*. It's not even a rookie mistake, happens even if they've been selling for years. Usually, people assume that the ladies don't know. And that's a 100 percent untrue statement.

Say hello to both. They say, "We're just looking." That's a defense mechanism. I saw this in a movie, that's where I got it: I say, "Hey, that's how it starts."

And they start laughing. Now they're relaxed. "My name is Jerry. You want to look around, Camrys are here, Lexus is over there. I'll be floating around; when you have some questions—which you will—I'll be over here. Now I'll leave you alone." You ever been to a dealership, the guy's trailing you?

Yeah, yeah, I have.

You're ready to leave, right? I generally tell any sales rep I'm working with that's new, "You're not trying to *sell* anybody anything. That's a bad word; you're trying to *help*."

I'm standing behind a salesman one time—who, for the record, he's not selling cars no more—he looks at somebody who pulls up. And he sees them get out of the car, and he says, "They can't buy nothing." I said, "Show me how you know. Show me how you know." People come in here, and they're not dressed all that exciting, sometimes those people are writing a big check. I don't know what you can or can't buy until we're on paper.

I had a gentleman walk in, and I'm taking him to a van he wants to see. And he looks at me, a Spanish gentleman, and he stops me and goes, "Why did you talk to me?" "Well, because you said you wanted to see the van." He said, "A guy in the showroom wouldn't even show me the van." "I got nothing to do with that." He goes, "Okay." We go look at the van. He likes the van. Then he tells me he owns a business. He leaves, goes to Chase, he comes back with a certified, I get paid cash for the van. (Laughs.)

You've used the term salesmen. Are there many women in car sales where you are?

No. Generally, ladies don't like the hours because the hours are ridiculous. And generally, ladies don't like rejection.

Does the competition [between salespeople] get mean-spirited?

Oh, yeah. Yeah, sure. I don't care about it, and I don't pay attention. One time one of my customers looks right at me. She goes, "Jerry," she goes, "they're loving you right now, right?" Meaning the other sales reps, and she was being kind of sarcastic. I started laughing. It was a Saturday, and we were just getting started with five customers in the store. They were all mine. They were either previous customers or someone said to see me. And I work with 18 sales reps. So yeah, so yeah, there's some love-hate. No doubt about it.

You seem to love this work. At least that's what you convey.

Yeah, I'm out of my mind. It's like you gotta be, you gotta be. My friend, she makes fun of me. She wants me to go somewhere where it's nothing but sand. How did she put it? "No cars and no phones and no roads and no pen." And I was like, "And no way." She's like, "*That's* what's wrong with you!" Whatever.

Do you ever feel like maybe she's right? That you might need a break?

Yeah, I've heard that. But I wake up, I'm going to work.

Do you think about retiring some day?

I'm trying to retire this year so I can be working for the most important person on the planet: me. But I don't want a dealership. I've got something bigger in mind.

You want to go independent?

One hundred percent. But even when I'm doing other things, I still will be, some kind of way, selling cars. I like cars. What do you drive?

A Prius.

A Prius. Look at you. You're a guy who knows. This is what I will tell you. When you decide you're going to buy something, even if it's not a Toyota, call me.

POSTSCRIPT: *A month later, I received a call from Jerry wishing me a happy birthday.*

"Oh, if my feet could talk."
KABIR ABDUL

He is a licensed and practicing cosmetologist, cosmetology teacher, barber teacher, and administrator as well as a salon owner and operator.
   "My clientele have been 90 percent women and 95 percent African American because of where I operate on the South Side [of Chicago]. I also had a place on the North Side, and it had a mixed clientele because [the population] is more diverse. I am known in the industry as Mr. Kabir. I am a Chicago guy. Born and raised here. My life, school, everything."

Did you always want to be a hairstylist?

No. When I was growing up, it just was not popular for guys to be a hairdresser. We were like the "guy guys," you know, the alpha male type, right? And hairdressing just didn't fit into that old thing.

I'm going to go back to the start, if I may. A friend and I were bumblin' downtown as 19-year-olds do, South Side kids, you know; we were all over the place, right? So, we happen to stumble up into a beauty school. And that's how it started. My friend and I, we looked around there in the school, and we saw nothing but pretty girls, right? The students? And I said, "Yeah, sign me up!" And I've never had to work for anyone else in a salon because I was lucky enough to go right into business right out of hair school. This is what happened.

The hair school that I attended, the owner at that time, his name was Mr. Lahti. He was a well-known hairstylist, African American man in Chicago in the early days, right? Many of his clients were like the Black celebrities of the time. He would show me the service list with people like Aretha Franklin, you know, Nat King Cole. When they [would] come to Chicago to perform, he was their hairstylist. He went into the beauty school business, and that's the school I went to. After we graduated—when I say we, it was three other classmates and me, so that made four of us—he came to me and said, "Let's open up a salon!" (Laughs.) Right? And I'm like, "Okay!" Now, guess what? None of us had any money, right? But I said, "Okay! That's good."

Mr. Lahti, he owned a lot of different properties. He said, "I got a place right now, been closed. You go in there, decorate the place, all that." So my first salon, I got with no money down. I mean, that was, talk about the stars lining up for me, man.

Once you have achieved any amount of success in something, it really does increase your love for it, and I've gotten success after success in the field. I'll say one big thing is this: I look at and measure my counterparts, my friends, peers, and what has happened with them in our life span of working, from my late teens right up to now. The majority of them, with the world economic situation or whatever else in our country, unemployment, and this and that, they have no jobs. And I have *never* been unemployed since I've been in the field. That's always worked for me.

The number one—you can say "talent" or really, more, "quality" or "attribute" that you need to be successful in this business is to be a people person.

Right? That's first. And so, I've always been a people person. With that being my main thing, I knew that I would succeed in this.

I also really always want to do a good job. I like the skill that's involved in it. And I like the challenges. And I say, "It's only hair." That's what I'd say to myself. I'm not asked to be a heart surgeon, right? "It's only hair." But I like what I do.

Do you get to know your clients well?

Oh my god, yes, you do. You're like the bartender, right? Meaning they tell us a lot, right? Many times, they tell things that we really don't need to know. Yeah, they tell us a lot. When they sit down in that chair, it's like you're their therapist. And so much so that it has even been shoehorned into our licensing requirements. We have always had to get continuing education in the skills and the business and all that. A few years ago, the state of Illinois made it a requirement for every license renewal period that we take a course, a one- or two-hour course on domestic abuse prevention. They teach you about all the red flags and what to say. And we have some literature we can share with them.

I also want to say that not being in the salon every day [because of the pandemic], I missed what we called the "shop life." Has a life of its own. There's going to be people that love to hang around the shop. It's just a part of the culture of the shop. Did you ever see the Ice Cube movie, *Barbershop*? That character that Cedric the Entertainer play? That barber that sits around and just talks about never having clients, and he just talked wild? There's always one of those, too. I had one.

We are taught in cosmetology school and barber school that there are subjects that we do not talk about. Number one, you should not talk about religion or politics because those are controversial. But guess what, that's *all* they talk about, right? That's where you would not give your own hard opinions. You want to keep your space neutral. Your clients are from every walk of life, right? And you don't want to tick them off. So you say, "Oh, so you voted for Trump?" You get a nice vocabulary of like, "Oh, okay, you don't say." And "That's interesting."

Is it ever hard to bite your tongue?

Yes, it is. Absolutely can be hard. Yeah, absolutely. I'll tell you, there was a big, big thing going in salons, a debate comes up. You know, it's always what the man should be doing and what the women should be doing. The male-female whatever you want to call it. Debate. The male-female debate. There's so many sparks!

I do a lot of "Oh, is that right? Mmm-hmm." But they also talk about money and a lot of stuff. You have to bite your tongue, yes.

As your own boss, do you build in vacations for yourself?

Boy, that's a great question. (Laughs.) That's where my weakness is, right? I have not. And that's not good. That's not good, right? I've done a lot of traveling with the hair business, traveling to different cities, states. I'm working for different companies but also been a technician and demonstrating for different product companies and hair companies, tool companies. I've been sent to places out of the country, too. So, I'm like, "Oh, well, *that's* a vacation." But really, it isn't.

Do you ever think about retiring?

I have not really thought seriously about retiring. I haven't. As long as I'm healthy enough to move around and think and do, I just do that. And really, when you look at the careers of many of the great mob of hairstylists or barbers, right? They work until they drop. There are very few of us who retire. It's not really laborious where you're doing heavy labor work that wears your body out, so. . . .

What about being on your feet all day?

You get used to it. In the schools, we have certain rules for what we call the clinic floor. That's the area where the students in the training service clients. And one of the rules is I don't let them sit in the hairstyle chair in between clients. They're like, "Why do we have to stand up?" And I say, "That's part of the job, so you got to get used to it now. It's sort of like boot camp, you guys. You *have* to stand."

Oh, if my feet could talk and tell you the hours. I'll say this: today, I wouldn't do the volume of clients that I used to do back-to-back. Those days are past me. That's a young man's game as far as doing just client after client. When I was in the salon every day, like, hard and fast, I did, Mark, 15 and 20 clients a day. And I don't mean quick haircuts. That's full services: hair color, certain styles, everything.

Nowadays, I don't see the young stylists and barbers working hours like we did. I tell you, things have turned so drastically with the pandemic that it just totally changed the way that the world operates, and my profession is affected as well. Meaning that people went into a lot of private services; you got a proliferation of private suites for individuals to operate out of now.

My clients, though, they don't let you stop. They don't let you retire. You know, when the lady wants to have her hair done, she just wants to have it done. I guess I must love it, though. I'm still hitting the pavement every day. Yeah. It has been very fulfilling for me.

"I mean, I love this work; I just love it."

CARY FRANKLIN

He is a consulting actuary specializing in pension consulting in Los Angeles. "I'm one of three founding partners. We now have 11 partners and a total of about 80 employees in nine offices around the country."

We talk on Zoom. He is in his office and arrives on my screen at precisely the appointed time, for which I compliment him.

"Well, hey, I am an actuary, right? (Laughs.)

There's all kinds of jokes about actuaries and accountants. I think the misconception is that actuaries can't speak English and people don't understand what they're saying. I was once at a meeting with a fairly new client. The attorney at that meeting passed a note to me, and he'd written, "An actuary who speaks English!" I love that. I saved it. When someone says, "Oh, I understood you!" that's the greatest thing. But most people haven't actually heard of actuaries.

It's funny, I'm a mathematician by trade but my favorite aspect of my work is actually the writing and the speaking. In a way, we're actors or teachers; we're trying to explain. I had an unusual double major. I was a math major and a film studies major. I often say that my film classes have helped me with my work more than my math classes because I had to do a lot of writing, you know, term papers. I think that really prepared me well for this role as someone who has to be able to communicate a concept to people.

I've been an actuary for the Screen Actors Guild–Producers Pension Plan for 24 years, so let's use their pension plan as an example of what I do. So you've got a group of people. In this case, you've got these actors who are working, and they're earning a benefit that they're going to get when they retire. Some of these actors are 5 years old now, and they might live to 100, right? The money that's being contributed into this pension fund is being invested, and, [as actuaries], we make assumptions as to how much it will earn, how long people will live, how long they'll stay in the profession, what kind of benefit they earn. We figure out, okay, how much should be contrib-

uted each year so that obligation, that promise can be met? It's obviously a
moving target, and we're adjusting it based on the assumptions we make. We
have to say, "Okay, how did the actual experience compare to our assumptions? Do we need to adjust our assumptions?"

This country is in the beginnings of a massive retirement crisis because
people go from one job to the next. They may take their 401k money and put
a down payment on a house or use it for college expenses, but they don't use it
for retirement. And then they get close to retirement age, and they realize, "Oh,
I can't afford to retire." And as fewer people have traditional pension plans, it's
getting a lot tougher for people to be able to retire.

Part of this is that they're living longer so they need more money to be able
to fund that long retirement period. If you have a 401(k) plan, you have a pot
of money. "Okay, how do I make that last? How much can I spend to make sure
that lasts?" Whereas a traditional pension plan is like a paycheck; you're continuing your paycheck, right? I have done some work outside of my job in terms of
some public policy things and other initiatives trying to promote different types
of plans that address this looming retirement crisis.

*I imagine that, in addition to mathematical calculations, you must also have to
make ethical calculations.*

Absolutely. Anytime we think about making a public policy statement, there
is a lot of internal discussion so that we're comfortable with what we're doing
and that, in the end, it's in the best interests of our clients, the best interests of
our firm, and, frankly, the best interests of society at large. It's fairly fluid. Each
situation is different. We're a small enough company where we don't have to be
[particularly] bureaucratic and codify everything. In terms of how we're going to
evaluate what we're going to say, we take each case as it comes.

I never have to deal with these by myself. So that's another thing I like about
the work. I don't work solo. I've got colleagues to discuss [these issues] with to
reach a consensus to figure out what's the best approach. I'm working with a team
on every client or every project. I like the give and take in the collaboration. During
the pandemic, like so many other jobs and businesses, we worked remotely for a
really long time. We haven't all come back to the office, yet, but a number of us
have. I missed working with everyone. We're a really close-knit group, and not just
in our LA office, here, but across the country.

I mean, I love this work; I just love it. I've been doing it for 46 years, and it's still fun and interesting. And I'm learning stuff all the time.

What makes it still so engaging for you after 46 years?

There's a few things: In my field, the plans are always changing. It's not static. It's like, "Okay, the stock market tanks, what's happening now? Can we improve benefits? Do we need to cut benefits? Do we need to increase contributions?" So, things are happening. There's also, every couple of years it seems, a fairly significant piece of legislation that affects these plans. And so, we have to evaluate: What's the impact of this legislation? What does it mean for our plans? I also have gotten involved in some of the lobbying for legislation, meeting with congressional staffers and members of Congress to say, "Hey, we need to do this to take care of this problem." The politics of the collective bargaining, the labor management, that's something that's also kind of lively and interesting.

And the other thing I really love is having to explain the work and what's different for our work versus, say, insurance actuaries, who work for insurance companies who may be talking to other actuaries or other technical people in the insurance company. In my work, our clients' boards of trustees are the representatives from these different industries. So I can be talking to screen actors; I can be talking to the cement masons; I can be talking to hotel workers. And I have to be able to explain what's happening, what the implications are so that they understand it well enough to be able to make informed decisions because they're making important decisions about the benefits for their people. I love the challenge of having to be able to communicate this work.

Wearing your actuary hat, do you predict you'll be doing this work for quite a while longer?

You know, I'm getting older. I've been doing this a very long time. But as you've heard, I really enjoy the work, so I envision myself slowly phasing down. I want to continue to work because I enjoy the field, but it's also because we started this company 14 years ago. The company is kind of my baby, so I don't want to walk away from it. As long as I'm able to and healthy and sharp, I imagine I'll continue to have a hand in it. Maybe at some point it'll be only a day or two a week. But yeah, I still get a lot out of it.

I have been told that the passion comes through; people see it. And with the younger people here that I work with, I think it helps inspire them and motivate them. But I just find the work so interesting. Plus, I feel there's a value to what we're doing. As I said, the nation is in this crisis. Some rough statistics show something like roughly half of the U.S. private sector workers have no access to a retirement plan from their employer in their workplace. So what does that mean for the future in terms of all these older workers who are going to have to stay on the job when they're not as productive, not as healthy? Are they going to have to have their children take care of them? So there's all kinds of societal implications for that, and if we, as multiemployer pension actuaries, are helping make sure that these workers are getting as secure a retirement as possible, I feel there's some social value to that. So, I am proud of that.

"The tattoo spirit."

KLAUS ZHANG

He is a tattoo artist, born and raised in China, where he got his first tattoo at 16. "I don't know how many tattoo I have gotten since, but other than my face, I'm covered. I know some people do the face. I can't. I get married. (Laughs.) Last week I was talking to her. 'Baby, I want to get a head tattoo—around here and go under my ear.' She just look at me. 'All right do that. Try it.' She doesn't mean try it, she mean, try it and see what happen. (Laughs.)"

He apprenticed with Mr. Kou of Wen Hua Ren Tattoo in Tianjin, China, for three years and later opened his own shop. Four years before we talk, he and his wife, an American, and their 8-year-old son, who was born in China, relocated to America where he now works. He is 36 years old.

How is working here in America different from working in China?

Oh, a lot different. It's more professional. Clean. Professional. Work schedule is always full. Much quick. And I'll be honest, customer here, they have their own taste. I'm most of the time doing black-gray realism. They show me a picture sometime. I don't have to do design at all. For some of the work, I need totally to find lots of picture and get all the ideas and draw it out by my own idea.

Is that what you prefer? Creating your own designs rather than copying a picture?

Yeah, that's true. Right now, because COVID we are only take appointment. No walk-ins. Right now, I'm doing all custom tattoo. I love it. But before [COVID] when we take walk-ins, there's half and half. Before, we take a lot of U.S. college students, teenagers; they just show me a picture. "I want this, I want that like my friend." It's interesting, some special holidays like St. Patrick's Day, oh my god. Whole group of people come in and want the same thing.

When they come in on a holiday like that, does it seem like they're being impulsive?

I feel like—I be honest, they just don't really deeply understand the tattoo spirit. But I will do a good job, clean line work for them. That's no problem.

What is the tattoo spirit?

That it is not only a job. That it's not only a way to make money, feed myself, feed my family. Is more like a duty. My client's happy, I'm more happy than them. I think the tattoo spirit for all different artists, they can feel a different feeling or same, but this is what I feel. I feel every time when I'm working on somebody, I should be focused and taking care like I'm tattooing myself.

Have you given yourself a tattoo?

I did. Is on my arm, this side. I did this because I need to feel it. I need to feel it. I need to feel what my customer feeling by my hand. Even how it heals. How it look. I need to tell myself which part I need to pull the needle, make the needle shorter or longer, or turn the power down a little bit. How to move to get color in and people not screaming. I need to teach myself.

Do you think that your customers sense that level of care from you?

Oh, yeah, they feel that. Yeah, sure. Sometimes, on the street, they call my name, "Klaus!" I'm: "Wait a second. Do we meet each other before?" And they show me the tattoo. Then I'm: "Yes! That's my baby!"

How does it feel when you see your work walking down the street?

Oh my god, that feels amazing. Yeah, that feels amazing. In the airport one time, I was holding suitcase, and somebody tapped my shoulder. "Hi, Klaus." "What's up, dude? Do I know you?" "Look at this!" And he started taking shirt off! I'm with my kid! And he showed me. "Oh, man! I remember, yes!" That feels awesome, really.

I would think it also means he's proud of it.

Very much, because I put all my focus, energy, and all my art feeling on it. I don't really talk too much with my customer. When I'm working, my habit is have my headphones and focused on the work. I'm very enjoy when working. I'm very enjoy and mute when I'm working. I don't pick up phone call. I don't look at my phone. I don't even talk. I'm enjoy shading dark to light, light to skin color. I'm enjoying changing the ink color on the skin. I just enjoy the art. I feel very proud with the work.

Double Duty

"The dead don't care."
THOMAS LYNCH

He is a "mostly retired" funeral director, following in his father's footsteps along with his brother. He has been the director of the Lynch & Sons funeral home in Milford, Michigan, for over 45 years. It is one of six Lynch funeral homes in the state. He is also the author of five critically acclaimed collections of poems and four books of essays.

I never saw the writing and my work as a funeral director as an either/or thing. I think it was Yeats who said, "The only thing a studious mind considers are sex and the dead." And I thought, "How nice for me, because the dead were everywhere, and I approve of sex wholeheartedly."

I've noticed the ones that are really good at being funeral directors have a "side hustle"—I think the millennials call it—and it's not something they do necessarily for money. I think they need some way to step back and catch their breath. It's something they do to divert their gaze from the existential. For me it's reading and writing.

When you were growing up, was the assumption that you would go into your father's business?

On the contrary, my father didn't own a funeral home until he bought the funeral home in Milford on Walled Lake in 1974. When all of us went to work with him as teenagers, it meant that he could have the best use of teenagers and could pay them less. But we all looked good in black suits. He would tell us how to work 14 or 15 hours a day, and how to get the smell of onions and mustard off your breath if you had had the Coney Island next door.

And I have to say this, Mark: when you're 14 years old and you're swinging the door open in the funeral home and wearing your wingtip shoes and some widowed person, woman or man, comes to you at the end of the evening after everybody's gone home with their casserole dishes, and they take you by your shoulders and look you in your eye and say, "I couldn't have done this without you. Thank you so much," you feel immediately necessary. And all you've done is swing the door or carry the flowers. You haven't done anything particularly important, but you've been there, you've attended. You've done your part, and they feel as if they've been served by you, and that's very seductive. It was for me anyway.

I was raised by Irish Catholics—which sounds like wolves. I didn't have the sort of religious-slash-spiritual inquiry baked into the pie. I always saw [this work] for what it really was, which was a deeply human effort to get rid of the dead guy and let the living return to their lives, bereft of one person, but intact and remembering the dead guy. I can disappear any body as long as I get a credit card number and the expiration date and the three-digit code. But if we want to say something about the who, what, when, where, why of it all, then we have to organize an event, and we process this mortality in the person of the corpse among the living so that they become the witnesses.

We're counting on the [funeral] to provide comfort, but I think it's way more basic than that. I think that funerals are the acting out of things that we do not know how to say properly. That's why it becomes incumbent upon cultures to organize behaviors, conducts, and they become traditional. And that's helpful because if you're, say, an Italian American lapsed Catholic and your grandmother dies, you don't have to wonder what you're going to be doing or what you're going to be wearing or who you're going to be talking to and seeing the next four days because the culture provides that. The culture has built the wheel that works the space between Grandma living and Grandma dead; all you have to do is go along for the ride.

Our problem is that, as a culture, we keep trying to reinvent this wheel, and we're clumsy and awkward and so we end up having these sort of memorial cocktail parties to which everyone is welcome except the dead guy. We want him out of the way because it's an unpleasant reality and smells before long and he's not smiling and he doesn't laugh at our jokes which we keep telling about him. We want people to grin and bear it or laugh and carry on. A lot of times people need a chance to yell out loud or weep out loud in the face of God and say, "What the fuck did have you have in mind here, God?"

My father died weeks before the pandemic closed everything down. We were not able to do the rituals you're talking about until two years later. So I'm wondering what you see as the impact of the absence of those rituals.

I do think the pandemic itself has made it difficult for people to do the needful things of witness and participation and process and procession, and I think we'll have a whole generation a few years hence who are stunted, more or less, because of the damage. Because they've not been able to grieve or participate in these things.

The sort of unspoken contract among humans is that if I do right by you, maybe my children will do right by me, and their children will . . . down the list it goes. We are doing this to show our children how it's done. When my father died in Florida, my brother and I flew down there and prepared his body to bring him back to Michigan. And people would say, "That must have been really hard to embalm your own father." I said it was really hard, but what we did seemed to be a comfort in a way.

My daughter jumped from the Golden Gate Bridge to her death in July of 2020. Getting her home to bury her was the only consolation of an otherwise desolate circumstance where my adult daughter had found herself at wit's end, without hope of any improvement. She'd been hospitalized just a couple of months before this happened. It was not shocking, but it was horrific. Getting her home to us to let her go again into the space we wanted her to go was the only sense that we had some agency in the matter because, as we know, we don't control these things.

Putting her in her coffin, taking her to the graveyard, lowering her into the grave, and filling the grave by hand with the rest of her family . . . it's sort of bittersweet, of course, but we do what we can do. I think when someone we love dies, we get stuck between the will to do everything possible, and the will to do nothing at all. I think doing what we can is better than doing nothing at all.

Another funeral director told me she doesn't want to be cremated herself because she sees the process. Do you feel that way?*

---

* Marysue Reardon, p. 383.

I don't know. I mean, one of the better sentences I started a book with was "The dead don't care."* They don't. I mean, I've checked on this. No one's ever proud of the pinstripe suit or the walnut casket. If you're dead, whether you're burned, buried, or blown from a cannon, what difference does it make? You're the dead guy.

You know, no one ever says, "Cremate me." They say, "*Just* cremate me." Operative word *just* because what they want is for you to have no trouble. We don't want to be a burden to our children is the interior mantra of most of the people who die and not one of my own mantras. I'm going to be a burden to my children, I hope, because they've been a burden to me—a lovely, lovely, substantial burden. Really the most important thing I've done with my life.

You witness a lot of tragedy and heartbreak in your work. Does it sometimes get to you?

Of course, it gets you if you share in humanity. I suppose some people try to completely disengage. But I have found that, actually, engagement is the better bet. If you sort of immerse yourself in what's going on, at least for me, it seems like a better strategy than trying to numb myself to it. Although, I'm 33 years sober so I must have been trying to numb something, but the thing about being around people at the worst time in their life, there are things that happen that so sparkle of humanity that you just feel glad to be alive, glad to be in the room when it happens. The astonishing moments far outweigh the ones that make you desolate.

Did your father share with you his wishes for his own burial?

We'd ask him. We'd say, "Eddie, what do you want when you're dead?" And he'd say, "Well, you'll know what to do." That's all he ever said. And we did, we knew exactly what to do.

"I had the motivation of a worker."
RODERICK "RICK" LETT SR.

He is a furniture "reupholsterer" (his preferred term) and an ordained minister of Jesus Christ. "I came from real humble beginnings, you know, like the average young minority raised in Chicago in the '50s and '60s. Didn't have a whole lot. I probably seen my dad once in my lifetime. We lived on the lower part of Chicago, 43rd 'round Cottage Grove and Lake Park and Drexel. But wasn't as bad as most people say it

---

* *The Undertaking: Life Studies from the Dismal Trade.*

was because parents in those days, they may not have been able to give you a whole lot, but they helped you keep your integrity. I didn't have to beg. I mean, what we had we had, you know?

"As far as I knew as a child, we were okay. I was too young to think about any prejudice or being poor because Mom always put something on a plate. We served people that was poorer than us. Gave them food, our clothes. So we didn't have much, but I would say basically everything I am came from home, came from my mother, you know?"

At first, I did furniture reupholstering in my one-bedroom apartment on the third floor. It had the living room and dining room and one bedroom. Me and my wife and my little daughter and my baby son. I turned the living room to an upholstery shop. I knew everybody in the building, so the noise I was making was okay.

Then by 1989 it was like a transformation. I say that because it wasn't just me getting lucky. I figured it was destiny for me to do what I did, because God loved me that much. In 1989, what I did, I gave my life toward Jesus Christ. I don't know how this fits anywhere in this conversation, but this is what the reality of it is, and it gets where we're going. My lifestyle changed—better man, better husband, better hungers and desires for doing the right thing. Not thinking about hustling anymore. Thinking, "Hey, I got a business, you know, let's make the best of it." So in 1990 I just heard a voice say, "For your effort, I'll carry on with your success; go out there and find you a place." So I left my house, went down 79th Street across Western. I seen storefronts with *for rent* signs up there. I didn't have much money. I just went there, and I put my hand on the building, and I just prayed. I said, "Lord, I really love this building."

I called the man and he gave me a real nice price. I went home, and I told my wife, I said, "Look, I found the place, and we need this amount of money for the rent and security." And I said, "I don't think we can handle that, Baby. I don't think I can do it."

She said, "If God opened that door for you, we can do it. Just go ahead and do it." And I went in there, stayed there 11 years at that place.

I service my community. Ninety-five percent of my customers are African Americans. So, you have a percentage like that that's paying you, what do you do? You take care of them. I'll take care of anybody, but if you're choosing me to service you and you pay me, why not treat you like a king and queen, you know? I appreciate you. I can't pay *myself*, you know?

If you go on the North Side, most of those guys take a $250 couch and they'll charge you $1,500 for it in the name of upholstering. But it might've cost them a few hundred dollars for material and their time. I mean, I can make that money too. I can do that, but the Lord never made my heart like that. I couldn't just go around and make up stuff and beat people out. You know, I might not be rich and nothing like that, but that's just not me. Never been money hungry. Never want to hurt people. You know? So, it works out fine. When you speak my name, my name is good. My name is good out there. You won't hear anybody sharing something bad, like "He beat me out."

And I've met *so* many people, and I still do. I meet people [who] will become friends. And it's just a wonderful thing. I've been all over the city. I've done things for the Staple Singers; they live in Chicago. I did things for Jesse Jackson, Hermene Hartman of *N'Digo* magazine. It's a good, friendly, enjoyable business that can bring happiness, joy, and beauty. I just love it, I love it.

Sometimes I tell my wife, "I can't even stop sitting back looking at my work and smiling and thinking, "God, thank you for this gift. Thank you. Thank you for this." Because that's how important it really is. It's more than work, more than a job, it's a passion, and I'm able to spread it out to customers.

I pick up and deliver. I don't charge people for picking up and doing that. So I get a chance to go in people's houses, meet family, sit down. I've had people ask me to sit for dinner, and I've got a chance to pray with people. I had two people that I met, older people, and they actually asked me to do their funeral. And I'm shocked. That was so far from my mind. But it is how much they liked me and the kind of conversations we had. They were Christian people like me, and we became friends and I'm friends with the children now, today. It's just a good time to meet people and to be friendly, and it's business, too.

Is there a connection between your work as an upholsterer and your ministry?

I'm glad you asked me that. I was *hoping* you'd ask me this question. This question is the apple of my existence. What made me get away from the name *upholsterer* and stick to *re*-upholsterer is because it lined up with my life in ministry. The Bible calls it "reconciliation of Christ." You're reconciling people back to Christ. So you're not *making* people, you're just redoing what He done, healing the broken-hearted. So, *re* means to redo something. When I go and minister somebody, I'm really doing what God had done, but *re*-interjecting that love into that mistrust and everything that they've gone through.

So, when I meet people, it's kind of like both go hand in hand. I'm coming to reupholster your furniture, but I'm also coming to reconcile you to God. As the Bible says, "Let your light so shine, that men would see your good works and glorify God which is in heaven." So, when they see my good works, they begin to glorify God for that. So yeah. They go hand in hand. They all go together. That's who I am.

Has your mother been able to see what you've made of your life?

My mother ended up getting bedridden for some years, so she wasn't able to get out and things like that. But she seen all the changes in my life. She seen I went to school, did upholstery. She seen the fact that I opened me up a business. She seen that I changed my life over to the Lord. But she never had got a chance to visit the place where I worked. I wanted her to see it because I named my place Lett 10 Reupholstering. That's her last name, and the 10 means I'm the 10th child out of 13.

So, one day what I did before she passed, I went and got her, and one of my brothers, he helped put her in my van with the wheelchair. I go by my shop. I said, "Look, Mom. There go your name." So I'm blessed. I got a chance to let my mother see me change from the streets, from running around hustling, things like that, and give my life up to the Lord. So she got a chance to see all of that. And not only that, when I made these changes in my life, and because I became a minister, I was the one who buried my mother in 2001.

It sounds like it was very important to you for your mom to see your shop.

Oh, number one, number one. That was number one. That was so important because she raised nine boys and four girls. She had to deal with Chicago, and we wasn't good kids, you know? We wasn't *bad* bad, but we wasn't where you can just sit back and relax. So for her to see some accomplishment come from her womb, I think any child in the right mind would want that. For me, there is no other success greater than that. I don't care how far I go. My greatest success is the fact that change came to my life and made me see who I was, and I embraced it. What I make of it, it's on me. It's not on anybody else.

I tell young people, I say, "Listen, you only get one chance to make your parents feel good about them giving you life and raising you. When you get out of this selfish mode and begin to say, 'It's not all about me,' then you begin to know how to please others." So. That's just who I am.

"I just enjoy the process."
CHRISTIAN RODRIGUEZ

He is 25 years old and a "futures trader slash pizza delivery driver."

My delivery hours are actually pretty short. I'm only on from 5 to 9. We used to close at 10, but we close at 9 now because of COVID. So it's only a four-hour shift. We have an hourly base wage which is pretty low. It's only like $3 an hour, and then $3 for delivery fee. But after tips, because it's so busy, I'm still coming out to about 15, 20 dollars an hour. I'm super thankful for that.

Which job occupies most of your day?

Oh, trading, for sure.

Do you make good money doing that?

More than my job currently. I'm hoping to be out of that job soon. Actually, I'm just using the delivery position to cover some bills until I reach the desired amount in my brokerage account. But it's definitely performance based, so it depends on how I'm doing. I've really honed in on my tactics and strategies over the last year, so my risk management has gotten way better. I pretty much threw myself into the fire, like two years ago.

The way I started doing this was crypto. Funnily enough, Bitcoin and Ethereum were going crazy a couple years ago. And I threw a little bit of money at it, won, and that's when everything tanked. I had no idea what I was doing. But my interest was there.

I only dedicate maybe one to three hours of my day to actual trading. But there's a lot more time that goes into looking into the market, seeing what different indexes are doing, or what different sectors are doing. So there's a lot more research that goes into it than my actual trading time. It ends up being like maybe an 8- to 10-hour day, but from the comfort of my own home.

I still have three or four alarm clocks, just to make sure that I'm up at the right time. The market opens at 8:30 central time, so I'm usually up by 6:30, 6:45, just to get my brain active, shower, drink some coffee, maybe exercise lightly.

I like the challenge. I love it. It's a passion. I wouldn't call myself good yet, even though I'm consistently profitable this year. But I feel like I still have a long way to go. It's fun knowing you got the trade right.

A shot of dopamine?

Oh, absolutely. Absolutely. I mean, it *is* gambling in a sense.

Could it be dangerous the way game gambling and drinking are?

It can be. But I don't see it being a problem, personally. I enjoy it so much, but not in the sense of always looking for the dopamine hit. I just enjoy the process. If I hit a big trade, I'll clap my hands. I actually have a goal per day that I want to hit on my account percentage-wise. And once I hit that, I completely shut my computer off because I don't want to risk losing any of that.

Have you ever lost a lot of money doing this?

I've taken some bruises, here and there. I think the biggest loss I had was back when I was actually trying to trade stocks and not futures. I was shorting Twitter and it just kept going up—it kept going up. I was like, there's no reason for this to go up as much as it is. This was before I really had my emotions and my risk management in check. So I added to the short position to increase my base price, but it kept going up and then forced me to take the loss. I lost about maybe $3,500. That hurts on a single trade. At the time, that was almost 50 percent of my account. So that was a big setback.

How did that make you feel?

Oh, it's demoralizing.

Did it make you want to quit?

If I ever have that thought, it's quickly gone. I don't actually stick with it. It's more the initial sting gets to me.

What do you hope to be doing in, say, 10 years?

In 10 years I'll be 35. I would definitely hope to still be doing this full time, but I want to do more. I hope to have a charitable account where I give away pretty much all my gains. That's the goal. I'll have my separate personal account that I'll be trading from, but I want to have an additional fund that I'll allocate to grassroots organizations and things that I think are interesting. Like, there's a Black youth program I know about that does a lot of work with incarcerated people and families.

I think maybe it comes from being a person of color and understanding the struggle. I mean, racism is definitely still rampant. I deal with it on a daily basis, often in the form of microaggressions. That's a motivating factor. If I'm in a position to help people by working two hours and making way more money than anyone should, I feel like I should give something back.

POSTSCRIPT: *In an update, he tells me he is still trading, but instead of delivering pizza, he is now a rideshare driver.*

"The thought that this is not a sustainable life."
LAURA PARKER

She is 40 years old and lives in Los Angeles. "I do a lot of things, I would say. Usually, to just to boil it down, my elevator pitch is to say I'm a singer and an Alexander Technique teacher. Post-COVID times, I really am mostly a teacher. I'm a teacher who still performs occasionally."

I had resisted being a teacher because my mom was a middle school teacher for 40 years, and because for my whole life everybody said, "You're gonna be a teacher!" So I was like, "No, I'm gonna be . . . (spoken with appropriate flair) a *star*." I wanted to be an opera singer starting around age 16. I got my master's in voice at USC, and then started my career artistically here in Southern California with LA Opera, Long Beach Opera, some small companies down in San Diego. And then when the financial crisis hit in 2008, all my contracts just disappeared.

I went to New York because a studio apartment was like $1,000 because of the crash. I knew I'd never be able to afford an apartment in New York unless I went right away. I was singing small gigs, pursuing my opera singing career, auditioning for regional gigs, sometimes going to Europe for auditions. Making a living at it. I had a day job, but I was still performing. I could never make enough to afford New York rent without a day job.

It became a kind of turning point. I started studying what's called Alexander

Technique* to help myself as a singer. I was working multiple jobs to make ends meet because every artist does, but then I moved back to LA to be certified as an Alexander Technique teacher. That's when I knew I really wanted to be an adjunct professor and work with college students. It's been about five years now that I've had multiple adjunct positions.

I have to go, "Okay, it's Monday. What school am I going to today? And what time am I teaching?" because sometimes the courses I teach on Monday will be at a different time on Wednesday. I really have to keep on top of my calendar. One of the schools I teach at is right downtown, maybe 30 minutes away. I will get there for the first class at 8:30 in the morning, and then I will teach until about 5:30. I'll do maybe a group class of Alexander Technique, and then I'll do a few voice lessons for the musical theater department. I'll have a break, which I don't get paid for [because I'm not salaried]. And then I'll teach another Alexander class and then I'll come home, and I'll teach a couple lessons in my private studio.

Then on Tuesdays and Thursdays, I have to drive an hour and a half to get to the other school, which has a wonderful performing arts program. That's why I do the drive. But I have to factor in two hours to get there in case there's an accident. I drive to Orange County, and I will teach a group class in the morning and then the students get to take private lessons with me for the rest of the day. I try to get out early enough to beat traffic coming back and then I'll teach a couple private lessons [in my home studio].

Does it ever seem like it's too much?

Yes. Last year, I said, "This is too much. I can't keep going at this rate. It's too much. What do I want to do so that I can still make a living, but not be so exhausted?" I just I don't have a work-life balance during the year.

I wish I could drop something, but because nothing is stable enough, I don't feel like I can drop anything yet. Sometimes it feels like my life is fragile, that if one job disappears, it's all going to be suddenly over. If we're not rehired in the fall, then it's going to be a rough year for me. I would love to not worry about that.

But the joy I get from watching my students perform is infinitely greater than anything I experienced when I performed, because I don't have any sense of self wrapped up in it. It's just because I'm so hard on myself when I perform.

---

* A method for improving posture, reducing tension, and enhancing movement by increasing people's awareness of their physical habits.

But when I watch my students, I'm just like, "Look at you! You *did* that! That's incredible. I'm so proud of you."

I don't want to leave either of my academia jobs. I just wish one of the schools I teach at could give me enough of an opportunity to make it so I can teach at only one school. Sometimes I think [what I'm doing] is crazy because there are no benefits. I'm still considered like a freelancer in all senses.

Do you have health insurance?

I buy it as a freelancer. I go through Covered California and have health insurance through there. I've never had dental or vision insurance, so I take really good care of my teeth and pay out-of-pocket. I'm allowed to work [up to] 20 hours at one of my schools.

If you worked 21 hours, would you get insurance?

Yes. But I'm capped at 20 hours.

Before you became an adjunct professor, did you have an expectation of what that life was like?

Yes, and I feel very naive. I thought working in a college as a teacher was so revered, and I did not imagine the pay that came with it, how low it would be. I thought, "This is my dream! This is such a huge accomplishment. I'm so honored to have this job." But it definitely feels like I'm just a guest there.

Do you ever feel resentment about that?

I don't know if it's resentment because I think I've just accepted that that's the way the system works, but sometimes I get mad at *myself*. Like, why didn't you [get a doctorate]? I remember trying to decide, should I get a doctorate, or should I become a certified Alexander teacher? My Alexander training took three years. People sometimes think that I just did it [quickly]. It took three years! So I do think sometimes I should have gotten the degree, and I would have had some stability. I don't know if that's true, but it's something I tell myself.

But I do get so much energy back from my students. I keep all of my thank-you cards in a box so that if I ever feel like "what am I doing?" I just pull out that box. I love the connection to them. I do get dispirited, though. The thought that goes through my mind the most is that this is not a sustainable life. I'm working six days a week because I sing at a church on the weekends and then in April when all my students are performing, I'm working every day without a break because I have to see them perform. I love seeing them do what they do, so I just wear myself out until finals. And then I kind of crash.

There's a part of me that loves it. There's something so magical to me about having a group of people for 16 weeks who you see twice a week, and you're seeing their progress over that journey. That's just something that feeds me emotionally. I just love it. So, I can't imagine letting academia go.

Do you think about retirement?

When I talk to my mentors or friends who are a little bit older, I go, "Wow, I don't have a retirement built in, so I have to save on my own." I try to be smart about that on my own, but it does feel a little bit like living without a net.

My teachers are in their 70s and 80s and are still working. I hope I have the energy and good health. I hope I'm still engaged in teaching in my older days, because really, my mentors make it look good. They don't make it look like they're doing it because they have to. They do it because they want to.

What do you dream ahead to?

I dream of working like, four days a week and being able to end up not having to work a 12-hour day. I feel like I have no flexibility during the year because I'm overworked. I would love to have flexibility and to not have to worry about what I call "the quilt" of my jobs. I would love to not worry about if they're going to come out to a good—to a livable wage at the end of the year.

Sometimes I think about—I guess we all romanticize the past—but at one point I had a day job in customer service in New York, and the thing that made me very happy when I did that was I had my hours, I worked, and then when I left, I didn't think about it until the next day. I was able to put in just the right amount of effort, and then I left it alone.

Do you think you would ever get to a point where you'd go back to customer service or a job that would give you stability and the benefits?

I was thinking about that when we were told that they were not sure what our jobs will be in the fall, and my first thought was "God no, please don't make me go back to [customer service]." Because I've now created this identity. It's my identity to teach. I lose that, I lose my identity.

I'm so glad we got to talk about this, Mark. I never get to talk about my job. It's so easy to complain about little things. Usually, I just complain about my commute. But to talk about how much I love it! It kind of makes my heart swell. I never get to say that I love my job. But I do!

You do light up when you talk about your students and teaching.

My mom will be so proud!

"That's just me; I'm a helper."
SHANNON DREW

She is a caregiver and has developed several enterprises of her own, including offering shopping services. She has received assistance from Connections for the Homeless[*] to maintain an apartment.

They say you can't have a testimony without a test. Well, that's true. I definitely have a testimony. I've been through some stuff. I would love to really talk about it and be able to help somebody else get out of a situation like I had and know you don't have to go back. I was never one of those females to want to be in a relationship like that.

I ran for my life because [a man I knew at the time and I] had a fight that morning. He ended up—he kicked me with steel toe boots. My whole left thigh was bruised. I ran to my daughter's room, and he told me if I went in there he would quote/unquote "fuck her up too." My daughter [who was 3] had seen him hit me. And that just was not sitting well with me. I was like, she shouldn't have to see that.

We took my daughter to daycare, then I dropped him off at work. And I kept anticipating this backhand smack to the face, but I never got that, thank God. I had a WIC[†] appointment, and the whole time, I'm just like, "I've got to get out of this. I'm leaving today. I can't take it. I can't do it." And I did. I took what I could. It was just horrible. It was absolutely horrible.

But it's my story. It's my . . . escape, so to say. My rebirth, my new start. My dream. Because I used to dream of the day I would do this. I could *see* my daugh-

---

*   See Betty Bogg, p. 85.

†   Women, Infants, Children—a federal program providing nutritional assistance.

ter and I driving down the highway in a U-Haul or whatever. But yeah, it was just my time to go. I just couldn't take it anymore. I'm very proud of myself for that. And I just don't want to see anybody else go through that.

[Today] I work for an agency that helps the elderly. I go in, and I help people for a couple hours. They're given six hours of my time a month. Twice a month I go in, and I'll do the bathroom, or I'll sweep the floors or do dishes. I can go to the store for them or run an errand for them. I can't take them there, but I can go do it for them. One lady, I do her laundry for her. It takes me a couple hours, and then I'm done.

They call it "chore aid." I don't like that term. I think they're trying to change it. There's a lot of clients that tend to think that we're a maid service, but we're not. We do light housekeeping. If you think I'm coming in there to fully scrub floors—no, I'm not going to do that. I'll vacuum. I'll do your bathroom, your dishes, mop your floors. Just light housekeeping. I had a client that needed more than what I could give her. It was like every time, every two weeks, I go to her. And she has a long house, and she wants all these things done. But I'm only there two hours. And then she's waiting on me every two weeks to clean her bathroom and do these things . . . and that's a lot. That's a lot on me. It's not fair to me. She needs a caregiver, somebody to come in and do these things every day.

Most of the time, they just want the company. Somebody to talk to. So that's gratifying for me because I don't have my grandparents anymore. My grandfather, I took care of him. He had dementia. I took care of him for two years before he passed away. And that just taught me a lot. I would do it all over again in a heartbeat.

During COVID, I also started my own errand service, grocery shopping. It's called Girl on the Go. I'll send you that flyer. Some people can pay what I'm asking, other people, I'm like, "Just give me what you can," you know. I'm not trying to shortchange myself, but I'm also not trying to break somebody else that really can't afford it. My mom says I'm too nice. (Laughs.) They always say that. "You're too nice, Shannon." But that's just me. (Laughs.) I just love helping people. I'm a helper.

My service has been like nonexistent now because [after the lockdowns] people want to get back out themselves, which is fine, but I definitely would like to have that in place for elderly people that can't get out or don't want to go for whatever reason. And as I'm thinking about it now, that probably would be a good thing because my daughter had the accident in May. My 20-year-old daughter was shot in her right eye. So she lost sight in her right eye, and she had a stroke on her left side. Now she has no sight in her eye, and she's still working on this left side, the arm and the hand, to get back full use of that.

You refer to it as an accident.

Well, that's how I'm getting through this. I don't think that it was purposeful. But then again, I don't know. I have a 16-year-old, her sister, that was in the car with her who actually witnessed it and called the police. So, it's a lot. It's just a lot. So I just say that it's an accident. That's what I'm going to choose to believe. I don't want to think that somebody did this deliberately to hurt her. That would just change the whole game for me, so I just say it was her accident.

If I could get the [grocery] service going again, that probably would be a good thing for her because it could be something that she could possibly do. She could do the grocery shopping, and then we'd have somebody with her to drive and get the groceries delivered.

Do you feel like you're living the life you want to live?

I'm trying. I'm trying. Yeah, I'm trying. It's hard. But you know, it's life. Life has its ups and downs, good times, bad times. Some people have it better than others and some people struggle and work hard for what they want and need. I'm one of those that's struggling to have what I want and need. It's really been challenging because I haven't been able to work as much because of this accident that happened to my daughter. I've got this GoFundMe going, I've had help from the city, I've had help from Connections for the Homeless. I've had help from churches just to be able to pay my bills, but it's a lot. It's really a lot.

Are you able to make the rent?

Well, I've had a lot of help with that. Connections paid a big chunk of it. I think I still have a credit. I've got a car note. I've got insurance. I've got the gas, the lights, food, and other stuff, you know, and from May when she had the accident to August, I really wasn't working. So I've had to just depend on these services to help get me through. And I'm still dependent on them.

Do you feel yourself moving toward the independence you were seeking?

I'm trying. That's why I need to pass and get my CNA* certification, because

* Certified Nurse Assistant.

that's going help me in the long run. And then I've got this teenager, she's a sophomore in high school, she wants to do this and wants to do that. And it's just hard. I've got family that helps, and their dad helps.

The girls are here with me, and then I have a son that's 26. He goes to a veterinarian school in Grenada. That's the best thing of my life to see him doing that. I would always say, "Oh, you're gonna be my little veterinarian!" He is going to be an amazing veterinarian. I'm so proud of him. I mean, I'm proud of all of them. My oldest is still struggling, trying to figure out his life, but we'll get through that. And then the girls and me, we'll get through what we're going through, so it'll be okay.

What does work mean to you?

The idea of working is not so much about the money to me. The money helps because it helps you provide, but there's so many people out here now that are just doing jobs just for the money. I get it, because things are hard and expensive and all, and you're trying to survive, but if you don't remotely even like what you do, you shouldn't be doing it.

You know when you go to work, everybody has bad days. Everybody has things that are on their mind that are bothering them or they're going through, but when you go to work, you need to leave that outside the door, leave it in your car, I don't care where you leave it, but don't come into work with it because it affects everybody. And it just isn't fair to other people for you to bring your crap to work.

I try to instill that in my kids and myself. To just keep that mindful. I learned that because I worked in Nashville, and I was doing telemarketing, selling the newspaper over the phone. And they said to smile. And then I also learned that in Tupperware because I am a Tupperware consultant as well. So, you know, *just smile*. Nobody will ever know anything's wrong.

"It's not all trail rides and cookouts."
TIM KELLOGG

He works on a cattle ranch. He is also a chocolatier and owner of a small artisan chocolate shop in Meeteetse, Wyoming, "a one-block town of 300. We still have the wooden sidewalks. I am a one-man band. I do it all. I make the chocolates every day using locally sourced ingredients and flavorings when possible."

No one ever got into ranching to make a lot of money. You're definitely not going to get rich quick, no matter what level you are, from ranch hand to ranch owner and anything in between. You have to have a passion for it or a love of cattle and the land.

One of the really nice things about ranching is that by the time you get sick of one aspect, it's time to move on. The work changes with the seasons. Like you had night calving, which droned on, and when you got sick of that, it was time for irrigation, and when you got sick of that, it was time for haying and baling; got sick of that and then you had the winter maintenance.

I think people probably over-romanticize calving more than they should because if you saw it, when we pull the calf, I have to have both my hands inside the cow to get it out. I'm just covered in mud and blood and afterbirth kinds of stuff, but it's just the reality of what we have to do, because if that calf dies, that's money that the ranch has lost, and also, it's not good for the cow. We all have to do things sometimes that are unpleasant. I don't really like being covered in afterbirth, but it's just part of the job.

When we move cows, though, we're on horseback, and the notion of moving them up the valley and all that stuff is all very cool, except for the fact that you're usually up at 2:30 in the morning. You want to start moving at first light, which, in the summer here, is 4:30-ish, give or take depending on the month. And those are fun days because you're just spending the day on horseback and moving cows up into the mountains in the summer, and then back down into the valley in the fall. You don't want to stress the cows and also don't want them to be running because you don't want them to lose weight or get injured. So it's a very leisurely trip.

We stop at ponds, let them drink, and then we'll sit there in the grass and have lunch, and the horses kind of meander around and eat. But it's not all trail rides and cookouts. I've had friends that have come out, and I've taken them horseback riding. They're like, "This is so great! You get to do this every day!" (Laughs.) I think it's over-romanticized. Regardless of the weather, we're out there. It's snowing, we're out there. If it's a hundred degrees, we're out there. You can't just say, "I'm not going to work today," because the cows need to be fed. The horses need to be fed. I'm not just responsible for myself on the ranch. I'm also responsible for the animals and all the other guys, just the same as they are. We have to do our jobs.

But even the worst day on the ranch is a thousand times better than the best day most other places because of the remoteness. There'll be days where you'll look up and there'd be 400 elk crossing, you know, or we'd see a bald eagle or something crazy like a pelican or just really random wildlife. Every spring the sandhill cranes come in. I love sandhill cranes. They're the most bizarre, prehistoric animal.

I was doing that for about 15 years, and then, as my chocolate business took off, I was starting to work there a little bit less. I still help out from time to time on different ranches.

How did you become a chocolatier?

It started about 17 years ago, 18 years ago. I was a saddle bronc rider in the rodeo, and I needed to get a new bronc saddle, which is like a modified saddle meant specifically for that sport. They're not cheap by any means, and I didn't have the money.

During the first week of July in Cody, there's one of the largest rodeos in the world. It's the Cody Stampede, and it's a professional rodeo. It's basically a week where tens of thousands of people come through Cody every single day and they have all these local vendors, like craft beers and stuff like that. And so, my mom suggested that I make a bunch of chocolates and brownies that I used to make with her mother, my grandmother, and sell them. I believe my exact words were like, "Hell no." But as luck would have it, I sold out every single day, and I raised more than enough for the saddle. I just kept doing these booths around Wyoming and then after a while people were like, "You should make a business out of this."

When I opened the business officially, Saturdays were my day off from the ranch, so the store would be open Saturday morning and early afternoon. I'd cook through the night, then fill the cases and open, and then I'd go up to Cody for the rodeo. And then over the years the business slowly grew. I'm in what used to be an old saloon that burned and was rebuilt into a very nice kind of café. I bought the building 13, 14 years ago. It still looks like an old saloon from the front. A funky, funky building. Now we're open Wednesday through Saturday, with the exception of Easter, which is really busy. The hours expand and contract with the holidays—Christmas, Valentine's. The seasons are very bipolar; either you're overwhelmed, or you're bored out of your mind.

I want to say 10 or 12 years ago, I had really kind of hit a wall because there was only so much that I could learn off of the internet and YouTube and the Food Network. I was having a very hard time because nobody, at that time, that I was aware of in the United States, was making chocolates the way I did. I was making my own extracts. I wasn't adding sugar or additives or preservatives or stabilizers. For two reasons: one, I didn't want that stuff in my chocolate, and two, that's also a lot of expense to get all that stuff. I just liked the texture and the flavor, but my chocolates have a very, very short shelf life because there's no added sugar and there's no additives, preservatives, or stabilizers.

People are so used to buying a box of chocolates at the grocery store and throwing them in a cupboard, and six, eight months down the road, they'd still be fine. I used to get such horrible, angry emails from people that were like, "We bought these chocolates in April, and we just opened them, and they're moldy." And I'm like, "It's August!"

Now we have like a "born on" date that we stamp it with. We told people they're good for five days. It took years and years because people were so used to manufactured chocolate that was made months ago somewhere else and brought in. My chocolates are very much a niche market, but I'm going for mouthfeel and flavor.

When people bite into my chocolate, it's like nothing that they've ever had before. And that's what I want. I'm going for quality, not quantity. And so, it was about re-educating the consumer and being like, "Listen, this was made by hand by me this morning. I'm using organic butter. I'm using local eggs, local dairy, cream, and milk. I'm importing the best cacao I can get my hands on, and I'm making my own extracts for every single batch. I'm steeping the herbs or the flavors in the cream. I'm not making a massive batch of alcohol-based extracts that I'm going to keep for months at a time." So now, finally, 99 percent of the customers have finally been beaten down by me over the years. (Laughs.) They've come to understand what I'm trying to do here.

I've been doing this for 18 years, but I promised myself that when I got sick of it, I was done. I'd walk away. I'm not going to live my life doing something I don't like doing.

THE WORK OF ART

"Individuals are important."
MARGOT MCMAHON

She is an environmental and public sculptor working in Chicago. She is also the author of several books.

Almost every one of my public art pieces is a social justice statement for a city that is still greatly troubled. The remarkable thing is that I have gotten to represent people who have made a huge difference in Chicago. These are people who dedicated their lives to trying to nudge the world in the right direction.

When I'm looking back on my life—and I hope I have as many years ahead of me as I've had behind me—I realize I've gotten to do what I thought was important. I got to say people are important. Individuals are important. You don't have to be well known. Did you see, [on my website] I was called the "Studs Terkel of sculptors" [by the Lincoln Park Community Art Initiative]?

Most people don't know who Father Jack Egan is, for example, but he was a superstar for the civil rights movement, and he was exiled [by the church after speaking out against the Archdiocese]. I sculpted him for DePaul University.*

I had an exhibit at the Chicago History Museum called Just Plain Hardworking, and it was five men and five women—a packinghouse worker, a steelworker, a homemaker, a restaurateur—and it wasn't Charlie Trotter! It was Florence Scala.† The idea is that *these* are the people who got up every day and made this city an integral and interwoven group of cultures. And *this* is why we like Chicago and why we want to live here.

I sculpted Delois Barrett Campbell. She was part of the Barrett Sisters,‡ who are still performing, but she was the oldest and had this amazing way of taking you to another planet with her singing. It was 300 years of woe that she was able to put into her voice. So, I sculpted her. The National Portrait Gallery selected it

---

* Her sculpture of Father Egan stands outside the DePaul University student union building.

† A political activist who waged a political battle with the city to prevent the demolition of the Near West Side neighborhood, which included the Hull House Settlement. In 1980, she and her brother opened the Florence Restaurant in what had been their father's tailor shop.

‡ Gospel singing trio.

for their collection of 10 Chicagoans who have made a difference. We cast that one in bronze for them.

I sculpted everybody in person. That's one of the criteria of the National Portrait Gallery. So I'd talk with them while I was working. Lois Barrett Campbell had told me, "I walk around Chicago, and nobody knows me. I'm just another face on the street. But when I go to Europe, I'm treated like Michael Jackson—driven around and protected. Here, I can go anywhere, and nobody says hello." She said it's very strange to live in both worlds.

Flash forward to 2016, I was invited to go to a meeting to plan the Gwendolyn Brooks' centenary. Her daughter came up to me at the meeting and said, "You know, there's a park named after my mother; it would be nice to have a sculpture of her there."

I wanted to create the impression of being in the room with her. Usually, as I said, I *am* in the room with the people I sculpt, but I couldn't recreate that with Gwendolyn Brooks [who had died in 2000]. I did sit and talk with Nora Brooks Blakely [her daughter], though. I had overheard somebody at the centenary event say, "Nora, you sounded exactly like your mother [when you spoke] today." So I started to watch Nora for her gestures, her actions, her intonation. She told me, "The top half of my face looks like my mom and the bottom half looks like my dad." Of course, I used photos that she sent me because that is what she thought best represented her mother, so I had images of Gwendolyn, but I wanted the *feeling* of Gwendolyn. And I wanted to capture her at the age when she received the Pulitzer Prize.

I think it was when she was poet laureate of Illinois that she went into every single classroom she could, and she listened to every single story she could. She heard those students talk about their experiences, and I'm sure a lot of that informed her own creativity. *That's* the person I had to capture. And those are the things that kind of settled me into sculpting her as somebody who's looking into your eyes as you sit down in front of her, and she already knows your story, but she wants to hear it fresh.

Public art is an individual piece that's been made for a purpose *in situ* that has been designed for people to gather at. There's been a discussion amongst artists about if you take that piece out of its location, you're taking the meaning away from it. It's meant for *this place*. For example, there are a couple of churches

* A poet (1917–2000) whose work often addressed the challenges of so-called ordinary people.

and two or three schools [near Gwendolyn Brooks Park]. Gwendolyn was not allowed to go to this park growing up, which is another reason I thought it's important for all of these students growing up and playing around the sculpture now to see a Black woman ... in bronze ... on a pedestal. I mean, there's no other place you could go in Chicago to see that, that I know of. And I would say, there was no other place in the country you could go and see that. We have a *few* sculptures of women who have been installed since the year of the Gwendolyn Brooks monument, but I don't think there was another image of a female in a public park.

We actually did a study, and this was shocking to me. Here I've spent decades sculpting women, and there was no sculpture of a real woman in a major city in the United States. In a public place. Not in DC, not in New York, not in Chicago, not in LA.˙ So that became a big deal. A really big deal. Why would I bring my daughter to parks when there's all these sculptures of men and none of women? There's no Jane Addams! This was a human being who devoted her life to helping immigrants get settled in Chicago. So, I have an issue with that. I mean, how could you have this city without Jane Addams represented?

As you're working, how do you know when you've captured what you wanted to capture?

It's the feeling. You model it in clay; you destroy it over and over again. And so, it's a constant creation and destruction, creation and destruction. And then finally, you have a product that's hard and lasts. A lot of times, I'll be going along, and I'm like, "Oh, I could get the proportion different or this or that, but it feels right to walk away now." That is what the maturity of an artist is, knowing to walk away at the right time, because [if you keep going] you could kill it. You just work it until it's got its own life. Egan could have turned out many different ways, but there was a moment when he came to life. And that's the moment that's out there.

And then you've got to make sure you walk away.

---

* Approximately 8 percent of the statues that depict historic figures in the United States are of notable women.

"Some terribly dangerous ideas."
BARRY BLITT

He is an editorial cartoonist and illustrator whose work has appeared on more than a hundred covers of the New Yorker *since 1992. He illustrated Frank Rich's weekly column in the* New York Times *from 2003 to 2011. In 2020 he received a Pulitzer Prize for editorial cartooning.*

"I grew up in Canada idolizing hockey players, so I spent most of my young life drawing hockey players. When I was 14, a friend in my class said, 'I'll be your agent' and he wrote letters to all the NHL teams, and the [Philadelphia] Flyers wrote back. (Holds up a magazine.) This is the Philadelphia Flyers' 1974 yearbook. I did all of their drawings on every page. We charged them $5 a drawing. What did we know? It was my first published work. Pretty exciting. Back then, my work was reverential; it was hero worship really. I've since become such a sarcastic bastard."

We talk on Zoom six months into the pandemic. He is 62 years old.

I keep a sketchbook. (Holds up a notebook and flips through the pages.) It's like a classic safe space where I don't have to worry. I hash out a bunch of ideas without any regard, really, to the drawing itself. I'll scribble, trying to express an idea so that [an editor] can see where I might go with it.

I have some terribly dangerous ideas in my sketchbook. Things I wouldn't show anybody. I did an idea recently that almost got me into trouble. I don't even know if I should talk about it. It was an obese Donald Trump in bed on top of Melania, and she's saying, "I can't breathe." I sent it to the *New Yorker* and Françoise* said, "So I love this. It's really funny, but I don't even want to show this to the editor. It's not the right time. And probably there's never going to be a right time."

I put it on Facebook. It got a lot of nervous and angry comments. Immediately, there were 600 or 700 comments. I took it down. You're using a murdered man's last words as a punchline, and I felt pretty bad about it. I had sold it to Graydon Carter[†] at *Air Mail*, his new venture, and I told him I don't think it's a good idea, and he was fine. Yanked it before it went up.

When I told Françoise, she said, "I understand your taking it down, as long

---

* Françoise Mouly, *New Yorker* art director since 1993.

† With Kurt Anderson and Tom Phillips, he cofounded *Spy,* a satirical magazine, in 1986. In 2019, he launched a weekly newsletter called *Air Mail,* which Blitt contributes to.

as it doesn't lead to you to being more cautious and to second-guessing yourself."
She wants me to center all of my worst impulses, and she'll decide whether it's
too raunchy or somewhere we shouldn't go. I've sent her a few things that are
quite horrible. And she's up to the task of just rolling her eyes and letting me
know that that's really not anything that is remotely publishable. But she does it
with good humor.

This isn't my insight, but lots of people have talked about how humor is
looking for the line, and then putting a toe over it. That's an interesting place
where it forces you to think. It's nice to laugh at something and then think, "Um,
should I be laughing at this?" Then: "Yes, I think it's okay to laugh at this."

I've only recently started putting things up on Facebook. I do it sporadically
and very rarely, but I'm finding it's a good way to get instant feedback. Because,
god knows, it used to be you were sitting in a room working, and before email,
you'd get *no* feedback. You'd send a drawing out with a courier and then there
would be no reaction until it was printed. But Facebook is pretty immediate. You
get to see a reaction in real time. I think I have the same reaction as everybody
who puts things on Facebook or on social media. It's a shot of whatever chemical
it is, dopamine or whatever. I'd say it's probably a discipline, though, to not be
governed by that too much. Anyway, I'm aiming for that.

Remember that old photograph on V-E Day of the sailor kissing the girl in
Times Square? Around the time of "Don't Ask, Don't Tell," I drew that with two
male sailors. And that was sort of before the internet; it was around '96. So I was
getting angry phone calls, which was alarming, but not like the reaction to the
cover with the Obamas doing a fist bump in the Oval Office ["The Politics of
Fear," July 21, 2008]. That came out, and immediately my AOL inbox went to a
thousand, and that's when you couldn't get more than a thousand. That was kind
of alarming. It's dizzying when that happens. It happened so fast, and it was so
negative. We thought we were trying to do something noble, you know. It seemed
obviously a parody of all the ridiculous things being said about the candidate
Obama at the time. But almost nobody got the joke, not immediately.

Do you regret doing it or is that response just part of the game?

It's just part of the game, I guess. Françoise was very gung-ho about that one and
it seemed funny to me. It still seems funny to me, but a lot of the reaction was
like, "*I* get it, but what are those other people going to think about it?" Too often

I'll beat myself up for not pushing hard *enough*. So, with this one, at least we tried something a little bit different, and—I hate to use the word "edgy"—but it was at the edge of something. But also, I have to say I regret every cover I do. I always wish I could have another stab at it so I could refine it a little more. Or maybe reimagine it.

How might you have reimagined the fist bump?

I wish what we were doing could have been more overt. One of the early sketches of that was Barack and Michelle fist-bumping, and in the window we've got Rush Limbaugh and Bill O'Reilly and Ann Coulter looking in. And you can tell that [they're seeing] their worst imagining come to life. That just seemed like one step too many in the final drawing.

Did the Obamas respond?

Yeah, Barack Obama responded officially when he was asked about it.* I think [Senator John] McCain said it was deplorable and disgusting or whatever it was. But since then, I've seen a picture of [Obama] standing in the White House with another cover of mine beside him. So I don't think he holds a grudge. Michelle was quite unhappy with it, which I understand and which makes me feel bad because I think they're both the greatest. But I can't get too deep into worrying about offending people I'm drawing. I guess if it doesn't connect necessarily, maybe it's not a great piece of satire, or else, maybe, people were just too sensitive at that time, and I can understand that as well.

Jon Stewart, on *The Daily Show*, talked about it and said, "You know, we're getting upset about a cartoon. It's obviously satire." Then it stopped. It would have been hard to have something like that go on for several months.

As you work, are you conscious of how a political cartoon can shape public perception?

Well, I'm aware that that's part of what a cartoon can do, for sure. I mean, I don't know if I would ever have looked at Donald Trump and thought he had small hands. I think that's something that's used to annoy him. And it's certainly shaped public perception about it. Everyone draws him that way now. You establish a cliché, basically, that's not necessarily based on a truth. It came from Graydon Carter, I think. He was the first to call him a "short-fingered vulgarian." Now

* "I have no response to that." *New York Times,* July 13, 2008.

it's part of the way he's always depicted, and it's thought of as practically truth.

Graydon told me that Trump would regularly send him photographs, Xerox pictures of himself on magazine covers and he would, with a gold marker, circle his hands and write, "See? Not small." But the only reason something like that sticks is because he's so sensitive about it.

There's people getting "canceled," and I think about how that easily could happen to me. Every so often that pops into my head. Someone could pick up on something I drew 20 years ago or more recently. I think about that sometimes, thinking, "What if I didn't have a career?" I can't imagine not drawing and not trying to make myself and others laugh with infantile drawings. I can't stop that somehow. So I do ponder it, but I'm not overly worried. We'll see. Anyway, there's really no point in thinking about this.

"I really need to sing for people."
KURT ELLING

He is a Grammy-winning jazz vocalist. We talk on Zoom eight months into the pandemic.

I'm always working pretty hard. In a regular year, I do about 200 nights on the road. In January and February of this year, we were gearing up to release a new recording project and to tour behind that project. So I was gearing up to do what usually would be a ferocious round with the record—do the road, a bunch of interviews, a bunch of duet concerts, and then wait for the summer when we'd go with the whole band to Europe. Yeah, I was gearing up for all of that. It was all scheduled. It was all in the books and everything was budgeted and ready to go.

I remember hearing about a new virus coming out of China and feeling very concerned that our own leadership wasn't going to take it seriously and would blow it off. I was in Palm Springs, where I had just done a gig with Patti Austin and some other cats, some friends of mine, at this little performing arts center there. I was sitting out on this beautiful deck at the performing arts center between the sound check and the performance. I had just gotten to meet Rita Moreno. I was having this beautiful steak dinner, and I was thinking to myself that this, what I was experiencing, is not going to last. I could see it in the news. You could read it in the cards. And I said this out loud: "This is going to be a really beautiful day out here in Palm Springs, and it's probably going to be my last gig for a while. I just hope it's not too long." That was in the first part of March. And that *was* my last gig. I was hoping that it would all be done by the summer and that our summer plans would still happen. And then they didn't. I feel like quoting Ferlinghetti, you know: "I have suffered, somewhat."

I'd grown used to having a regular performing schedule to guide and orient my waking hours. I'm so used to the opportunity to sing for people, to sing right out loud, to collaborate with my musicians, to be challenged in that arena, to do my best work every night, to literally reverberate with sound in a way that is very healing and meaningful and . . . *identity-giving*. To have that rug pulled out like that has been—I won't lie about it. It's been excruciating at times. I can't say that this has been my finest hour. I haven't been the most up individual I've ever been. It's been hard. It's been a lot of pouting.

I really need to sing for people, and I need *that* exhaustion. I need to be exhausted by my work. I'm built for *that* challenge. I'm not really built for this challenge. I'm 25 years into a career of trying to sing in tune with grace and power and authority every night, and to sing music that has a purpose and that is worth listening to, *really listening* to. I know I haven't reached the potential of what that is. I have so much to learn and most of that has to come from the experience and trial and error. And if I can't keep doing *that*, then—well, I won't say it's lost time because it's certainly not, nothing's lost. There are things to be learned here that I clearly need to learn. But these aren't comfortable lessons.

You said you need *to sing for people.*

I've had these occasions over 25 years where I had to be on the stage [at momentous times]. Four days after 9/11, I was in Chicago. It was the Saturday, and I was the first thing that people came out to hear, a record release for a romance record at Park West, and they all wanted to be fed and they all wanted to have something happen that's salutatory, that's an act of mercy, somehow. Everybody just wanted to be together. They just wanted to be together. And it just happened that I was there.

We had an arrangement of a Stephen Sondheim song called "Not While I'm Around," which, in the context of the show it's from, *Sweeney Todd*, is very twisted. But my collaborator at the time, Lawrence Hughley, was able to put this into such a beautiful arrangement. Even standing alone, it's a thing of beauty. It's a gorgeous, gorgeous musical statement. But I adjusted the whole set list that night. We all stood, we sang the national anthem, sat down, and then I had him improv on the piano. I told him, "I'm going to say some stuff; you know what to do." I don't remember all the words I said, but I wanted to broadcast a fellow feeling and to remind everybody that we had survived a whole lot of things in the past. And that this event is incredible and shocking, but it's not the end of us. And it's not the end of what we believe in.

And then, because I had been in divinity school, I could fall back on some stuff. I said, "I remember a quote. Something like, 'We're surrounded by a circle whose center is everywhere and whose circumference is nowhere. And we bathe in this, and it's our birthright, and it's the birthright of everything that's alive. And the God that created this doesn't want us to forget that. What do you think a God who created this much beauty would want us to hear?' And then, (he sings:) "*Nothin's gonna harm you. . . .*"

That's one of the times when I feel like I can really do my best when I'm there, that's what I'm there for. It was a moment. It really was. I think of that as being as much a part of my job as helping a guy propose to his girl. I've had . . . I mean, maybe I'm overstating it. . . . No! No, I'm *not* overstating it. I've had the *privilege* of investing as much time as I've wanted to when those moments arose. But who am I? Just some guy trying to sing in tune and trying to do triage for 90 minutes a night to people who choose to show up.

"*It felt worth trying.*"
MARK HARRIS

He is an author who writes for New York Magazine *and the* New York Times Style Magazine *and has published three nonfiction books. We talk on Zoom shortly after the release of his first biography,* Mike Nichols: A Life. *He sits in his writing space, which he shows me with a 360-degree Zoom pan. Behind him are two framed posters. One reads: "Get up you lazy bum." The other: "I can't, I don't feel well."*

Those two signs are kind of the two halves of my writing personality: the whiner who doesn't want to do it, and the scold who tells the whiner to focus and get on with it. I like writing with my back to them because it's like having the devil and the angel on my shoulders. I also have an office in Provincetown, Massachusetts, that also has two signs. One says, "Give it all you got." And the other says, "Fuck it."

Did the idea of writing a biography for the first time scare you?

Oh, yes. Very much. Yeah. But I should say, I definitely want to go into any book I do half-scared and half-excited. I have huge respect for biographers, and it was never something that I imagined myself doing, not even something I was sure I would know *how* to do. But it seemed worth trying.

What kept me up at night was not a question as vague as "Do I know how to write a biography?" But "What happens if I don't understand him [Mike Nichols]? What happens if I can't figure him out? What if I can't make him make sense to me?"

How did you wrestle your way through that?

I told myself not to think about it and just do my research. My job wasn't to have figured him out before I started work on the book. The whole point of doing research was to *give myself the ability* to figure him out. So, I thought, let me kick my own question about whether or not I can make him comprehensible to myself down the road until I have as much information and understanding on my side as I possibly can. Although I didn't research the book chronologically at all, because that would have been impossible, I do keep everything I learn from interviews, from reading, from research, from movie watching, whatever else, in a chronological timeline.

One thing I didn't realize, but which turned out to be true is that. . . . Well, I actually *did* know this from my first two books, but it was especially true about this one: that even if you think you've figured everything out in advance before you start to write, the writing always teaches you things that you didn't know you knew, and the writing will sometimes take you in a direction you had no intention of going. I think it's a good thing to listen to that. Themes can emerge that you didn't realize were themes until you find yourself coming back to them again and again. And that is a really interesting part of writing to me: that your own writing isn't just this thing that you plan in advance and orchestrate. It's more like what you've written becomes this separate thing that can teach you something.

To what degree and in what ways do you manage and shape real characters and events?

I do think a lot about the question of narrativizing things because I want my books to be stories. But I tried very, very hard not to fictionalize him, not to put ideas in his head that I had no evidence were actually in his head. And, at the same time, I'm aware that writing a biography is always, to some degree, presumptuous and that you *have* to make connections, you have to take some leaps. You can't just do a dry recitation of facts and dates and events. It was mainly about finding a balance between making sure that I understood to my satisfaction why something followed something else while resisting glib, overall psychological explanations that would uncover everything in this, what I call "Rosebud" way. You know, the single childhood event that makes everything that follows make sense. I don't think lives really work that way. So walking that line was a challenging thing for me.

You said you "tried very hard" not to fictionalize him. Was there a temptation you were fighting?

Yeah, I think there *is* a temptation to do it. And I don't think it's important to never be tempted. I think it's important to recognize it as a temptation when it comes up. Often, if you feel that temptation, the reason is that you haven't figured something out, and you're looking for an easy answer. That temptation is a good signal to you to go back and report more, or think more, or research more until you don't have to invent something to patch over a period that you don't understand.

What is the role of serendipity in your research?

I think it plays a big role. I interviewed 250 people for this book. And if I had had another year to research, I probably could have interviewed a hundred more. Would those hundred people have changed the nature of the book? Or would they have just made it a longer book? Did I get the people I needed to get in order to feel like I could do the book? I don't know. These are really unanswerable questions. And what if I hadn't gotten to talk to Elaine May? I don't know what I would've done. It would be a very different book. It would still exist, but I would have lost the knowledge and understanding that she gave me, which informed huge, huge parts of the book that she isn't even in. There are also things in the book that are there because I decided to look at one extra old clipping file in a library, and there are things in the book that are there because I later happened to notice something in a movie.

So serendipity plays a huge part, and all you can do is—It sounds contradictory to say, "plan for serendipity," but what I mean is put yourself in a position where you can be exposed to as much serendipity as possible. The more people you talk to, the more work you do, the more you're opening yourself to the chance that you can be surprised.

Your husband is also a writer, playwright, and screenwriter. *How does your work inform his and his yours, if at all?*

I'm really fortunate because it's great to live with another writer, and it is also great to live with a writer who does not do precisely what you do. Tony invents characters and situations from scratch, which is wildly different from what I do. We both like each other's writing (laughs), which is a good thing. I think it would be really rough if we didn't. There's no sense of competition because I could never do what he does, and he has no desire to do what I do. But I think the struggles of writers have a lot of things in common. We both know what they are and what that's like.

I think we both like how the other reacts to our work. I will tend to show Tony things that I do early [in the process]. He tends to show me things that he does late. We have different ways of critiquing each other's work. Tony, frankly, is much nicer than I am. I tend to go at things as an editor because that had been such a big part of my life. He tends to go at things as a *listener*.

But I think we both find each other helpful. There are ways in which my approach as a writer is very journalistic: cut what's not necessary. And there are ways in which his approach as a writer is creative: keep what's delightful—although, he will also say that one of the first rules of playwriting is come into a scene as late as possible and leave as quickly as possible. I've learned from him to sometimes leave something in just because it's kind of wonderful and a great detail, even if it doesn't feel essential, that maybe, instead, it's essential *in that moment* that the reader be delighted by that little detail.

I should add that we work in separate rooms now, but we did share an office for a few years, and it drove him crazy. (Laughs.) He said he could not stand the sound of my typing while he was stuck, which I totally understand.

---

* Tony Kushner, *Angels in America* and the Steven Spielberg films *Lincoln* and *The Fablemans*, among others.

What does it mean to you to have pulled this biography off?

(Long pause.) I don't know. That's the answer. I don't know how to tell you any-thing that's more truthful than that. I *think* I pulled it off. I know that the book has been very well received, but I think what you're asking me is how does it feel inside? And I think that I'm not letting myself have those feelings. The book being well received is something that I have to keep a distance from because, in advance of the book coming out, I had worked so hard to figure out how I would not feel destroyed if the book was really poorly received. I worked really, really hard to think that the way this book is received is not who I am, and so now that it's been very well received, I still have to stick to "that's not who I am."

"I like to disappear into a film."
DENNIS SCOTT

Since 1992, he has been house organist at Chicago's Music Box Theatre, which was built in 1929. He plays weekend pre-shows and intermissions, sing-along events, and themed film festivals. He is the official organist for the International Buster Keaton Society. We talk on Zoom 11 months into the pandemic. The Music Box has been shuttered the entire time.

There are people around the country who identify themselves as theater organists and travel around playing programs on theater pipe organs, but they've never actually played in a theater for *movies*; they're concert organists. Some of them think what I do is not legitimate because I don't have to go out and play concerts, but I'm just very comfortable being at the Music Box and playing intermissions and accompanying silent films.

It was Roger Ebert's favorite theater in Chicago. He used to write about it all the time, and he said that many times. The theater looks like a much bigger theater because there's a full proscenium and the grand curtain, but about three feet behind the curtain is a brick wall. We have a domed ceiling that's painted a midnight blue, and there are twinkle lights up in the ceiling that flash to look like stars. And then they have a machine which projects clouds slowly crossing the ceiling. Plaster facades on both side walls create this ambience of a Spanish courtyard. The main curtain is down when I'm play-ing which is traditional. Before the show, I always play music written in the same year the movie was introduced. For *Hello, Dolly!* with Barbra Streisand, I played all of the music of Jerry Herman. For *The Untouchables*, I played all movie music from the 1930s.

A lot of people recognize me in the lobby because they're regulars. And, in fact, some of them are like family because we see them all the time. So that's always nice, to visit with people in the lobby. But generally, I just blend into the woodwork. I like to blend into the woodwork because people should be paying attention to what's on screen and not to me.

For me to do a good program for a silent film, is to get out of the way. Just let the film speak for itself. I attended a performance about three, four years ago by a very, very well-known concert theater artist, who, I don't think, really enjoys playing silent films. It's a way of making money, so he does it. And he basically played a *concert* during a silent film, so he missed a lot. He was accompanying *The General*, which was Buster Keaton's masterpiece. And in some of the very quiet scenes where there's a sense of mystery, he just played furiously through the whole thing and missed the subtlety of the moment.

And then during the battle scene between the North and the South, he was playing the *1812 Overture*, which he played flawlessly. He has wonderful technique, so he played it wonderfully. But it was inappropriate. He missed a lot of Buster's little pieces of business that he was doing in a serious scene. That's one reason the movie is such a masterpiece because during this very serious battle scene, Buster was managing to do all these little bits that were funny with swords and cannons and other things, and the accompanist just missed all of it.

When I'm playing a film, I like to disappear into the film. One of the biggest compliments people can give me is at the end of the movie, they come on up and say, "Oh, we really enjoyed that film." And then they'll say, "I forgot you were playing!" I say, "Thank you! That's the whole idea!" You're supposed to forget that I'm playing because I'm supposed to enhance the scenes on screen, but not overpower them.

There's a theater organist named Gaylord Carter who was famous all over the country. He played a lot of radio. He played for *Amos 'n' Andy* and so forth. He was from Los Angeles, and he was befriended by Harold Lloyd. He said they were doing an appearance someplace where Lloyd was there in person to view *Safety Last!* where he's hanging from the clock on the side of a building. And

Gaylord played a little snippet of "Time on My Hands." He was a very young man then, and he said that Harold Lloyd came up to him after the film and said, "Gaylord, I'll do the jokes." (Laughs.)

Are there passages of silence, too?

Sometimes you want to make the organ as quiet as you can, where you're just playing one or two notes and let the action on screen speak for itself, basically. If there's a scene where somebody is on the verge of dying, for example, you just get quieter and quieter and quieter. The camera will linger on someone who is dying, and sometimes it's appropriate, not for long periods of time, but for several seconds, just to play nothing. And it's interesting because when I get to that point, I swear I'm in an empty room because the people behind me, sometimes I think they're not even breathing because it gets so quiet in the house. And I think, "Ooh, look! I got them!"

Now during the pandemic, it kills me not only not being able to play, but not to see all of our regular customers and our old friends. It really hit me during the Christmas season. The previous year we did 34 Christmas sing-alongs, officially, sometimes four shows a day. People say, "How do you keep the energy level up to do those?" I say, "I get the energy from the people because they're having such a good time." I sort of feed off of their energy.

Do you ever watch silent films on TV at home and find yourself scoring in your head?

Oh, yeah. My partner, Tom, and I watch film every Sunday night on TCM. We have a seven-foot screen down in the basement, and we have an organ similar to the one in the Music Box. Some of the films have the most hideous scores, and if it's bad, but the film looks interesting, I'll turn it down and play along with it. Many times, between movies, I'll play an intermission, and then Tom and I will sit with our popcorn and watch the next film. And if it's a film I really like, I'll sit and watch it over and over.

I'm certainly missing all that energy from playing for an audience. I'm missing the whole thing. I mean, I can sit and watch all the movies I want to here at home, but it's just not the same thing.

"What else is there?"
HOLLY MULCAHY

"I'm a violinist first and foremost. And among the many things that I do with the violin, I'm a concert master, which is the first chair of an orchestra. It's basically the quarterback of an orchestra, the liaison between the music director and the rank-and-file, and also liaison to the audience. I'm the second most visible face right after the conductor."

In addition to her work as a concert master and a soloist, she recently founded Arts Capacity, a program that brings live interactive performances and art to prisons.

As I talk with my colleagues, I think that it is not uncommon for most people in my shoes to have a feeling of inadequacy, constant inadequacy. I think it's part of being a musician, feeling inadequate. And there's a lot of, what's it called? Impostor syndrome. You think, "I only won that one audition because I played something accidentally better than somebody else. I should not be here." There's a lot of that. And those who say they don't feel that way are lying.

I grew up with this [feeling]. Growing up in Colorado, partially from the environment, but partially from the idea that was in my own head that if you are not on the East Coast, and you're wanting to be a classical musician, you won't make it. And so, I went to the East Coast and then I thought, "Oh, I'm just from Colorado." I didn't grow up with this serious, you know, classical music heritage. I must be lesser than my colleagues. So it was partially peer pressure, and partially my own manufacturing of this idea. But at this point, I don't care.

I think there's a point in a career where if you've reached what you had imagined at a young age would be your goal, if you get that goal, you either stop and just say, "That's it. I've reached my goal, I'm happy," or you say, "I've reached this goal, what else is there?" I think I'm that person: what else is there? As soon as I hit goals, I'm like, "Huh, what else?" It's dangerous.

How is it dangerous?

Theoretically, I should be extremely happy and just ride this wave of playing concerts, but I'm always like, "Maybe I should start a nonprofit. Maybe I should start a series. Maybe I should. . . ." Dangerous.

Why do you think you're compelled to keep reaching for more?

I don't know why. I think I'm trying to prove something. I think self-worth. Trying to prove that what I have to offer to my profession is worthy of my existence, which sounds really trite. But as a musician, you don't *have* to have music. You're not going to die without it. You need food and shelter, but you don't *need* music. So my goals have always been about: how is this relevant to somebody's life?

I feel like I've been given a lot, even though I grew up in a middle-lower-class kind of home. My mother was a part-time dental assistant to pay for my violin lessons and for trombone lessons for my brother, and my dad worked for United Airlines ground control, cargo. I was never hungry and never forced to make a decision between two bad choices. I think that I've been lucky. And music has played a good part in that. It's given me a place to put an energy that may have been spent other ways. And so, I've thought that I should share what I have.

That sounds like what you are doing with Arts Capacity. How did that program come into being?

It started very simply. I was sitting at a donor dinner, one of these symphony functions where the donors are sitting at round tables; nobody really knows each other, and an artist or executive also sits at the table. Because nobody knows each other, the questions usually go to the artist at the table, and it feels very self-centered to me to constantly just talk about myself there. I found that if I ask people about themselves and what brought them into music and about their lives, we could generate some real conversation instead of just enjoying rubber chicken together.

So, this one time, after people were done asking me about my career and what I thought about Beethoven and whatever, I asked, "So, what do *you* do?" And a couple of people at the table said they did prison mentorships. I blurted out, "Oh, I'd love to play at a prison," which I had really wanted to do. Then two months later, a gentleman contacted me, and he said, in a long email, "I don't know if you remember me, but we'd love to have you come here."

This particular prison that we went into is a place where all faiths are recognized. There's 13 different faiths, not just Judeo-Christianity, so atheism and Islam and Buddhism and Hinduism.

Did your initial experience in the prison match your expectations?

It exceeded my expectations. When one thinks of prisons, one imagines the worst-case scenarios, you know, really awful situations. If you watch *Orange Is the*

New Black or *Shawshank Redemption* or any number of those TV and movies, you would expect the worst. I was expecting the place to be smelly, loud, but I was met with very respectful, kind, helpful people that just had prison uniforms on. They were excited to greet me. They were excited to hear what we had to offer. And they were *present*, which I can't say about some of my audiences on the outside.

At the first performance, we were able to invite about 20 community members with us. These people were regular Chattanooga Symphony concertgoers, plus several members of the board of the symphony, the then-interim executive director, and some other volunteers. It was really fascinating because this was where I learned about the power of listening through somebody else's ears. When [these visitors] heard the impact of composer Jennifer Higdon's piece through the ears of somebody who was listening so fervently like their life depended on it—I mean, you listen different after that. It shifts the way you listen forever. And you don't take it for granted.

At first, I was taken aback because it was so quiet, and the prisoners were all just staring and listening on the edges of their seats, listening with *such focus*. It felt weird because I'm used to people checking out or falling asleep. But here, after certain pieces, they would give a standing ovation because it felt that good to them.

My philosophy of sharing music is always to listen to what *you*, the listener, think of it. I don't want to say, as sometimes happens in programs like this, "Here's serious music; here's what you should feel; here's what you should think, and if you don't, you're an idiot." Normally, people go in and play some music, tell the audience how to feel, and then leave. We've discovered that there is great value, therapeutically, in allowing people who don't normally get to share their opinions to share their opinions. Not only do they have great opinions, I learned from *them* how to listen to music. It taught me more than I learned in conservatory about how people listen.

There was one man who was new, who was virtually in tears. He said, "You know, this reminds me of my daughter playing violin. I haven't spoken to her in 20 years." And he couldn't finish the sentence. And some of the people around him were like, "Go on; it's okay."

We've had prisoners say things on their surveys, like one of them said, "I had pushed my emotions so far down, I didn't think I had them anymore until your violin recital." You know, saying that was "nice," doesn't really give it the gravity it should have. It gave depth to my career, that comment.

As satisfying as it is to be a performer on the outside, when the houselights go on at the end, people are already walking to their cars. The orchestra is still on stage! So, to have that kind of raw emotion shared [in the prison]—we never get that from the paying audience ever. People will applaud and then leave, and then that's the end of that relationship until the next concert. But this experience gave me validity; it gave me purpose, a new kind of purpose, a sense that I mattered. That I could bring those feelings out [with music] matters.

We had a recital right before COVID. We brought in a composer and my brother, who is a trombonist, and a saxophone player. The four of us played, and then I invited the prisoners to listen to the textures, the tonality, the colors, the story, everything, of each of these instruments and each of the pieces. And then we would compose on the spot, improvise a new piece with the prisoners' help. The pianist started to play. Then my brother came in, and the saxophone came in, and then we stopped and asked people, "What do you want to hear next?"

Somebody says, "Can you make more of a fiddle sound?" Somebody else: "Can you make a bagpipe sound?" "Can you make it more jazzy?" "Can you make it more solemn?" And then one prisoner said, "Can you make it sound like I'm with my daughter on Family Day, and we're releasing a balloon?"

That was our last performance before COVID. I came back after the lockdown, and Tim, the composer, had written this piece called "Release" and it felt really good to premiere that piece that those men helped write. It's that collaborative kind of art where I'm listening to you, you're listening to me, and we're going to create this together.

One thing over the pandemic that I've noticed is a lot of orchestras, their executives have said things like, "We need to get out there and reach the community and play in prisons and play in hospitals," but they don't know how to do this. And a lot of times it looks like virtue signaling if they play a prison and then don't come back. I think that's one of the worst things any organization can do is to play one time and never come back. Because it's insincere.

And so, the eventual plan [for Arts Capacity] would be for professional orchestras to partner with Arts Capacity. We would provide training to the orchestra members and be the liaison to the prisons, all in an effort for Arts Capacity to branch out, to have chapters around the country. We would guide these members on deep listening and communication and collaborative skills so that they can come up with something that's unique to that prison in that cultural environment.

We're not just doing this to give free concerts to murderers, rapists, drug dealers. We're giving free concerts as an investment in society.

A Better World for Our Children

"My dad would always say, 'We're not going to let you quit.'"
SANTIAGO SÁNCHEZ

He is an assistant principal at an elementary school in Virginia. He is 34 years old, and a father of two, ages 2 and 6.

I came from Mexico 21 years ago, when I was 13, from a state called Guanajuato, a beautiful part of Mexico that is very much like the valley where I live here, with lots of mountains and beautiful scenery. When my four other siblings and I were getting ready to go to the middle school, my dad figured that he wanted something better for us, and so he decided with my mom to bring us along to this country.

We crossed the border illegally when I was a child, so my dad began the process, as soon as we got here, to legalize our status. He initially brought my two younger siblings. My two other sisters and myself, he left us behind for about six months until he would be able to earn some money to pay to bring us here. He came directly to this area because of the poultry industry. It's still a pretty large part of the businesses around here. We have a lot of people working in poultry. We lived in a small trailer when we first got here, at a trailer park where a lot of the Latinos in the area lived, mostly Mexicans. First six months or a year, we lived with another family related to us, my uncle and aunt and three other children.

I came with no English. I was put into a middle school in eighth grade, and first year, really nobody knew how to help me, what to do with me. So I spent a lot of time on my own. At high school, I was one of very few Latinos in the school. It was a county school. It was not a very pleasant experience. I was little, I was different, and I was a perfect target for kids who were looking to bully another.

I almost quit a couple times, but my dad would always say, "Well, we're not going to let you quit. That's your only choice: school." A couple of times, in the summers, he said, "So you think you want to quit school? I'm going to take you to work for the summer." He would take me into the poultry industry, and I would work there for the summer. He would make sure that I would do some of the harder jobs so that I would really be able to experience what it would be like for the rest of my life if I chose not to go to school. They would always say, "Is this what you want for the rest of your life?" So every opportunity my parents had, they would say, "Just imagine yourself doing this your whole life. Now imagine yourself learning English and having a better job."

How have these experiences growing up shaped who you are as a school administrator?

I just keep thinking about my parents and thinking about seeing my dad coming from work on a regular basis with his hands swelled up because he had been hanging turkeys the whole day. Raw turkeys. And we're talking about 40- to 45-pound turkeys, hanging them as they were going down the line at the poultry plant. I'm just thinking about the pain he was going through. Seeing my mother coming from work after a long, long day at work and seeing her pain, you know? I always thought, "I may not have what it takes, but I have the desire, I have the perseverance, I have the courage."

[Where I work, now], we have about 440 students, pre-K through fourth grade. We have about 85 to 86 percent free and reduced lunch. We have about 65 percent children who are speaking English as a second language. It's very diverse, very diverse. We have kids coming from some of the most wealthy neighborhoods in the city; we have homes on this one side of the school that are half-a-million-dollar homes.

Whereas on the other side of the school we have a lot of subsidized housing and low-income neighborhoods where a lot of the kids are living with single parents, a lot of times single moms, and with a lot of challenges. A lot of the children who we serve, they're not only behind academically, but their background knowledge is also very weak. They spend a lot of time unsupervised. These children don't have the opportunities to go places in the summertime when a lot of the other kids have their parents take them places where they can actually gain some learning. This is probably one of the most challenging schools in the city at this point.

When I think about what I do here at school, I really have to put myself in a lot of different positions. I have to think as a parent. What do the parents expect from us for their kids? How can we get the parents more involved? A lot of times, parents are not reading to them. They don't have access to a lot of books; they don't have access to high-quality daycares and after-school programs. Their homes are very challenging as well. They don't always have the clothes they need to wear to school or food to have on the table. They come with a lot of emotional needs. This is a huge challenge.

So, when they come to us, we've got to take care of them, you know? We've got to make sure that 86 percent of those kids come in and go to the cafeteria for breakfast, because we've got to meet those basic needs. And once they feel safe, and they have a full belly, then we have a much better likelihood of them being successful.

We care about our kids 100 percent so our kids *can* be successful. The biggest trouble is when the kids and the parents don't have the legal means. I'm talking specifically about some of the Hispanics in this area. They don't have the legal means, so they know that their kids can go through school, all the way through high school, graduate, and then what? Because of their being illegal, they're not going to be able to go to college. Being here illegally and not having a path to become legalized because their parents are not residents or citizens, they really have no opportunity. So we're seeing a lot of our kids in the high school and middle school level who are just dropping out of school left and right. And graduation rates are not the best. [As a student], you know that your vision and your goals may not be able to be attained because of this huge thing, this law is in the way of you getting there, then why bother? So they think, "I'll get a head start on working [a job] right now and get a head start on making some money."

In kindergarten we're asking kids, "What do you want to be when you grow up?" A lot of times kids will say, "I want to work at a poultry plant just like my mom." Or "I want to become a construction worker just like my dad," or "I want to go to the apple orchards." That's how they see themselves. They see their grandparents, they see their parents, they see their older siblings who've been in the same neighborhood forever; they don't have jobs, they may be out of housing, so they kind of see themselves already failing because they really haven't seen anybody in their family be successful. It becomes one of those cycles that you wish you could just get out of.

I think we're doing a lot of great things nowadays in our division to allow kids those opportunities to really try to be challenged and to give them a vision about a bright future. We try that, but we've got to have the parents in this with them. We've got to have the community in this with us. We can't do it alone. I can work with kids 180 days out of the year—and more with summer school—and I can really work myself to death, but we can't do it alone. We can't change kids alone.

I see kids now that I used to teach five, six years ago, and when I see they're doing great, I'm proud of them, and I feel great about them. But when I see kids that made the newspaper because they got in trouble with the law, I mean, that really frustrates me. I know that we did what we could with those kids, and unfortunately, we were not able to do enough. So it's a struggle each day.

I go home every day, I have two children of my own, one is 6 and one is 2, and my wife. She will ask me every day how things went, and I'll say, "It was a busy day." A busy day as always. There's never a slow day at our school. But I know at least I am at the place where I know I can continue to make a difference.

I'm a man of challenges. I love to be pushed because I feel like there were times in my life when I really wanted to show people and show myself and show my parents how capable I was of doing things. I was always struggling just to get through the day. But now I feel, as a grown man at 34, I feel that I have the confidence, I have the educational background, I have the passion, I have the desire and the will to do well. I really do think that I have so much to offer yet.

"It's not easy, but it's not impossible."
MIMI MARTINEZ

"I'm a full-time program assistant at a community college. I'm also a student, and I'm a single mother of a 4-year-old son. Luckily, I have a babysitter. I trust her with him. He goes with her Monday through Friday from 7:30 a.m. to 5:30 p.m. I pay her $200 a week. I know it's cheap compared to some other people. But for me, I don't make as much as other people. It's kind of tough, but she does great.

"I cannot say that it's super easy [having a full-time job and being a single mother] or that everyone should be doing this, because it's not that easy. Nowadays, everything is really expensive. And you have to be very careful who you trust with your kid, you know. And then work could be stressful and hectic as well. But I just take it one day at a time."

I grew up here [in the U.S.], and I also grew up in Mexico. My mom sent me and my sister to Mexico for nine years to live with my grandparents when I was probably 8, 9. And then I came back here when I was 15. I was there because they were older, and they had some health issues. My mom couldn't really help them because she had us here. She was also a single mother and she works, and then my brother is autistic and needs help. So she decided to send us over there so they could take care of us while she was working here and helping them with financial goals.

I thought I wanted to work in medicine, but after being 10 years in the field—I was an activities assistant in a nursing home, a CNA nurse, and then a pharmacy technician—I decided that that wasn't my field.

At the time my son was born, I was working in a nonprofit that helped non-accompanied kids between zero to 18 years old who crossed the border. It's called a detention center. I used to work there as a medical person and case manager just helping with medications and doctors. After that I was working at a nursing home. I was the administrative assistant for the therapists, doing their paperwork, timesheets, payroll. And then when COVID happened, they explained to us we needed to be working from home and sometimes go visit sites. I was just like, "Whoa, that's just going to put my son at risk of catching COVID. You need something more safe and secure for him."

After working at the community college and working with so many students, helping with computers logging in and problems with their browser or what-ever, I was like, "Wait, I'm good at this, and I enjoy working with technology. Yeah, this is a field where I should be." But I was like, "Are you *sure*?" I mean, in a Hispanic household, it's not very common for someone to be in the IT world. It's more about business or law or medicine. But I was like, "No, *this* is what I really like and enjoy, so this is what I'm going to become."

Is it hard for your son when you drop him off in the morning?

I think it's harder for me than for him. He goes in, doesn't really care. Like, "Bye, Mom." And I'm the one that's usually having a hard time, like, "Oh my god, I have to go to work, and I'm leaving him." I don't get to see him when he goes to preschool or things like that. But then I'm like, "One day, one day, don't worry, one day you'll be able to see all the little things that he does, don't worry."

Not having a car or whatever, to me, it's just a common normal thing, you know, because I didn't grow up having money or having luxury or cars. I'm used to not having things, so for me, that's not much of a challenge. Through the years, I learned how to manage everything, so I can pretty much say that I'm stable. Of course, once I'm done with school, I have goals in my mind. In a couple years, I want to buy a house or whatever. But for now, I think myself, my son, my mom, and my brother, we're pretty okay.

What do you wish people understood about your being a single working mother and student?

At least in my experience, once someone says, "I'm a single mother," people feel that I, as a single mother, don't have the good job, that I don't have health insurance through my work, or that I'm on food stamps, that I need help from the government with whatever. "Oh, she must be struggling, going through depression and anxiety, and she doesn't have a place to live, doesn't have a car. She's taking drugs." And I'm like, "No. I'm not poor. I'm not any of that."

I just want to make sure that they understand that not all single parents or single moms, especially the Hispanic or Latinas, have that [challenge]. I'm working really hard to make sure that I'm covering all the expenses. I don't qualify for any of their systems because I'm salary-based. I have insurance through my work. I have a pension. So, to me, it feels really bad when they say that. I'm just like, "Oh, god, they really think I'm in a bad position." I'm just struggling with some other stuff, but financially, I'm okay.

I think it's really hard to get rid of that—stigma? Is that what it's called?—of all single parents, that we need help from someone else. You know, it's just a little bit harder, but it *is* possible. [People] are not being educated or informed correctly that a single mom can become an engineer or, I don't know, an attorney.

How do you feel when people make those assumptions about you?

To me, it feels really bad. Yes, there are single parents that need the help for whatever reason, but *my* situation—I mean, okay, if the government doesn't think that I need the assist, I don't want to take it. But nowadays, I think I'm used to getting "the look" or the smart comment. I'm like, "Oh, whatever." I can't really educate people every single time. They can think whatever, but I'm fine.

[People think that] a lot of immigration and single parents are crossing the border with their kids and that they're here just to ask the government for food stamps and whatnot. I mean, it's not every case. My mom, yes, is an immigrant, came here, she is a single mother, but she's also not able to collect any assistance from the government because she doesn't have documents. My mom came, did whatever she did to get to be here to provide for her family back then.

When I was working at the detention center, we had people outside the facilities saying that "you're not helping" or "you're making it worse" or "you are also an immigrant." My color skin, my dark hair, my last name—so they're like, "Well, you're Hispanic." "Yes, I'm Hispanic, but I was born here. I'm a U.S. citizen." I had people tell me, "Why do I have to pay taxes for you to have a job?" I'm like, "I pay taxes, too. And you also are using *my* taxes to retire, so. . . ."

Yeah, but, I try to be very mellow, very calm. I stay back. I try not to interact. I obviously do stand up for myself. Obviously. "Yes, I'm Hispanic, and just because I'm Hispanic doesn't mean that everything is given to me. I have to work very hard to be where I'm at. And it's not easy, but it's not impossible."

What have your learned from your mother about being a single parent?

My mom made the decision as a single mother to send us to Mexico not only to help my grandparents financially, but for them to help her with us. I have thought about the things that I *wouldn't* do as a mother. And that's one of them. I have never, never separated from my son. He is my responsibility. I decided to be a mom. When they were telling me that I was pregnant, I was like, "Okay, so I'm going to be a mom. This is not a game." So that's one of the things I learned. I'll never, never send my son somewhere else so I can work and gather money. I will struggle with him and be with him to make sure that he's okay. But I will never separate from him.

And another one: my mother never went to school because in Mexico and here, money was very tight. So she's always saying, like, "Go to school, go to school; do better, do better." So I'm going to school, getting my degrees to make sure that I'm at a higher level of pay so I can afford more things for my son. Education for me, it's like a high priority so I can make sure and guarantee that he'll have a better future. I always want to be part of my son's life. I'll never be apart from him, so he can see that I'm working, going to school, and I'm sacrificing a lot to be with him and making sure that I'm a better person in the long run.

So going to school, working hard, and never being apart from my son. Well, maybe those are the three things I learned from my mom.

"How do I make sure that I prepare my children for this world?"
MECOLE MCBRIDE

She is the advocacy director for The Policing Project, implementing an initiative that aims to bring police and community members together. Her career path has been around community organizing on social justice, criminal justice reform, racial equity, and police accountability.

She is 40 years old and has three children, ages 2, 5, and 9. In her Twitter profile, she writes, "Doing my part to leave the world a better place for my children to live in."

I remember when I was young, thinking I wanted to be a pediatrician. I may have thought that because my pediatrician was also an African American woman, and I thought that that was pretty cool. But as I grew up, that was just not my career path. But I knew I wanted to help people. I've always been into helping people.

My great-grandma used to say, "You always make enough food for the person who may show up." So that was just innate for us, this idea of always helping other people. I never grew up being selfish, because that's just not who my mom was.

I started out working at a Target store as an executive for assets protection. That was my first shot at employment out of the gate. Then, at some point, my mom was volunteering for a nonprofit that was started by our church, and they were working on statewide legislation for drug reform, specifically to create more equitable sentencing practices for Black and Brown people who were either caught with drugs or convicted of having drugs, and having those individuals go through drug schools, as opposed to having a criminal record.

My job at Target was making sure that we prosecute to the fullest extent of the law someone who has taken from their store. And I get it, it's a for-profit. But it started conflicting with my internal [idea of] why I'm doing work. After about two years at Target, I left, and I started working at a nonprofit doing street-level intervention as well as some prisoner reforms, and it kind of just blossomed from there.

Now, I work with community members and with the police department, independently. We're implementing a policing initiative which, on one hand, is trying to work with the police department to embrace a different idea of community policing. The core of it is that *every* officer should be a community policing officer. Every officer that walks into the community should have a sense of "I'm here to serve this community." So detectives, officers, whomever. I think historically, you have the community policing officer, and then everyone else who does the "real" police work. But *every* officer should have a sense that every time I come in, I'm either going to enhance our relationship, or I'm going to destroy it.

Does the police department respond well to this initiative?

The reality is that change is hard, right? We're introducing something new to the police department front that's different from how it has operated in the past. We're asking the department to work cohesively with each other in a different manner, having a subset of officers who are directly responsible for working with the community, but then sharing, bringing those relationships back to your beat officers and detectives, so that there's more unity in how police are showing up in the community, and more shared understanding of the norms and the concerns of the community at large. That's a new concept.

We also are asking beat officers to work with community members more deliberately, as opposed to what has happened, particularly in the most recent history of just sitting in a car as a deterrent. And that's fine; their presence is fine to a certain degree, but you can't occupy a community, you have to partner with them.

How do you feel when you hear a phrase like "defund the police"?

I think that I understood the spirit when it was first used because that was heavy after George Floyd. I understood it. I think that *defund* has also been weaponized in a way that I don't think is healthy. I think in my heart that when people say *defund*, I hope that it means ensuring that adequate funding is happening for officers, but also every other social support that's needed in our community to make it safe. Public safety isn't just about more police. Public safety is about adequate housing, it's about food access, it's about clean communities, it's about adequate lighting on train terminals. All these kinds of things make up public safety.

Officers are an agent of the city who are there to help create a response to or be a deterrent of criminal activity. But what we have seen historically is that police budgets increase as every other social service decreases up to and including after-school programs—all these things that were around when I was a kid. We can't continue to fund one entity at the expense of every other social need that helps determine public safety outcomes.

This is especially important to me in "inner city" schools where some children have seen more violence than some war vets, probably, in some of these communities. You look at some of your hyper, extremely violent communities, and in some of these, kids hear gunshots regularly. You cannot tell me that that does not affect their psyche. And we don't have adequate trauma response in schools, or counselors, or things like that. So, when I hear "defund the police," my hope is that the spirit of that is that we can't continue to balloon that one budget and completely ignore everything else that plays a huge role in this.

How were you affected by the killing of George Floyd?

I guess the answer is in two parts. You've got your professional, and you've got your personal. The reality is that my husband is six-foot-two, 340 pounds. He's a big guy. When you see those kinds of things happen, you can't help but to see your own family. The George Floyd, the Philando Castile, all of these different things that have happened from coast to coast, every time you see it—Oh, god, I almost got emotional. (Pauses.) Every time you see it, you can't help but to think, "God, cover my brother." He's six-one, and 290, so another big guy. So that's how that affects me personally. And that's not to say that a woman of color can't be a victim as well. But I think that is a harder thing for the men in my life.

On the professional side, that moment in time was compounded by the pandemic when everyone was at home, and everyone *saw* it. I think that it had almost—please don't mistake what I'm about to say—but I think it had almost the same effect as what Emmett Till had in the '50s. Meaning, you couldn't ignore it anymore. If anyone wanted to say, "Oh, these things don't happen," we had a moment in time where everybody for the most part was at home and weren't distracted by work or life or what have you. And to see something that blatant. He literally sat on this man's neck for that long . . . with other people around! This complete disregard even for *having witnesses*? So, if you did this with disregard for witnesses, what are you doing when there *aren't* any witnesses?

We live in a hyper-, *hyper*-surveillance society now. *Everybody* has a camera. And he *still* would be this blatant with that level of abuse? You wouldn't do that to a dog. You sat on someone's *neck* . . . who was *handcuffed* . . . for that long? And the whole world saw it. So I say with complete respect: Mamie Till said, "The world is going to see what they did to my child." And I think 2020 gave us a 21st-century view of that.

But in a lot of ways, this moment has poised us for the change that we need. So maybe that's good. I mean, you hate tumultuous times and for bad things to happen, but I think that sometimes, when the tree shakes, things get cleaned up, right? For me, it's also like, how do I make sure that I prepare my children for this world? How do I make sure that if, at any given moment, the political winds change, we survive that? I do spend a lot of time thinking about this and having conversations with my family about it.

I think that I am slowly introducing my 9-year-old to understanding race and her being a Black woman, what that means for her. We have a book of 100 Black women who changed the world through history, and we read a story each night, starting back from Harriet Tubman through to now. I think that's important to me, because we don't live in the city, we live in the suburbs where the majority of her classmates are not her color, nor the teachers. So it's hyper important to me to make sure that she's grounded. I think that book is how I'm slowly introducing her to a lot of these concepts. I'm also careful about how much I say in front of any of the kids because, to a certain degree, I don't want to steal their innocence. I think that it's important to figure out ways to reinforce who they are, without it being a tumultuous thing.

Does this work satisfy what it is you wanted to do with your life after you left Target?

It's definitely satisfying. I think that there is, though, this feeling of, is it ever enough, right? Even though you know that the work that you do is making a difference, you also know that there's just so much difference yet to be made. So it is fulfilling, but it still kind of leaves you feeling like you've just got to kick the can further down the road to make things a little bit better for my kids.

What is the biggest obstacle to your goals?

Honestly, fatigue is probably our biggest. It's easy to become fatigued or to lose hope that things will change. So one of the things I can do, and it doesn't take anyone else, is I can always look for someone for help or support, and that's all on me. Systems change is something different. I can do the best that I can, but if it doesn't happen, it doesn't happen. But you won't say I didn't try.

"What are we going to do about this? Are we just going to live with it?"
SISTER CANICE JOHNSON

She is a Sister of Mercy and project director of the Mercy Education Project in Detroit. "Some people call me 'founder,' but I would prefer that you use project director of the grassroots start-up group, a group of a dozen, which grew to about 40 volunteers." The project provides support for low-income women and girls who have experienced educational failure.

She also led a grassroots effort to open the Detroit Cristo Rey High School for low-income students when multiple Detroit Catholic schools closed. We talk in the living room of her small, comfortable home in the near east side of Detroit. Of the 39 homes on her block, 15 are burned out, boarded up, or have been removed, leaving overgrown vacant lots. Three more, she tells me, "might be occupied."

I feel that I'm following a call from God. I believe that. And it's a call to be part of a community which serves. All religious sisters take three vows. The Sisters of Mercy take a fourth vow in addition to poverty, chastity, and obedience. Our fourth vow is service to the poor, sick, and, when I made my vows, it was "and ignorant." But ignorant never meant what we typically use the word ignorant to mean today. We mean those who are poor, those who are ill, and those who need education. That's who we serve.

I was born in Detroit and grew up in Detroit. My mother was a homemaker. My father was a pharmacist. He had a drugstore here, lost it during the Depression, and went bankrupt. We were poor, but I didn't know it, which was good. We had a lovely family growing up in Detroit, west side. It wasn't too much later that I began thinking about becoming a Sister of Mercy. The Catholic schools were booming then. You know, it was Depression time, but still. It wasn't the kind of poverty you see around here now with the run-down houses and all.

So many of the businesses that were then in good shape have moved out of the city now. There are some that are moving back in, and that's helpful. So we have hope, and there are a lot of wonderful, wonderful people in Detroit. But when I tell somebody I live in Detroit: "Whoa, you live in Detroit? That must be scary." (Laughs.) Like they think it would be totally impossible to live in Detroit and be safe. Well, in a sense, you can't live *anywhere* and be safe these days. And there probably *is* more violence in the city of Detroit than there is in the suburbs. However, I've lived in this area for almost 20 years, and I do feel pretty safe.

A lot of this devastation that you saw coming here, all these empty houses, has happened in the last eight or nine years that we've been in this house. When we first moved in here, almost every house on this block was occupied. People move out or get foreclosed on. Then it just falls apart or somebody sets a fire in it. Or people break in and they take the metal out of the house. That house [she points toward a home that we can see through her front window] has just totally fallen apart since they left. It makes me very sad.

The family down the street who has since moved, the man and the woman both lost their jobs. And they had three teenage children. He owned a truck. A nice truck. All of a sudden the truck was gone, so I said to him one day, "What happened to your truck?" He said, "Oh. Well, we had to sell it, because we needed food." I'm thinking, "Oh no! Now you don't have transportation. If you get another job, how are you going to get there?" Because that's another problem in Detroit: the bus system is bad. He would sometimes come down and ask for a ride because he needed to get to the drugstore to get his wife's medications or go to the soup kitchen or the pantry to pick up food for the family.

I know I could actually move out of here, but I choose to stay here. Most of the rest of the people on my block *couldn't* move. They don't have anywhere else to move to, or the funds to do it. So it makes me feel sad. Sometimes we talk about the fact that children growing up in this area, this is all they know. All they know is houses falling apart.

Detroit is one of the worst places in the country in terms of graduation rate. In fact, it has been named the worst in terms of the public schools. Somewhere between just 25 and 30 percent of students have been graduating over the last 10 years. I think the reasons are very, very complex. The problem is much bigger in terms of a whole system. We're not putting enough resources into it. But that's not Detroit's fault either, because Detroit is practically bankrupt. I mean, it's very, very poor. If there were a greater tax base, that would help, but the people have moved out of Detroit because of the problems over the last several years. As they do, we have fewer and fewer children in the schools, then you have these large buildings with not enough children and therefore not enough state money coming to the educational system.

We started the Mercy Education Project when the Sisters of Mercy came together, the ones in our area who were educators, and said, "What is it that we really need to do? What problem do we need to address as educators that maybe our skills and our energies can address in some way or other?" So the decision was that we were going to establish a new program in the city of Detroit which would be for women and children. Part of that is because one of our interests is to help turn around the problems of women, whatever their needs are, to try to address them, to bring women to fuller participation in society. It became such a nurturing program for these women and girls, and I'm very proud of it.

In 2005, the Archdiocese of Detroit closed 15 schools, some of them in the city of Detroit and some of them in the near suburbs. One fell swoop. There were only two Catholic high schools left in the whole city of Detroit, and both of them were Jesuit schools for boys only. There was nothing for girls. All these kids were going to be without a school, and all these teachers were going to be without a job. So there was a group of us that came together, people who were concerned about the closures. I was actually part time teaching at one of the schools at that time and chairing the board. So this group came together and said, "What are we going to do about this? Are we just going to live with it? Is there some way we can do something?"

We decided that we were going to start a new Catholic high school. We didn't know how we were going to do it, and looking back it seems kind of naive, but we were going to try to raise the money. We immediately established a development committee, and we actually raised about $300,000 in six weeks. Much of it was from a couple of large religious communities.

In the process, we learned about the Cristo Rey model of schools. There are 24 across the country. When we learned that they are schools in which every student works one day a week at a local corporation, we said maybe that's the answer. Because the students work the jobs, the employers pay for those jobs, and the money goes to the school. The family signs that over. The typical tuition at a Catholic school is seven, eight, nine thousand dollars. And there's no way that most of the families in the city of Detroit can pay that kind of tuition. That's actually one of the reasons why the schools were closing in the first place. They couldn't manage it financially. So the idea of Cristo Rey is that eventually 60 to 70 percent of the school's costs come from the student jobs. We were very, very excited about this and said, "Let's do it!"

I had no salary, but I said we have to have enough money to hire one staff person, and then I need lots of volunteer help. And that's what happened. So we had a planning committee of about 20 people, all of them volunteers, and we had another 20 people who were on various task forces. We had about 40 people altogether that worked for the next two years. We opened in 2008, and four years later we graduated our first class! Every single one of those students was accepted into college. They're told from the very beginning, soon as they walk in the door, they're told, this is an eight-year commitment. Four years of high school and four years at the college of your choice.

There is no stopping you, Canice.

(Laughs.) That's what people say. Well, first of all, I love to learn, myself. And since I find learning exciting, I want to help others have that kind of excitement in their lives. But the other thing, the other part of it, perhaps it's even deeper, what keeps me going is the *need*. My drive, I think, is to address the needs of at least some of the kids in our city. Again, it's a small number compared to the huge numbers that need a better educational possibility. But it makes a difference for them.

What's next for you?

(Laughs.) Well, I'm almost 79. I think I'm moving toward a little more rest in my life, a little more leisure. I'd like to have more time to just learn new things. But I guess maybe I'm saying a little more leisure in my life would be welcome. However, some people doubt that'll ever happen. (Laughs.)

POSTSCRIPT: *Sister Canice died of cancer two years after this conversation at the age of 81. She had been a Sister of Mercy for 64 years.*

"It's time to write a new story for humanity."
TRUNG LE

He is an architect specializing in school design. He is 57 years old and a father of four children.

In this time of rapid change, you're designing a physical object, a building, that could be here 100 years from now. How does knowing that affect your work?

We often refer to architecture as a Trojan horse because, yes, you're building this physical object which you're going to inhabit now, but you have to think about the human condition, and then you have to think about the whole living system, not just your own, and not just the human condition of that community. I think that we have to recognize that we are part of one ecosystem called planet Earth. We're not separate from it. So when you think over time about that physical structure that you're going to build, you need to think about building it for the people that are not even here yet. It's like that First Nation saying that any decision that we make, we have to think about the impact on the next seven generations. I think that good design now is starting to think about that as a core design principle in anything that we build.

We really want to base our work on the idea of telling a new story. I've always said that architecture is a very old profession, not just in terms of time, but also in terms of culture and mindset. The training of architects and the working lives of architects really haven't changed all that much. It's very prescriptive, it tends to have a certain rigor around it, it's very enclosed within a certain culture in terms of ritual and other things. And in that way, it's very similar to the field of education. The idea of school hasn't changed in a long time. It's time that we all need to write a new story for humanity. That's the foundation of the work that we're doing. So we really want to base our work on the idea of telling a new story.

For example, I'm on the board for this tiny little public charter school on the southwest side of Chicago, and we're building a new campus that's going to meet the Living Building Challenge [to design structures that contribute positively to their local ecosystem]. We will try to think about water differently, for example. Every drop of water that falls upon that piece of land, we're not going to call it stormwater, we're not just going to divert it into the sewer. Water is now precious, so we'll use it. For example, in the working farm we're planning.

We're also trying to change some pretty status quo policies and building codes in the city. So, a specific example: the city of Chicago still does not allow a gender-neutral bathroom, so we're designing our student bathrooms to have a wall that could be dismantled once that rule changes. We're also [being more equitable about who will] have the opportunity to come and help us build this campus. I think that we have to constantly think about those things. So that's how architecture becomes a Trojan horse for us to think about changing policy, to think about how we deal with resources, how we make the idea of beauty and nature accessible to everyone, not just a few.

We want to live those values in building this campus and in *how* we're going to build this campus. Every step of the way we want to create this new ecosystem [that will demonstrate] how you *can* build this 21st-century school that will meet the Living Building Challenge that is on-cost with a typical public school. We want this to be a formula that other communities can actually follow in their community, rather than think that, "Oh, that's just a one-off thing, and they got lots of money from some wealthy donor, and we could never do that." We're saying no to that; we're saying that here's a formula that we have created. And it's dynamic because you can change things within it for your own needs. So, this physical thing, this building, gives people messages about how we feel about the people that belong in this place.

Are you talking about writing a "new story" through architecture?

I would say writing a new story, period. How we start to think about *what* we build, *how* we build, and why we *shouldn't* build should be part of that conversation. A recognition that architecture is a very privileged thing. It tends to serve the 1 percent throughout history. It always bugs me at the end of the year how architectural magazines put up a graph about where the tallest buildings are. It's like, okay, but that doesn't serve humanity, that just serves somebody's ego. So these are the consequences that I think we have to realize more and more.

I recognize that, especially in the U.S., you can't separate the education system that we have created from the idea that it has emerged from a place, historically, of social injustice and environmental injustice and racial injustice that is deeply embedded in the structures that we have, so you can't separate the system that we have right now from the history of this place, right? Because it does have this *intention* of inequality from the first moment of conception. We've lived with the old story, we accepted it completely, and we never questioned it. That's the capitalistic, societal aspect of our current education system. America is more about freedom than about equality. We embrace freedom much more than we embrace equality.

So when we say that we want educational reform, that doesn't go far enough. We want an educational *transformation*, not just reform, because reforming is still just tinkering. I don't think we have a new story yet. But we have to be busy deconstructing the story that we have now in order to create that new one.

I'm curious about how your own personal story has impacted your thinking as an architect. You were 11 when your family fled Vietnam. Do you remember your childhood there well?

I remember a lot. I remember the good and the bad. I remember the day-to-day experience of growing up in Saigon and having a family life with my grandmother living next door. I remember my childhood being magical in some way, but I also remember 1968 with the Tet Offensive. We left our home because the fighting was very close. I don't know at this point if I made it up, but I remember coming out of the house and having this helicopter shooting a rocket right over our heads. I also remember really horrific propaganda on TV. It still haunts me a little bit to this day how they bury a lot of people alive. And that black-and-white film was constantly being played on TV. So as a kid, seeing that is terrifying. And it was designed that way; it was designed to terrify you. I don't think it will ever leave my long-term memories.

How have these early experiences helped shape the professional you became?

(Sighs.) Well, the last four years, living the life of an immigrant and reflecting upon it in the era of Trump was very powerful. That brings out a sense of epiphany in terms of what you have to do as an immigrant to survive in a country like this. I think one of the most powerful things I recognize is that I really suppressed my Vietnamese identity to a point where it virtually almost disappeared, because you just want to be accepted. You just want to be part of it. We spent most of our time, especially when we were younger, trying to blend in, trying to be not different. We had to be quiet, we had to not stand out: try to be successful, but not too successful. Try to work much harder, because we had to work much harder; we had to prove ourselves, because we look different, we talk differently. But now that we're adults, I realize that hadn't even come to the surface for me until this Trump era emerged.

We have to recognize that there's a whole group of people that came here in very different circumstances. We really have to embrace that, [in this country], we've come from a history of slavery, of genocide. That's just part of our history. And yet, the opportunity is that, here we are now, and we can build something new that maybe will accept and honor the past by making it a remarkable human story for the future.

Do you see ways that you can do that through your work, or make movement toward that, or urge that?

Now what gives me hope is that if you change yourself, the larger world will change. It doesn't require us to be activists. It doesn't require us to join movements. But it does require work in personal transformation, in continuing to learn and continuing to understand, continuing to be curious. Through that work, you can change yourself, and then when all of us go through our own personal transformation, a new society will emerge because we will be interacting with each other differently, we will have different relationships with each other, we will think about each other differently. I think there will be just a greater sense of . . . love, right? So that makes things more manageable for me. (Laughs.) But, boy, it's a battle every day to be hopeful. It really is, now more than ever. How can we maintain that sense of hope?

You seem to have a strong social conscience that informs a deliberateness about what you do in manifesting [what you believe] in a building.

I love what Victor Hugo said about Gothic architecture. I think this was around the time that he was writing *The Hunchback of Notre Dame*, and he was inspired by the Gothic cathedral. He said that architecture is a "book of stone." It should be able to tell stories of the people that lived within that period and built it because before the invention of the printing press, architecture embedded sculpture that tells stories. These physical things we create give people messages about how we feel about the people that belong to this place. I think that spirit is really powerful. We're hoping that the children of this charter school we're working on will be able to take a group of adults around and tell the stories of this place that they helped create.

PART FOUR:

AFTER WORK

LINDA MACLENNAN

"Well, I'll say 'retired,' but I don't usually identify myself that way. But since you asked, I would say I'm a 'retired news reporter and anchor.'" From 1987 to 2003 she was on the air at Chicago's CBS network affiliate. She received six local Emmy awards for her work.

I've never cared for the word *retired*, not because it connotes some sort of age thing, but because I didn't retire. I was fired. So that always bugged me. People say, "Oh, so you decided to leave to spend time with your family?" No. That was decided for me by a man with an agenda. So that's been my issue with that word *retired*. Obviously, at 65, *now* I'm retirement age, but I've been retired for a long time, which definitely has its benefits for sure. But in terms of feeling relevant or involved or having a purpose—sadly, I don't feel any of those really, sadly.

You'd like to.

Yes! I would *love* to, to be perfectly honest with you. Yeah. I don't want to get too maudlin, but yeah, being fired was life-altering. That was a very difficult time because [that work was] all I had done. I knew since I was in college what I wanted to do, because I started as a Sunday reporter in my last year of university in Ottawa. So that's all I'd known. I mean, I didn't get married and have a family until I was in my mid-30s. I can't cook; I am *still* learning to cook. (Laughs.) My children were still [in single digits] when I left CBS. I have no organizational skills, so to run a household and run three kids' lives growing up, I was really out of my element.

    I have a very thin skin. If I'm ever in some sort of trouble, or if I'm ever being criticized for something, I take that very seriously. So I was seeing all this happen and it was hard. From August until I finally sued them and was successful in February, it was hell. It took a career that I *absolutely* loved and that was so much a part of my persona, and basically put it through a shredder, and said, "We don't need you anymore." It was awful. I still grieve it. It took such a toll. It took a toll on my marriage, took a toll on me.

    I wish—and this is not a big deal—but I just wish in hindsight that my kids had been old enough to see me when I was working. And I especially wish that for my daughter. If she could have seen me in my prime being a female anchor in a big market and just loving what I do. I would have been a really good role model for her.

As a nightly viewer, I remember sensing what I believed was a strong camaraderie among your anchor team.

Oh yes! When [sportscaster] Tim Weigel passed away, I was putting together reminiscences from his coworkers. I was upstairs in the archives going back through old show tapes. And what struck me *was* the camaraderie, the respect; I mean, *joy* is not overstating it, the joy of working together as a team on the air. That was the best part of my day. It was being part of an anchor team that I really cherished.

It's a unique work situation. There was a lot of mutual respect and support and fun. At the end of the evening, Lester [Holt, co-anchor] and Steve [Baskerville, weather forecaster] and I would leave the building—we all parked in the same garage across the street—and we would be standing in that silly underground garage till midnight. Just chatting. So, when I watched those old show tapes, I thought, "Yes, this is what people liked. That camaraderie."

When I think back to then, though, it was easy to underestimate the female co-anchors. The model you had in local news was of the avuncular man* and the younger, attractive female. And so, even visually, it's easy to subconsciously underestimate the female part of that pair. They look more glamorous, they're younger. And here's the guy with gray hair and all the experience. He's the heavyweight. And then here's the, you know, the female tossing to the weather and tossing to sports and whatever. So visually, I think it was easy to underestimate us. They used to call us "news foxes" and "news babes."

I think people saw me like the girl next door. That was always my thing. But you know, there could be worse things. Because I think that suggests a relatability, which I think really worked for me. I wasn't the beauty queen. I wasn't the sexy whatever. I was the girl next door that your mom wanted her son to marry, right? "She's really a nice girl. She's smart. She's got a sunny personality," you know, all that stuff. The men thought I was—you know, cute. The women thought I wasn't a threat. They thought it was funny to tell me, "My husband goes to bed with you every night." So I think that in the long run, the reason why people responded to me was because I was relatable.

* Her many co-anchors over the years included Holt and Bill Kurtis.

But it sounds like it took a long time for you to appreciate that.

Probably because I didn't really want to. I didn't really value that at the time. But I really did value the idea of communicating with average people who were watching us. I now finally understand the whole thing of people saying, "Oh, I watched you every night." While I was working, I never really got that. But now I get it because *I'm* at home watching. That connection and that trust is deep, it can be *really* deep. People who are watching you believe you, and trust that you're going to tell them how it is and tell them what's really happening and why they should care.

Did you get opportunities to show your true value as a reporter?

I remember sitting in 10 Downing Street in the private quarters of the prime minister waiting for Margaret Thatcher to come in the room and talk to me. I was doing an interview with her about sanctions in South Africa. I knew I was going to be intimidated by the surroundings. We got there about an hour early, and I'm just sitting in my chair, trying to get comfortable. I thought of my dad, whose parents were both immigrants from Britain, and we were very, very working class. And I thought, "You know, Dad, this is your daughter. I'm about to sit down at 10 Downing Street with the prime minister, and I'm going to try to put her on the spot about the sanctions."

And then in she comes, finally. She was totally, totally in control. At one point, she tried to catch me up on something. She leaned forward and said to me, "Linda. Do you know what 'the necklace' is?" And I said, "I do know what the necklace is. They take a tire, put it over your arms, and they fill it with gasoline, and they light it."

Did you feel she was underestimating you?

That's what I thought it was. I think if a male interviewer had been sitting there asking the same questions, maybe she wouldn't have challenged him like that. But I don't know.

I can tell how much you miss it. And why.

Anytime there's a big story now, I want to be back in that newsroom. It's the electricity when a story is breaking, the electricity in the newsroom, and all the pressure and how people managed to pull together and get something on the air under really short deadlines and really trying circumstances. It's being part of a team. When you're part of the team, and you're doing good work, there's nothing like it. When you're cast adrift, you're not part of a team anymore and that's so sad. I'm not part of a team, now. And I want a sense of relevance and purpose.

During the pandemic it was really hard because I couldn't visit my family in Canada. Then, after two and a half years, I finally drove up there with my dog just in time for my dad's 90th birthday. One of the reasons I loved it was not just the time with my dad, but because I felt like I had a purpose. A *purpose*, right? Even if it's caring for an elderly parent, helping organize the kitchen, or getting rid of stuff or whatever. I felt like I had a purpose.

It's been the downside of what may look to the outside world as this long, well-funded retirement. The downside is no purpose. I've done all kinds of things. I've been oil painting for the last year. I had no idea that I could oil paint. And I've been doing my photography. All this time I've been self-indulging, which is wonderful. But at a certain point, you go, "I need a purpose. I need to be feeling valuable, I guess. I still feel like I have a contribution to make somewhere. I don't know where, but you know, at almost 66, I feel like I'm a 45-year-old who has lots of great experience. And just because it's taken me 65 years to get all that experience, don't *discount me*, right? I think we all feel that way. The desire to feel that you *matter*. You're sitting there with this reservoir of experience and talent and insight and wisdom at this age. *This* is why we should be sought after, right?

"I don't need a boss."
WENDELL DEW

He is 68 years old and has been a doorman at the John Hancock Center in Chicago, a high-rise with some 700 units and 2,000 residents, for 20 years. When we spoke on Zoom, he was two weeks from retirement.

I am a people person. I've always been a people person. My father worked at the steel mill, and my mom was a stay-at-home mom. They had seven kids. I was third. Two sisters before me. My father had a record shop, too. I worked in his record shop, and so there's a lot of people coming in and out all the time. Oh, my father loved people. He loved to talk, could talk about anything. Oh, yeah. It was one of the great things he did.

What was your career aspiration as a kid?

I was a street guy. I hung out in the streets. I didn't really work. I didn't have no desire to really work outside the hustle. My first full-time job was washing dishes at a restaurant up north. The guy would really be cruel to me. And he'd be screaming and cursing at me. I think there was some racist stuff going on, too. But I would come out from behind the kitchen and help people out with taking their dishes away and stuff. And then a young lady who would come in there often, she said, "How do you take that stuff from him?" She didn't appreciate the way he talked to me, and she's saying that I was a nice guy. But my son was just born. I wasn't going anywhere because I was gonna have to feed my son and put some diapers on him. So I just go ahead and take it. Figured something would open up soon.

She said, "How would you like a better job?" I said, "I would love one." And she got me a job at Loyola University. I was so excited to start this new adventure. They asked me if I knew how to do janitorial work. And I told them, yeah. But I really didn't. So, I learned a lot.

Later, when I was working at Marriott, the Residence Inn as a houseman—busing tables, cleaning up, collecting all the garbage—there was a gentleman, he was a lawyer and architect, and he would come over at night, and he and I would talk. And he loved the John Hancock. He told me some stories about the people in the John Hancock. And I would just sit there, and I was just listening. His stories was beautiful. I said, "I want to go work that!" (Laughs.) I would come past the building, and I would see the sign on the door. It says, "Being monitored by cameras." And so I was like, "Wow, look at that! *That's* where I want to be." And that's where I am, now.

My days is Thursday, Friday, Saturday, Sunday, and Monday. Those are my days. And these days fall around holidays, people traveling back and forth. And so, if I started on Thursday, they'd be leaving [to travel] on a Thursday, coming back on a Monday. So my day is just running. A lot of luggage, a lot of grocery shopping. We take people up to their door, come back down, and somebody is waiting on us to bring them up. And so, it's just busy all along.

I have a gentleman that I work with, his name is Greg. We've worked together for 20 years. One of us is gonna be at the desk. The other one's gonna be at the door. One of you is on the phone calls. The other one's gonna be having the driveway. And he's a people person, too. I've watched him over the years. When you have conflict, he tried to calm everything down before anything got too . . . you know. He's very good at it.

My thing is I'm always wait and see. I don't judge anyone. You walk in the door, I'm not going to make any assumptions about you. I'm going to watch and wait and see how you act. [In this job] if you have a lot of problems with people then you're probably not a people person. I'm gonna do whatever I can to help you out. We have to work with each other so everything can go smooth and easy. You just work with one another. That probably comes from me having a large family. You have to work together. It's important that you are able to work together. Everybody in this around you, you need. You need each other.

But I don't need a boss. I've never needed a boss. I'm gonna do what's supposed to be done. That's what I'm gonna do. Yeah, you pay me for a job, I'm gonna do it. I don't need nobody bossing me around.

Do you make a fair wage?

It's okay. Yeah. I mean, you know, it ain't that great. As a doorman you depend on tips. The tips come by daily. I made a lot of money from tips; you would make sometimes 100, 200 a day. That's why I like working weekends. Yeah, because everybody's moving. The tips, they can help a lot. With the pandemic, though, you ain't getting those hundreds and hundreds of dollars every week. You know? Well, it hurts.

Are there aspects of your work you don't like or dread having to do?

(Pauses.) Not really. I really enjoy it. I really do enjoy it. One of the things [the lawyer and architect I met at Marriott] always spoke about was how much knowledge is in that building. There's so much knowledge. He said the libraries that these people have [in their apartments] is amazing. Oh my god. Every subject that you really like or care about is in the John Hancock.

So, when I started reading about Egypt, people will come down and say, "What are you reading now?" It would be something about Egypt, and then they go upstairs, and they come back down and bring me another book. They say, "You're on the right page with that, but check this one out."

I just had a gentleman; I was talking to him, and he went and bought me this book, *The Fortunes of Africa*. And I'm reading it now. A lot of the things that have gone on in Africa, I have seen, like the slave dungeons that were in Ghana and then Gambia and Senegal. I traveled to these places, and I was curious as to what happens with the people, most of it done in the name of religion. And that tears me apart. Traveling is so important. People that don't travel, they can't really see the world. They can't really do the world. People talk about third-world countries. Have you *seen* a third-world country and seen how lopsided this whole world is? I thank God for being able to go to the John Hancock and receive the knowledge.

The one thing that I promised myself. . . . Back while I was at the hotel, I was putting people's luggage in cars, and they were on the way to Europe or India or Asia. And I would I say, "You know, if I can put their luggage in cabs and send them off, how come I can't go?" So I started traveling. A doorman at the hotel used to tease me. He said, "You've been everywhere, man. Where you going next, the moon?" (Laughs.)

You seem like you're very good at seizing the opportunities this job offers and are making the most of them.

Oh, yeah. Oh, yeah. Oh, yeah. I mean, because I have to go in with my eyes wide open. Yeah. I have to. I'm watching. I'm looking for everything. Everything.

And you're a thinker.

You *have* to be a thinker. You *have* to be, man.

You said you're retiring in two weeks. Is that going to be a challenge for you, to separate from this work?

It's very painful, the thought of leaving. It's very painful. Because as I told you, I love people.

I imagine they will miss you.

Oh, man. I tell you, man. They tell me all the time. One time, I went to midnights when a night shift had opened up, and I did that for a couple of weeks because I had time to read. During the day, I [don't have time to] read. But the boss came back, and she said, "Wendell, [the residents] want you back on days." (Laughs.) Oh, yeah. I'm gonna miss them. Yeah. I will miss all of them. Well, I'll miss most of them. But these are some of the things that you have to do in life. I mean, I have so much that I have to study. And that's more important to me right now.

"I had to keep working."
WILLIAM GREAVES

"There are three distinct parts to my career. I began as a chemist and scientific editor, branched into patent searching in support of scientific research, and finally was appointed by Mayor Richard M. Daley to be the director and community liaison for what is now the City of Chicago's Advisory Council on LGBT Issues.

"At present I am the executive administrative coordinator for the director of the Superfund and Emergency Management Division in Region Five of the U.S. EPA. That's a mouthful. Basically, I'm a secretary now."

We talk on Zoom. He is 72 years old.

I received a PhD in inorganic chemistry with a minor in journalism in 1978, a time when the country was in a recession, so it was very difficult for people to find jobs in chemistry. This was also the time when the chemical industry was moving overseas, where labor was cheaper, and things were not as regulated. All the graduating chemists had difficulty finding a position. I was lucky enough to have the minor in journalism. When representatives from the Standard Oil Company of Indiana came to Iowa State [for] recruiting, they saw my resume, called me, and asked if I would be interested in joining Standard Oil as a technical editor. I did that for four years.

Then I became a physical sciences editor for *Science* magazine. I started just as the Gallo-Montagnier paper hit the editor's desk; that was the paper that identified the AIDS virus. The editor at *Science,* Philip Abelson, understood that AIDS was the most important scientific story of the period, so he had a policy to rush to publish anything having to do with AIDS. There were only eight scientific editors at the journal; we were the ones that obtained peer reviews of all the scientific papers that were submitted to *Science* and decided, on the basis of those peer reviews, what would be published.

What was it like for you personally to be among the first to read these findings?

It was difficult because I had just come out publicly [as a gay man] while I was in Washington, and I was reviewing and editing the papers while my friends were dying around me. I stopped counting those deaths at 40. I watched as many of them died, which was really difficult. And I have regrets about a number of them; I feel that I didn't do enough for them.

Later, in the '90s, I got involved with activism. My current body notwith-standing, I was a jock. I used to be a long-distance runner, and while in Washington I joined Front Runners [an international LGBTQ+ running and walking club]. Later, after returning to Chicago, I became president of Frontrunners and Frontwalkers Chicago. From that experience, I ended up being invited by a member of the Chicago Police Department to be a member of the gay and lesbian advisory council to the police. And from there I was invited to be a member of the mayor's advisory council on gay and lesbian issues. I served in that capacity for about six years, I think. Mayor Daley appointed me the director and community liaison for the advisory council in 2000.

When you look back on your career so far, do you think of it as eclectic or do the distinct parts feel related?

I'd call it eclectic because I don't see how the different parts connect, and certainly I didn't plan any of it. Who would have a career plan that ended up with being the mayor's liaison? I mean, especially as a scientist. "Oh, I'm going to go get a PhD in chemistry because I want to be Mayor Daley's liaison to the LGBTQ communities"? No, you don't think that. So it's eclectic, but I would say that I took advantage of opportunities that came to me. I don't mean that opportunistically. I mean things happened and opportunities arose, and I followed them as best I could. I think the part of my career that really influenced my success as Mayor Daley's liaison were the *Science* magazine years where I first dealt with the public in different ways and learned to listen.

Then 2008 happened, and it destroyed my IRA. I lost more than a third of what I had saved, and it never came back. Some of it came back but not completely. And then when [Rahm] Emanuel became the mayor in 2011, he eliminated my position. Luckily, his administration allowed me to work till the end of the year, when I reached my retirement age and had the 10 years of service with the City that I needed to retire.

My idea was I would find a job and work until I got my Social Security benefits at age 70. With that and my pensions from Amoco and the City and my IRA, I would be able to live off them.

Unfortunately, I didn't find a job right away and had to live off my IRA for four years, which reduced my savings even more. Then I had a problem getting my Social Security benefits, and when I did get them, they had screwed them up a little bit. They didn't take out the taxes for my first payment, which was large, so I had to keep working because I didn't know what my tax liability would be that year. At that point, I saw that I really would have difficulty living on just those four streams and that I needed extra income now. I had to keep working. But looking for a job after age 60 is not easy.

What was it like for you when you realized that your plan couldn't happen?

When I first retired from the City and was not finding a job, I had a hard year where I was pretty depressed and coping the best I could. I knew that if I didn't find a job it was going to be difficult, like really difficult. I was scared, basically, about that. I *panicked*. Yeah. I industriously looked for a job and found nothing; people wouldn't even answer my inquiries. I mean, that had never happened to me before. The ways of recruiting for jobs had changed during the last five to 10 years I was working, and I just simply didn't know how to do it anymore. All my jobs after my first I had basically learned about through my network of people.

I found a job at the EPA through a friend who saw an ad in the Trib for an opening in the senior citizens program at the EPA and sent it to me. I applied for it and didn't get it, but I was later hired in the Superfund division as a technical editor. About a year after I started, the Superfund director's assistants came to me and said, "We think we have a position that would interest you. We think you'd be really good at this, and we want you to take it. Would you be willing to apply?"

I went up and talked to the deputy director, and the selling point for me was that by changing jobs, I got a 50-cent-per-hour raise. (Laughs.) But hey, every penny counts. I got the job.

They were surprised that I was so good at being the director's assistant. But I mean, try being an assistant to Mayor Daley. (Laughs.) Everything I learned working for the City and working for the mayor, I've used here. I know how to talk to people. I know how bureaucracy works. I know how to navigate that.

It strikes me that they got really lucky. Here you come with this wealth of experience and honed skills.

Frankly, I think they did. Yeah. I think my boss would agree. They usually staff this position with somebody in their 20s, an intern or someone right out of school.

Essentially, this is a retirement gig for me. At some point in the future I will retire fully. Either at the end of January 2024 or the January after that. My contract terminates on January 23, so that's how I've set those dates.

Do you feel secure to retire at that point?

No, not really, but I think I need to retire, mentally. I'm really ready to retire, and so I will make it work, as I've always done with everything, but I will not be in a position to be really comfortable. I will not have a lot of extra income.

Have you had to downsize your life?

Physically, the answer is no. I can still keep this home, for example, but I have lowered my expectations. I realize that I won't be able to do some of the things I'd like to do, such as travel extensively. So I manage my wants to meet my means. I won't be able to travel as much as some of my friends do, but I'll be able to take the trips that will mean the most to me, attend theatrical productions and concerts that mean the most to me, and be creative in ways that are meaningful to me. I've had a rich life. I hope to continue to have one.

What do you plan to do with your retirement?

During the four years that I wasn't working, it took me two years to figure out how to be retired. I flailed for two years. I had to learn what I could do that made me feel happy, that made me feel productive. Fulfilled.

[Years ago] I had gone to a doctor because I was stressed, and the doctor looked me over and he said, "You're an A-type personality, and you're obsessive." He said, "I can tell you right now, you need to do something with your hands. I don't care what it is. You need a hobby, and you need to be able to do something that will take your mind off of work and really absorb you." And I thought, it also has to be affordable, and it has to be portable. So I took up needlepoint. I'd always been interested in weaving. Hang on. (He steps out of frame and returns with a square pillow with a needlepoint cover.) This was the first one I ever did. Now I want to make a needlepoint rug. I've actually designed one in my head.

I've found I really enjoy it and even more importantly that it calms me down. For me, it's a meditation. The repetitive motion. Stitching is like a meditation to me. I can really focus on it. I'm obsessive, what can I say? It does take an obsessive [personality].

People say, "How do you have the patience to do that?" I always answer with a quote from Maggie Lane's book *Needlepoint by Design*: It takes *impatience* to do this. You want to know what it will look like, so you keep working at it. So that's what I want to do in my retirement. I want to do my genealogy research into my family, which I find satisfying and that has always intrigued me, and my needlepoint, and I want to go back to the gym.

You actually kind of glow when you talk about it.

(Laughs.) People tell me that, yeah.

"Finding a place to be."
LAURIE ZRENDA

She opened one of Connecticut's first six medical cannabis dispensaries in 2014. She is 57 years old. "I'm retired. I didn't want to be."

I'd been working for a chain retail pharmacy for 27 years. You're on your feet 13 hours a day, and you're fighting with insurance companies, and it just was getting old after 27 years. Originally, when I went to pharmacy school, I worked at an independent pharmacy, and I worked for a woman owner. I kind of admired that when I was in college. Independent pharmacies had gone by the wayside by the time I started working in the late '80s. All the chains were gobbling everybody up. The idea of owning my own business, not a pharmacy, but sort of a pharmacy with marijuana was my way to own my own business and do something different and probably, hopefully, profitable.

I only heard about [medicinal marijuana dispensaries] by accident because my neighbor was a manager at a Walgreens, and she said to me one day, "My pharmacist is applying for a marijuana license." I hadn't even heard about it till then. So that's when I was like, "Oh!" And I went online and started looking into it.

My biggest problem was getting people to allow us to open in their town. I had to search around to find a town that would be willing to host us. A lot of them were very nervous about it and didn't want us there. So it took a little doing. That was probably our biggest challenge, finding a place to be. I think they worried about crime. I *think*; I don't know. They worried about how their friends in their town would feel about it. It was just a big unknown to them, and they didn't want to deal with it. The town where I had worked with a [chain pharmacy], the zoning lady there was a patient of ours at the store who would come in once a month or whatever to get her stuff. So I started talking to her, and I told her I was having trouble with some of the bigger towns that I was looking at. And she said, "Well, I won't give you any problems." So we started looking in that town. It was a smaller town, but we kind of took on the mantra, "If you build it, they will come." And they did.

Were you a marijuana user, medicinal or otherwise, before you started your business?

Not at all. (Laughs.) I went to my high school reunion after we opened, and I think everyone was shocked that I was even doing this. I would have been voted "least likely to sell marijuana." I never tried it in college or high school or anything. But I knew from being a pharmacist that a lot of people with cancer were using it to help their nausea and build their appetite when they were going through chemo. And so I knew it had its medical benefits, but I never really gave it much thought otherwise. I still don't have any interest. I don't need it for anything. I'm pretty healthy, and I'm not stressed, so. . . .

What do you remember about the day you opened?

Well, I didn't know if I was going to have a line of a hundred people deep when we opened our doors or if we were going to have nobody. I'd seen recreational places with long lines in Colorado and places like that, but I didn't know what to expect. We didn't get our first delivery till late in the afternoon, so we opened from like 4 to 8, and we had about 40 people. That felt like a rush because we didn't know what we were doing. But then it dropped off.

In the beginning, if we saw 10 people, that was a normal day. We would watch *General Hospital* on TV, trying to pass the time. I mean, it was very slow at first. Either people didn't know we were there, or maybe doctors weren't into registering patients for the program yet. But later, we would see about 350 to 400 people a day. We went from making less than $1,000 a day to about $40,000 a day. It was, you know, a very busy place. On a busy day, like a Friday, we could see 500 people. We'd have all six registers pretty well hopping on the first Fridays of the month. People get their disability checks and their government checks. I think our record was 712 in one day. Nonstop. Crazy.

I felt guilty at first about someone's paying $200 for this and paying cash.

I would feel bad. And then I'm thinking, well, if they're buying on the street, they'd be probably buying it for $200, too.

Did you enjoy this work?

Yeah, I did. It's different than regular pharmacy in that we really get to help people. In the regular pharmacy, I was just checking if the technicians filled the prescription, and I just had to make sure it was right before it went out the door. I was at the computer constantly with my head down. I didn't get to talk to people. I didn't very often get to tell someone who might say they have a cold, what they should take or whatever.

[At our dispensary] we kind of counseled people about what to use. If it's your first time in, you would have a half-hour appointment with one of the pharmacists, and we would sit down and go through all that with you. People would come back in tears thanking me for making a difference in their life, that nothing has ever helped them like this before. It was life-changing for some people.

I had a girl who was in the Twin Towers on 9/11 who had post-traumatic stress. And she came in, and it just made a huge, huge difference in her life. I mean, she could take enough to not be high and function and yet have that level of calm in her life. And on top of that, her blood pressure went down and then she could get off her blood pressure pills because she wasn't so anxious. It made huge differences for her. It's pretty cool. I'm getting to know people and owning my own business. It was all fun. You had your regulars and you made friends and it was just, it felt like home. Plus, I had a bunch of family work in there, too, so it was really nice.

I left the store in January, just a few months ago, because we sold the dispensary to a larger company. They made us an offer we couldn't refuse. I never planned to sell the business, but, you know, if you're going to get more money than you'd ever make in the next 20 years, you kind of have to sell it. But they gave me a two-year employment contract to continue to manage it for them. I had never expected to leave, but when my contract was up, they wanted to bring their own manager in and they said, "Thanks, bye." And so I'm retired, but I didn't want to be.

It's weird to think it goes on without you when it's something you poured your heart and soul into. When I was selling it, I kind of compared it to having a baby and giving it up for adoption, and then watching that other family raise it because they live next door. I mean, it had been everything for me for so many years.

"I broke some rules."
SUSAN HARRIS

She was a television writer and producer, and is a Television Hall of Fame inductee who created such classic shows as The Golden Girls, Benson, Soap, Nurses, *and much else.*

Listen. I wasn't curing cancer. I don't think of myself as doing anything important in those years. If I managed to make people laugh and could also spread a few ideas around, that was my contribution. And that was okay. It's good to make people laugh, but you know, as far as contribution to humanity? I would say, negligible.

But to television?

Well, I would say that I was among the first female comedy writers. I broke some rules, and I always tried to do the hard stuff. The abortion episode I wrote for *Maude*—there was a lot said about that at the time. And there was the first gay character on TV—Billy Crystal in *Soap*. *Golden Girls* focused on women of a certain age who were a forgotten demographic. So yeah, maybe in some ways, I did change the face of TV. But I would give Norman Lear the same credit.

Is there anything you'd still like to accomplish, professionally?

I think the best thing I've ever done was I had two sons. That was my greatest achievement because I loved being a mother more than anything else, and to have found Paul [Junger Witt], the love of my life. The writing started out as a way to earn a living because I just had no money in the bank, and then it became something else. When we did shows, it was a lot of hard work, a lot of late nights, but we had a good time. And yeah, now I'm done with that.

EPILOGUE:

REST

"I'm here."
SAYDA RAGHEB

She is currently working in a hospital in a progressive care unit to expand her skills and experience but looks forward to returning to assisted living, where she worked until recently, because she prefers to work with geriatric patients in long-term care.

We talk on Zoom one year into the pandemic.

I always knew what I wanted to be at the end of my training. I wanted to work in long-term care and geriatric care. That's always been my love. I do like the younger populations, but I really prefer anyone over the age of 70. I can connect with them a lot better, which is interesting because I'm going to be 31 on Friday, so I'm pretty young for that.

Why do you think you connect better with the older folks?

Well, so, I was adopted from Peru. My mom was 42 when she adopted me. She was a widow at that time, still is, and she really wanted to be a mom. Peru was one of the few countries that allow single parents to adopt. We had found out in a letter that came with me that my birth mother had passed away when I was about 3 months old and that I had some siblings.

I recently connected with them about five years ago. They're very, um, on the poor side. On this most recent trip that was about three years ago, I saw where I was born and where my parents passed away. They didn't have running water. They didn't have bathrooms. I mean, we lived very much in the mountains, worked from the earth, the ground. It's humbling to be over there. It's emotional, too, very hard to see it. I've always had this sense that I didn't want to end up in a situation ever like that, again. It's like a fear; I don't ever want to somehow end up where I started. So that's why I save money like crazy.

I was very close with my grandma, and I was with her to the end, which is actually interesting because the assisted living home I work at is actually where she lived her last couple of years. So I've been running around that place since I was 10. I really like working there.

I know all the halls, all the floors, but my favorite actually is Memory Care. I love, I *love* dementia [care]. If I could, I would work with them all day, every day. I'm very close with them. So that's primarily where they put me because I have

377

the patience for it. It doesn't always work when you come home, though, because you've used up all your patience at work. (Laughs.)

I see them so much that some, especially with dementia, they won't go to their family member anymore. They'll come over by me and want to be by me, as bad as it sounds, because they trust me. Sometimes it's like caring for a child because I get them up in the morning. I brush their teeth; I brush their hair. I pick out their clothes. I clean them when they're dirty. So they trust me. They trust us.

When people with dementia, or anyone whose memory just starts going when they get older, a lot of times they refer back to when they were younger or when they were new parents. I think 90 percent of my residents at some point ask me where their mom is or why their parents aren't here. I had a resident who was over a hundred years old who said, "I have to go." And I said, "Where are you going to?" "My mom needs my help. She's down the street. And I need to help with my siblings." I'm like, "Listen, we can't get there yet because there's construction." It's just reorienting them.

Does it ever feel like you're lying?

It does. A lot of the times I feel like I'm lying to them. But I've seen it when they've been told the truth, and I'd rather live in their reality than make them realize, all over again, their mother's passed away or their father. Sometimes, though, you can help them get to that truth. You can say, "Well, you're 91, how old would your parents be now?" But yeah, it does feel sometimes like I'm lying to them, but I rather them be happy than crying all day, feeling, again, like they just lost their mother. You have to tune into what their reality is.

What makes your job difficult for you?

I've had pretty combative dementia residents. We did have some gentlemen, they forget what's going on. They're at the very beginning onset of it. So they don't know who you are, why they aren't with their wife. Why they're not at their house. Why you're keeping them here. They can become very combative because they don't know, and that's not their fault. I've had to call the police once or twice because I can't personally restrain them. I'm five-foot-one. I really don't like calling the police, so the only time I do is if I fear for my residents.

But the hardest thing is when we don't have the staffing we need. It takes a toll. And COVID, when that hit, was our biggest test because we lost quite a few nurses and CNAs* because of medical conditions they had, or they had other jobs and they kind of work both jobs, or honestly just from the fear of getting COVID. We had staff members that were pregnant, and they had been trying to be pregnant for a long time, so they obviously stopped working because we didn't know what the coronavirus was going to do. So, being short-staffed and also having no PPE,† or not enough PPE, and having sick people and not understanding the disease, that seemed to be like my own pushing point; I didn't know what to do. None of us knew what to do. People were dying; we were sending people to the hospital, you know, trying to save people. And I was just so past the point. . . . I mean, I didn't have as much compassion as I had before. I had to just block it all out, block everything out because it was so hard to watch. It was very hard. That was my limit. And I'm like, "I can't do this. I don't have the people I need to help me. I don't have the equipment to do my job, and so I can't help them." That was the worst. I want to be able to do something more than just sending them out and not knowing if they'd come back or not.

And then, I actually ended up getting COVID, myself, at the end of April. I knew pretty fast something was not right. Whenever I would get home from work, I would always shower right away and throw everything in the laundry. Lysol the whole place. I used soap and water and bleach as much as I could. So, this time, Mom had just come in with my daughter, and my daughter said, "What's that smell?" And I'm like, "What smell?" It was the cleaning products, but I couldn't smell it. And the other sign was the start of a fever. And I said right away, "You guys need to stay away from me."

I called my boss. She's like, "Well, you're instantly off for at least 10 days." I was laid up in my bed. I had horrible fevers. And I have asthma already, so I was using my inhaler like crazy. I was more terrified for giving it to my daughter because she is immunocompromised. She has juvenile idiopathic arthritis, so we have doctor's appointments all the time. And my mom is over the age of 70. That was my biggest fear, is that I would give it to them. I think a lot of health care workers don't really think about themselves as much. They worry about who they're going to hurt.

* Certified Nursing Assistants.
† Personal Protective Equipment.

What do you find most rewarding about your job?

This might sound weird, but the most rewarding part of what I do is when I'm there at the end. I want to be there at the end of their life because I've been there since some of them have come in, and I want to be there when they need someone in the end. I am the one who gives them the morphine or the lorazepam to help the pain and the anxiety; it's going to calm them enough to be ready to go.

When it's someone I might have known even for just two weeks, it's hard to watch them pass, to watch anyone passing away, but if I've known them for years, it's—There was one, her passing away really hurt because I was there when she still remembered my name and now she didn't know anyone, and her family wasn't around. So that was really hard, her being by herself. But at least I was there.

I think the best way you can let go and leave this world is to be not in pain, to not be anxious, and to be with someone that cares and helps with all of that. I'd like to be a hospice nurse later on.

"I don't need to take this burden home."
ROSEMARY OLAIREZ

She is 44 years old and a hospice nurse. "I also do admission, so I bring them onto hospice and educate them of what we can do and what we can offer them. I really like giving them that information."

She has a 24-year-old daughter. We talk via Zoom on Rosemary's day off.

I've seen a lot of deaths from a very young age. My grandparents adopted me because my mom left me with them when I was 1 year old. My grandpa died when I was 7 years old. As a young child, I kind of learned to take all these emotions in and know that death happens. I don't know if it's a good thing that I experienced so much grief as a child, but it has helped me in this career. I don't know. Maybe I felt death less. I don't take it as hard as the first time somebody had died.

I came here to America from the Philippines when I was 13. In the Philippines, we have open caskets. Where I lived was the main home, so when my two uncles died, the casket was right there in our home for 30 days. We would go in front of the casket and see my dead uncle's face every day, and we would pray in front of him. So I think that kind of desensitized me a little bit. You know, about dealing with death.

I actually didn't want to be a nurse. I wanted to be a doctor, but I had my daughter early. I got pregnant at age 20. I ended up giving birth right before I turned 21. So I stopped school for a bit, and my mom was like, "Oh, you know if you really want to be a doctor, it's going to take you a long time, and it's hard with a baby. So why don't you switch over to nursing?"

I did end up liking it. I like the relationships I developed with the patients in the oncology floor. But it's funny, I had a different view of doctors as a child. It's different when you're actually in there in the field and in the hospital. Doctors are so in a hurry, most of them. Well, from my experience, most of them don't really care about the patients. They have so many jobs, like they don't even have time to listen to you.

So that's not what you imagined doctors were like?

No, no. It was kind of like a lot of them don't have bedside manners. And a lot of them in the hospitals are so angry. Like, they're so mean to the nurses. It's terrible. Especially new doctors. *Especially* new doctors. The older doctors have learned to rely a lot on their nurses. So they ask the nurse what they should do. But the newer doctors don't know that the nurse has a lot of inputs. So they're like, "I'm the doctor. Don't tell me what to do" kind of thing because, you know, they went all through school, so they think they have all this knowledge when it comes to the real world.

But I've learned so much from my coworkers, the nurses, especially in the hospice field, because there's things that I've learned that I would never have thought of doing. So we are each other's resources. They're caring, and you have someone to talk to and really help you out. I know in some hospitals, the older nurses eat their young. You're kind of like an enemy. Even the managers are like that, too. When I became a manager, the person orienting me was like, "Oh, you need to put a distance between you and your nurses. Think of them as your enemy." I was like, "But they are the ones who are working on the shift. I have to work with them. I can't treat them like my enemy." It's probably because she hadn't been on the floor for ages. She's been doing this for forever. They forget how it is to be a nurse.

You're with patients and families in an emotional time in their lives, and you're part of that. Do they ever become emotionally attached you?

Actually, my family I'm working with right now are so attached to me. Instead of calling the triage or the weekend nurse after hours, they would rather wait for a different day so I can see them. It's really sad because some of them really need help right at this moment, but they want me to be the one to do it. So they wait for a day or two or three. I'm like, "No, you can't do that. You need to stop doing that." A lot of times I give them my email, and I give them my phone number so that I can at least help them understand, "Hey, this can't wait until two days from now; you need to call After Hours. You need to call triage." They get so attached to their nurses that like, "Oh, I only want to see you; I don't want to see anybody else."

Do you become attached to the patients and families you work with?

Some of the patients are nonresponsive, nonverbal, and bed-bound so they don't really interact with you so much. I do get attached to the families, but I do put boundaries on our relationships. When families cry when I do death visits after somebody has passed away, sometimes they share with me their stories. It's very touching, and I do end up crying with them. But after I leave that door, I don't know, a switch turns off and then it's like, "Okay, I'm okay. I don't have to take this burden home with me." It helps you when you do it that way, when you try to put up boundaries. It's for yourself. It's self-love. You don't want to take on the burden that they have because that's more stress for you.

You have other patients to think about, and you have your own problems. Especially like after you do a death visit and then you have another visit after that. You kind of want to show [the next family] a good face and that you're there for them. You don't want them to know that, "Oh, I'm sad because somebody just died."

Are there times when you can't help taking that burden home?

That depends on the situation. I've done some death visits where it reminded me of my own situation. My grandpa—I was really close to my grandpa—and I still cry when I think of him, because he's passed on. I cry every time I visit him at his grave. So when I see like a grandfather—(Pauses.) See? I'm getting all teary now.

(Pauses.) When a grandfather and the grandchildren are there, it reminds me of my situation. It does take me a while to kind of get over it, and I do take it home because then I start to remember my grandfather and the feelings that I've had for him.

But whenever I walk into my next patient's room, I clear myself so that I don't have any anything with me, any burden that they could feel present. I want them to just have this positive energy with me.

Can you explain to me how you "clear" yourself?

Well, for me, it's just deep breathing and kind of clearing my thoughts. I think of my happy place and think of a positive outcome going into this room that I'm about to walk into, and about giving them some good news, at least. You know, or some hope.

Have you ever imagined yourself doing anything besides being a nurse?

No, I don't think I could imagine doing anything else.

"Life's short, you know?"
MARYSUE REARDON

She is a funeral home director, embalmer, and crematory operator.
After her divorce, a friend had offered her a job answering the phone in a funeral home. "I fell in love with the business. Then, at 47, I decided I'm going to go back to school to get licensed as a funeral director and embalmer."
She is 60 years old and has three grown children.

It's been a crazy few days. We had, in 24 hours, seven calls, death calls. That's a lot in 24 hours. It goes in spurts, you know; we might go for a week or two and have nothing, or minimal. And then, as soon as somebody says, "You know, we're slow," then you tend to get the call and you're up all night.

Holiday time is a bad time. Christmastime people hang on for one last Christmas. Or maybe they're alone, and they pass before Christmas because they can't bear another holiday alone. It's kind of interesting. My kids always said there was never a time that we didn't have a Christmas morning opening gifts when the phone wouldn't ring. I'd tell them, "Somebody's having a much worse day than us. So why don't you eat breakfast, and I'll be back."

When I arrive [at a home], I meet with the family, but as I'm talking to the family, I'm observing my area. Okay, how much furniture do we have to move to get to the deceased and get them out? Is the spouse going to not want to leave the room? We always recommend that they leave the room, just because anything can happen when you move a body. But more importantly, I was taught in a continuing ed class, especially today, no one knows where cameras are. We always want to be completely respectful no matter what, but in the back of our minds we make sure we are always attuned that someone's watching. We always treat our deceased as though they were our own family, but things happen. People "purge," it's called, fluid comes out of the mouth and the nose when they're moved. It's not something we want the family to see, so we cover the face gracefully with a sheath. There are times when the family wants to help, the sons or the grandsons, they want to be part of it, and we never turn that down. You have to love what you do because you're meeting with people [at a terrible time in their life].

I don't mind embalming, but that's not my niche. My niche is the family. My niche is walking in that home when someone's passed. There's a lot of emotion when you are standing there with a widow whose husband went into heart surgery and just didn't come back out. She's crying, and she says, "I've just lost my best friend. What am I going to do without my best friend?" [My boss] Mike said to me, "You just have this, like, way." I have families that come in to see me, later; they bring me flowers at the anniversary of their loved one's passing. I have people that come back in because this was the last place that their husband or wife was.

They always say you shouldn't cry along with someone. Well, I think that sometimes there's an appropriate time for that. I probably take more into my heart and soul, so I probably struggle more at night sometimes where you feel like, is there ever anything good going on? You get home and you think, life's short, you know, life's short.

It's very difficult to date when you're in this industry. It's kind of weird that I'm even throwing that into our conversation. I'm on call a lot, and if I'm having dinner with someone, it's like, "Speed it up, I've got to go to work." And it's hard. Most men struggle with what I do. I think they struggle with a couple of things. When you tell them what you do, they'll say, "You just work in the office, right?" "No, I make removals." And they're like, "You pick up dead people?" "Well, somebody has to." I've had a couple guys that I was going to go on a first date with, and finally, they're like, "I can't; I just can't." People ask, "Do [corpses] really sit up?" "No, they don't sit up." But most people genuinely have questions, just out of pure curiosity, because when they were in high school this job was not one of the topics on career day.

I remember when my grandparents died, my dad looked at me, and he goes, "You're not working right now, right?" It's very hard to take that hat off because this is what I do every day, so I look at things a little differently. We're all going to die, but I see it every day. I see how I would want things done, how I wouldn't want things done. I wouldn't want to be cremated, by the way.

Why?

Because you see the process. None of the directors I know want to be cremated. Isn't that funny?

[I tell her that two people I talked to in emergency services said that even though they've learned to adjust to tragedy, it's different when a child has died. She nods slowly and describes a case in which a young girl suffered a devastating and disfiguring fatal injury in a head-on automobile accident caused by a drunk driver. She asks that I not use specific details out of respect for the family.]*

It was horrific. And the girl had the same coat that my daughter had. That night I threw my daughter's coat away. And at that time, I didn't have a lot of money to be doing that, but I couldn't bear to look at it again.

But the strength of those parents. They wanted to see her, and I said I can't do that in good conscience. I can't. There were other family members who came in, and I asked if it was ok for them to see her. The mother said, "Yes, because I need to know it's her in there and know that she's not somewhere else." Your brain knows she is there, but your heart doesn't. These are two very different things at death, two very different things.

So I brought them back to see her, and the girl's face was badly damaged. And the woman said, "You fixed her hair." And I said, "Of course I fixed her hair." She's still a little girl, you know. I dressed her in a dress. (Pauses.) It took me a long time to recover, as you can see, probably. I'm still not totally recovered from that one. Because you can't. It can hit you to the core.

---

* Meghan Hilliard, p. 105, and Alex Hilliard, p. 102.

Do you see the cadaver as a person?

The first funeral home I worked at had a sign that the owner put up [in the prep room] that said "This room is to always be treated with respect." This is someone's mother, someone's daughter, someone's dad. Always treat them with respect. There'll be no TVs on, there's none of that. We have music going on, especially for an embalming case that might take us longer than the average time to do it. It gets pretty crazy after a while, so the music is just something to keep you sane when you have an open cavity in front of you.

But the prep room is a very sacred room. The deceased is always covered up; the sheet goes up to the neck. After the embalming takes place, they're cleaned, their hair is washed, they're propped properly, there's lotion we put on their face to keep their face moisturized, and we wait till the next day and then check and see how the body took and how everything has gone. But that is the most important room of the building. No one is allowed in that prep room unless you're a licensed embalmer, or you're a student, a doctor, a nurse in nursing school. My daughter had been in there; she was always intrigued with it. My son, he's like, "I'm not goin' in there. You can't make me." I'm like, "Please help me with the removal." "No way." (Laughs.)

It's not for everybody.

It is not for everybody, yeah.

There are no cameras in that room. It's you, the deceased, and whoever the other staff is.

Sometimes it's just me.

In that private space where you're not being watched, why the emphasis on respect?

First of all, the majority of the time, I've already met someone that loved that person. Ninety percent of the time, I've already had a connection with their son or daughter or spouse. That's number one. Number two, it *is* a human being. That's a human being for eternity in my eyes. Someone loved that person whole-heartedly and would want us to take the utmost respect and care of that person. I would expect the same respect for my loved ones.

I think I carry a lot with me. I think it makes me who I am today. Good and bad. Somebody asked me once, "Will you put [your occupation] in your obituary?" I kind of thought about it a little bit. And I said, "Gee, I don't know." My son said, "Why would you *not* want it in there? I think for your industry, Mom, it should be in there because you served a lot of families." And then I asked my other kids what they would do. And they both said, "Oh, I would put it in there. I would definitely put it in there." I said, "Why?"

My daughter, Katherine, said, "Mom, this has been your life. This is not a job. This has been your life. You've raised great kids. You've been a great friend and a great daughter and a great sister. But this has been your life." (Pauses.)

What did you think when she said that?

That she was right. So I think I would probably say, "Proudly served as a licensed funeral director" for however many years it turns out to be.

ACKNOWLEDGMENTS

I owe a large debt of gratitude to the many people with whom I collaborated to make this book. My first debt is to Doug Seibold, president and publisher at Agate Publishing, who conceived the idea for this book and trusted me with it. I always appreciate his reliably sage guidance along the way. I also thank Agate's managing editor, Amanda Gibson, who was my editor and trail guide, for her keen eye and sound judgment; Jacqueline Jarik, publicity manager, whose goodwill and creative energy is always a joy to work with; production manager, Jane Seibold, for her striking cover and much else; and the entire capable and caring Agate team.

I am also grateful to Dick Streedain, whose suggestion that I base my dissertation on oral histories helped get this ball rolling years ago.

To every individual who shared their stories so generously, my deep gratitude and respect are due for their often-surprising openness to my probing their work lives and their willingness to explore aloud their feelings about what they do. I will never take their trust lightly.

I spoke to many more people about their work than I am able to include here, but my gratitude, respect, and appreciation are no less.

I also wish to thank those who answered my call for conversation and invaluable assistance and advice along the way, especially Daryl Anderson, Ed Asner, George Drury, Steve Fury, Elliott Hurtig, Rick Kogan, Jude Leak, Sydney Lewis, John O'Connor, Pemon Rami, Scott Silberstein, Treva Silverman, Scott Tennant, Laura Washington, and Alan Wieder.

I would not have been able to find and connect with the people I did without the assistance of many connectors, including Kim Adamle, Masha Alexander, Raul Amezquita, Bill Ayers, Dominick Belmonte, Sara Berg, Erika Berkey, Ann Bines, Jordan Blackburn, Tanner Blackburn, David Bremer, Joannie Lamb Callahan, Lori Cannon, Karen Collins, Nils Collins, Amy Crider, Carole

Dibo, Cathy Donnelly, Cate Dunlap, Kurt Elling, Vicki Engonopoulos, Timothy Evans, Emma Feldman, Richard Feldman, Beth Finke, Tony Fitzpatrick, Jen Feuer-Crystal, David Futransky, Sandra Gaynor, Laurie R. Glenn, Deb Granite, Marilyn Halperin, Alison Hawley, Mollie Herman, Kristin Hettich, Meghan Hilliard, Marvin Hoffman, Ina Jaffe, Lovella Carol Hughes Johnson, Beth Kligerman, Joanna Klonsky, Susan Klonsky, Delia Kropp, Emily Larson, Sarah Larson, Denny Lawton, Nancy Lawton, Amber Lingenfelter, Penny Lundquist, Reggio MacLaughlin, Gwen MacMillan, Amy Mall, Margie Marcus, Nancy McDaniel, Tina Menendez, David Moromisato, Fran Uditsky Moss, Holly Mulcahy, Mary Ellen Munley, Anne Zrenda Murphy, Victor Musoni, Simone Nathan, Diane Prokop, Pemon Rami, David Razowski, Kelsey Rhodes, Kim Sanzo, Jaime Saunders, J. J. Sedelmaier, Marla Seibold, Nick Shih-hseih, Aretha Sills, Sarah Slavin, Rusty Steiger, Dick Streedain, Scott Silberstein, Sara Sugihara, Cheryl Watkins, Steve Weinstein, Victoria Zielinski, and Laura Zurcher.

And finally, I want to thank my parents, whose incalculable contributions included introducing me to Studs Terkel, both the man and his work, when I was 15. Thanks are also due to Sarah Larson for photographically documenting many of my talks and interviews, and Emily Larson and our grandsons, Nicholas and Tilden, whose many adventures and creative endeavors are a constant inspiration to me. Most of all and forever more, I am grateful to my wife, Mary, whose astute advice, tender patience, and steadfast support and encouragement since the day we met, keep me intact.

ABOUT THE AUTHOR

Mark Larson is a Chicago-based writer and educator who holds a doctorate in educational leadership. He is the author of two books on education and *Ensemble: An Oral History of Chicago Theater*, for which he conducted over 300 interviews with Chicago theater artists, past and present. He lives in Chicago with his wife, Mary. They have twin daughters, Sarah and Emily, and twin grandsons, Tilden and Nicholas.